Some annotation!

32 → Brittain – *late* full-scale pacifism. Her ambivalent statements?
For (SJ)

46 → Jameson
64 → Jameson
85 SJ + Mitchison in PEN
205 SJ re Europe.
See Rathbone articles (206)
246 SJ's Black Laurel. + Before the Crossing.
250 *VIP*. + 251.

35 Stevie's crit of VB's *England's Hour*
37 Stevie – re NYP + Frontier. + 38 [Little Woman tone w gt relevance to issues].
41 Implicates self in Britain's 'oppressive colonialism'.
(see link w Mannin 44)
197 Lengthy critique of *Frontier* [Woolf/Kafka]
274 see fn 13
249 *Holiday* + 250

(1) See Acknowledgements for Archive references.
(2) Horizon Oct + Dec 1941 (Tom Harrisson / Koestler etc
(3) New Feminist Discourses: Critical Essays on Theories Texts ed Isobel Armstrong (London: Routledge 1992) esp Laura Marcus
(4) Englishness: Politics + Culture 1880-1920 eds Robert Colls + Philip Dodd (London: Croom Helm 1986) esp Dennis Smith
|| (5) Periodical New Leader
(6) VIP Jameson ed Challenge to Death (1934)
Peace Pledge Union 1937
The End of this War (1941)
|| (7) Periodical Lilliput
8 SJ No Time Like the Present 1933
9 SJ Letters to Vera Brittain
(10) VIP Jane Waller + Michael Vaughan-Rees eds Women in Wartime: The Role of Women's Magazines 1939-1945 (London: Optima 1987)
(11) Look at Mitchison correspondence?
(12) See SJ biting policeman ~~before~~ 1913 for feminism
SJ 'Women on the Spot' Atlantic Monthly Feb 1941
See Bibliog for TLS etc for SJ (see poems etc
(13) See Bibliog for VIP Mosley. + 5 + 7 (VIP)
(14) See fn 4 p 261 for VIP Mosley. + 5 + 7
(15) See Andy Croft.
(16) SJ 'Silchester' TLS 3000 1943; 'Cloud Form' TLS 29 July 1944
(17) Leavis 'Lady Novelists + the Lower Orders' Scrutiny 4, Sept 1935
(18) See Robillard fn 44 p 265
(19) SJ Left Review 2 (Nov 1934). + 4 (Jan 1936).
(20) See fn 48 p 265
(21) SJ Time + Tide, 6 June 1936.

Also by Phyllis Lassner

ELIZABETH BOWEN

ELIZABETH BOWEN: A Study of the Short Fiction

(22) See Birkett fn 57 p 265 (VIP) & Albinski.

(23) Malcolm Cowley, The New Republic 29 Jan 1936
Forum 95 (April 1936) p vii
Manchester Guardian 7 Feb 1936, TLS 1 Feb 1936

(24) N Mitchison 'Eye Opener', New Statesman 27 Jan 1984

25 SJ 'New Europe', Fortnightly Jan 1940

(26) CHECK LIDICE 1942

(27) Martin Ceadel, in Frank Gloversmith, ed., Class, Culture & Social Change (Harvester, 198

(28) SJ TLS 7 Oct 1939

(29) Lidice: A Tribute by Members of the Internationa PEN (London: Allen & Unwin, 1944)

30 see fn 6, p 273 & fn 18 p 274 re attitudes to Jews in war time

(31) See Eleanor Rathbone (fns 19, 20 p 275)

British Women Writers of World War II

Battlegrounds of their Own

Phyllis Lassner
Senior Lecturer
Northwestern University
Evanston, Illinois

First published in Great Britain 1998 by
MACMILLAN PRESS LTD
Houndmills, Basingstoke, Hampshire RG21 6XS and London
Companies and representatives throughout the world

A catalogue record for this book is available from the British Library.

ISBN 0–333–72195–0

First published in the United States of America 1998 by
ST. MARTIN'S PRESS, INC.,
Scholarly and Reference Division,
175 Fifth Avenue, New York, N.Y. 10010

ISBN 0–312–21241–0

Library of Congress Cataloging-in-Publication Data
Lassner, Phyllis.
British women writers of World War II : battlegrounds of their own / Phyllis Lassner.
p. cm.
Includes bibliographical references and index.
ISBN 0–312–21241–0 (cloth)
1. World War, 1939–1945—Great Britain—Literature and the war.
2. Women and literature—Great Britain—History—20th century.
3. English literature—Women authors—History and criticism.
4. English literature—20th century—History and criticism.
5. World War, 1939–1945—Women—Great Britain. 6. Patriotism in literature. I. Title.
PR478.W67L38 1997
820.9'358—dc21 97–40947
CIP

This book is printed on paper suitable for recycling and made from fully managed and sustained forest sources.

10 9 8 7 6 5 4 3 2 1
07 06 05 04 03 02 01 00 99 98

Printed and bound in Great Britain by
Antony Rowe Ltd, Chippenham, Wiltshire

As always
to Liz, Jason, and Jake

Contents

Acknowledgements

I would like to thank Northwestern University for supporting the writing of this book in so many different ways: through a faculty research grant which enabled me to finish my reading at the Bodleian Library, a Hewlett grant to develop a course on Women and War in the Twentieth Century, and for a Fellowship at Northwestern's Center for the Humanities where colleagues listened to my overall argument for this book. I am also grateful for the hospitality at the Oxford Centre for Hebrew and Jewish Studies which provided an idyllic setting in which to complete the writing of this book. It was because of my stay there that I was able to travel and benefit so much from responses to talks I gave at John Moores University in Liverpool and at the University of London. For those opportunities and their expertise I would like to thank Frank McDonough and Jean Radford.

To those who read chapters from this book and listened and commented so patiently on a subject that became only more compelling to me, I am infinitely grateful. I would especially like to thank Paul Holsinger, who has supported my work through the World War II sessions of the Popular Culture Association and with Mary Anne Schofield, publishing my essay '"A Cry for Life"' in the volume *Visions of War*, my women's history friends, Anne Summers and Joan Perkin, for their necessary and pungent questions, and what have been encouraging talks and moveable feasts with Karen Alkalay-Gut, Marcia Gealy, and Chanita Goodblatt. I would also like to express appreciation to Charmian Hearne, my editor at Macmillan for her enthusiasm, good advice, and good humour.

Finally, as always, so much of what has made writing this book such a joy has been the loving support of Jake Lassner, who may have a very different idea of war but has energetically and enthusiastically shared mine.

My thanks to the following: Christopher Storm-Clark for permission to quote from the unpublished letters of Storm Jameson, and the Vera Brittain Papers, William Ready Division of Archives and Research Collections, McMaster University Library, Hamilton, Canada, for Brittain's copies of Jameson's letters; Anne Ridler and Carcanet Publishers for permission to quote from her 'Poem for a Birthday', Naomi Mitchison for permission to quote her poem '1940'. I would also like to thank the Popular Press, *Mosaic*, and *Woman: A Cultural Review* for permission to reprint sections of earlier work I published with them.

If any copyright holders have inadvertently been overlooked the publishers will be pleased to make suitable arrangements at the earliest opportunity.

PHYLLIS LASSNER

Introduction

As recently as 1983 it was still assumed that English literature had somehow glossed over the century's most cataclysmic event. Salman Rushdie made the point:

> If you think of World War II – America, Germany and Italy all produced extraordinary novels about it; England didn't. Perhaps that also has something to do with the fact that the end of the war and the end of the Empire happened at almost the same time. There's a certain amount of living in a green world of the past in England. . . . There have been few attempts to come to terms with contemporary England, though perhaps that's beginning to change.[1]

In the years since Rushdie's claim, we have only begun to recognize that for women writers the World War II home fronts were fertile grounds for the production of a varied and powerful literature. As their writing is studied, it is reshaping critical debates about war literature. Among many others, the work of Stevie Smith, Storm Jameson, Elizabeth Bowen, and Phyllis Bottome dramatically refute Rushdie's assumptions. But equally important, these writers question ongoing approaches to the cultural politics of war and its representation by women.

The assumptions supporting Rushdie's contention were already established in 1941 by Tom Harrisson, who collected British home front testimony for the Mass-Observation Archives. Writing on 'War Books' in *Horizon* magazine, and claiming to have 'read literally every book which has anything to do with the war, reportage, fiction or fantasy', Harrisson concludes with mocking despair, 'Never have I felt that I owed so little to so many.'[2] In this case as in Rushdie's, such a claim holds up only when women's war writing is not taken seriously. With 'hats off to Naomi Mitchison quietly cultivating harsh lands in the Mull of Kintyre', Harrisson goes on to dismiss other women as part of 'the large number of different writers who have poured out indifferent material' ('War Books', p. 418). Harrisson's plaint can be seen as the result of a self-fulfilling manifesto he co-signed in October 1941 with other male colleagues, 'Why Not War Writers?'[3] After calling for government support of war writers in order to 'implant consciousness' of 'the relation of our every action to the conduct of the war', the co-signers prescribe war writing by delimiting the meaning of action: 'Why are there no novels of value about the building of shadow factories, the planning of wartime services, the operation of . . . an evacuation scheme? Why are there no satires on hoarders, or the black market? Why no novels of army life?' ('Why Not', pp. 237–8).

Harrisson's manifesto and Rushdie's statement, like so many surveys of British World War II literature, reflect critical values that predetermine the neglect of women's war writing. These surveys polarize the war fronts so that women's debates and experiences of the war do not figure in the studies which define war experience.[4] By defining war literature as representing combat experience, critics omit the writing of those who merely suffered through the Blitz, the aerial bombardment of British cities in 1940 and 1941, and for whom home front and battlefield merged. Although some, like Stevie Smith, Elizabeth Taylor, Betty Miller, and Katharine Burdekin have been reprinted, too many remain out of print and unavailable in most libraries. As a result of this neglect, much of this complex 'world of the past' remains invisible, and so it seems, an entire front of the war is still buried.

Instead of living 'in a green world of the past', most British women writers represented their wartime lives in a grey and stormy present. Because this difference emerges with so much interesting complexity, I decided to concentrate on women writers themselves rather than compare them to their male compatriots. Instead, I offer a reading that argues for the value of British women's World War II writing as a distinguished and multiform literary tradition and as individual novels of political and social analysis. Avowedly political, these writers tested the ideological and aesthetic grounds of traditional genre definitions in relation to their own ideologies and the language of wartime representation. Most studies, however, give them only a single voice or ideological framework.[5]

Despite expanding canons of women writers, British women writers of World War II remain at the margins of literary movements and ideological concerns with war. To complicate matters, many of these writers preferred the margins to the mainstream, and as a result were either trivialized or ignored. To recover them requires that we see their literary and political differences both as they identified them and as they were defined for them then and now. I maintain that exploring their individual and group differences takes us into uncharted literary and cultural territory. To group them testifies to the collective power of their arguments and contribution to the broad range of literary productivity in Britain in the thirties and forties. The result will be to expand our historical and cultural knowledge about a time we still find so compelling.

I contend that in their writing about fascism, the Nazi blitzkrieg [the coordinated campaign by air and ground forces] and Allied responses, many British women writers represent a challenge to two dominant cultural discourses: (1) British national and cultural identity and relationship with Europe; and (2) theories and practices of literary and cultural critics of women and war today. In response to the political discourses of their day (and Salman Rushdie's echoing voice), women writers ask: How does one reconcile a thriving British imperial identity based on claims of moral hegemony with the politics of appeasing Hitler and misogynist domestic ideologies and social policies? The failure to confront what Storm Jameson called 'the reality of evil men' causes these women to wonder whether Britain was ever justified in its claims to moral rectitude.[6] And finally, even as the war ended with the Allies' victory, they asked: Was this indeed a just conflict and what difference will victory make for the women and men on British and European home fronts?

Of particular interest to cultural debates is how these writers challenge the project of recovering women writers and women's wartime experiences. For while studies of women and war have exposed the masculinist ideologies of all wars and all kinds of women's resistance, they ignore the particularities of World War II that engendered a new definition of resistance. Many British women writers resisted policies of making peace with Hitler by insisting that this war, unlike others, was the only way to save the führer's victims. With full recognition that women rarely influenced government policies, many became active resisters through writing that questioned their social and political status in relation to accepted definitions of victimization. Even as their writing became political, however, many British women were intensely concerned about whether being active made them resisters or complicit with aggressivist policies. In their dilemma, they might very well have agreed with Elizabeth Bowen's declaration that all war writing is 'resistance writing' as it works out its own politics of concern[7]. We see this as they debated definitions of liberal democracy, international peace, offensive and defensive intervention, and British imperialism; as they resisted complacency towards the political and social effects of wartime disclocations, about victims on all sides, and about postwar social planning.

This women's discourse of World War II destabilizes the universalist anti-war conclusions of many influential studies of women and war.[8] Those studies, which are based on World War I as the foundational anti-war text and Virginia Woolf's *Three Guineas* as the canonical feminist anti-war theory, assume that all wars are wrong and that they destroy women's culture. While many British women shared this assumption after World War I, many also changed their minds as they recognized that the uniquely horrific consequences of Nazi policies differed from the self-deceived aims, purposeless losses, and uneasy peace that had justified their denunciation of 'the war to end all wars'. These complex and sometimes wildly divergent responses challenge Woolf's metahistorical and pancultural construction of fascism as well as essentialist theories that women are only passive war victims, war protesters, or complicit with the power of a masculinist war machine.

In recent years, rediscoveries of neglected women writers have led to cultural debates about the power of literary texts to be transformative, even revolutionary, about new definitions of modernism, and about extending aesthetic criteria to include didactic or political effects and popular culture. As Carole Snee reminds us, however, even with its inclusionary moves, literary criticism 'from Leavis to Althusser' is wedded to the idea of a canon for its 'self-definition of good art'.[9] Most significantly for British women writing World War II, whatever canon we privilege – feminist, modernist, realist or postmodern – the writing valued in our time is that which questions or transforms traditional forms or conforms to those currently privileged. When it doesn't fit or if it challenges the new criteria, the writing remains ignored or is reconstructed.[10]

British women writing World War II have also suffered from literary study that engages writers' political and social alignments; methods that combine literary and ideological analysis show concern for authors' unconscious or conscious implication in the dominant ideologies of the day. In the case of the thirties, critics often assume that writers' references to liberalism cohere in a universal definition and voice. As a result, writers are judged, not by their own arguments, but by their attention to liberalism's gendered social construction or debt to collectivity.[11] In the case of the forties, women's support of the war can be construed as a conservatism that all too easily aligns them with a masculinist war machine and alienates them from modernist forms.[12] The convergence of a critical debate about ideology and literary aesthetics, about accepting one literary period as political and dismissing another on aesthetic and political grounds, marks a point where we can see each period in the light of the other, discover new discursive terrain, and create more fluid boundaries of literary and political definitions.

In addition to individual differences, as a group, the writers I found in the course of my researches are distinct from canonical writers and categories of the period. Though my study begins with the thirties, only Virginia Woolf claims the modernist camp as her own. And while so many novels experiment formally with political aims, they do not invite new definitions of modernism; instead they invent new literary responses to modernism and to the era's socialist and proletarian fictions. They accomplish this in glossing their literary writing in polemical book reviews, newspaper and magazine letters, in forums on war and peace, and as volunteer war workers on the home front. The corresponding political goals of their writing and actions invite us to rethink the aesthetic criteria implicated in our ongoing concerns with the ideological and genre boundaries of literature.

My assumption in constructing this British women's literary tradition has been from the start that our debates would be complicated by integrating additional perspectives. While there is always the danger that readers will reject positions that challenge their own, I have worked within the inclusionary ethos of contemporary feminists. As challenging as women's war writing is to male-centred canonical interests, so is it to today's theories of women and war. For this reason, I felt it was imperative to prepare my responses in relation to debates on women and war over the past 20 years. My strategy, therefore, is to address questions raised by these debates through my analyses of British women writing World War II. In turn, these writers raise issues that enrich the texture of these debates by destabilizing their terms.

It may not be a coincidence that only since the Vietnam War have scholars been exploring war as a gendered discourse and experience. That war, on a home front so far away, invaded western homes only through TV screens, but the nightly show of decimated homes and families and the absence of women in war discourses lent dramatic irony to the simultaneous liberation struggle of western women. Those who served and died were noticed only when women lobbied for a memorial. That attention exposed a wide range of women's war attitudes. Just as public opinion stopped blaming soldiers for the war's problems, so we now understand that women participate in war for reasons other than those canonized as coercion, complicity or resistance.

Current feminist debates on women and war

For more than 20 years, research and theories of women and war have modelled women's representations, roles, and attitudes on cultural and social codes of motherhood. While it is acknowledged that these codes vary across cultures and time, they are usually interpreted as prevailing upon women to internalize and act upon universalized images of caregiving and selflessness, not to mention self-sacrifice. Despite their emphasis on nurturing impulses, these images do not present motherhood as strictly peaceloving. Jean B. Elshtain, a pioneer theorist of women and war, shows how these images may rely on and justify biological imperatives of motherhood, but they inscribe aggression as well.[13] She argues that because women internalize social and ideological pressures to participate in war, they are neither biologically nor socially constructed as innately pacifist or innocent bystanders. Elshtain, like many feminists, locates the source of these pressures in a romantic discourse that encourages men, figured as 'Just or Beautiful Warriors', to go to war to protect and defend women, who in turn embody virtues that constitute righteous causes ('Women and War', p. 3). As a result women are easily made to justify war's violence.

Recent study shows that this model elides the actual wartime behaviour of men and women. Wartime records of women's behaviour reveal that they are not passive bystanders, but participate and actively fuel war's support. But even here, a problematic maternal model prevails, implying that women justify their war work not only to nurture men, but to rally for their sacrifice.

Despite critiques of polarized 'Good Mothers' and 'Good Soldiers', the 'central, powerful image of the Moral Mother – nurturant, compassionate, and politically correct' has had enormous staying power.[14] But if 'the Moral Mother' image legitimizes women's place in public spheres, it also ties them to domestic ideology and roles. This maternal double bind seems an inevitable outcome to theories that keep women in line with notions of either their innate or constructed natures. Either nature essentializes them or prescribes, as such models do, what women ought to feel and how they ought to act. The prescriptive ordering of these formulations denies women the struggle for self-determination other scholars are gleaning from women's actual histories and self-representations.

Sara Ruddick's concept of 'maternal thinking' revises essentialist concepts by viewing women's war responses historically. But because that history is only about pacifism, even women's struggle against violation is seen as a 'maternal principle of reconciliation, resistance and refusal to injure', the only alternative being 'failure'.[15] Because Ruddick's revision is based on a universal idea of 'warism', she sees 'the cruel realities of war engraved' with the same intent and result, and therefore can find no justification for women's support of any war (See note 15 above, p. 113).

Women's war experiences have been further polarized from men's by viewing both through the prism of literary images. In their compendious study of women writers over the two world wars, Sandra Gilbert and Susan Gubar expose an internecine battle of the sexes. Pitting women's writing against men's, they argue that their separate spheres of suffering drove them to project their victimization onto each other in a war of words. Most recently, the collection, *Gendering War Talk,* focuses on both the historical moment and the symbolic representation of gender as it is constructed in and through war. Here again, however, because the aim is peace and reconciliation, its contributors see warlike values as a universal force overwhelming the historical contingencies that shape different origins and aims of wars. While the writers complicate the impact on gender by locating the pressures of warlike values in both men's and women's behaviour, the values of peace and war are themselves polarized. As a result, so are men and women, who are made to seem so susceptible to either peace or war values that they cannot see each in the other's light, much less question or revise them.

In response to the pitfalls of such polarized models, feminist scholars have called for analysing war culture and ideology through devising more categories. In order to demonstrate a wider range of women's wartime roles and representations, women's 'material reality' must be considered in terms of historical and present 'relations between gender and militarism', including women's military service and work in military production, and the effect of militarism on women's daily lives (Leonardo, p. 603).[16] Jane Marcus argues for the place of imperialism and race in the story of women and war, while Claire Tylee, on World War I, includes class and age distinctions.[17] Marcus criticizes any analytical model that ignores the historical context. If we foreground 'the metaphorical war between the sexes', argues Lynne Hanley, we lose 'sight of the real wars, of the massive, global human slaughter actually going on in the world outside these duels of the pen'.[18] Without understanding how the shifting grounds of wars and different players vex dualistic categories, we cannot understand the complex attitudes that support various kinds of war resistance and participation.

War, gender and the historical moment

It is my contention that British women writers interpret their World War II experiences in ways that unsettle our conceptions of political differences, social change and gender. As they show again and again, even as 'the discourse of wartime social policy worked to limit gender disruption', their own literary discourse very often resisted traditional gender relations and expressed a yearning for social change (*Behind the Lines*, p. 8). Their acute sense of the particular historical moment links their critique of dualistic gender relations to the geo-political shifts that marked changing constructions of ally and enemy. We see this dramatically in their diverse and complex responses to the enthusiastic participation, complicity and victimization of women living under the Nazis.

By considering wars as specific historical events, each with its own destabilizing battlegrounds, we can see that to identify women as pro- or anti-war or, to use the old labels, conservative and liberal, prevents us from noticing the nuanced questions women writers asked of their own politics and participation. Moreover, while many women writers use language generally attributed to conservative, socialist or leftist platforms, they challenge their precepts as well as our own use of political labels, especially as they remained sceptical about any tradition or reform schemes. Identifying their concerns allows us to see that their choices, while pressured by prevailing ideologies and what has been called 'the Man's House of militarist social organization', also involve questioning those ideologies as the material conditions of specific wars shape social parameters[19]

British women question the aims and direction of World War II through a range of literary forms that interpret the moral and political implications of actual events; theirs is not a war of the sexes or of literary or symbolic images involving only the production and history of literature. Thus, though women responded to wartime changes through the lenses of 'existing cultural resources', they also became agents of cultural change, analysing actual domestic and foreign policies that were perpetrated by and affected the lives of both men and women. And instead of feeling victimized or discouraged by being labelled 'selfish, divisive, or even treasonous', they often took great relish in their revisionary representations (*Behind the Lines*, p. 7).

Attending to a historicized range of women's self-representation also shows how changes in war and society do not, as so often claimed, always polarize men and women but provide ways of seeing how their responses intersect and are often interdependent. Jana Thompson and Scharf and Woollacott argue that the historical perspective shows how social changes, however fleeting or lasting during wartime, both alter and reinforce conceptions of masculinity and femininity.[20] An example of this would be how women's independence and self-esteem were spurred by wartime paid work but also undercut by prevailing domestic ideology.[21] Widening our perspective even more is to see how gender constructions are complicated by seeing the military discourse of this particular war in relation to other cultural texts and symbolic icons of the era, and not as solely determining in itself.[22] In interactions between women's self-portrayal and their consciousness of propaganda and social codes deployed in broadcasts, newspapers and women's magazines, we can see how women do not merely ingest images of victimization or power, but act, react, and represent themselves in both roles, sometimes all at once. So themes of 'women's complicity and and resistance to war' are not discrete, but overlap (Cooper *et al.*, p. XV; note 8, above). If we consider how literature and other cultural artifacts are implicated in both war and gender systems, we will see how war changes imagistic and linguistic meanings of categories such as gender, and how women debate and challenge those meanings. In literary representation, as Cooper *et al.* (p. 82) observe, war, narration, and characterization work together so that gender roles not only reflect prevailing social codes, but question and revise them.

Literature and other cultural artifacts are implicated in war, not as universal themes, but as expressions of particular historic conflicts working in tandem with the historical memories, concerns, and ideologies, not only of writers, but of readers at different times. So our readings of the specific past of World War II must be shaped by our positions in our present. In the case of current theories of women and war, while categories expand to include women of different class, ethnic, ideological, age, and religious identities, there has been no attempt to see war except as a universal category of aggression, bellicosity, terror and violation. My hunch is that because our theories of war are so invested in memories and constructions of the tragic wastes of World War I and the Vietnam War, World War II must either be ignored, dismissed as an exception, or integrated as one more debilitating experience for women. As Pierson (p. 85; note 22, above) argues, however,

> [T]he term "war" is, of course, an abstraction under which we subsume a bewildering variety of activities, only some of which could rightly be viewed as "gendering." For instance, in extreme situations, such as running for cover from aerial bombardment or seeing one's loved ones led off to a gas chamber, the social category of sex/gender would undoubtedly shrink to insignificance.

In light of these World War II examples, the proposition that meanings of war and gender shift according to their discourses should expand the reasons women choose to fight for their country and unite with the very forces they hold responsible for war's terrors.

I argue in this book that those British women writers who construct World War II as a unique onslaught find their own reasons to participate in or resist the war effort, reasons that develop out of their experiences in domestic and public spheres.

These reasons, moreover, do not accord with the manipulative messages of government propaganda, popular media, or with their traditional gender roles. The cumulative effect of reading British women's writing about fascism and World War II is to see that they took no meanings for granted or as global. Writers such as Betty Miller, Elizabeth Taylor, Lettice Cooper, and Margaret Kennedy drew upon their liminal position as women in an unoccupied but embattled England to question the aims and costs of war. I maintain that it is from within the complex and ambiguous conditions of middle class privilege, the blitzing of middle class private life, and their marginalized political and literary lives that many British women writers constructed their responses to the war.

Though they often respond in the language of caregivers and protectors, the safe haven they imagine for their children reflects an idea of home and homeland that does not comply with official war aims or prevailing domestic ideologies. Those who unite with the war effort create narrative voices which define their country, their homes, and family on different grounds. And in their vocation as writers, as part of the sacrifices this difference moves them to, they demand a greater public role and recognition by the state, not 'to prove themselves worthy' and therefore patriotic in any conventional sense, but to redefine patriotism as an emotional and political commitment to a nation and to social roles they would change (Thompson, p. 66; note 20). For these writers, the myth of a People's War must be revised to become the truths of women's home front realities.[23] These realities, moreover, would reflect a different truth about the emotional resonances of nationhood. Just as the People's War was now a woman's war, so women demonstrated that national identity was gendered.

The proliferating dichotomies of gender and war only prove how powerful and determining are those images dividing women into passive and innocent victims or complicit with the 'military state', either in their war work or in 'bearing the children that will replace the Nation's fallen manhood'.[24] Such dualities undermine the challenges of feminist and cultural critics to the hierarchies contained in binary categories. But it is also difficult to escape such images when the model of analysis for women and war continues to be World War I, with its haunting archetypal resonances of self-defeating loss. If we invoke a historically discrete approach for the study of war's literary representation, we discover not only that women write from 'every conceivable ideological position', but that they invest wars, both continuous and discrete, of different times and places, with different meanings (Marcus, p. 50; note 17). We can therefore see women's changing attitudes towards world war primarily as an evolving and recursive cast of mind, a moral philosophy and world view, especially in terms of understanding history and the processes of social and political change which had begun but not ended with World War I.

The painful separation of World Wars I and II

Differences are clarified when we examine responses to World Wars I and II. Vera Brittain, Virginia Woolf, Ethel Mannin, and other women became lifelong pacifists as a result of the tragedies of World War I, and viewed World War II as a continuation of its horrors, with dress rehearsals in the Spanish Civil War. Others, whose careers also span the two world wars, changed their minds; in so doing, they 'destabilize' what Jane Marcus calls 'the standard plot of the literature of World War I' ('Antaeus', p. 50). If we follow women's varied and changing views, we see that they responded in language that marked the policies, propaganda, events, and symbols of a history of change even as some complained of stagnation. To globalize or abstract these responses by fusing them with their responses to World War I would betray their struggles to publicize their revisionary political and moral consciousness.

It is unclear how much the regeneration of domestic ideology which marked the post World War I backlash against women affected the attitudes of British women writers towards another world war. At the same time that the interwar years produced economic and political crises, domestic ideology and women's traditional roles were regenerated.[25] As women's fiction of the twenties and thirties reveals, the English middle classes retreated to traditional attitudes that celebrated the domestic sphere and its relations, and this produced the effect of putting 'women and the home . . . at the centre of national life'.[26] By the time fascism was taking hold in Europe, with its emphasis on women's childbearing and caring roles, many British women writers came to fear that its radical conservatism accorded only too well with traditional attitudes at home. Vera Brittain's 1936 novel, *Honourable Estate*, intended as a feminist drama of women's 'private destinies' in the interwar period, reflects her 'painful awareness that the rise of fascism and the return of militarism marked a reaction in politics' that 'revived hostility to feminism'.[27] Women's writing about fascism shows that many imagined it exploding into another war, but that this time, home and battleground would become one, ruled by a combined ethos of militarism and misogyny.[28] It is this imaginative coalition that makes their dystopic fictions of the thirties part of British women's literature of World War II.

Naomi Mitchison worried that British liberalism, always subject to internal dissent and lack of cohesive popular support, would dissolve if conservatives yielded to a fascist takeover. Her fears, however, merged with her belief that whatever polity prevailed and oppressed them, women would survive a fascist war only if they continued to fight for equality as well as for expression of their differences. Her fiction and non-fiction of the thirties and forties represents women as both victims and agents for change. In her 1934 dystopia, *We Have Been Warned,* women are brutalized by a British fascist takeover that could easily have been inspired by Oswald Mosley's fascist emphasis on women's maternal and domestic perogatives. His split statement, 'We want men who are men and women who are women', reflected the backlash feminists feared and resisted as well as their division about valorizing sexual difference or equality (Kent, pp. 141, 142; note 28, above). Feminists like Eleanor Rathbone argued that women benefited more from valuing their sexual difference and wanted special economic assistance for women's family responsibilities. Rathbone's apprehension about another world war was allayed in part by her belief that if women were paid for domestic work, they could offer the home as 'an effective antidote to the anxiety created by the threat of war, even to the fact of war itself' (Kent, p. 142; note 28, above).

If women writers of this era connected their views of women's domestic roles to issues about war aims, they did not do so with any symmetry. Whether they saw the domestic sphere as a site of regeneration or resistance did not lead them to support or protest the war. As their depiction of the British home front reveals, both home and street, whether bombed or intact, are imagined as places where women can just as easily be victimized, be self-determining or implement social change. Just as women's wartime roles were as constraining as they were liberating, so their reactions were mixed. Even as they were conscripted into agricultural and factory work, they were also subject to government policies that denied them equal economic compensation or adequate childcare. And yet, as so many have reported, women found these work experiences liberating. While such reactions reflect similarities to World War I, feeling liberated into new spheres as well as abused by primitive working conditions and persistent misogyny, their writing reveals important departures.

The structure of this book reflects the myriad views and forms of the writers I consider. What began as a survey of attitudes towards a second world war came to reflect women's changing definitions of war and pacifism as peace turned to crisis in the thirties. It is because of this transformation that there are so few women writers who declare themselves pacifists. Most never stopped feeling that war is loathsome but many also found that they must give up their pacifist principles. Learning about Hitler's victims, many concluded that not only could pacifism not help, but that it coincided with what they felt was the cruel indifference of Britain's appeasement and war policies. In their passionate reaction against the conservative political culture Storm Jameson labelled 'old Park Lane', pacifism itself appeared bound to the same romanticized past to which reactionary forces aligned themselves.[29]

The tension between a revolt from the past and present and fears for the future produced a radical form of writing examined in two chapters following a survey of war attitudes. These are the dystopias that envision apocalyptic ends to the reactionary past and stagnant present. In the thirties, which saw a proliferation of politically engaged fiction, women's dystopias grapple with political and social unease in radically nonrealistic forms. Although speculative fiction was already an established genre by the mid-thirties, what distinguishes these dystopias is the conjunction of a gendered political analysis, the historical moment, and imagined experience. Together, they form a feminist political polemic that represents a rejection of the technologically bound dystopias of H.G. Wells and Aldous Huxley. Women's dystopias remain earthbound, where evil forces have evolved, not in test tubes, outer space or under a rock, but in Parliamentary halls. Their imagined fusion of political and social disorder and war relates women's prescribed biological destinies in the past to a projected horrific future. As female characters are portrayed both individually and collectively, they embody and question the myths that shape political culture. For Naomi Mitchison and Storm Jameson, the political becomes personal as they imagine traditional values translated into state policy with fascist takeovers. Written two and four years before Virginia Woolf theorized the origins of fascism in *Three Guineas,* the dystopias of Mitchison and Jameson dramatize the catastrophic consequences of fascism, but with differences that mark their political and literary inquiries as a reaction against modernism as well. Recoiling from modernism's search for mythic wholeness at the expense of *realpolitik,* these dystopias dramatize the historical moment as disrupting a trans-historical continuum.

The linkage in women's dystopias of political and literary analysis and polemic follows the war years in imagining a world dominated by Hitler and Tojo. It is here that my chronological sequence assumes the projective shape of these fictions, for one of the most powerful dystopias about the protracted desolation of the war's outcome was written in 1937. Katharine Burdekin's *Swastika Night* takes us into the 700th year of the Reich while delving into the past that represents the historic reality of so many women writers' fears. That past is in fact the present of the 1938 *Three Guineas,* Mitchison's 1934 *We Have Been Warned,* and Jameson's 1936 *In the Second Year.* A far cry from the domestic conservatism of Britain's interwar period, the future in *Swastika Night* and Jameson's 1942 *Then We Shall Hear Singing* is orchestrated by imagining its most radical consequences as they spill over from the home into the disorder of communal life and international politics.

Because so many women writers view the home as consolidating the political, social, and cultural concerns of the home front, my next two chapters consider domestic fictions of the war. With their wartime settings, these novels represent the ground on which interwar and wartime imperatives meet domestic ideology. For writers such as Betty Miller, Lettice Cooper, Marguerite Steen and Elizabeth Bowen, however, this is not a fiction that promises to soothe the aching wartime soul. Despite many rural settings, these novels do not promote a sense of 'living in a green world of the past', as Rushdie claimed. The domestic quietude of middle and upper class life cannot be retained in wartime, even if its doyennes so wished. Amidst the pressures of shortages, evacuation, and maintaining the stability to which these classes were committed, all staples of their lives are dashed. Gone is the solidity of the manor, the quaint village, or urban neighbourhood, with their self-contained, reserved, and decent populace. Its heirs are disoriented and decentred by wartime conditions, the sum of which blasts all containment, reserve, and decency into social and psychological shrapnel. Even as oppositions of masculinity and femininity are maintained, even exacerbated by home front conditions, this does not guarantee social stability or confidence in the social order. The exposure of domestic disorder in these fictions allows us to explore how the end of self-confidence and the quotidian invites new definitions of community and empowerment among women. As the grammar of social life becomes political, these domestic novels also reveal new perspectives on the genre.

My study of English home front novels moves to the European scene in the chapters that follow. In a sense they follow the political trajectory of many British women writers who lived and travelled in Central Europe between the wars. For Ann Bridge and Olivia Manning, Europe is no longer an exotic site of romantic adventure, but one in which to recognize a new world disorder. The result radicalizes the conventions of genre fiction to deploy a political critique that links British foreign policy and domestic ideology to the fates of aliens and women. On the foreign grounds of these texts, British national identity is both gendered and racialized, bearing critical weight in its relation to the Nazi enemy.

In the light of these revisions of gender and national identity, my book can be seen as a celebration not only of many neglected women writers of a submerged literary site, but of their moral and political courage which evolved in what Henry Louis Gates Jr calls 'the politics of identification'. This position contrasts sharply with identity politics, which 'starts with the assertion of a collective allegiance' and being

> . . . about the priority of difference . . . is – by itself – dangerously inadequate. A politics of identification starts not with the possession of identity, but with the capacity to identify with. It asks what we have in common with others, while acknowledging the diversity among ourselves. It is about the promise of a shared humanity.[30]

British women writers who lived through and looked back at World War II wrestled with a politics of identification in response to the identity politics of the liberal tradition they inherited. This tradition, despite shifts in emphasis over time, continued to combine an ideal of freedom with 'the imperatives of achieving decency and achieving order'.[31] Within this purview, liberalism had also produced social codes which kept women from being as influential as they would have wished. 'The image of decent traditional English folk' did not include Storm Jameson or Eleanor Rathbone refusing to accept a polite 'no' from officials and notables they pressed to rescue Hitler's victims (D. Smith, p. 256; see note 31 above). In one sense, women's behaviour travestied a hallmark of British decency – restraint. Compounding their bad form was the cause for which women were stretching the bounds of propriety. Rescuing aliens defied a cohesive identity politics on which 'the management of a decent communal life' depended (D. Smith, p. 256; see note 31 above). The refugees looked to England to fulfil its 'promise of a shared humanity', but as the nation rallied around feelings of national unity in the emergency of war, it rejected those who represented difference, and either refused them entry or interned them as potential threats (D. Smith, p. 256; see note 31 above).

It was their identification with these Others that drove so many women writers to redefine patriotism, with its emphasis on national identity and denigration of women's rights and needs as 'selfish and divisive'. Government and popular rejection of refugees reminded these women writers of their own marginality, a position that drew ironic attention to the idea of national solidarity. In the sense that women and refugees were granted a kind of alien status, they could not be considered integral to that part of national identity which stands united. In wartime, when the nation defined itself as an island – England, fighting a defensive war alone against a colonizing enemy, women and refugees represent its ironic opposite: a colony of Others representing the nation as the empire – Great Britain.

What happened, British women writers asked their Janus-faced nation, to the liberal ideal of individual freedom in harmony with 'a decent, rational, and ordered community?' (D. Smith, p. 256; see note 31 above). What they saw were signs of civil tensions that did not bode well either for Britain's war aims or its projected plans for peace. If women and refugees were seen as alien Others, threatening the myth of a united nation, then also threatened was the propaganda that there was a united front to beat back the enemy and build a liberal society. Parallel to the condition of interned refugees, women's political writing and activism were contested and opposed. The oppositional status granted women and aliens suggested a nation at war with itself.

And yet despite their alienation, many British women writers forged a detente with the nation which was 'interfering now with their liberty', as Virginia Woolf noted.[32] But instead of remaining 'shut up' and 'shut out', many women writers represented this condition in their debates about the war (*TG*, p. 103). From their unrelenting writing, we learn that women's engagements with internal crisis and world war affected their consciousness and identities permanently. Having politicized and publicized their identities and writing, many remained aggressive proponents of political and social causes for the rest of their lives.

What I have come to value as the heroic lives and writing of so many British women of this era could easily fuel nostalgia. As so many have testified since, especially during its 50th anniversary, World War II was a time when so many boundaries did dissolve that the effect was liberatory for many women, regardless of government constraints. But any possibility for nostalgia is undercut by tensions that define these writers' identification with their nation, 'a kettle on the boil', as Betty Miller put it.[33] It is because the issue of English and British identity plays such an important part in women's war debates that I also decided not to include writers like H.D. (the nom de plume of the poet, Hilda Doolittle), who wrote movingly about her wartime experiences in Britain, but did not assume its identity. As home front and battleground merged, meanings of the nation at war expand for many British women beyond the factory and home, beyond the borders of national interest and 'existing cultural resources' to redefine nation, homeland, self and other. As women writers either acknowledge openly or embed, their ambivalent identification with alien Others shifted the meaning of this war.

The writers I consider created various narrative forms in response to their ambivalences about the nation and the Other. In all cases, however, they represent nation and Other as a relationship between the outbreak of a new and foreign tyranny and a very old style of oppression at home. This portrayal was founded on the place of women's experience and attitudes in the political culture of total war that monitored and censored their voices. In a mirroring effect, British women writers depict this multilayered experience as their ambivalent identification with representations of self and Other. That these writers recognize both similarities and unassimilable differences between themselves and Others such as evacuees or refugees and victims, adds even more moral complexity to their polemical fictions. Whether they write from a prewar, wartime, or postwar position, their moral template remains the same: how women's responses to the presence or absent but haunting presence of the Other offers criteria for their determining the moral aims of the war.

Although the concept of the Other is threatened by overuse, the work of Emmanuel Levinas sheds particular light on the moral complexity in women's responses to those they cast in that role. Describing the Other as 'a face looking at me as absolutely foreign', Levinas establishes that 'the absolutely other is the Other. . . . The alterity of the Other does not depend on any quality that would distinguish him from me, for a distinction of this nature would precisely imply between us that community of genus which already nullifies alterity'.[34] As so many British women writers realized, with varying responses, despite their own status of Other, the absolute foreignness of Others meant that not only was the state of difference between them immutable and absolutely constant, but that any bridge between self and other would still keep them separate, both at the level of experience and identity.

The moral gauge used by Levinas and with which British women writers grapple is located in a relationship of responsibility, where the Other might appeal for help but 'resists possession, resists my powers' (*T&I*, p. 197; see note 34 above). The struggle results because the Other will always demand both separateness and empathy, and '[t]o welcome the Other is to put in question my freedom' (*T&I*, p. 85; see note 34 above). Levinas claims that his concepts of the Other and moral responsibility transcend historical experience; his persistent references to the Holocaust invoke a sense of timelessness as a 'drama of Sacred History'.[35] And yet, as Theodore De Boer has noted, the reason why Levinas is so concerned with such social institutions as 'the political order of citizens in a state' is because 'In the years 1933–1945 we experienced concretely what it means when institutions forsake justice. Man was left to the guidance of his own conscience. This was the predicament of the Jews.'[36] Pinpointing 'an explicitly Jewish moment', Levinas extrapolates a moral question profoundly rooted in both sacred and profane history: 'The essential problem is: can we speak of an absolute commandment after Auschwitz? Can we speak of morality after the failure of morality?'[37]

Many British women writers speak of the morality of a second world war as a relationship to Others threatened by a holocaust they fear and whose reality they ponder long afterward. They ponder the absolute commandment of not killing as they dramatize the absolute alterity of both the Nazi enemy and the Jewish victim. In its dramatic form, their ambivalent identification with Others is played out as problematic relationships between women whose sense of self is prescribed by government and social policy and men and women marked as unassimilable aliens. Women's depictions of these ambivalent relationships provide a distinctive cultural key to the social and literary contexts and concerns of women's wartime writing. Constantly facing rejection of their own social platforms, some writers recreated their experience in fictional Others who become victims of an oppressive politics of identification. Instead of expressing empathy for those who have also been subject to an ongoing history of persecution and marginality, this writing recapitulates and reinforces that history even as it pleas for the rescue of aliens and refugees.

The ambivalence that drives this writing produces rhetorical effects that are equally ambiguous. On the one hand, caricatures of alien Others often act out a rejection of the marginalized self. Typical of a kind of self-loathing in which rejection is internalized, in constructing these stereotypes, the rejected also acts out her identification with the oppressor. And yet in most cases, these caricatures play alongside polemical pleas for sympathy and support for the Other. The multifarious ways in which these ambivalences play out in many texts create moral and aesthetic complexities that challenge our own constructions of the past. They do so by enriching our understanding of the relationship between British women writers, the historic moment in which they wrote, and their construction of it.

In view of our own contemporary critical concerns with representation, rationality, and the truth of historicism, we would have to consider these narrative depictions in and through their changing permutations. This does not relegate these writers' fictions to a falsely polarized position of subjective, partial, ideological, or even irrational responses to history. As Paul Ricoeur argues, while 'traditional dichotomies between historical and fictional writing' problematize our ability to find 'a truth claim' in each, there is a stronger relationship between historical and fictional writing than supposed:

> Just as narrative fiction does not lack reference, the reference proper to history is not unrelated to the "productive" reference of fictional narrative. Not that the past is unreal: but past reality is, in the strict sense of the word, unverifiable. Insofar as it no longer exists, the discourse of history can seek to grasp it only indirectly. It is here that the relationship with fiction shows itself as crucial. The reconstruction of the past . . . is the work of the imagination. The historian, too, by virtue of the links . . . between history and narrative, shapes the plots that the documents may authorize or forbid but that they never contain in themselves. History, in this sense, combines narrative coherence with conformity with the documents. This complex tie characterizes the status of history as interpretation.[38]

I contend that British women writers of World War II create historical fiction that performs the act of historical interpretation through the lens of the social documents that shaped their experience. These 'documents' include the wartime situations and policies that drove them from their homes into evacuation or war work, that called for refugee internment, and that both liberated and constrained their sense of self and Other. In their ambivalent constructions of the fates of many Others, these writers not only reconstruct and verify the past, they interpret it as part of their discovery of new meanings in their own lives. In order to give credence to these writings my analysis will not problematize their representations of World War II to the point where they are in danger of disappearing once again, only this time, in a theoretical debate. Emphasizing writers' changing perceptions, ambivalences, and figuration does not mean that we can only speak of them primarily in terms of destabilizing or demythicizing discourses. To do so has produced the effect of merging the experiences of different wars into one experience or plot. As experiences of different wars are discussed as having been decentred by the exigencies of language and competing discourses of war, it has been all too easy for the former to disappear into the story of the latter.

My perspective on the particular historical events that comprised the British and European home fronts for British women writers not only distinguishes their experience of World War II, but also questions the relation between my literary analyses and historical inquiry. The literary and critical representation of lived experience become matters of historicity and its shaping into a narrative.[39] For example, there are obvious differences between writing that is recorded during the war's events and that which represents them in retrospect. Like historians who make sense of the past by reconstructing it into narrative and then subjecting that reconstruction to analysis that might include the present and even the future, literary writers, as Alison Light reminds us about interwar British women writers, feel not only the pressure of their own 'heterogeneous present' (p. 2; note 26, above). They also respond to their sense of the future as it positions them to read 'into the entrails of the present signs of what was to come, and how far they were moved by the forms of the past, aware of it as loss, as comfort, or as an invisible force in their lives'.

I would therefore agree with Alison Light that

> ... to read literature as history would be to invite the reader inside a culture, and yet to insist on listening to its own heart beat.... Because novels not only speak from their cultural moment but take issue with it, imagining new versions of its problems, exposing ... its confusions, conflicts and ... desires, the study of fiction is an especially inviting and demanding way into the past.

This book explores a past that is very much with us even as it recedes with the deaths of its survivors and their memories. Debates about the 50th anniversary of World War II have challenged those memories, striking painful chords in both survivors and heirs. Those who fought for the Allies and many of the defeated and their heirs, as well as those whose loved ones were brutalized or killed under Nazi and Japanese occupation, celebrate the Allies' victory at all costs. Others, as we saw with the Smithsonian's Enola Gay exhibition, find the costs of victory's strategies prohibitive. By returning to British women's writing of the war we can begin to construct a cultural history that raises significant questions about our own responses to that era and its relationship to waging any war. To consider the complex range of women's voices and experiences as individual sets of political and social identities as well as products of historical constructions and local culture leads to a method that 'shows women choosing war ... and writing from every conceivable ideological position from the patriotic to the pacifist' (Marcus, p. 55; note 17 above).

I maintain that in representing and bearing witness to this war as distinctly horrific, these writers create disturbances in our ethical, ideological, and emotional understanding of any war and our attitudes towards its other players. Analyzing the complex ambivalences of these writers did not, therefore, lead me to neatly divide them into opposed camps, taxonomies of women's war literature, or into extant categories of women's wartime roles and responses to World War II. In my view, these British women writers and the fictional women they portray cannot be considered as either consenting to or resisting war in terms that contemporary debate criticizes or celebrates. Indeed, they assert over and over again that while they are aware of themselves as gendered subjects, as women writers, their identities are just as bound up with the contingencies of the larger history of both men and women on both sides of the war. It is therefore my goal in this book to suggest the need to review this writing of World War II as identifying more complex frameworks and forms of written expression in which to discuss women's responses to war.

All together, their writing represents an epic of moral clarification, working as a self-reflexive document that transverses human experience, memory, and history. In its relationship between individual consciousness and historical event, this writing gives us access to a past that for these writers must remain imprinted on the collective consciousness of future generations. To do this, these British women writers construct its meaning in a combination of political, historical, and fictional discourses to produce a literature that reaches beyond pleasing forms to shape an ethical/political aesthetic.

1

'Differences that Divide and Bind'

In these days when there is a bad name for detachment, it is hard to assess the detached man.[1]

Elizabeth Bowen, 1941

The title of this chapter is the title of a 1942 essay in *Time and Tide* by Rebecca West.[2] Like so many British women writers, her inspiration to find meaning in a second world war began with the losses of World War I. Their painful memories were often similar, and not just because so many lost loved ones. It was also because they remembered how their struggles for equality lost ground to the lure of supporting the nation last time it was threatened by world war. Many had rallied to that earlier war effort on behalf of brothers and lovers who risked their lives for it. When the war invaded the home front with a dreaded telegram, many women, including Vera Brittain, Storm Jameson, and Virginia Woolf, turned their anguish into rage against all wars and became pacifists. But just as World War I garnered impassioned differences among women, the awful possibility of an even more engulfing war moved them to weave memory into different patterns for world peace. So Vera Brittain crafted her 1933 odyssey of feminism and pacifism, *Testament of Youth*, out of her diaries of World War I's inexplicable waste. Storm Jameson wove her despair at her young brother's senseless death into many later narratives, each of them arguing the justice of a new and different world war.

Many who were feminists as well as those who were not used the rallying cries of English national identity and destiny as a language of opposition against Nazi Germany. In turn, they were divided from women who found no meaning in victory, especially since the declaration to save the world for democracy sounded like the same old jingoistic propaganda. Many of the latter felt that their earlier losses were degraded by recycled slogans of military moralism, and saw this as a betrayal of the *realpolitik* that extended across the home front and international relations. Even when war finally erupted, women's writing invoked historical and personal memory, the power of which shaped their visions of the world's future.

Though many women writers would reach different conclusions once war broke out, in the thirties, as they witnessed the promises of peace and prosperity emptying into economic depression and the rise of fascism, most blamed Britain's leadership as a sign of their nation's decay – impotent at best and fascistic at worst. Phyllis Bottome, for example, found 'There was a part of England determined on a peace to be paid for by her fellow democracies; arrogant with the sloth of a quarter of a century; steeped in victory; guilty of money-conditioned thinking . . .'.[3] Others, like pacifist socialist Ethel Mannin, found historical reasons for both guilt and decay while blaming a more universally self-destructive imperialist system; in Mannin's view, Britain's leaders were merely taking their long-running role as self-righteous dupes on the road:

> . . . "fascism" – that convenient scapegoat. As though before such imperialist-nationalists as Mussolini and Hitler came to power the world was a safe, sane, happy place . . . as though without Adolf Hitler the conflicting materialist interests in Western civilization would never have reached the peak of crisis which topples over into war. We had entered upon a period of decadence long before Hitler's rise to power. It is a decadence which goes back to the Industrial Revolution. . . . Hitlerism is merely an offshoot of "the secret dictatorship of money" which began in the nineteenth century.[4]

In 1938, after Hitler moved into the Sudetenland and threatened Czechoslovakia, the sight of Neville Chamberlain waving his white paper accord with Hitler made many women feel that British women and children would also be sacrificed. Like Mannin, they found their government leaders guilty of hypocrisy and duplicity, but for a different and more ironic reason. Bryher, Rose Macaulay, and many others felt that the 'old boys' preferred to placate both their nervous electorate and a committed conquerer rather than risk Britain's military ego once again. The historic irony of this policy drove Phyllis Bottome to write to *Time and Tide* in August 1939: 'We have strapped upon our backs today adolescent statesmen, the fathers and sons of those we lost in the War – the generation that might have saved us from the cowardice and irresponsibility that seems to be our doom....'[5] Such political immaturity led Rebecca West to condemn 'a pervasive weakness in the liberal forces that oppose cruel races or systems of government', which she traced to their 'frivolity' and 'failure ... to stiffen their opposition to militarist tyranny after the Great War of 1914', an 'indecisive campaign'.[6]

Many women writers were divided not only among, but within themselves about theories and then realities of waging another world war. They continued to abhor militarism and imperialism, but many also found World War II different enough from the confused aims and results of World War I to support it. Where millions of soldiers in World War I had lost their lives to gain a mile of mud, Hitler's blitzkrieg made it clear that untold numbers of defenceless civilians and children would be ground under every mile. Because women writers were now torn by fears of German conquest, many felt contempt for the political paralysis that issued from the bad marriage between British imperialism and appeasement that threatened the lives of too many. The interplay between criticisms of British self-interest, the widespread support of a war against Hitler and wildly diverse reasoning destabilizes much of the opposition in women's views. On the one hand, many women distinguished this war from the last by defining it as a defensive battle to save not only their own lives, but those of Europeans and Americans they hoped would join in finding new solutions for a more humanely secure future. So Pamela Frankau enlists support for the war in her upbeat broadcast to North America in 1941. As she recalls her own work 'enrolling people for National Service', she exhorts: 'we must prepare. Because if you had a tiger living in the garden next door you wouldn't wait till he came into your garden to find out the best way of dealing with tigers.'[7]

Other British women, representing a wide range of pacifist beliefs, resisted the idea of this war's uniqueness. They felt that the League of Nation's inadequacies opened the road to Mussolini's invasion of Abyssinia and Franco's junta in Spain, all spans in the bridge to Hitler's blitzkrieg. In their agonizing over this history, however, some women pacifists also shared sympathies with those war supporters who worried about ideals of social equality and Hitler's victims. Other pacifists felt that since this war was but a continuation of the last, to fight it would also subvert the struggle to eliminate the causes of all wars. Still others promoted peace through negotiation or appeasement. Many women were torn between their rejection of any form of state violence and anxiety about the destruction of their own nation. So many authors, as well as their narrators and characters, would thus share Virginia Woolf's fear and rage at the ubiquity of Hitler's war. Woolf's 1941 essay, 'Thoughts on Peace in an Air-Raid', invokes Hitler's name for every mention of 'tyranny, the insane love of power'.[8] But instead of allowing fear and rage to paralyse them, British women writers became agents for change, not only in domestic life, but in public politics and in the shape of their ideologies and writing.

THREE GUINEAS PLUS: VIRGINIA WOOLF AND HER WAR CORRESPONDENTS

Like Woolf, many women writers felt that the war was a wrongful validation of a still potent patriarchal political machinery. When Woolf's nephew was killed in the Spanish Civil War she linked its betrayals and losses to World War I. Giving credence to the political ideals at stake in Spain, she nonetheless finds war abhorrent as a method for achieving them. She recalled that

> . . . we were all C.O.'s in the Great war. And though I understand that this is a 'cause' . . . of liberty & so on, still my natural reaction is to fight intellectually: if I were any use, I should write against it: I should evolve some plan for fighting English tyranny. The moment force is used, it becomes meaningless & unreal to me.[9]

Attributing meaningless force to a universal masculinist militarism inspired Woolf to create a pacifist counterforce. She fought 'intellectually' by writing her 1938 anti-war pamphlet, *Three Guineas*. By 1936 and 1937, when she was researching and writing it, Woolf's memories of protesting World War I made her weary and disdainful about signing petitions and appearing on public platforms: the futility of such efforts to influence government policies had already been proved. As a second world war drew near, her polemic went behind the scenes of geo-politics and statesmanship to challenge the ethos that peace can derive from war.

Woolf located the cultural core of this ethos in male only chambers of politics and education. She defined the core as a tradition which encourages war as the culminating act of courage, patriotism, and nobility. For Woolf, these abstractions, glorified in the rhetoric of manliness, were dangerous in what they reflected and effected. Because the romance of courage and patriotism was kept aloft by Britain's class and gender hierarchies, it ensured the mobilization of political and economic power that governed women's lives, indeed governed them so totally as to be equivalent to fascism. She concluded that fascism was endemic to any nation that 'shut out and shut up' those who could not be identified with the dominant and dominating male 'advance guard' (*TG*, p. 103). If her equation of fascism with parliamentary politics seems a bit slippery to us now, we must remember that by the mid-thirties Woolf had witnessed enough bungling in all political parties and processes to conclude that politics was 'all phantasies ... only mudcoloured moonshine', and that instead of acting on the ideals of democracy, most politicians have 'watery and wobbly minds ... always afraid to say what they mean' so that all their 'best feelings are shrivelled'.[10]

Although *Three Guineas* could not have been taken as anything but provocative and polemical, Woolf found readers' negative responses personally and politically painful. Perhaps most upsetting were the portentous silences of her friend Maynard Keynes and of her husband. By not saying anything, they confirmed her belief that men were closed off from the influence of women and therefore predisposed to carry on their business as usual. Woolf's use of ellipses in *Three Guineas* suggests the two-way silences that prevent women from shaping, much less influencing, political culture. Her ellipses also imply that to join a male-led anti-war society would only replicate women's inferior status in all social and cultural spheres; once again their responses would be overwhelmed by men's exclusionary rhetoric: 'But what analysis can we attempt of the emotions on the other side of the table' (*TG*, p. 129). For Woolf, ellipses indicate not only what women cannot say to men and what men will not hear from women, but a space in which to imagine the healing effects of a woman's language of peace.[11]

Woolf was also concerned about women who filled in ellipses, either by identifying with patriarchal society or by acquiescing to its principles as a pathway to their own self-determination, power and authority. As Jacqueline Rose points out, in wartime this compliance is particularly heinous to Woolf because women would be 'supporting war as one of the few opportunities to escape the tyranny of the home'.[12] What Woolf advocated instead was to fill in the ellipsis with a lethal silence of rejection – 'complete indifference' (*TG*, p. 107). The actual range of women's World War II writing shows us a different scenario. Women's escape from the tyranny of compliance was often the result of doing war service, not the motivator. The majority of war support derived from other reasons. Though many would agree with Woolf that the 'fear which forbids freedom in the private house . . . gives the lie to the moral superiority of the democratic world', such writers as Rose Macaulay and Naomi Mitchison responded differently (Rose, p. 32). They also won their freedom by resisting domestic tyranny, but they theorize that their reasons for supporting the war also resisted the government policies and practices they found oppressive to themselves and to the war's victims.[13] As many British women attested, these writers were not alone.

In our time, *Three Guineas* has become the ur-text of feminist anti-war writing. It has been canonized as a trenchant and far reaching feminist analysis of the militarism inherent to the patriarchal culture of Woolf's England. The very efforts to rescue and validate Woolf's voice have created other problems, however. Claims for Woolf's unique courage situate her on the margins not only of male-dominated debates about war, but as the only credible feminist position on war. Such an approach ignores the vibrancy of a more historically accurate and complex set of responses to World War II – including Woolf's own ambivalences once the Battle of Britain began and other women's anguished analyses. As we shall see, Woolf's was not a lone voice but one of many in a vital feminist debate on war and fascism in the thirties. My attention to Woolf will therefore focus on her voice as one of many women, as a correspondent with others concerned about war and peace, and in this way we can recuperate a more representative and interactive range of women's views.[14]

Before we attend to those other voices, we owe it to Woolf to understand her responses to World War II as not only theoretical and polemical but as personal and ambivalent. Between the moment war was declared and Woolf's suicide in March 1941, she anxiously witnessed the Battle of Britain in the skies above and fields around her Sussex home, and picked up the pieces of her blitzed London home. An even greater threat lay with the real possibility of Hitler's invasion of England; for the Woolfs would undoubtedly be rounded up and killed, both because of their angry and loud responses to fascism and because Leonard was a Jew. If Leonard's Jewish identity was inescapable, both because he acknowledged it and the Nazis decreed it, Virginia was also aware that antisemitism was a danger that could not be condemned as either foreign born or a thing of the past. Indeed, her strong sense of her own English identity reflected how being English and Jewish was not always a secure fit. In a 1930 letter to Ethel Smyth, she recalled how she felt marrying Leonard: 'How I hated marrying a Jew... how I hated their nasal voices and their oriental jewelry and their noses...'.[15] Woolf's added note – 'What a snob I was, for they have immense vitality and I think I like that quality best of all' – acknowledges her sensitivity to what is usually referred to as genteel social antisemitism. But that postscript also situates Woolf's identity in the mostly safe and stable space of 1930 as a culturally secure Englishwoman who does not question her stereotypical judgements, even if they replicate the politically destabilizing act of 'shutting out' she rages against eight years later. As danger did draw close, she faced the brutalizing implications of her identity position. When Woolf links English patriarchal oppression to Hitler, the 'monster Tyrant, Dictator', who 'is making distinctions not merely between the sexes, but between the races', she also calls upon women to reject the aggressive feelings towards others that produce a 'subconscious Hitlerism' (*TG*, pp. 102–3; *Diaries* V, p. 169).

Along with Woolf's rage at Hitler's monstrousness and her rejection of an exclusionary English society, she allows herself to feel her identity in her abiding love for '*my England*': 'if a bomb destroyed one of those little alleys with the brass bound curtains and the river smell and the old woman reading, I should feel – well, what the *patriots* feel.'[16] If it is a bit startling to find Woolf using the sentimental language of national identity, her maternal concern for English soldiers – 'grieving and tender and heavy laden and private – bringing our wounded back carefully through the green fields' puts her in even stranger company (*WD*, p. 322).

Now she is sharing the affective ground of those who would find her Society of Outsiders (*TGT*, p. 106) an affront to their sense of Englishness and its history. But just as we would expect, Woolf also questions the meanings of patriotism. For the material and human objects of her elegy were not only treasured in themselves, but as Karen Schneider has so importantly observed, they were part of 'her cultural roots'.[17] If soldier and city represented a male-dominated culture, so did the English intellectual tradition from which she formed her own critical methods. Recognizing her debt to this heritage even as she resisted it, Woolf allows herself to betray and us to witness those feelings that necessitate our reassessment of what this war meant to her. In fact, she feared 'the encroaching apocalyptic demise of that culture by a fundamentally similar but far greater tyranny from abroad' (Schneider, p. 94; see note 17 above).

Unlike Woolf, there were many women writers who analysed war by beginning but not ending with a universal condemnation of male militarism. Many shared Woolf's belief that in order for militarism to end, men and women must realize the need for equitable social and economic structures. By the late thirties, however, Woolf's call to 'attack Hitler in England', to stop his 'savage howl' with 'the emancipation of man' seemed like an exercise in futility.[18] Just as Hitler's invasions raised doubts for many feminists about universalizing the meaning of patriarchal fascism, it also created new and overlapping definitions of self and Other and victim and enemy. Writers such as Storm Jameson, Bryher, and Rebecca West felt that saving their loved ones and other potential victims required a total war on Hitler, and therefore, for as long as it took, it was necessary to put anti-war beliefs aside. They also distinguished the rise and power of Nazi Germany from Britain's patriarchal history and contemporary politics. As a result, they decided to play an active role in both the war effort and war criticism, and whatever reservations they had about their effectiveness, they continued to appear on public platforms, sign petitions, and write letters and pamphlets throughout the war years. Lady Rhondda, for example, felt that her anti-war views were best served in her active role as editor of *Time and Tide*, rather than as a member of Woolf's Society of Outsiders (Silver, p. 263; note 14, above). Other women wanted to be involved in the war effort in their own personal lives, by 'looking after people rather than [being] . . . looked after' or, as

Naomi Mitchison felt, it was sometimes necessary to join 'revolutionary actions arising from "intolerable situations" that one shares with one's "fellow-beings"' (Silver, pp. 263, 264). Like Mitchison, Phyllis Bottome and others envisaged such an intolerable situation in the Nazi drive to conquest, an event that ensured such world-wide suffering, it made it impossible to 'stand aside indifferently... when bombs are killing their families and destroying their homes' (Silver, p. 267).

In their texts and actions, these writers succeeded in redefining the meaning of homeland, patriotism, citizen, and 'outsider' – revisions that both complement and comment on the work of Woolf. This does not mean that they formed a consensus about war aims. In fact, their debates were often heated, if not embattled, expressing so many different warrants for either participating in or resisting the war.

SACRED AND PROFANE 'REARGUARD ACTIONS': VERA BRITTAIN AND STEVIE SMITH

By the late thirties, as the possibility of war became more of a reality, feminist concerns increasingly intertwined with those about pacifism and the welfare of men and women on either side of the battle lines. Vera Brittain's anti-war commitment, which grew out of World War I from the overwhelming losses of her brother, fiancé, and friends as well as from her nursing experiences in France and Malta, did not evolve into full-fledged pacifism until 1936. At first she wavered between advocating collective international security through the League of Nations and criticizing its domination by the French. Gradually, she became more pacifist, and although she held fast against the pressures of the Blitz and Nazi domination of Europe, she also rejected the argument that doing medical work supported the war effort. Brittain's pacifism shifted from the agnostic scepticism that had gripped her after the Great War's losses to a belief in a politically grounded idea of collective security. Finally, influenced by Dick Sheppard, Vicar of St Martin-in-the-Fields, she was moved to explore a Christian basis for her belief in making a 'disinterested' contribution to the cause of sound human and political conduct.[19] At the beginning of February 1937, she signed on as a Sponsor of Sheppard's Peace Pledge Union.

The model of Jesus's life which shapes much of Brittain's political language is neither romantic nor sanguine about the transformative possibilities of pacifism. As her memoir records, she was aware of the dangers of an anti-fascist pacifism: 'to follow Dick meant treading the Way of the Cross in modern guise. He pointed to a path which might end, not in crucifixion or a den of lions, but at internment, the concentration camp, and the shooting squad'.[20] This statement reveals how Brittain always tied her faith in pacifism to a reading of the past that eschewed happy endings or sentimental interpretations. In 1934, writing about her commitment to peace, she highlighted the problem of romanticizing the pacifist struggle, implying that women should not capitulate to the stereotyped mindsets assigned them in the private sphere but should take an assertive role in war's public debates. She found that 'Even amongst avowed women supporters of the peace movement, there is a depressing tendency to emotional rather than well-informed allegiance.'[21] Her corrective for this emotionalism was to recognize 'an urgent need for more women to speak on politics and to understand thoroughly what they are speaking about' ('Peace', p. 60).

Even with the 'swastika flying from [the] Eiffel Tower', and clear signs that the Nazis had invented a uniquely despotic brutality, Brittain's own research found the war no different from the one in which 'Twenty-two years ago to-day Edward was killed', the reminder of which drove her to exclaim: 'What futility!'[22] She deduced that this war could accomplish no more than the last when

> . . . all the suffering and service of those nightmare years failed completely in their purpose. Far from smashing German militarism and making the world safe for democracy, their long-range consequence has been to smash German democracy and make the world safe for militarism. The war to end war has resulted in a greater fear of war than the world has ever known. The attempt to smash militarism by force has led to more of it – and not in Germany and Italy alone – than at any period of history. The Europe that was to be made safe for democracy has only 150 million people living under democratic governments, and 350 millions under different forms of despotism. (*Wartime*, p. 19)

For Brittain, World War II was historically unique only in its proportion – monumental proof that war reduced all political systems to despotism.

During the Second World War, Brittain's pacifism was intensified and complicated even more deeply by her motherhood. Frightened for the safety of her children, but also concerned about those unable to escape, she now found 'how difficult it is to draw the line between courage and responsibility' (*TE*, p. 216). Knowing that her writing targeted her and her family as Hitler's enemies, she sent her children to the United States, a decision so painful that she replayed it again and again in letters, memoirs, and in her wartime novel published after the war, *Born 1925*.[23] Knowing also that this decision and the economic and social privilege which underwrote it made her vulnerable to criticism, she risked her professional reputation further by publishing her 'Letter to Peacelovers', a newsletter focused on peace aims. To discuss only war aims, she felt, would support the escalation of war and its technology as though they had a will of their own.

Despite her unwavering opposition to war, Brittain expressed a fair amount of ambivalence not only towards war and peace aims, but about strategy. On 20 April 1941, she responds to 'Worse news from Greece' by focusing on military tactics (*Wartime*, p. 81). As Germany was about to overrun Greece, it would have been consistent for her to have accepted a Greek appeasement policy, especially when as late as 1942, she was still regretting Britain's lack of 'sense to make peace when Hess offered it' (*Wartime*, p. 127). Instead, Brittain bemoans the probability of 'Greek capitulation', a phrase which not only recalls the fall of Paris, but implies that a better course would have been its opposite – armed resistance (*Wartime*, p. 81). With this response, it is not surprising to find her rallying to 'our own forces fighting rearguard action' once 'Greek capitulation' is a *fait accompli* (*Wartime*, p. 82). And yet for Brittain, what was good for Greece and its protection was not permissable for the Allied forces. And so she views every Allied bombing of German sites as not merely effecting 'further reprisals on heads of people in Bermondsey & Bow', but as the narrator of her war novel, *Born 1925*, concludes of the 1944 London raids, 'The Nazis seemed to be copying some of the more malignant devices used by the Royal Air Force on Hamburg and the Ruhr cities' (*Wartime*, p. 81, *Born*, p. 279).

When Brittain abstracts moral principles from the war, she begins by refuting any language that would distinguish Germany's war aims or practices from those of the Allies. An Allied victory would only perpetuate the idea that war is a solution to military aggression, and this would elide the ways in which Nazism is 'an old evil, once known as "Reason of State"' and which cannot therefore 'be overcome by military weapons' (*Wartime*, p. 125). Brittain's critique here, which locates the problem of war in European political ideology, recalls Ethel Mannin. Brittain's solution is not, however, to turn away from history, but to find inspiration in the Sermon on the Mount as a history lesson, to 'neither hate nor condemn the Germans for everything that has passed'; instead, we must find out where we ourselves 'were at fault' (*Born*, p. 301).

The pacifist hue of Brittain's wartime writing drew criticism from other women writers, some of whom used their responses to clarify their support of the war effort. Stevie Smith for one, argues for the necessity of this war in her criticism of *England's Hour*, Brittain's survey of England's blitzed population. According to Smith, the belief that all war is wrong, and 'that th[is] war need never have happened', leads Brittain to find nothing of value either in the war effort or in the possibility of an Allied victory; for Brittain, World War II will be tragic for all.[24] Smith shares the conclusion of poet Lorna Lewis that for Brittain, what will be the tragic consequences of World War II are derived from World War I. In a letter to *Time and Tide* responding to *England's Hour*, Lewis calls Brittain a 'tragic sightseer' and condemns her comparison of London's 'ruined areas' to the Western Front of 1914–18.[25] Such a comparison, Lewis argues, only ignores the 1940 Blitz on civilians who were victimized not by the misguided militarism of their leaders, but by the Nazis' design for world conquest. Brittain's linkage of the two world wars did allow her to distinguish her nation from Germany, but only as a right-minded world leader gone wrong. Stevie Smith interprets Brittain's argument in this way: since 'the Treaty of Versailles [is] the root of all our troubles', Britain as a framer and signator is responsible for the outbreak of World War II ('Brittain', p. 176). For Smith, assigning such unilateral responsibility could lead to only one bitter conclusion, that 'if we are still alive we really ought not to be' ('Brittain', p. 76). Brittain identifies as a Londoner under siege, but where, Lewis asks, is her sympathetic identification with her neighbours?: 'does familiarity breed – but in this connection, pride, affection, a desire to protect and serve our city?' (p. 170). What

Lewis finds in *England's Hour* is not the morale that in fact kept Londoners going, but Brittain's 'despair' that the war had to be fought to save Britain (Lewis, p. 170).

Throughout the war years, Brittain's concern for bombing victims on both sides was consistent with her pacifist 'belief in the ultimate transcendence of love over power. This belief comes from an inward assurance'.[26] For the novelist, E.M. Delafield, reviewing *England's Hour* for *Time and Tide*, assurance could only come from Hitler's defeat: 'It will be much easier to forgive the Nazis when we have delivered their victims.'[27] Brittain's emphasis on 'transcendence' takes her analysis of war beyond that of geopolitical strategies to social theory. Like Virginia Woolf, she analyses the structural elements of power which all too often and too similarly govern the lives of men and women in different nations unjustly. From the social codes that structure human relationships to the economic forces that pit haves against have nots, Brittain finds sources of conflict that lead to the outbreak of fascism and war. Brittain also understood that the antipathies underlying political violence and specifically, Nazi racialist policies included a visceral hatred of Others. The realization that such feeling could not always be explained by political defeat or humiliation or economic deprivation led her to rally to the rescue of Hitler's victims, and she wrote passionately on behalf of European Jews. She would not, however, advocate military strategies, including more bombing, as effective ways of stopping the Nazi death machinery. Indeed. she holds to the idea of complicit, and sometimes even active Allied guilt despite her unequivocable statement in 1940 that 'Even if there had been no war, no Jewish persecutions, no concentration camp at Dachau, I need not explain to any other lifelong feminist my reasons for detesting the Nazi regime.'[28] Her condemnation of the Nazis intensified as she learned from her publisher Victor Gollancz the extent of Jewish persecution, but she never relinquished her belief that the solution was to rescue the Jews (not only into Allied nations but into Palestine) and not to escalate the war. Indeed, she held the 'war itself, its length and its geographical vastness . . . responsible for the deaths of [Jewish victims]' and figured out early on that whatever this war was about, the Allies were not planning their battles to save the Jews (*Peace Lover*, p. 135). Once the Allies' saturation bombing of German cities became known, she risked public censure by protesting it in public speeches and in writing. Her pacifism also transcended the particular circumstances of this war or any other. Like Woolf, she envisioned a society in which feminist principles would lead to the end of militarism and the emergence of social, racial, and economic harmony.

While Stevie Smith also felt that the march towards another world war was tragic, her view is differently transcendent and also historically particular. As she developed it in her two novels, *Novel on Yellow Paper* and *Over the Frontier*, and in essays and stories, Smith impugns the imperialist agendas of both Germany and Britain for being oppressive, but her insistence on their separate political ideologies and systems leads her to assess the Second World War differently than Brittain. It is on the basis of these national profiles that she also finds World War II distinct from World War I and the grounds for championing the Allies' cause. For Smith, differences erupt in Nazi Germany's political policy, a fascism so totalizing in its mythical vision and so micromanaging in its technocracy, that it squashes any reformist vision. Britain, as she characterizes it in her poetic and narrative voices, works like a debating society, the rules of which constrain but encourage the push and pull of reform and counter-reform. Nazi oppression, for Smith, is therefore mortally different in its consequences from Britain's economic or social inequities. Combining mechanistic and brute force, the implementation of nazism leads Germany, not just to 'battlecruelty', but to 'doing people to death in lavatories'.[29]

Smith depicts the emotive force which propels the Nazi machine as spawned not only by male militarism, but by a form of cultural romanticism tied to a triumphalist nationalism. The fusion of retrograde myth and historical self-righteousness was deadly, in Smith's view, because it offered the palliative of restoring pride and honour to the damaged cultural identities of German men and women. This gendered but all-embracing romantic nationalism was encouraged by the Nazis by mythologizing the nation's history in order to satisfy 'a dream or something that is out of focus'; for Smith, this myth emerged in Germany 'with its Movements, and Back to Wotan, and Youth Youth Youth' as a 'neurotic' cruelty, and therefore deserved to be debunked as a childlike dream of family romance which denies its own brutality (*NYP*, pp. 116–7):

> ... beneath the Gemutlichkeit and the health-dance and the papa-love-baby there is all of this menace and the memory

> always of the Nazi martyr memorial in Munich where two sentries stand night and day and the passer-by must salute. Yes but he must salute, papa, mama, baby, they must raise the hand and make the absurd and revolting spectacle of a fascist discipline. Or they can cross the road and pass by unsaluting, unmolested. But to do this too often, is not this rather dangerous, is it not the thin end of the wedge of the beginning of incorrect thinking.[30]

In her 1936 *Novel on Yellow Paper* (see note 29 above), Smith was not only mocking the 'idealismus' that marked 'incorrect thinking', but warning that it would lead to 'a whole race . . . gone run mad'; she bemoaned, 'Oh heaven help Deutschland when it kicks out the Jews, with their practical intelligence that might keep Germany from all that dream darkness' (*NYP*, pp. 117–8). That the Jews would be singled out as enemy and victim of Germany's 'dream darkness' is presaged in Smith's fictional interrogation of militarism and war. And while she condemns militarist ideology as self-destructive, her assessment of Germany's plans moved her to appeal to a fighting spirit: 'God send the British Admiralty and the War Office don't go shuffling on with their arms economies too long-o' (*NYP*, p. 117).

Stevie Smith's published voice, with its combination of serious analysis, obsessive refrains, zany flippancy, and send-up of the 'old boys', has struck many readers of today as dated. And it is, but not so that we should dismiss it. As the crisis of another world war drew closer, she, like some other women writers, expressed her anxiety by deploying a wish-fulfilling romantic patriotism which she also undercut with ironic absurdity. The result is a political and historical critique that corrects the woman's defensive and damaging emotionalism it also dramatizes. Even as Vera Brittain would have deplored Smith's political conclusions, she would have applauded the drama of a woman emerging into acute and learned political consciousness.

'A WAR OF DOGMA': DOROTHY L. SAYERS AND ETHEL MANNIN

From a position that would appear to be even further removed from Brittain's pacifism, in a voice that not only resembles Smith's acerbic and cavalier tone, but asserts the authority Brittain wished women to assume, Dorothy Sayers also entered war debates as a polemicist. In essays, meditative books, and poetry, Sayers departed from her extraordinarily successful career as creator of Lord Peter Whimsey and Harriet Vane to explore the Christian religious and ethical need to defeat Nazi Germany. Analysing how Hitler used Nazi ideology to appeal to the Germans' need for retribution, she brashly asserts her political voice: 'Any demagogue can carry fools with him by over-simplifying the issues into a slogan.'[31] Once war started and Sayers's writing carried the British flag into rhetorical battle, it took on a tone that could easily put off many readers today. With as much romanticism as swagger, her writing enthusiastically endorses the war in terms that accord all too comfortably with propaganda. Very critical of King Leopold, who ordered the Belgian army to capitulate to Hitler, she also saw the forced evacuation of the British at Dunkirk as 'a colossal military disaster'.[32] Her plan for British victory was to transform the Dunkirk evacuation into a 'heroic failure [that] stirs the pulses of free men in free countries' ('Notes', p. 633). Sayers's belief in a righteous military offensive against the *blitzkrieg* moved her to write poetic sermons in the hope that the power of words would 'issue in deeds' ('Notes', p. 634).

In September 1940, nearly a year after Britain entered the war, Sayers published a deeply patriotic poem, 'The English War', which constructs a national identity of uniquely defensive valour. Invoking key points in England's military history, the poem builds on the swashbuckling tradition of standing alone, swords drawn against the invading enemy. Sayers's identity politics here presents England as 'The single island', threatened by the very 'men who love us not, yet look / To us for liberty'.[33] As though England alone is God's reserve for 'decency' and 'justice', so it is called upon 'To fight . . . the English war' no matter how many times ('EW', pp. 45, 46). Wherever else she distinguishes between the world wars, her poetic invocation dissolves boundaries between past and present to construct an English national identity based on a heritage of justified military engagement. As Ralph Hone notes, the poem expresses 'bulldog courage', and indeed suggests the rhetoric of Churchill, whose words she found 'really stirring and inspiring'.[34]

By 1943, when England had been through the Battle of Britain and the Blitz and its airborne European offensive was in full swing,

Sayers found it 'marvellous' how technology improved the chances for the Allies' precision bombing.[35] At first she identifies with the village landscape that resembles her own 'Isle of Ely', but then she shifts her perspective so as to distinguish the enemy landscape from her own ('Aerial', p. 269). This happens when the narrator focuses on a photograph showing the Other village broken 'up into dots'; the photo image reflects how the village has been made 'fragmentary' by the Allies' bombing ('Aerial', p. 269). The narrator's stance, which seems empathetic, emerges as 'delighted' with

> . . . what it means, [to] understand it,
> because I can see exactly what we have done
> we have blown up the dams,
> burst the sluices, unshackled the waters ('Aerial', p. 270).

The omnipotent power of the bombs has created a safe distance between the narrator's island and the enemy and reinforces a national identity of aggressive isolation. Despite victory, however, the island/nation remains haunted by a presence that reflects the political and ethical implications of the poem's aggressive rhetoric. As the narrator exalts in the idea that 'The land' itself 'was not . . . a primary objective', she draws attention to the fact that not once has she mentioned a human presence in the bombed landscape ('Aerial', p. 270).

Part of what enabled Sayers to valorize military aggression was her sense that 'We are waging a war of religion . . . a life-and-death struggle between Christian and pagan.'[36] Elevating the geopolitical conflict to an eschatological drama enables her to topple the trinity of professed war aims – 'freedom and justice and faith' – by asking 'what economics and politics are to be used for', when what is at stake 'is a violent and irreconcilable quarrel about the nature of God and the nature of man and the ultimate nature of the universe; it is a war of dogma' (*Creed*, p. 8). While she admits that most Christians are not exemplars, she insists that they do recognize their wickedness and are dissatisfied at not practising Christian ethics. Not so the Germans, who have not merely abandoned both Christian dogma and ethics, but have embraced sin and evil in the form of 'bestial ferocity' (*Creed*, p. 31).

Not in contrast, but in tandem with Sayers's audaciousness is her well-tempered argument for a Christian analysis of nazism. Like Vera Brittain, Sayers casts her attitudes towards World War

II in a Christian hue, but with different conclusions. Sayers's entire career, as mystery writer, dramatist, poet, and scholar, is shaped by her inquiry into Christian creed and dogma. By the late thirties, she combined Vera Brittain's transcendent belief in a universal moral philosophy with the kind of political distinctions made by Stevie Smith, to form reasons for supporting the war. In 1939, Sayers wrote *Begin Here* (see note 31 above), a meditation on what she believed to be the ideological bases of 'the truth about our present troubles' (p. 5). Admitting that war is the ultimate evil, she nonetheless finds reason to 'say that the war against Germany is a just, and in the most terrible sense, a holy war' in it being 'a war for our national existence – though not (one hopes) for national profit – and for the existence and liberation of other nations' (*Begin*, p. 90).

Though it is all too easy today to find Sayers naive and therefore troubling in her zealotry, her romantic conservatism assumes a self-critical edge in attacking Britain's imperialist self-interest. As James Brabazon points out, however, her glib admissions of her nation's wrongs pale beside the thunder of her 'eloquence about "our blood" and "the bones of drowned sailors"', especially when she 'steered clear' of involving herself in the war effort other than to lecture near London occasionally.[37] Unlike Stevie Smith, whose fictional introspection implicates her in Britain's oppressive colonialism, Sayers breezily champions Britain's imperialism in contrast to other conquerors. Sayers's essay, 'The Mysterious English', applauds the English as superior traders, whose 'spirit of lighthearted adventure' leads them at worst, to piracy, but their own 'very long memory of national consciousness' also motivates their respect for the differences of others.[38] Perhaps it is because of her contradictions that what Sayers's war writing gains is analytical value. Applying her Christian model of analysis, she exposes Britain's 'hypocrisy' and 'oppression' and in so doing, creates distinctions that recognize Germany's expansionist motives as deadly in a new way and castigates those who fail to do so (*Begin*, p. 90)

For Sayers, moral failure and political difference are both constructs of a Christian vision – the recognition of two kinds of sinners. Like Vera Brittain, she saw Britain as a power which 'knows what is right but does what it knows to be wrong'; unlike Brittain, she cast Germany as 'that more desperate condition of sin that honestly believes the wrong to be right' (*Begin*, p. 90). Embedding historical context in her political theology, Sayers traces the road to a second world war back to the end of the first, when peace terms humiliated Germany. This created a wrong that 'is not only a direct contravention of all Christian principle but a neglect of all political experience' (*Begin*, p. 139). Accepting moral responsibility for the past does not, however, lead Sayers to conclude that World War II is simply an outgrowth of World War I. Convinced of historical change, she sees Germany as a political entity and as a people losing their distinctions as they collectively respond not only to geo-political humiliation and economic suffering, but to a new outlet for vindication: Hitler's supremacist ideology, which drives him 'to impose [Germany's] will-for-peace upon an inferior majority' (*Begin*, p. 89).

Just as past and present are not coterminus for Sayers, so she sees the possibility for positive change growing out of the differences of World War II. In order for peace to be formed, the critical mindset that distinguishes past from present must be applied to plan for the future. On the domestic front, the particular circumstances of evacuating people from the cities exposes Britain's urban poverty, but rather than blame the poor, as so many did, Sayers sees the exposure as an opportunity to begin planning for reform. On the international scene, like so many other writers, she wants 'a United States of Europe', but as always, Sayers's writing is infused with a patriotism that places Britain at the helm of international reform (*Begin*, p. 51).

To link reformist patriot Dorothy Sayers with socialist antinationalist Ethel Mannin except as political opponents challenges the tolerable boundaries of feminist literary history unless we include their equally powerful identifications with Christian ethos. This religious identification, moreover, while it leads these writers to different conclusions about this and all wars, also binds them to a universal vision of spiritual indomitability in the face of tyranny. So Phyllis Bottome would argue that 'The really stubborn core of what Hitler is fighting against in Great Britain is the unconscious Christianity of the British people', a moral psychology in which 'only unselfish and courageous people want to act in immediate sympathy with their neighbors, at a moment of personal danger' (*Tyrants*, p. 272–3). The conservatism of this Christian psychology does not lead Bottome, Mannin, Sayers, or Vera Brittain to the reactionary abyss sacrificing women's public stances for a life of submission. Instead, these women offer an exegesis of Christian teaching that not only activates their self-determining political critiques, but in their influential positions as widely read authors, makes them agents of political and social change.

Less known today than Brittain or Sayers, Ethel Mannin (1900–84) has only recently been rediscovered. Celebrated for her romance fiction, she published 95 books in her lifetime, including serious meditations on politics and morality and on sexual freedom. She was also a regular contributor to the Independent Labour Party's weekly, the *New Leader*. Andy Croft argues for her importance to the literary history of the thirties by showing how her 'novels suggest . . . the unavoidable presence of contemporary events in almost all aspects of British cultural life – even in the world of romantic fiction'.[39] The reverse of Croft's statement is also true for Mannin if we examine her response to the contemporary events of World War II as informed by her cultural identity as a Christian.

Like Vera Brittain, Ethel Mannin found pacifist inspiration in the life of Jesus. Instead, however, of focusing on the sacrificial aspect of his suffering, Mannin celebrated his inspiring a 'spiritual revolution which alone can lead man to universal love and security and peace' (*CorC*, p. 234). Her writing attests to her abiding belief in the power of the spirit over that of the body, even as the shadow of another world war spread. As Mussolini marched into Abyssinia and Hitler annexed the Sudetenland, she came to believe in Gandhi's non-violent resistance as '"the spirit of God in man"'.[40] Even as Hitler's armies drove towards the English Channel, between January and September 1940, Mannin felt that his power could be challenged most successfully, not by validating it through equally violent means, but through his followers' collective rejection. What kept Hitler in power was

> . . . the submission of those who permit themselves to be dominated by it. Individual revolt does not break the force of this illusion; only the community which created the illusion can do that. In the final analysis, therefore, it is the community which has power, not the government or dictator . . . the force that governs and dictators command is none other than the power of the people themselves . . . (*CorC*, p. 127).

Mannin argued that if the people's power followed the example of Jesus's principles to love, the result would be not only political self-determination, but social change. Wedding her Christian vision to her socialism, she believed not in 'a personal Deity, or in a life hereafter... but in Life, the living spirit' as a collective struggle to build a classless society based on social, economic, and gender equality (*Spectator*, p. 299).

Like most British women writers of her generation, Mannin's rage against war grew out of the bitter end of World War I, but like Sylvia Townsend-Warner, she was also drawn to support the struggle of the Spanish Republicans against the Fascists. Though Mannin never joined the Communist Party as did Townsend-Warner, her socialism led her to define 'the Spanish struggle' as 'a social revolution behind the anti-Fascist struggle... for a new social order' (*Spectator*, p. 61). The Republican defeat and its internal conflicts and betrayals proved the futility of war for Mannin but sharpened her belief in the efficacy of a spiritual political consciousness.

Once World War II seemed imminent, like Virginia Woolf and Stevie Smith, Mannin felt that the new call to arms hid 'the fact that the so self-righteously indignant democracies had done the same thing in their time in the interests of "colonial expansion"' (*Spectator*, p. 122). Expanding Woolf's list of outsider/victims, Mannin denounces war on behalf of those who are 'ignored by the Press', the government, and even by people moved to support the war on behalf of Hitler's victims: the ignored are the victims of all colonial powers – 'the millions of subject coloured peoples... Arabs, Negroes, Indians... those vast masses of human beings... commonly forgotten in estimates of peace and war' (*Spectator*, pp. 295, 293). For Mannin, those 1939 estimates focused one-sidedly and therefore unjustly not only on fascist brutality but on a kind of victim privileged over time by being 'white and "educated", Western civilized', including 'an artificial state called Czechoslovakia' and 'a handful of Jews' (*Spectator*, pp. 295, 268). Despite her protestations that she is 'filled with compassion for these tragic people', Mannin does not hesitate to condemn the Jews in advance for being 'willing to see the whole world plunged into the unspeakable horror of war in order that there might be an end of the persecution of my people' (*Spectator*, p. 293). If, as Mannin admitted, 'the Fascist persecution of the Jews moves me less than it does many people, perhaps most people', it was not only because of the neglect of other victims, but because 'I do not, moreover, believe every atrocity story I read, and because I do not regard

Fascism as the greatest evil in the world . . .' (*Spectator*, pp. 293–4). Considering the Jews 'white' and 'Western civilized' enables Mannin to dismiss both fascist evil and the Jews in one fell swoop, for her inclusionary ethos ignores Hitler's Nuremberg Laws which justified the Jews' destruction by ejecting them from both categories.[41]

If Mannin's view in 1939 was shaped by the immediate past of the perfidious Spanish Civil War and the current rhetoric of her imperialist government, the end of the war did not change her assessment of its tragic losses. She concluded that 'it was no worse for a neutral country to be occupied by, say, Germany, than by, say, the British . . . but 1945, with the talk all of Buchenwald and Belsen, was no time to suggest it'.[42] This last statement was to appear as an epilogue to her 1946 novel of the European home front, *The Dark Forest*, but her publisher insisted she delete it. If Mannin is right about his sensitivity to 'the talk all of' Hitler's death camps, her own statements and tone show her consistent refusal to factor the emerging material facts of the Holocaust into her 'spiritual revolution'.

Mannin's refusal to believe atrocity stories coincided with her vision of the war as a conflict between body and spirit: 'For the pacifist the purely physical hazards of war are the least anxiety . . . it is the agony of spirit of living in a world in which there is no place for those who do not, cannot, believe in mass murder' (*Spectator*, p. 263). Even if an entire nation is attacked, occupied, and enslaved, 'the spirit of its people' cannot be possessed but will prevail (*Spectator*, p. 300). Mannin went on to explore the dramatic implications of her beliefs in two novels analysing the war: *Bavarian Story* (1948) recounts the spiritual and physical death of those who joined the Nazis and *The Dark Forest* (1946) is about the spiritual rebirth of a Central European village occupied by an unnamed army. Written from a postwar perspective, in the interests of a sustaining peace, both novels distinguish between self-deluded Nazis and those Germans who upheld the family and communal traditions that enabled ordinary people to withstand the brutalities of war. In its focus on the fate of the Germans, *Bavarian Story* humanizes them by showing the loving family life of its protagonists. Likewise, *The Dark Forest* depicts the psychological history and suffering of its protagonist, a young occupying soldier.

If there are no atrocity stories in these fictions, it is because war for Mannin means spiritual death. And yet the sole Jewish character in either novel – a tailor in *Bavarian Story* – is bodily removed by the Nazis early on and is never heard about again. Mannin's repugnance at Nazi antisemitism is expressed several times in this novel, but as her plotting also shows, what matters about World War II is not whether or how to save Hitler's victims, but 'the spiritual vision of those who survive the cataclysm' (*CorC*, p. 234). Thus the survival of her hero in *Bavarian Story* is ensured by his mode of resistance which becomes a model for the 'spiritual revolution which alone can lead man to universal love and security and peace' (*CorC*, p. 234). A musician, Gabriel Weber resists the Nazis by defying their orders to stop teaching his pupils Christian hymns. Just as he needs no armed intervention to be saved (he emerges unscathed from Dachau), so Mannin also plots the defeat of nazism by having its leaders succumb to a fated self-destructiveness. Mannin proves that armed resistance or defence can never have a justifiable purpose, and in fact is unnecessary; she does this by dramatizing a providence whose victims and heroes she selects to fit her model of spiritual victory. That this model excludes those whose bodies or spirit could not be rescued by providence is of no concern to Mannin, and so they too are fated to be destroyed.

'THE COST OF WAR': OURSELVES AND OTHERS

Within the dramatically disparate combinations of war attitudes among and within British women writers, many linked their arguments to their ideals of social justice and their constructions of their nation. Some saw the war as subverting those ideals and yielding to tyranny while others found the war itself a ground on which tyranny was defined and social justice could be affirmed. Within their inconsistencies and ambivalences, a figure in the carpet emerges that defines what they meant by social justice. Despite the different shapes this figure assumes, it is always identifiable as representing the outsider/victim. In its different permutations, the figure becomes the writer's touchstone for gauging and registering the justice of World War II. The ideals of democracy and social equality which these women connected to their attitudes towards the war were complicated by the unforseen and indeed, in some cases, unwanted entry of this outsider into their revolutionary and reformist scenarios. As many of these writers extended their sense of social justice beyond the borders of their xenophobic nation to include Europe and even wider international relations, they became more critically aware of the contested borders of identifying and defining who constituted the citizens of individual nations and the objects of international concern. Once Hitler's racialist policies became known, they struck a visceral chord in these writers who in turn were moved to identify with or exclude the outsider from the societies they critiqued and imagined.

One writer who staked her attitudes toward the war and social justice on the fate of the outsider/victim is Storm Jameson. Like Virginia Woolf and Vera Brittain, Jameson developed theories and analyses of political and militarist culture, but her conclusions led her to believe World War II was not only supportable, but necessary. Like Dorothy Sayers, Jameson saw opportunities for social and political reforms in the unsettling conditions of a Second World War. Unlike Sayers, however, Jameson rejected any kind of romantic patriotism. Jameson was also a close friend of Vera Brittain's until their different views of World War II brought them to an irreparable rift. Like Brittain, Jameson had also become a staunch pacifist as a result of the inconsolable losses of the Great War. In 1932, as she still mourned the death of her brother, she vowed that she would not sacrifice her son in another war: 'I shall tell him also that war is not worth its cost, nor is victory worth the cost.'[43] But once she travelled to Germany later in the year, she began to realize that her beliefs in war prevention were challenged by Hitler's plans. At the same time, however, Jameson could not bring herself to endorse an offence that might stop him, and merged her belief in international security with a kind of pacifism Martin Ceadel analyses as pacificism: 'It sees the prevention of war as its main duty and accepts that, however upsetting to the purist's conscience, the controlled use of armed force may be necessary to achieve this.'[44] Unlike Virginia Woolf's call to reform men's militarist consciences or Vera Brittain's and Ethel Mannin's Christian belief in love, pacificism holds 'that implementing reforms at the political level . . . offers the only realistic chance of limiting the use of force and of curbing warfare as a human institution' (Ceadel, p. 5).

Jameson's autobiography recalls how her ambivalences about the possibilities of another world war led her to 'live in equivocal amity with pacifist and combative supporters of the League of Nations. . . . My only immovable conviction was my loathing of war.'[45] As part of her loathing, Jameson enlisted the efforts of other writers to analyse the causes of war from the perspective of their various political stripes, and edited a volume of their essays in 1934, *Challenge to Death*. Her own concluding essay, 'In the End', moves towards a critique of Britain's isolationism and towards a kind of internationalism that would later crystallize in her devotion to the besieged people of Europe. As though arguing with Dorothy Sayers, Jameson averred that

> In the past there have been little Englanders . . . in love with an England which never was but could be, and, as if opposing them, internationalists of a country no smaller than Europe. It is time for the two dreams to grow together. The jealous lover of England can no longer separate her in his dreams from the other countries of Europe.[46]

By 1936, even as she joined the Peace Pledge Union (PPU), Jameson foresaw Hitler's appropriation of the Rhineland as a problem of taking moral responsibility for the fate of others: 'If I believe that concentration camps, the torture of Jews and political opponents are less vile than war, I must say so plainly, not pretend that the price is something less' (*J* I, p. 341–2).

Like Jameson, Rose Macaulay joined the PPU 'haunted by [the] thought the advocates of complete pacifism were doing harm'.[47] Macaulay resigned her membership in 1938, and in 1939 published an essay that shows her growing irritation with the chauvinism she saw in all claims for moral and political superiority. Though she found this historical moment particularly brutal, she was very critical of 'the British patriot', in whom 'self-congratulation and indignation with persecuting foreigners furiously rage together'.[48] On the other hand, she felt that excessive criticism of 'the shocking behaviour of their own side is less moral indignation than pro-enemyism', having been produced by an equal tendency to excoriate 'the ill conduct of others' while claiming the moral high ground for whatever position one holds ('Moral', pp. 179, 190). Macaulay remained a pacifist until the Nazi blitzkrieg of 1940, which convinced her that 'submission to an unreasonable tyranny' was a greater cost than 'the sacrifices that would have to be made in a "reasonable" negotiated settlement' (quoted in Ceadel,

p. 215). In 1941, in a short piece touched only occasionally by her usual irony, 'Consolations of the War', she still condemned war as 'a grotesquely barbarous, uncivilised, inhumane and crazy way of life', but distinguishes this war from a history of Britain's unjust forays as defensive: 'twentieth-century men and women who had hoped war to be for ever outlawed' have been forced to adopt the weapons and 'horrid incivilities' of 'outlaws' because 'the things we are fighting against are still more beastly'.[49]

It was this barbarity and its designated targets that ultimately made the difference to Jameson and others, and that drove Jameson to finally elaborate the abandonment of her pacifism that ended her friendship with Vera Brittain. In her letter to Brittain of 6 August 1940, she explained how her resignation from the PPU was a result of

> My loathing of concentration camps and the Nazi creed [being] as deep as my loathing of war, and I've never managed to achieve a single mind on the issue since after 1933. Such mental peace as I have achieved has only come since I decided that it was dishonest for me to try to be single-minded.[50]

By 4 September 1941, she was clarifying her views as she prepared a pamphlet she would publish for PEN, *The End of This War*, and wrote to Brittain:

> I hate war with as much venom as you do, but I have come to believe that there are certain values for which it may be necessary to fight. You do not believe this. That and that only is the difference between us. . . . You most certainly think the point of view I have reached mentally dishonest. I think that pacifists are mentally dishonest when they don't admit that Hitler's triumph would be a worse blow to humanity than war itself.[51]

Despite her rejection of Jameson's views and friendship, Brittain's pacifism was sustained by her belief in the very values for which Jameson would fight and in the British institutions which would uphold those values. *England's Hour* ends with her celebration of 'the process of British justice [which] I have seen function in a fashion as close to the ideal of human decency as the present stage of our spiritual development can be expected to achieve'.[52] Even as she distinguished her view of England's role in the war from so many other writers, she shares their underlying commitment to an abiding nation:

> And it is an England which neither the pitiful challenging paranoia of Nazidom nor that of any other invader can destroy. Those who call themselves our enemies may obliterate buildings . . . assassinate men and women; they cannot eliminate the flowers, the trees . . . the quiet inviolate spirit, of a whole countryside. Cities may vanish in a red fury of smoke and flame, but no conqueror by his bombs and aeropolanes can wholly remove the marks which immemorial centuries have laid upon our land. Whatever the future may bring of hope or despair, of sanity or suffering, of peace or war, the villages of this country will be England for ever (*E Hour*, p. 198).

The conservatism and identification with her nation that Brittain expresses in this statement recalls Virginia Woolf's deep love for England. Brittain, however, combines patriotism with religious faith in pacifism, the result of which shows how her ideas to reform her militarist society rested on a romantic image of England as a unified people sharing a pastoral vision of a continuously harmonious past.

Brittain's invocation, supported by the history and the diverse literature of village wartime experience, turns out to be more fact than fancy. The continuity of village life was not only sustaining, but its rhythms suggested a kind of rationality that coincided with and supported many pacifist beliefs. In his study of 'The Nation as Pastoral in British Literature of the Second World War', Simon Featherstone shows how the rural community defines and represents 'the necessary values of the nation in wartime . . . with the effect that traditional values are preserved and even heightened by a new singularity of social and hence national purpose'.[53] Among these 'timeless' values is 'the double purpose of pastoral – acting as a stay against the horrors of industrialized warfare and a representation of all that is threatened by such warfare' (Featherstone, p. 158). What is threatened by warfare is the continuity of community that is maintained by peace. For those who subscribe to a rural vision of English national identity, change always rests upon an essential moral and social foundation, and the language in which this foundation is figured depicts a timeless landscape populated by different classes of locals who merge elegaically into a seamless whole. It is on the basis of that timelessness that Dorothy Sayers was able to take heart in anticipating the bombardment of a European village in her poem, 'Aerial Reconnaissance'. Even if the village is flooded when 'we have blown up the dams, / burst the sluices, / unshackled the waters . . . it won't hurt the land,' which can always be reclaimed ('Aerial', p. 270). A distinct irony in Sayers's depiction of the Allies' bombing proficiency is that her image of a pastoral haven depends on a mythic British national identity that is opposed to Germany's romanticized nationalism and Nazi mechanization.

In Britain, whatever actual disruptions the rural areas experienced, especially with evacuated mothers and children, village life closed ranks around them as though women's traditional domestic roles were assuming the power not only of sustaining the local culture but reshaping it. And because the country could mostly feed itself and bombing raids concentrated primarily on the cities and ports, there was every opportunity for both sustenance and quiet reform as there was comparatively little suffering in rural areas. This is an England, as one critic of its literary landscape notes, that is often made to represent a 'quiet' place in which to be 'meditative', but then disturbingly turns out to be 'something more ancient and intractable'.[54] It is the 'quiet' England that Frances Partridge constructs to sustain her pacifism. She and her husband, Ralph Partridge, spent the war years at their home in rural Wiltshire, where even in April 1941, as the Battle of Britain raged, she could 'contrive to live much more within our magic Ham Spray circle':

> . . . sitting on the verandah most of the morning – the sky perfectly blue: peace visible, tangible and audible; the cows lying down in the field; Burgo and R.'s voices the bonfire under the glossy leaves of the Portuguese laurel, the bees buzzing in the grape hyacinths; far off the hum of a tractor. No aeroplanes. Positive happiness invaded me, and though I know that it is achieved at the cost of ostrichism I cling to it and do not want to lose it.[55]

Partridge insulates her idyllically domesticated natural scene from mythic glorification, a construction that would elide its more natural harmonies. For example, she criticized Vita Sackville-West's 'quiet natural-history attitude' towards 'Our village in an air-raid', as representing values that mystified 'the ancient English rural tradition' at the expense of human and military realities (*PW*, p. 55). For Partridge, the reality of this rural tradition was that it could not be separated from the human beings who perpetrate war, and so instead she finds a more valuable 'principle' in 'the processes of nature' which despite her complaints about Sackville-West, are heroicized to 'go on regardless of war and cataclysm; their resources against their own cataclysms of storm and frost seem boundless' (*PW*, p. 88). What Partridge does not express and therefore may not recognize, is that she has built her 'magic circle' in that same all too quiet 'ancient English rural tradition' that Sackville-West celebrates, and that while she creates a different nature story, her life and English identity follow the course of Sackville-West's myth.

As the war continued, and its regulations and news drowned out the hums of rural peace, Partridge came to believe that the peacefulness of Ham Spray had 'no future', and she retreated into feeling 'more detached and more fatalistic' about any good the war was doing or might bring (*PW*, p. 88). It may well be that the insularity of her charmed circle supported her retreat from a reality her diaries never mention and therefore about which there is no need for involvement. The sounds of suffering and pleas for help of the European refugees who poured into London daily and their fellow Londoners who suffered the Blitz along with them could not compete with myths of nature's infinite resources.

Other women writers clung to the mythos of village and domestic harmony as the hallmark of England's national identity and backbone of its stability, and out of this found reasons to support the war effort. And yet despite this concordance with government propaganda, many of their war aims were critical of the government's. Like Brittain, Partridge, and other pacifists, such as Dora Russell, most women writers of this period condemned the male-centred hostility and short-sightedness they felt had made war inevitable. Because their own war aims were more often defensive and anti-heroic, they also rejected any goals that could be associated with Britain's role as a postwar superpower. Still grieving the losses of the Great War, they saw such power as an imperialist sign of militarist aggression. Whatever sacrifices they felt had to be made to defeat Hitler, they did not, as one critic claims, wish to produce sons to die valiantly.[56] Despite the differences which ended their friendship, Storm Jameson and Vera Brittain nonetheless shared the view that 'on what [women] think . . . depends the future of this land, the future of all the children in it. Let no one tell you what to think. Think for yourself'.[57]

We can see that women were thinking for themselves in their articles and letters to the feminist journal, *Time and Tide,* throughout the interwar and wartime periods. In a series of letters from 11 November 1939 to 6 January 1940, two writers who identified themselves as pacifists, Rebecca West and Naomi Mitchison, debated the merits of fighting a war against Hitler. Like Virginia Woolf, Vera Brittain, and others, Naomi Mitchison was concerned that World War II would be a replay of World War I. Unlike Storm Jameson, who held 'the old men' responsible for appeasement, Mitchison found them guilty of perpetuating militarism: 'Are not the same privileged classes in control of our present war machine? Have they altered so much as to merit our trust?'[58] In response, Rebecca West identifies with Mitchison's 'Left-Wing' concern for the rights of the underprivileged – the 'unknown or unlikeable' Other – but she parts company with her correspondent's cynicism about another war accomplishing any more than the last.[59] For West, 'this is a war fought by all concerned "for some freedom and against Fascism"' ('War Aims', p. 1520). West agrees with Mitchison that Chamberlain's government is primarily interested in protecting the interests of English capitalism, but identifies a distinction that challenges the unified conception of 'all concerned', and that becomes crucial for her support of the war. She argues that one must not 'pretend that a Glasgow working woman would not notice the difference if Hitler and Goering and Himmler were governing her life. Are concentration camps and Jew-baiting then nothing?"' ('War Aims', p. 1520).

In the final analysis, both Mitchison and West gave profound recognition to the plight of Others. West's recognition derived from her journalism in the twenties and travels in Yugoslavia in the thirties, and Mitchison's catalyst was a meeting with English industrial workers and their wives and travels in Austria in the early thirties. As a result of this recognition, both were prepared to fight a war against Hitler and their quarrel reflects their individual and shared ambivalences about defining the relationship between their goals for the war and those of the government. In an essay, 'I Have Five Children', published in the pocket magazine, *Lilliput,* Mitchison presents her argument in the language of motherhood, but with a twist.[60] Stripping motherhood of any sentimental rhetoric, she assumes a public voice and role. She empowers herself and other mothers with a communal but critical 'we' who must share responsibility for ignoring the events at Versailles and their aftermath when they retreated into domestic insularity.

Mitchison's critical stance develops in relation to her eldest son and to other mothers. An 18-year-old science student, her son represents both the human cost 'of using a bad means for a doubtful end' and the hopefulness in recognizing 'certain moments in human history when a situation so intolerable arises that the only way out is by war' ('Five', p. 18). In language that shows the intensity of her love and attachment to her children – 'I feel that my children are more myself than I am' – but which also marks her independent life – 'I have always accepted any adventures which came my way' – Mitchison anticipates the wartime government slogans that would appeal to women's self-sacrifice ('Five', p. 19). But pitting herself against both the state and its enemy, she would save her children by appropriating the language of war and attacking 'the murderous madness of [the] idea that . . . the individual does not matter, but only the state' ('Five', p. 20). She refuses to play into the government's rhetoric of fear by protesting it in the language of a fatal retreat. Instead she launches her preemptive strike by tapping into her empathy for those Other mothers who have already lost their children in Spain and China. In the end, this war can be a fight for change through defeat of the old Moloch idea which has menaced mothers before"' ('Five', p. 20).

Rebecca West's readiness to fight a war not only anticipated the horrors Hitler would perpetrate, but was also consistent with her earlier stand on nationalism. In an essay published in *Challenge to Death*, Storm Jameson's 1934 anthology, she argued that the only remedy to the aggressive tendencies of a nationalism based on supremacist beliefs was an 'international spirit' that would mitigate against 'the spread of Fascism'.[61] For West, fascism implied 'a headlong flight into fantasy from the necessity for political thought' ('Necessity', p. 251). In the light of fascism's deadly dream of expansionist domination, West advocated an international police force which, by giving each member nation security against aggression, 'will enable all to live in this useful fellowship' ('Necessity', p. 260). West's pacifism would thus appear to be paradoxical if not contradictory, calling for a defensive threat of aggressive intervention as a solution to offensive aggression. And yet Mary Agnes Hamilton, in the same volume, argues that an 'international spirit' requires international policing of nationalist aggression because individual nations will always fear that another's assertion of sovereignty can all too easily translate into disregard of theirs.[62]

Validating the reality of this fear, Hamilton calls upon both pacifist and 'national patriot' to 'sacrifice' their conflicting priorities 'if, together, they are to achieve the co-operation on which peace depends?' ('No Peace', p. 270). Such priorities are isolating, Hamilton argues, and do not participate in 'the common world of struggle and effort' ('No Peace', p. 271). By implication, this mutual isolation mirrors the withdrawal of nations from the quest for 'common consent' that would ensure peace ('No Peace', p. 271). To work towards international cooperation, pacifists must concede their absolute rejection of force and 'national patriots' must yield their faith in the nation's armies to an international security force. If such a force suggests the self-defeating perpetuation of war, Hamilton distinguishes between 'force in the hands of the individual and force used through the consent of the community' ('No Peace', p. 271). The latter allows people within and among individual nations to understand, tolerate, and accommodate their differences.

Despite their differences, as the thirties drew on, many British women writers were shocked into the recognition that Hitler's rise to power was cohering into a new and unique kind of hostility that travestied the idea of international cooperation. Even as they empathized with the women of Germany and Italy, now consigned by the fascists to domestic servitude, they also recognized that those women who supported fascism had to be held responsible for its crimes. As we shall see from a closer study of their writing, many linked this recognition to the fate of victims beyond the boundaries of their island, the introduction of which challenges binary categories of opposition. The persistent presence of the Other in many fictions and non-fictional writing of British women of the thirties and forties suggests that the values for which Vera Brittain and so many others celebrate an abiding England must include the victims beyond its borders. In turn, identifying with the position of the Other, as did many women writers who lived in Europe between the wars, reframed their definitions of national purpose and war aims and used their redefinitions as political and social critique. Thus, writers like Bryher and Naomi Jacob, who had savoured the independence and privacy screen of European self-exile, returned to England to share the war's agonies with their friends, and challenged government policies and social attitudes with their continental perspectives. In Jacob's retrospective novel of the war, *Wind on the Heath* (1956), a woman who takes part in the Dunkirk rescue mission challenges the detachment made possible by doing one's bit in a safe place like Yorkshire: 'You read the casualty lists and say how terrible it all is. But you're safe – safe, tucked away here, miles from munitions factories, airfields, and the rest of it.'[63]

Bryher insisted that 'if you believe in freedom you must be prepared to defend it'.[64] Her method of defence included risking her career by criticizing the government, and while this 'made people angry and words could not bring back the things [she] had lost', she, like other women writers, chose to be 'in it' living in a kind of home front exile (*Mars*, pp. 4, 8). Reflecting on the 'Third Year' of the war, she highlights the ambiguous position of her alienation; she condemns the lack of moral 'will or vision of her fellow English who fail to adjust their 'dreams of a Victorian paradise to come' to 'the historical repetition of crisis, futility, despair, and further war'.[65] In her view, this failure produced a moral indolence that 'favoured fascism because it was easier for you to let them have their way than to fight them' ('Third', p. 20). Resigned but also energized to join the war effort as a necessity, Bryher regrets the failure of 'energetic democratic intervention up to 1935 [which] could have prevented this struggle, with its slaughter, its air raids, and its misery' with 'action, criticism, acceptance of personal responsibility' ('Third', pp. 20, 23). For Bryher, 'personal responsibility' does not stop at the border of self or nation, but includes other victims, alienated, not by choice, but by persecution: 'If you had been a free and independent citizen in 1933, for example, you would have thought it inconsistent with the liberty you prized yourself, to allow thousands of innocent people to be herded into a concentration camp, no matter what the geographical boundary' ('Third', p. 19). Bryher found fault with pacifists 'when they substituted battle is wrong for conscience, that necessary if somewhat Puritan virtue' because that use of 'conscience' showed the failure to grasp that the plight of these Others required aggressive action, to do battle against their enemy ('Third', p. 23).

Other women writers opposed the war because they found it painfully disruptive not only to their material lives, but to the social attitudes that had supported their sense of stability. Ursula Bloom, who mined the minutae of her often painful life for a prolific output of romance fiction, magazine articles, and biographies, recalled her war years in London as moving 'from one air raid to the next and ask[ing] no questions as to the possibilities of the future'.[66] Bloom expresses her criticisms of the war by constructing the nation's enemy as a sign of its own weakness and disharmony. Her 1945 novel, *The Fourth Cedar*, registers the nation's weakness as women's essential stupidity and the war's social disruptions as an unassimilable Other. Thus a woman commits a fatal error by falling in love with a Jew whose tortured English marks him as a threat to the nation's cohesion.

This plot manoeuvre could have been taken as either a joke or an attempt at realistic dialect – 'You was made for me' – were it not for Bloom's unfortunate rendering of the Jew through the image of 'a smear of grey ash' – and this in 1945.[67] Asking no questions betrays a fatalistic loss of faith in the critical process that would move other women writers to confront such misogyny and antisemitism as the cultural inheritance they would reject. This rejection would become part of their revision of Britain's war aims and national identity. The now irretrievable connection of the home front to Europe's victims became clear to many other women writers who chronicled the domestic war. For them, there is no retreat to private imagination, personal consciousness, or home sweet home and its individually created space. With searchlights and bomb fires glaring, even one's own neighbourhood becomes a city of disorientation. Like Bowen's 'Mysterious Kor', in which any sense of belonging, intimacy or insularity is shattered in the Blitz, the war experience for so many British women writers destroyed boundaries, not only between inside and outside and between social classes and regions, but between their sense of individual destiny and its connection to the fate of Others.

2

From Fascism in Britain to World War: Dystopic Warnings

CANONIZING DYSTOPIAS

Stephen Spender begins his account of the 1930s by declaring it 'the decade in which young writers became involved in politics'.[1] Reflecting his own turbulent political involvement, instead of assuming any harmony or consistency, he describes his generation's divided heart:

> . . . extremely non-political with half of themselves and extremely political with the other half. With the political half they really did try to see the world from the ideological viewpoint . . . a struggle between opposed interests, those of capitalist imperialism and those of the socialist revolution. Perhaps one might not in past historical situations have seen this, but in the thirties it was so highlighted by current circumstances . . . (p. 18).

Spender's bipolar image of a collective creative imagination is shaped not only by a sense of political crisis, but by his ambivalent political commitment. Deeply involved in one political camp and then another, and then claiming to be apolitical later in his life, he also distances himself from other writers by talking about 'them' and 'one' instead of 'we'. Even so many years later, his cool voice is aimed at stemming the surging apocalyptic vision of his generation of writers. Many others of his era, however, were less cool, and in a wide variety of literary forms, from documentary realism to moral and modernist fables, they express a sense of impending catastrophe for which there appears no solution. Even when writers avoided naming its historic realities, their work of the thirties is shaped by a voice of doom.

Many questions have been raised about this overwhelming pessimism, especially since the the apocalyptic vision had already spun itself out in the twenties, when writers like Lawrence, Yeats, and Eliot had prophesied a rough end of days.[2] The older writers, of course, were responding to the Great War; its incalculable losses still haunted them despite the fact that the twenties was a period of recovery and social ferment. It is the combination of despair and creative regeneration that drives the formal and ideological experimentation of the twenties. But by the next decade, political and economic failure overwhelmed any sense of a new dawning within existing political and social structures. It may very well have seemed that real recovery was more mythical than literary constructions of catastrophe. After all, by 1933 nearly three million were unemployed in Britain. Cuts in the dole and wages of government workers spelled crisis for the Labour Government and drove many of its intellectual supporters into a state of disaffection.[3] As fascism spread its wings over Europe and exploded into nazism, fears of another world war which led many to join the Peace Pledge Union in 1934, materialized when the Spanish Civil War broke out in 1936.

Anxiety and political violence were triggered not only by barbarians outside the gates. When Oswald Mosley led the British Union of Fascists at his Olympia Rally on 7 June 1934 and then on a march through the Jewish East End of London on 4 Oct. 1936, many must have felt that fascism could no longer be considered an alien political species, but home grown.[4] For many intellectuals and writers who felt that the Labour Party was enfeebled and liberalism in general 'associated with private wealth and with empire', it was easy to proclaim, as did Auden in 1939, that 'We are seeing the end of Liberal Democracy . . . and "this is a good thing": it will be replaced by socialism or fascism' (quoted in Watson, p. 66). Certainly, in the early thirties, the example of Soviet revolutionary politics was very enticing. For despite progressivist movements within the Labour Party and even the formation of the Socialist League within it, there was little coherence or power to its gradualist political and economic solutions, and so while the nation's problems seemed to originate within itself, its leadership appeared unable to generate its own solutions.

Cultural critics of Britain in the thirties agree that for many writers who reached adulthood during World War I, the continuing 'images of atrophy and decline' reinforced their loss of 'all faith in historical progress'.[5] In addition to problems that were all too visible, the period also produced a more diffuse but equally disquieting unease about rapidly accelerating technological and scientific progress. Rather than being viewed as a creative revolution, science and technology produced the feeling of being controlled by impersonal forces. For many, the equally dehumanizing systems of monopoly capitalism and mass communication lent a surreal aura to the decade.[6] Literary responses to this sense of surreality did not always end in a despairing whimper, but with a bang that reflected an intense ambivalence about social, political, and technological progress. If, as George Watson argues, catastrophe had already occurred for the older writers of the twenties, 'For the youthful optimists and utopians of the Thirties, by contrast, catastophe was a doctrine of revolutionary faith, and the collapse of the old meant the triumph of the new' (p. 100). However uniformly revolutionary this sounds, Valentine Cunningham's study of thirties literature shows a total lack of orthodoxy, not only in the political responses of Spender's coterie, but as a volatile shift of political allegiances within individual writers, such as Eliot, Waugh, Orwell, and Virginia Woolf.[7]

An example of how political ambivalence shaped the political writing of the era is that of Amabel Williams-Ellis, who expressed her disillusionment with political progress with an almost self-cancelling irony. After visiting the Soviet Union in 1933, she wrote *To Tell The Truth,* a novel that defends the Soviet system by satirizing the self-deluded smugness she felt made British anti-Soviet criticism ridiculous. Her ironies, however, almost backfire in the relationship between her comic education of a Soviet defector and her own changing political views. He becomes disillusioned about bourgeois democracy while touring an impoverished Britain in 1940, but even before the novel was published, Williams-Ellis was changing her mind. Once the Nazis took over, she combined her communist sympathies with a defence not only of 'a Popular Front against Fascism', but of '"English liberties"' and 'bourgeois culture'.[8] Her sympathies, however, remained imbued with a critical air, which lent the atmosphere of catastrophe an element of hope:

> Our democracy is far from perfect and complete but it gives us room to gather the hosts of the people for a fresh advance....

> Just because Democracy holds within it the promise of a new social order in which the happiness and well-being of the people shall be the single aim of government, all the black forces are now organising for the murder of Democracy. Over England are gathering the black shapes of reaction, of would-be dictatorships, of that concentration of every thought and thing most alien to English life – Fascism. (quoted in Croft, p. 225).

Ellis's collective voice embeds concerns shared by many writers of the thirties. As Samuel Hynes has pointed out, conflicts between political commitment and 'individualism' raised the question of how an artist could 'respond to the immediate crises of this time, and yet remain true to his art?' (*AG*, p. 207). It is therefore certainly no coincidence that this politicized literary decade was fertile ground for a type of imaginative literature which envisions horrific ends to scientific and technical invention and links them to misguided political process – dystopian novels.[9]

From the early thirties, British dystopias express a need to contain what they prophesied as destructive ends to a process of dehumanization. True to both art and politics, they use formal experimentation to serve moral and political ends. These dystopias dramatize a scenario first imagined in 1783 by Baptist Noel Turner, writer and churchman, who coined the term dystopia to signify what would happen if 'the cynicism of means and the utopianism of ends' could be united so that 'the ends justify all means'.[10] In the 1930s, dystopias dramatized fears that scientific technology would serve the aims of totalitarian demigogues and blow this world apart.[11]

Huxley's *Brave New World*, published in 1932, set the trend, and though more satiric than grim, it is a classic case of dramatizing the combined disastrous implications of scientific, social, economic, and political control. Its literary value as satiric fantasy, however, distances it from the present scene it indicts. As Peter Widdowson observes, Huxley expresses 'a vision of the present, but it is not about the present . . . [and] only signif[ies] Huxley's cultural pessimism, his rejection of history' (p. 42). A year later, H.G. Wells published *The Shape of Things to Come*, which imagines not only Hitler's European conquest but more world wars followed by a plague that leads to universal social chaos. The novel's epic structure reflects Wells's yearning for a new enlightenment built on progressivist assumptions. Combining the evolutionary theories of T.H. Huxley with a socialist vision, Wells's vision stakes the future on a planned 'evolution of humanity's intellectual and moral capacity', a vision of progress that could 'replace the blind warfare of natural selection'.[12] Wells's dramatic emphasis on cycles of human destructiveness, however, challenges his optimism. At the finale of the novel, as British leaders look skyward, their exhaustion lends a pessimistic note to their hopefulness. Despite his socialist critique, Wells's vision is tied to England's pragmatic political and scientific ethos, while his depiction of humanity's planned evolution could compare to Nietzsche's will to power. The combination of non-utopian democratic progressivism and apocalyptic hysteria underscores the disasters of the dystopic half of the novel.[13]

If the canon of modern British dystopias begins with *Brave New World*, it peaks with Orwell's *Animal Farm* (1945) and *Nineteen Eighty-Four* (1949).[14] Huxley's novel was easily adapted to classroom teaching with its hi-tech thrills and obvious dichotomies, while its allegorized arguments for and against the progressivism of liberal humanism and science made it easy prey to literary criticism. Orwell's dystopias were read as easy 'anti-Communist and anti-revolutionary lesson[s]', even if that was not his intention.[15] The success of these works, moreover, followed on the heels of Orwell's rising status among intellectuals; he had contributed pungent social and political commentaries on the British scene to the American *Partisan Review* throughout the war years.[16] Unlike Wells, who lost his cachet as he became more embittered, Orwell's appeal has increased the more ambiguous he becomes to contemporary readers.

As hallmarks of academic reading lists, these novels have provided the images and vocabulary that have educated the political consciousness of two generations. Hidden in the margins of this popularity, however, lies another story of *realpolitik*. Equally potent dystopic fictions by British women writers languish out of print, ignored by publishers and professors. The neglect and what we can therefore claim as the silencing of these women writers shapes a metafiction that dramatizes and inscribes a 'newspeak' Orwell never imagined. The silence, moreover, is particularly deafening considering the extent to which Orwell's reputation has been revised since the critical year 1984. Interestingly, those very critics who debunk him choose not to fill the vacuum, which they could easily do by studying dystopias by Orwell's female contemporaries.[17]

REVISING THE GENRE – QUESTIONING POLITICAL PROCESS

In contrast to the models of Huxley, Wells, and Orwell, the dystopic warnings of Storm Jameson, Naomi Mitchison, and Katherine Burdekin suggest that in order to prevent the crises of the moment from exploding worldwide, prevailing political and social ideologies must be revised. Moreover, Mitchison's *We Have Been Warned*, published in 1935, and Jameson's *In the Second Year*, 1936, do not represent the kinds of divisions which beset Spender and his coterie. In fact, what creates aesthetic problems for these novels is their total political engagement. Unabashedly didactic, they claim an aesthetic space by combining political argument with formal experimentation, and in so doing, refute Hynes's assertion that 'by 1936 . . . political commitment had produced no art of any importance' (*AG*, p. 206).

These women's dystopias represent political and moral arguments on behalf of historical progress, but because their stances are always critical, they also envision change that positions them in reaction against prevailing British ideologies, political parties and platforms. Their dystopias also represent reactions against traditional forms of the genre itself. Anti-utopian, these novels eschew the marvels of supertechnology while questioning both the despair and biting satire of dystopias by Huxley and Wells. Even those dystopias of the following decade – by Jameson, Katharine Burdekin, and Vita Sackville-West – which predict a protracted Hitlerian nightmare, are more taken with analysing the ideologies and conditions that produced nazism than they are with imagining the death driven technologies that represent its material consequences. Unlike Huxley or Wells, the major apparatus of the state in women's dystopias is not scientific control, but prevailing social codes, and psychological warfare does not materialize as hyperkinetic thought waves, but rather as a companionate marriage of misogyny and social control.

British women's dystopias of the thirties and forties revise the genre by questioning its underlying liberal doctrines. Committed to readings of the historical moment, they question the progressivist and universalizing gestures typical of utopian and dystopian literature. The result is to translate their fears of another world war into dramatic connections between British and European forms of political oppression. As they underscore similarities as well as differences, they show how political oppression resonates in social structures the English take for granted as liberal and progressive, even at the level of friendship across the classes. Seeing the present as regressive also leads to revising traditional forms of character development; instead of focusing on the individual in society, women's dystopias produce a narrative dialectic between individual and collective consciousness and experience. Privileging neither, these writers construct character to function as a fictional debate. At stake is an argument about the nature of progress and how the idea of utopia may intensify the damage individual and collective authority inflict on each other.

In these dystopias the characters of men signify a kind of stasis, as though their commitment to progress backfires when it materializes as a will to power and an authoritarian fight to the finish. Female characters, on the other hand, embody and narrate visions of this dystopic finale and its victimizing consequences. Unlike Huxley or Wells, or modernist novels of social and political critique such as Virginia Woolf's 1932 *The Waves*, the polemical and didactic purposes of these dystopias are not symbolically embedded in suspenseful melodramas or poetic structures. Instead, they are narrated as the characters' historically and gendered political debates, and dramatized as the disastrous consequences of these debates failing to affect political process. In a dramatic move towards a new feminist form, these dystopias analyse prevailing political and social problems by projecting them into the future as conditions of gender.

Clearly inspired by current events in Britain and in Europe, the dystopias by Storm Jameson and Naomi Mitchison predict fascist takeovers in England. Created with enough detailed allusions to remind readers of the historic moment, they warn that British democracy could not only collapse, but that if it did, the government would collaborate with a world-wide fascist conquest. Such a view was not far-fetched when a sign of the times was Oswald Mosley. Read in conjunction with these, other dystopias by Storm Jameson, Vita Sackville-West, and Katharine Burdekin show the terrible aftermath of World War II arising from Britain's failure to redirect its internal social and political goals and therefore defeat the fascism that explodes into the Third Reich. All of these dystopias dramatize British malaise in the thirties as marking the beginning of world disaster, but not its cause. As Storm Jameson writes in 1932, the danger signs were already present in those ‘anxious honourable men whose minds were hard set in 1913. For this reason and no other their remedies against social disaster are as much use as a roll of sticking-plaster in an earthquake’ (*No Time*, p. 97).[18] With 2 955 000 unemployed by January 1933, and a reigning Labour Party led by the increasingly conservative Ramsay MacDonald, these writers could imagine ‘no panacea, Socialist or otherwise’.[19]

Unlike H.G. Wells, who foresees such ‘honourable men’ developing viable ‘remedies’, many women writers of the period see the masculine definition of honour as the problem, and their dystopias predict its drastic political and social results. The structures of women’s dystopias, moreover, implicitly criticize Wells for taking solace in imagining new global visions of old political structures – ‘“the New Liberalism, World Socialism, Scientific World Organization or World Radicalism”’.[20] They would also thus stand in opposition to the way ‘the values of individual freedom and justice’ were been deployed by the leftist intellectuals of Spender’s coterie (Hynes, p. 262). Unlike Spender himself, who veered between condemning the Moscow show trials and joining the Communist Party, or those like John Strachey who refused to see anything wrong with the Soviet Union, Jameson and Mitchision were appalled by connections they saw between revolutionary violent means and ends, and so rejected Communism very early on. Their dystopias embed this rejection by deconstructing violent solutions that support myths of either catastrophe or progress. The alternative Jameson and Mitchison propose is nothing short of a revolution in social and political consciousness. Without such a non-violent revolution, they imply, Wells’s utopian vision, like that of the Communists, presages only another dystopia.

If a recalcitrant patriarchy could lead the world to disaster, according to these women writers, it was also responsible for persistent domestic economic and political inequities. In their dystopias, these inequities are shown to oppress both the men and women of England. This oppression, moreover, has an impact at such a fundamental level of consciousness and extends to such a broad spectrum of social relationships, that the sexes are driven apart in ways that parallel the brutalities of war itself.[21] Government and prevailing social codes are not depicted as the only culprits, however. These novels also take on the trade unions, which had proposed family allowances that polarized men and women. This program, designed to help working class families, was predicated on married women withdrawing from the workforce. Unfortunately, this solution only re-established women's dependency. Imagining a solution to this bind, Wells's *Things to Come* concludes with an equitable relationship between a man and woman who fly to the moon to create a new humane world. But like his hopefulness about honourable men, the future of his young people is also in doubt. Wells's new Eden resembles that of the trade union leaders; ignoring the social and economic construction of gender relations, it will be built on power relationships left over from the past. This is an inequity that will remain a potential threat to the future.

STORM JAMESON AND NAOMI MITCHISON: LOCAL AND GLOBAL POLITICS

The dystopias of Jameson and Mitchison warn of a future blind to the economic grounds of social and political inequity. It is on these grounds, they argue, that men and women victimize each other and the seeds of international injustices are sown. For Jameson and Mitchison, totalitarian power was not simply the provenance of evil empires originating elsewhere. Instead, they felt it could also arise from the totalizing effects of Britain's internal failures. In their dystopias, such failures weaken the moral and political resolve of leaders and populace.

Storm Jameson was Naomi Mitchison's good friend. Active members of the Labour Party and yet disturbed by its lassitude towards prevailing economic depression, they share a place in the literary history of the thirties and forties. Divided differently than Spender and his colleagues, the politics of Jameson and Mitchison are marked by their ambivalence towards prevailing socialist and feminist politics. The feminist book Mitchison could never complete and the sarcasm that Jameson aims at her fictional feminists express mixed feelings about the feminist movement. They applauded the change in consciousness that rescued the ambitions of middle-class women, but rebuked feminists for ignoring the fates of impoverished women and men. Mitchison always felt tensions between feminism and socialism, and only rarely found outlets that supported both, as when she joined the Women's International League in the 1920s and publicly advocated birth control for women of all classes. Her 1934 essay, 'The

Reluctant Feminists', a review of Winifred Holtby's *Women*, insists that the feminism of Holtby's protagonist has been 'firmly conditioned by the economic position of the section of society to which we belong. We started before the war as good little bourgeois feminists, determined to beat, or at least equal, men at their own game'.[22] Taking into account the effects on women of the great depression and the rise of fascism and nazism, she argues that feminism must change once again. Its forceful response to these new dangers must include the voices of working-class women, for to speak for them, assuming to know what they want, only subjugates them once again. Jameson's fiction and essays call for representing working-class women's lives without sentimental pity or polemical self-righteousness. Her essay, 'Documents', arguing for a new socialist aesthetics, castigates the 'self-consciousness' of writers who depict the poor, but render them as stage props for the drama of their own excited curiosity.[23] Instead, the 'emotion should spring directly from the fact', and tellingly, her example of a fact is one that runs throughout her writing – women's dirty work – a 'woman's forefinger . . . scrap[ing] the black out of a crack in the table or the corner of a shelf' ('Documents', p. 11). If direct knowledge isn't available, then identifying with women's work sympathetically will produce the fact.

Jameson's feminism remains focused on linkages between domestic and public politics. Her 1932 essay, 'Man the Helpmate', satirizes 'the legend' of the essentially 'superior' yet supportive patriarch, which is upheld by 'newspapers, art, literature' and 'the pulpit'.[24] Her humour, however, is mixed with both anxiety and pride in a feminist revolution that must take women beyond the domestic sphere: 'This cherished and precious independence – for which we fought, bit policemen (yes, this I did – in Hyde Park . . . in the year before the Great War)' means assuming painful responsibilities in the public sphere, not only in British politics, but 'bring[ing] order out of the international chaos' ('Man', pp. 124–5). From the time she began travelling in Europe in the thirties, Jameson became internationalist in outlook and urged women to see that their social and economic problems were part of a masculinist world order that would culminate in fascism. During World War II, as deeply involved as she was in Britain's responsibility to Europe, she also focused on the heroism of British women of all classes, as well as on the dangers and inequities of their working conditions in British factories.[25]

The attitudes of Jameson and Mitchison towards social and economic reform are equally critical and Janus faced. The Britain they wished to see transformed remains paradoxically essential and immutable in their writing, even as they dramatize how its 'roots turn and twist' in the maelstrom of its violent history.[26] Such volatility is the mirror image of Jameson's ambivalence and shapes her writing through alternating, sometimes superimposed backdrops of Yorkshire's craggy and indomitable landscape and its unstable industrial history. Suggestive of unresolved conflicts between nurture and aggression, these images encapsulate Jameson's acknowledged source of her shifting male and female identified narratives. Just as her parents fought endlessly throughout their marriage, so her dominant but beleaguered mother and weak but restless and independent father represent Jameson's own alternating moods and sometimes fused voices.

Mitchison's 1934 dystopia, *We Have Been Warned*, is as much a gendered history of her cultural identity as is Jameson's. For Mitchison, Scotland's tradition of political resistance cannot be understood except as a struggle between aristocratic and tribal imperatives and between Scottish nationalism and British sovereignty. Just as Jameson's narrative voice assumes male and female identities, so Mitchison identifies with her suffragist Tory mother and academic scientist father. Mitchison also uses her parents and her class identities as models of resistance against each other. In both Mitchison's and Jameson's dystopias two internecine battles join forces: between the desires of women and men for individual freedom and collective power, and between a male-dominated political sphere and women's individual and collective resistance. For both writers, the intersection of gender and political inequities in the 1930 reflects Britain's self-infected weakness, and so they dramatize the etiology of a home-grown fascism that is all too ready, like a fifth column, to be exploited by an external conquerer. In their fantasies, myths of an impermeable homeland yield to nightmares of the nation as decimated battleground. Presaging Britain's experience in World War II, Jameson and Mitchison show that as homeland and battlefield merge, the boundary between a brutal domestic politics and war disappears. The dramatic result, in which polarities between women's peacefulness and men's militarism also merge, implicates the gendered lines of both dystopian and war literature. Both men and women are depicted as lovingly protecting others even as they protect themselves by venting rage and hostility at the internal and external enemy.

The deep ambivalence both writers express towards aggression and nurture as both positive and negative forces is captured in Jameson's poem, 'Cloud Form'.[27] Published during the height of World War II, it invokes an aggressive action as both necessary and hateful. 'Night's double grain' is the trope that represents ambivalence as a radically generative force which embraces both aggression and nurture; its purpose is to propel women into active resistance against their own 'body's sterile salt and the fear of some betrayal' on the part of impotent men. This is not an ambivalence that produces emotional and moral paralysis as a result of being unable to choose between two opposing positions. Rather, it is a self-reflexive and critical vision that generates a complex understanding of the contradictory social roles women feel constrained to play while they also enact a resistant rear-guard action. A new perspective emerges in these fictions that is both a warning about the destructive potential of traditional domestic politics and a vision of reform. As Jameson's poem illustrates, women's complicity with men's destructive politics signals a sterile marriage, while men's betrayal of their own desire to nurture produces the urge to destroy. In its multiple cadences, this formulation defies essentialist assumptions, for it works in reverse as well. Beneath the rubble of a dystopic future lies the hope for a restored nation, a homeland that could nurture the urge for creative risk while also ameliorating the aggression that accompanies the passion for power.

SOCIALIST ARISTOCRAT: NAOMI MITCHISON

Resistance to political entropy is the hallmark of Naomi Mitchison's life and career. She was born in 1897 into the same class as Virginia Woolf, but came to define her feminism and socialism very differently. Her father, John Scott Haldane, the eminent Oxford philosopher and physiologist, became Mitchison's model for experimenting with her life 'in pursuit of her art and of her relationships, political and intimate, as well as in pursuit of the self she was to become'.[28] Her mother, Kathleen (Maya), had been a suffragist, but her Tory snobbery and insularity irritated her increasingly left leaning daughter whose own pursuits blended feminism into family life. Of fiercely independent mind, Mitchison also disagreed for many years with her brother, J.B.S. Haldane, celebrated scientist and communist. She herself read science at Oxford, but then left to become a nurse. In 1916, she married Dick Mitchison, a lawyer whose family wealth provided the means for the domestic ease that enabled her to write and follow the political causes she chose. The devoted mother of four children, she could also afford to travel widely and study history, activities which became the bases of her historical novels. Set in the ancient and medieval worlds, most of her fiction embeds questions of women's status within themes of 'female questing' (Benton, p. 26). This was a theme that also shaped her life, for by 1925 she and Dick began what today we would call an open marriage, and though the experiment was often disappointing, even hurtful, she felt it necessary for her emotional, creative, and political development.

By 1931, Mitchison had joined the Labour Party and published her masterpiece of women's historical fiction, *The Corn King and the Spring Queen*. Her commitment to women's sexual freedom was matched by her concerns with working-class life, the combination of which forms the basis of her many public speeches and the core of *We Have Been Warned*. Her combined sympathies also pitted her against the interwar conservatism that would drive women back into the home, a place she revered only when it could provide the economic and emotional nourishment for women's autonomy and creative drives. Her 1930 essay, 'Comments on Birth-Control' presents a wry but radical view of women's dependency on 'domestic prostitution'; along with her critique, she also portrays a fantasied future in which professional women and their overworked husbands would be nurtured by resident 'sexual mates' (Benton, p. 73). Of two minds about any reformist platform, even her own, she wanted to relocate the essentially physical 'she-values' lost in the civilizing process, qualities she dramatized throughout her historical fictions of ancient and medieval life and politics. Always self-conscious of her privileged status, she understood the dangers of romanticizing a mythical past even when it had a feminist agenda, and so she also indicted her own speculations as 'a bit of a tory' (Benton, p. 73). The feminist book she began at this time was pathbreaking even in its unfinished critique of the patriarchal construction of knowledge and its effects on women's place in culture and civilization. Benton infers that the implications of such a woman centred analysis 'seemed to overwhelm Naomi' at a time when feminism was suffering a backlash, and so it remained unfinished (Benton, p. 74).

By 1932, Naomi Mitchison defined herself as a socialist. While deepening economic depression affected more of the nation's populace, she debated whether socialism's commitment to collective and egalitarian well-being offered more of a solution than the Labour Party. Her decision rested on what she could discover for herself about the effectiveness of British political process, and so while she campaigned for Dick in Birmingham, she kept a journal, recording conversations and observations as she got to know labourers and their families. Under the influence of John Pilley, a communist and teacher at Bristol University, she developed a synthesis of individualism and socialism which focused on women's sexual freedom. Part of her agenda to discover the implications of socialism took her to the Soviet Union, a journey also about sexual freedom where en route, she offered to help a sexually dysfunctional young man. Such a gesture is typical of Mitchison's idiosyncratic and personalized investment in feminism and socialism. Throughout her career she would challenge the mainstream of political movements with critical positions garnered from personal experience; she would then express her reflections in essays, letters to newspapers, lectures, and her own political activism. Though her views targeted her as part of the backlash against feminism and communism in the thirties, she remained dauntless.

In 1938 Mitchison published her political philosophy in *The Moral Basis of Politics*. This work, like Virginia Woolf's *Three Guineas*, of the same year, analysed the historical and economic positioning of power. Focusing on relationships between individual power and a democratic polity, Mitchison 'realise[s] that the kind of equality which I have supposed to be necessary for right relationships is economic equality'.[29] Despite their shared concerns, however, Mitchison's economic analysis differs markedly from Woolf's. For Mitchison, fascism is not endemic to British patriarchy, but a political possibility that could erupt from the damage of long standing economic disparities among British men and women of different classes and the blindess that ensued from assumptions about the other's social expectations. Her response to Winifred Holtby's feminism is pertinent here, for she asks feminists to consider 'the woman whose husband is also owned, as much a chattel belonging to another man... as any oppressed female. That kind of woman may and often does feel herself at one with her man in the struggle against ownership' ('Reluctant', p. 95).

Mitchison's dystopia of the thirties, *We Have Been Warned*, dramatizes the possible effects of a decade that for the three million unemployed was summed up in the slogan 'Poverty in the midst of plenty'. At the heart of Mitchison's warning are relationships between women's sexual, economic, and political oppression and the economic power or deprivation that drives men to disenfranchize and brutalize women. Dealing with the social effects of poverty also allowed her to confront her own implication in their condition as a member of that intellectual aristocracy that fuelled so many dubious social reforms, but retained its self-satisfaction. She concluded that brutality was an outgrowth of gender inequities in all classes, but that the blindness that privilege afforded made it possible for the best intentions of reformers to become another form of oppression. In her view, both men and women can become either oppressors or victims, and they are both encouraged to impose 'their will' by class privilege, 'through money-power (often turned into physical violence)' (*Moral Basis*, p. 80). Mitchison's view of Virginia Woolf's feminism as 'bourgeoise value' derives from her indictment of what she felt was the arrogant gesture of the 'daughters of educated men' speaking for women of other classes (Benton, p. 75).

'A COLD SHABBY PURGATORY'*: NAOMI MITCHISON'S VISION OF BRITISH FASCISM

Although Naomi Mitchison was already a celebrated writer when she wrote *We Have Been Warned*, her publisher and editor rejected it. Edward Garnett, her editor at Cape, found the heroine's sexually free behaviour both unrealistic and unacceptable, while Victor Gollancz, progressive publisher of the Left Book Club, felt that women's issues in the novel should have taken second place to those of class. The novel was finally published in 1935, two years after completion, but then reviewers echoed the earlier complaints. Even today, when Mitchison's wartime writings have been reprinted, this novel, which compellingly dramatizes a

* Storm Jameson, *Journey from the North II.*

modern British civil war, remains out of print.[30] *We Have Been Warned* remains startling, but not because it advocates women's sexual freedom. Rather, its narrative power emanates from the novel's linkage of this theme to a critique of interwar British politics and its relation to the European rise of fascism. While it can be argued that Mitchison's European travels enflamed her critical approach to Britain's political horizons, any examination of her non-fictional political analyses in the thirties shows her cautious and subtle comparisons. In her 1934 *Vienna Diary*, for example, Mitchison examines how progressive Austrian leaders, acting 'in complete good faith', needed to compromise to advance their policies but when the fascist Dollfuss government pressured them ever more strongly, the result was 'snatching away one freedom after another'.[31] This functionalist approach allows Mitchison to survey the operations of a society's political institutions in the light of the conciliatory needs of liberals. She sees the results backfiring at the hands of autocratic political leaders, and translates her European observations into a warning to her own nation.

Written before Hitler's 1933 consolidation of power and Austria's fascist takeover, Mitchison's dystopia expresses fears that Britain will fall prey not only to the inadequacies of the Labour Party and socialism, but that combined with the Tories' commitment to the status quo, the rise of a fascist right in Britain is inevitable. It is through a woman's sexual and political odyssey that we learn that the nation's retrograde social codes are implicated in totalitarian politics.

The plot of this dystopia turns on the murder of Daniel Coke-Brown, a right wing newspaper baron. The murderer is Donald Maclean, a gardener's son radicalized by communism (the naming more than 20 years before the real Donald Maclean's defection to the Soviet Union is also startling but apparently only a coincidence). Mitchison's Maclean is rescued by an upper class couple, Dione and Tom Galton, who are drawn to him by their concerns about deepening social and economic injustices in Britain. The Galtons devise a plan to smuggle Donald to the Soviet Union, using the passport of Dione's brother, whom Donald resembles. With this plotting, *We Have Been Warned* may be as melodramatic as other dystopias, relying as it does on fateful coincidence and the inexhaustible power of personality. But it also revises the genre by gendering the dystopic future. Unlike Huxley's or Wells's dystopias of this period, or Orwell's postwar *1984*, where women are subordinate to man's fate, and therefore the plot, Mitchison showcases her dystopic future as a distinctly gendered place where the historical and social complexities of women's reactions question the assumed charisma of powerful men. In her vision, a woman's mind and body become objects of revolutionary politics.

Borrowing from Scottish gothic lore, Mitchison uses the spectre of a female witch, Green Jean, to prophesy dire consequences for a problematic present. Whenever Green Jean appears in a vision to Dione Galton, connections are drawn between the violent suppression of women in the past and the revolutionary forces that produce only new forms of oppression. As if to confirm the material reality of such foreboding, the vision is internalized as Dione's political consciousness and the narrator invokes historic memories of burning witches in the seventeenth century. With this combination, the novel points to the growing intolerance of dissident voices in the 1930s as symptomatic of Britain's continuing moral decay.

Mitchison's inspiration for gendering both history and the dystopic future was her 1931 experience campaigning in mining and industrial towns for her husband, who ran unsuccessfully for a Labour seat in Parliament. Visiting homes and talking to workers and their wives moved her to explore and question her socialist beliefs, a practice she never abandoned, as when she worried about the poor women of Glasgow in her 1939 letter to *Time and Tide*. At this earlier date, she already concluded that prevailing social and economic injustices were inextricably tied to inequities that affected men and women differently, but in such interrelated ways, that they were driven apart by their suffering. She then wrote her dystopia in a self-consciously double voice, viewing working-class experience from the perspective of her own privileged background and from that of her feminist consciousness. As Benton reports: 'She was trying to write about the contradictions inherent in British socialism as it was lived by herself and those around her' (p. 51). The result is a scathing portrait of a self-deceived British socialism and its complicit role in the rise of a brutally vindictive fascism. In its double voice and echoing effect between Dione and Green Jean, women embody not only the victimized Other, but as Other, represent a perspective from the margins that is both critical and resistant.

The foreword invokes the novel's exploration of 'social morality' as its goal, and this is carried out by alternating and then synthesizing private and public voices. The opening scene, for example, scans a Scottish upper class family reunion, shifting perspectives of power, collusion, and resistance as men and women vent feelings about sex and politics. Instead of remaining distinctly separate, however, the narrative voices form a synthesis of individually gendered and collective social consciousness. The novel then alternates Dione's unspoken thoughts with those of a nameless and ungendered narrator, dramatizing the tension between them and offering readers a seat on the sidelines of a debate about historical narrative as a predictive force. On the one hand, Dione's political vision fuses a subjectively emotional response to historical injustice, while on the other, the narrator dramatizes history as impersonal events and uses them to deliver an impassioned but objective warning to readers.

The name Dione, which in Latin means law giver, suggests that female agency is as inseparable from rationality as the latter is from her emotional responses, but despite the intellectual power Mitchison claims for this combination, Dione is still constrained by male-centred interpretations of the law as well as by male-dominated lawlessness. The ungendered narrator, who understands and has the power to warn of impending violence, nonetheless has only limited agency. In not being able to protect her subject, the narrator illustrates a liminal position between the authority of those who have access to power and the powerlessness of others. In relation to her narrator, Dione is left alone to interpret and respond to the events which envelop her. The narrative thus takes her on a feminist odyssey as she must live through and interpret political stasis, revolution, and counter-revolution. All along the way Dione questions relationships between contemporary political culture and the idea of human progress.

She begins by naively hoping for a revolution where 'afterwards everything will be planned and reasonable, and we shall all want to help with the plan – all the people of good will'.[32] But as Dione's own class-bound assumptions are implicated in the failure of such high hopes, Mitchison is mocking the claims to goodness and light of her own class. As a corrective, her heroine's character must enter a revolutionary phase. To begin, Dione expresses a radical ambivalence when her 'reasonable we' is exposed as the privilege of the intellectual aristocrat: 'Have I got to be torn, one half of me wanting brotherhood, demanding it as the only sensible thing, and the other half realizing the plain fact of intellectual inequality?' (*Warned*, p. 62). 'Fact' here marks Mitchison's ironic juxtaposition of snobbery and socialist sentiments. Instead of working through Dione's ambivalence, Mitchison uses it to expose how class-bound hierarchies entrap women along with the uneducated poor. 'The fact of intellectual inequality' turns out to be socially constructed by 'the people at the top' on whom upper-class women depend for the stability of their identity and for the leisure to develop socialist sympathies. Like her author, Dione's struggle to form her political consciousness begins as she campaigns for her husband's election and meets industrial workers.

This struggle became the target of Q.D. Leavis's attacks on the novel and on Mitchison's 'innocently bourgeois background'.[33] Leavis was contemptuous of the novel's attempts 'to arouse revolutionary feeling', and indicts Mitchison's upper class 'assumption of authority' to speak on the workers' behalf; by implication, Leavis valorizes her own empathy for the 'workers of England'.[34] Biased by her own identity politics, Leavis cannot see Mitchison's critical irony. In fact, Mitchison is being self-critical in her portrait of the Galtons, and so portrays them as realizing that for their class, poverty is comfortably theoretical compared to others' material privations. The novel illustrates this self-criticism in Dione's shocked response to the mindless work of miners and labourers, the meagre rewards of which cannot relieve their wives' despair over the smell of their poverty. Contrary to liberal and socialist sentiments, Dione comes to see that the conditions of industrial workers and their families cannot be explained by social science paradigms. While categories of the underprivileged may generate sympathy, they also condescend to the poor and comfort the privileged. Hence Dione discovers that while it is all too true that the workers are exploited to pay for the 'fine feelings' of the privileged, their impoverished condition also fails to numb the worker, either intellectually or aesthetically (*Warned*, p. 397). Leavis insists that Mitchison's portrait of the poor is condescending, that the novel makes their lack of 'fine feelings' 'a mark of superiority because it comes from closer contact with reality' ('Lady', p. 134).

Mitchison's critique of 'fine feelings' does not, however, suggest that the perceptions of the poor lack subtlety or complexity, that they are noble savages. Instead she argues that the subtle and complex perceptions claimed by the upper classes are no more than 'elaborate hot-house feelings' which are expressed in a vocabulary and syntax they are educated to believe is superior (*Warned*, p. 28). With self-directed irony, she has Tom tell Dione: 'a lot of our fine feelings are just a very unimportant by-product of too much money. That's why I can't stand all those novels and poems about them' (*Warned*, p. 20).

The unadorned, journalistic language with which Dione's working-class encounter is represented strips away any effort to validate the perceptions of the intellectual aristocracy or ennoble or sentimentalize the poor. If anything, it coincides with Mitchison's memory of her defensive need to distance herself from the London poor, whom she first saw in 1914, and who struck her as 'another race, frightening'.[35] Her dystopia dramatizes how the power supporting such antipathy can not be disassembled either by 'reasonable' politics or revolution (*Warned*, p. 62). Tested in the novel in various ways, both traditional and revolutionary political culture come under attack for resisting the reform of their intersecting hierarchies of gender and class. For Mitchison, Britain and the Soviet Union each encompasses a 'dream [that] means war and oppression and owning things and owning people' (*Warned*, p. 68). It is this 'dream' that had earlier provoked her to urge 'politics-shy women into the field of political action' and 'to consider the economics of feminism as part of the general economics of possessors and possessed' ('Reluctant', p. 93). Translated into dystopic drama, this means that the socialist desire to help the poor masks a middle-class noblesse in which every representation of the poor, whether fictional or reportage, threatens to take over their lives.

Mitchison later theorized the social contexts that produced this 'general economics' in *The Moral Basis of Politics*. Here she observes that both men and women desire power, but that those 'at the top', upper-class men, have exclusive access to economic and political power that corresponds to their control of such institutions as all-male public schools. These landmarks of privilege train the country's leadership 'in the old-fashioned sense of taking and using power . . . with its tacit assumption of power by men over women, who, poor things, can never be English Gentlemen' (*Moral*, pp. 336, 337). This feminist analysis coincides with that of Virginia Woolf in *A Room of One's Own* and *Three Guineas*, but Mitchison parts company with Woolf in implicating her own position as an upper-class woman. The social and economic privileges which sustain her depend on working-class men, and the need for this sustenance could easily drive her to conceive of wanting 'power over people' (*Moral*, p. 336). In her dystopia, both Tom and Dione thoroughly enjoy their privileges, but also worry about their complicity with a system that uses her dependency and his power to exploit the less advantaged.

Mitchison's dystopia examines an alternative to capitalist exploitation and fascist persecution in the model of the Soviet Union. Dione's tour of the Socialist Republics begins with enthusiasm for its principles, but when its practices are exposed as the violent exploitation of women, the idea of a communist revolution turns sour. In a startling scene, borrowed from Mitchison's trip to the Soviet Union in 1932, Dione is shocked into realizing that the revolutionary state disguises its 'power over people' in its 'propaganda' about women's equality (*Warned*, p. 295). What shakes her is the sight of a woman enduring an abortion without anaesthetic. In its promise of granting women choices for their bodies and destinies, the communist state exacts a price of unbearable pain. That women are singled out to pay for revolutionary struggle is central to Mitchison's warning. Exploiting a woman's body for the purpose of celebrating the state's body politic testifies to the retrograde nature of a male-centred progressivism. That it should be women who bear and recognize state-sponsored punishment reflects Mitchison's historical interpretation. The Soviet abuse of women echoes Dione's visions of witch burning as well as the narrator's depiction of women sacrificed on the altar of Britain's fall into fascism. Mitchison's view of the Soviet Union as 'a lot of Sparta' left her feeling 'ambivalent about the Communist Party' (*Ask*, pp. 188, 191). While many intellectuals in the thirties were championing a Soviet struggle to build a classless society, Mitchison views it through the lens of a society based on one class: the military.

Caught in the lens as well and connecting communism to its supposed opposite is the image of a 'Spartan' goosestepping fascism. If left-leaning readers were put off by this juxtaposition, conservatives would have been incensed at Mitchison's linkage of communism and Britain. Reflected through Dione's observations, Soviet Russia ironically reflects the 'cocksuredness' of her own class divided and misogynist society, and no better: 'Sometimes it seemed to her that the whole place was... becoming more and more imbued with that public-school spirit which all sensible women are up against ...' (*Warned*, p. 295). When Mitchison's male publishers found the abortion scene offensive, it only highlighted the link between women's oppression in the Soviet Union and Britain. The 'public-school spirit' that supports the male stiff upper lip inflicts as much pain on women in Britain as it does on Soviet woman. Both the revolutionary left and traditional and liberal centre oppress women by prescribing what should be desirable and fearful.

Mitchison constructs Dione's empathy so that it marks a feminist resistance to male-dominated public policies, a revolutionary state of mind that leads to her decision to declare sexual and political independence. Mitchison's publishers may have found this development jarring and unrealistic, but it is actually based on the Mitchisons' open marriage and serves the novel's linkage of revolutionary and sexual politics. Dione offers Donald Maclean a sexual relationship, and though he refuses, she also supports her husband Tom's liaison with a Russian woman despite feeling terribly hurt as a result. The effect of this complicated sexual politics is to dramatize the revolutionary impact of a woman choosing her own desires and pain. Unlike public policies that shaped women's lives in either Britain or the Soviet Union, the policies governing this fiction allow Dione to assume her own responsibility for the consequences. By implication, the narrative questions codes of conduct that deny women responsibility for their sexual decisions and consequences.

Dione's relationships with Donald Maclean and with her husband express desires which run counter to those prescribed by either 'the fine feelings' embedded in English conventions of romantic love or in myths of maternal sacrifice to Mother Russia. What emerges instead is an upper-class self-consciousness about the privilege that supports the ability to assume personal responsibility for sexual decisions. This takes place in the form of Dione's cherished memories of having her children and husband safe and secure while she explores her independence. The desire for independence embedded in Dione's memories repudiates the myth of women's wish to lose themselves in either sexual passion or selfless patriotism. While the novel validates her independence as important to all women, it also shows that Dione's wealth makes it possible. Because Dione can afford domestic servants, she doesn't need to be her family's primary caregiver. Concommitantly, she does not have to rationalize the middle-class dictum that her husband and children should be her primary passion. Dione's sexual decisions revise entrenched beliefs about women's psychological desire for marriage. Instead, the novel situates a woman's power to define herself in her revisionary construction of family and community, one that belies the state's idea of family welfare. When Dione becomes pregnant with Tom's child, the event is not naturalized as an automatic cause for celebration. Instead, the couple deliberate about having the child or aborting it. Their decision is based on working out a definition of mutuality; they must choose between their sense of a collective social conscience – knowing this rests on their economic security – or their definitions of individual and mutual emotional attachment.

Working out the ambivalences in this construction enabled Mitchison to understand why she desired both continuity and change.[36] In her memoir of 1920–40, she confessed that she wanted to see 'economic liberation' bring 'a fairer world', mixing people of all classes, but she did not want a socialist revolution destroying 'our way of life' because it would hold her children 'hostages'; so while 'change was necessary', 'we went on planning for things to go on as they were going' (*Ask*, p. 192).

In her dystopia, choosing the child leads the Galtons to reimagine parenthood as a synthesis of personal and social imperatives. The child neither makes nor breaks their marriage or the state, but represents a promise to make each interdependent, not dependent on the other. Making this decision, however, does not represent a resolution to Mitchison's radical ambivalence. Instead, the structure of Dione's odyssey is like a dialectic, in that each of her experiences produces not only a lesson, but an alternative perspective that serves as its critique. In this sense, her communist, socialist, and feminist sympathies are used to question their political practices. A case in point is Dione's sexual independence, which is supposed to fulfil her personal desires as well as her feminist and socialist ideals. Instead of being a 'shortcut' to intimate and interdependent relationships, however, her sexual freedom only highlights the economic oppression and social alienation that drive people apart (*Warned*, p. 363). Dione's sexual adventures disclose that such values as sexual and political freedom are not only gender based and politically governed, but the 'economics of possessors and possessed'.

What the novel executes very didactically, and what Dione learns, is that social and emotional connectedness carry very different meanings for those whose oppression cuts so deep what is desired is a victim to share the misery. Dione learns her lesson by being subjected to a more violent shock than the sight of the Soviet abortion. She is raped by a British communist party worker. In this case, her upper-class status provides neither protection nor connectedness, for it has both implicated and targeted her in her violation. The rape enacts the worker's rage against the woman who embodies his oppression by those 'at the top'. Dione symbolizes the consumption of goods for which he breaks his back but cannot afford, and worse, her pity for him sentimentalizes his condition and robs it of any reality.

Collapsed into capitalist and communist dehumanization, the objectified and emasculated worker suffers his own violation from Dione's efforts to recuperate him. Her unquestioned reliance on empathy, her assumption that she can feel his pain, denies his difference and his experiential reality. To be rescued by her means being remade in the image of what the upper classes consider human, but denied their privilege, he is only fit to serve as a mascot to their faith in social progress. Ironically, the effort to rescue him desecrates the very individualism prized by the free enterprise system, and therefore exposes the feudal assumptions supporting reformist ideals of social justice. In the dialectical patterning of the narrative, in order to assert his reality, the worker blots out the sense of a unique self and the struggle for agency that represent Dione's competing reality. The worker's sordid economic reality is then reflected in the bruised face of the upper-class woman. After he rapes her, Dione looks in the mirror of his primitive bathroom and sees the imprint of the oppressed's wrath against the face of aristocratic largesse. Instead of an ideal of empathetic and interdependent 'brotherhood', they have played out the distrust that leads to mutual coercion and hostility. In short, this is the aggression that mocks both the 'fine feelings' of her class and the possibility that empathy could bridge their social and economic gap. The upper-class woman and the male labourer are estranged bedfellows in a dystopic war of sex and class. In Mitchison's warning, this is a war that will produce no victory, only the emergence of fascism.

Mitchison's understated depiction of rape, suggesting that it is an ordinary, everyday event, was particularly shocking to readers because it discloses how a protracted history of irremedial brute force is deeply embedded and unquestioned, not only in revolutionary practice but in traditional political language.[37] The sentimental language and 'fine feelings' that often underwrite liberal beliefs in progress, coupled with the seductive voice of revolutionary polemics, disguise the violent feelings at their source. Through Dione's visionary meeting with Green Jean, the seventeenth-century witch, Mitchison argues that it is recognition of women's historical and continuing experience of violation and rape that leads to recognition of a nation's moral decay.

The translation of this experience into a dystopic warning, albeit fictional, was clearly not welcome news. This was especially true for readers whose language Mitchison blames for denying that the cause and effect of such violence lay in their power. Mitchison's book *The Home and a Changing Civilization*, written in angry reaction to publishers' rejection of her dystopia, produced even more ire from reviewers, who rejected her analysis of the home as 'a gloomy picture of a prison with a male gaoler at the head . . . where the almost universal patriarchal system of government is produced in a microcosm: women and children are possessed physically and psychologically by a father who, in his turn, is slave of an economic system'.[38]

In her dystopia, Mitchison pictures the convergence of personal and political violence as the only logical and imaginable consequences of physical and psychological possession. At the end of the novel, Dione imagines a counterrevolution in which old Tories, now wearing fascist colours, take over, and the naive labourite socialists are executed while their wives and daughters, including Dione's, are raped. Working as a kind of narrative counterpoint, the horror is both distanced and brought home to the reader. We picture the scene indirectly, as Dione's nightmarish vision, and then, only as it is recounted by the unnamed narrator in understated language, as though in a newsreel as one more event in the scrolling of history. Instead of blunting the effect, this strategy invites us to imagine the worst as it connects every woman's violation in the novel. In Dione's vision, the brutality of a fascist junta becomes the mirror image of her rape by the Communist worker, and Britain's inertia is no alternative. Particularly important here is the synthesis of Dione's heightened imagination and the ordinary quality of the dramatized events, the effect of which challenges the idea of men's politics as 'reasonable'. The synthesis thus provides the warning that a dystopic future is grounded in the lengths to which Britain's leaders rationalize the failure of its pragmatic and bellicose politics of self-interest. As a defensive strategy, rationalization backfires, subsumed by its relationship to the dangerously emotive appeals of revolutionary ideologies.

The explosion of a counterrevolution out of the more liberal social reform advocated by the Galtons is explained in Mitchison's *The Moral Basis of Politics* as 'the easiest kind of change – that towards Fascism' (p. 310). Having feared that they will get caught on the wrong side of a failed revolution, Tom and Dione face the impotence of their good intentions. Mitchison's worst case scenario is contained in the dystopic implications of rationalistic and romantic socialists. They dream of a democratic process of social and moral transformation but fail to understand people's unyielding need for order, direction, and cohesion. Her dystopia questions the assumption that the hallowed British traditions of parliamentarianism and pragmatism would save the nation indefinitely from a destructive revolution. Although her imagined revolution is identifiably fascist, Mitchison embeds in it her distrust of liberal and left sentiments. This is especially revealing in the failure of her fictional British governments, ideologues, and the Press to recognize and deal with their most fundamental social and economic problems. Certainly depicted as a man of integrity, Tom Galton berates himself for the kind of inaction that can only lead to disaster: 'My generation are about due to stop making the war an excuse for everything they do badly' (*Warned*, p. 145). The disasters of the Great War produced not only pacifism but in Mitchison's view, a dread of risking decisive action. On the left and the right it was more comforting to ignore the ignominies of Stalin and Hitler than to involve oneself in the fates of the victims.

Mitchison's warning of a collective political failure is unlike earlier dystopias which sacrifice character to elaborate plots. The disasters of *We Have Been Warned* are filtered through an individual woman's emerging political consciousness while an anonymous narrator questions the ideologies that privilege either individualism or collectivism. In this sense, the formal and ideological bases of Mitchison's dystopia synthesize her ongoing political ambivalences into an argument for the experiential foundations of political theory. In its historic and dramatic shape, Dione's journey to political critique includes sights of the violent ends and means of political revolution, the impact of which strengthens her individual resolve, especially as she experiences revolution as the violation of the individual.

Despite these achievements, *We Have Been Warned* ruined Mitchison's literary reputation. According to Jill Benton, the novel's 'invaluable first-hand description of British politics and morés in 1932' was also shocking and unwelcome news to her readers (p. 105). Even the progressive feminist journal, *Time and Tide*, felt that 'many a good Socialist will be profoundly shocked by Dione Galton's sexual unreticence and her assumption of an intense importance in material surroundings'.[39] There were no favourable reviews, and even negative ones smugly admitted 'a feeling of embarrassment' at having to trash the work of such an esteemed writer.[40] This condescending reaction was already predicted in Victor Gollancz's letter to Mitchison explaining why he could not publish the novel. Feeling 'ashamed' at rejecting what he considered to be 'the first piece of genuinely social art . . . that has been done in England in our time', he nonetheless 'shrink[s] before the certainty of jeers and abuse [and] fear that my efficiency as a publisher of socialist books would be seriously damaged by my association with the publication of a book which will undoubtedly be widely described as "filthy"'.[41]

Mitchison knew that her dystopia would irritate readers. 'In fact', Benton reports, 'she was aware that her novel would be unappealing to most political positions, including that of "correct" communism' (p. 93). If readers were not put off by Mitchison's political critique, they objected to the novel's depiction of women's emerging sexual independence (Benton, p. 93). Connecting social and economic justice with women's sexual freedom was inflammatory, and Mitchison's plot never veers from this path. Her strategy tests prevailing ethical norms and liberal ideals of social change from the structural perspective of women's personal lives. The novel's conclusion is that moral abstractions underlying the political theories of socialism, communism, and fascism – the good of the people, for example – are exposed as replications of 'the authoritarian ideals' of the old guard.[42] Mitchison's challenges to the political left, centre, and right continued unabated and unabashed. Her criticism of the Soviet Union in the early thirties turned to outspoken expressions of distress by the end of the decade when she recognized the brutal truths behind Stalin's show trials. From her travels in Vienna in 1934, she saw how the rise of nazism had to be stopped, even if it meant war. In a 1935 debate on pacifism and war preparedness in *Time and Tide*, Mitchison wrote: 'Some of these people never faced what they would do with their pacifism if England were invaded' (Benton, p. 108). Even before England was invaded, Mitchison had joined Storm Jameson's efforts through the British chapter of PEN to rescue people who would otherwise have become Hitler's victims.

Mitchison's critical view of British political life never waned even as she supported the war effort against the Axis powers. In 1936 she published 'The Fourth Pig', a moral fable predicting a universally cataclysmic war.[43]

However deep her political despair, she rallied around the cause of the war's victims and the need to be an informed critic. She contributed financially to the Mass Observation research archive and became one of its participant observers because she saw the need to collect and disseminate information about attitudes towards Germany and the Soviet Union that were not tinged with propaganda. In her own decisive actions she embodied a living alternative to the political impotence and disasters she had imagined.

STORM JAMESON: 'SPLENDID POLEMICIST'*

Jameson's dystopic view of Britain began when her frustration with its social and political failures turned to anger after World War I. In her autobiography, published 50 years later, she describes the 20 years between the wars as an 'interregnum' buoyed up by hopeful 'dreams [and] experiments', but endangered by an 'intoxicating illusion of freedom' (*J* I, p. 292). By the early thirties, she identified the major symptom of her nation's impaired political sensibility as 'a moral stench – 'on one side Dachau, on the other the "distressed areas" with their ashamed workless men and despairing women' (*J* I, p. 293). The bitterness of her hindsight is only an epilogue to the apprehension that drove her life and fiction to become politically engaged the moment she recognized

> . . . two principles . . . struggling for mastery of the future. On the one side the idea of the Absolute State, with its insistence on total loyalty to the words and gestures of authority, its belief in the moral beauty of war. . . . On the other all that was still hidden in the hard green seed of a democracy which allowed me freedom to write and other women freedom to live starved lives on the dole (*J* I, p. 293).

---

* Storm Jameson, *Journey from the North I.*

Jameson's double edged vision mocks Salman Rushdie's assessment of World War II British writers as living in a 'green world of the past'. Her image of a 'hard green seed of a democracy' encapsulates the conflict between self-interest and social change that defined British political culture for her in the twentieth century; and it was this image that would prevent her from romanticizing the past. Recognizing political conflict was not, however, a matter of detached analysis for Jameson, but rather part of her identity. This is expressed in much of her writing when she personifies her Yorkshire background as a moral template.[44] Her family had lived in the seaport of Whitby for 600 years, and she attributes the fortitude and willfulness of her fictional nation and characters to the spirit of the north country. Her idea that nation and character reflect each other's moral and political temperament derives from her portrait of her parents, who struggled throughout their married life against each other's domination. In so much of her writing, as Jameson struggles to understand and resist their overpowering influence, she creates characters to whom she ascribes a sense of individuality and personal responsibility, as though through them she is holding herself accountable for how well she could withstand the pressures of personal and political history.

Her struggle for moral and intellectual growth never abated, beginning with winning one of only three County scholarships to Leeds University in 1912. And then, despite graduating first in English, she was only awarded a research grant to attend University College, London, and not a lectureship. Though she would often react to personal slights by feeling inadequate, she was just as likely to move beyond that to recognize both a larger problem of institutional inequity and her own responsibility. And so she transferred to King's College, and wrote, without approval, a thesis on Modern European Drama which was accepted by Leeds University for a Master's Degree and was then published by Collins in 1920. Jameson's life continued to be driven by dissatisfaction and self-criticism. Her marriage to a classmate at the University of London was unhappy from the start, and when she finally wrenched free, she made the painful decision to leave her son with her mother in Whitby so that she could make her way as a writer in London. Feeling she had abandoned the boy only added to her growing anxiety about writing too many unsatisfactory novels. Though she never resolved her conflict between motherhood and writing, she gave herself the chance to begin anew in 1925 with a strong and happy marriage and politically active literary career. Her husband, Guy Chapman, shared her passion for history and supported her activist needs. These culminated in 1938 when she became the first woman president of British PEN, an office she used unabashedly to promote anti-nazism and rescue writers from Nazi-occupied Europe.

As intensely critical of British politics as Mitchison, Jameson's allegiances were even more volatile. Although she declares that she became a Labour Socialist 'at school and my first membership card was dated 1917', she never stopped criticizing both its leaders and rank and file.[45] Guided by socialist principles, she 'thought that my own job began and ended when, as a writer, I upheld pacifism and the classless State. I was a pacifist because I hated war, and a Socialist because I hated poverty and the injustice and waste of inequality'.[46] Beginning with 'the collapse of the General Strike' and climaxing with the Labour Party's refusal to demonstrate against a Fascist rally in 1934, she not only questions her Party's definitions of pacifism and injustice, but revises her own ('Crisis', p. 156; 'Labour', p. 32). Her autobiography invokes her Yorkshire disdain for 'dogma' to explain why she 'disliked and distrusted Fabians' and never became a Communist (*J* I, p. 65). At King's, she had already bypassed the political mainstream, joining a group of young men, the Eikonoklasts, who 'were sceptics, unavowed anarchists, self-dedicated to the unmasking of hypocrites, politicians, clericals, reactionaries, bigots, and dogmatists of all ages and conditions' (*J* I, p. 65).

By the early thirties, however, she felt that Britain's impassive response to poverty and fascism required active confrontation, and so she asked other writers to join her in public debates. Despite this activism, her 'violent self-contradiction' continued, only now she felt used by Communist groups; she felt it necessary to share their anti-fascist platform but deplored the practices of the Soviet Union (*J* I, p. 294).[47] She admits that her choice showed her loss of faith in the liberal humanism with which she had aligned herself.

Jameson's trilogy of this 'interregnum', *The Mirror* of *Darkness*, portrays the social and political conditions of the General Strike. The three novels, *Company Parade* (1934), *Love in Winter* (1935), and *None Turn Back* (1936), interweave two major characters – England in the 1920s and an Englishwoman. Hervey Russell, androgynously named like Jameson's nom de plume, comes to

London from Yorkshire and like her creator, struggles, with little money and no literary establishment connections, to become a writer. In her ordeal with words and politics Hervey's character demonstrates that no love story or *bildungsroman* of her time can develop in isolation from stories of self-interest and poverty. For Jameson, the latter comprised the political history of Britain after the Armistice. And yet despite her sustained passion for critiquing British politics, Jameson abandoned plans to continue this realist saga. *None Turn Back* ends on a melancholy note, and almost instantaneously her work of documentary realism mutates into dystopia, imagining a 'hard' fascist seed in democratic soil. It is as though her socialist aesthetic had exhausted its imaginative possibilities in the anxious hope that Britain would not continue to squander its political resolve. Instead, she wrote the dystopia that performs an analysis of thirties political culture by imagining its apocalyptic demise.

Like Mitchison, Jameson's aesthetics are always politically engaged and reflect a struggle between forms of traditional realism and concerns with the writer's responsibility for the representability of language. In 1937, after her dystopia, she published her socialist aesthetic, 'Documents', calling for a synthesis of objective representation and personal experience that would stress their relationship. She wanted a literature that would faithfully record 'the lives of men and women in a world which is changing and being changed' while it would also reflect the writer's 'experience of it and his understanding of his experience' ('Documents', p. 9). The result, however, is not like Orwell's *The Road to Wigan Pier*, which she criticizes for serving 'some fancied spiritual advantage' ('Documents', p. 12). Like Mitchison, Jameson felt the risk of exploiting others' abjection. At a loss to find models in fiction, Jameson finally turned to documentary film, a medium that could represent the artist's observations but not his or her presence or personal struggle with social and political consciousness.

Her 1936 dystopia employs such a technique. In order to register the material substance of political consequences, *In the Second Year* evokes close-up portraits of its major players and the epic sweep of large-scale events as though alternating between long-range and zoom lenses. Instead of merely presenting 'talking heads' who debate each other to death, the novel achieves dramatic effect through the emotional impact of each major character on another's life. Calling upon readers to draw a relationship between historic events and the formation of character, the novel presents the unselfconscious and uncensored self-serving dialogue and actions of political leaders and the unspoken and fearful reflections or anguished voices of their victims. Similar to Mitchison's dystopia, this technique intertwines public and private political consciousness with the narrators' processes of understanding and predicting the political consequences of their historical moment. For Jameson, this hybrid form remedied the 'combination of hard lying, fear, and greed' that 'passed for realism in the "twenties and thirties"'.[48]

What Jameson is reacting against is the sloganeering rhetoric that passed for serious questions on political platforms and in the press: 'Fascism or democracy, Slavery or freedom, Tyranny or liberal humanism?' (*Y*, p. 41).[49] Such easy dichotomies, in her view, deny that the cruelties against which so many writers were protesting 'had roots in our society far deeper, far older, than the new rotten growth in Germany and Italy' ('Writer's', p. 4). For Jameson, those roots were grounded in the liberal humanism which was not prepared for the 'cold bestiality' of acts formerly 'held to be too obscene' (*J* I, p. 301, 302).

Writing this from the hindsight of the 1950s and 1960s, Jameson implicates herself in such blindness, but in fact, all her writing of the thirties and forties resounds with challenges to the specious simplicities of dualistic thinking and the separation of language from act. She felt that to talk about 'the dignity of man in a world' where 'the term final solution impl[ied] the methodical killing by slow suffocation of six million human beings, old and young' was to empty words of their meaning ('Writer's', p. 4; *J* I, p. 302). By 1936, Jameson's writing was impelled by recognizing that events had altered the meaning of words like justice and freedom and complicated the self-serving dualities that pitted 'angels' against 'devils' ('Writer's', p. 3).

In her dystopias of the thirties and forties she struggles with the politicized literary problem of how to situate moral responsibility in a fiction that would not only reflect Britain's relationship to fascism, but the role of the individual in global political crisis. The result was to divide her characters among those whose lucky circumstances allow them to defend freedom and those who 'were silenced, imprisoned, killed . . . because to a Nazi conqueror, the free intellect is the enemy of enemies' ('Writer's, p. 4). The political analysis of *In the Second Year* reflects Jameson's view that responsibility was being denied not only on the fascist right but throughout the liberal centre and among fellow travellers of the Communist Party. Indicting them all, this dystopia upset many of Jameson's friends, including those 'on the far Left, who expected a direct attack on Fascism, with a Communist hero, and the rest of it' (*J* I, p. 336).

In the Second Year imagines a fascist junta in Britain as it is consolidating its gains in an apathetic and fractious society. Such a vision is neither unique among women writers of the period, nor, according to A.J P. Taylor, among those 'Left-wing socialists [who] really anticipated a Fascist dictatorship in England' (p. 319). Taylor characterizes the political mindset of this generation as believing and deploying the political catch phrases bandied about in the media. This belief guaranteed victory in the 1935 election for the Conservative candidate, Stanley Baldwin, who stood for democratic values by supporting a League of Nations he had actually written off as unworkable. Taylor's view that such a 'facade became a reality for a generation trained in cinema palaces' coincides with Jameson's savage jibe at British complacency (pp. 319–20). Holding people responsible for their ability to sort out 'face' from 'reality', she was appalled at people's dismissal of 'the tinny words' coming from both 'hero-gangster[s]' of the silver screen and lackadaisical politicians.

Jameson debunks such hallowed myths of British political culture as the moral superiority of its electorate and leaders and exposes instead, a deadly 'inertia', characterized by 'dreary indifference, worse than malevolence' (*Y*, pp. 215--16). At a time when Hitler is already in power, Jameson warns that unless the slogans of democratic ideals translate into social reform, even the British could be swayed by the 'penny dreadful' language of a demigogue promising 'the regeneration of his country' (*Y*, pp. 40–1). Like Mitchison, Jameson criticizes both Tories and Labour, but identifying with the latter, she fears and imagines that the 'failure of the Labour Party to turn the nation around after its (second and last) general strike' will produce 'the eventual triumph of reaction by the default of the Labour Party'; these are concerns she also expressed in a letter to *Time and Tide* the same year (*Y*, p. 20).[51] The propensity for 'Labour bosses [to] have accepted the ends and means of a mechanical civilization', and their inability to 'offer anything more' leads her to imagine a dictator aptly named Frank Hillier (*J* I, p. 35). Like his Nazi counterpart, Hillier rejects modernity but relies on military industrial technology to solve domestic problems. The dehumanization that results leads to the dead end of his nation. Jameson's demonization of scientific progress had coincided with many writers in the twenties, and by the early thirties she saw events in Europe as an objective correlative to her fears. She was afraid that even in Britain a democratically inclined electorate might prefer a coherent but mechanized order of totalitarianism to the messy and uncertain process of parliamentary debate and backbenching.

In her novel, fears that pluralism and the struggle for social and economic equality would bring social chaos leads to disaster. On the second day of the general strike, with its news of communist outbreaks in Glasgow and Liverpool, the conservative government becomes as paralysed as Labour. The leaders, 'old men, had obeyed a sound instinct to do nothing . . . aware that any step they took must be a step nearer autarchy . . . they held their hands' (*Y*, p. 216). Signalling their 'unliving spirit', they sign their own dismissal, setting the stage for economic chaos (*Y*, p. 216). The widespread rioting that results from the workers' economic fears are stopped by an army of National volunteers led by the charismatic and impetuous Richard Sacker. An old friend of Hillier's, Sacker believes England's internal victory and stability will guarantee world order, but both victory and order are unified into fascistic oppression. In its efforts to maintain supremacy, the fascist government resorts to violence at every hint of a threat. At the end, Hillier consolidates his power by having Sacker executed while dissidents either flee or are incarcerated.

Jameson's dystopia expresses her fear that British democracy will dissolve into fascism as a result of the impotence of the old men who lead parliament. This is not pure fantasy, however, if we see their 'inertia' as both cause and effect of the infighting among the left and the recalcitrance of the right in the thirties. Although a National government was formed in 1931 to demonstrate Britain's unity, still raging economic problems were overshadowed by fierce divisions over foreign policy and national security within and among all the political parties. In Jameson's view, the persisting domestic and international problems were also symptomatic of the failure of Britain's left and right to understand that its national culture does not represent a universal standard, is not univocal, and cannot afford the narcissism of protective isolation.

The motto of Hillier's regime signifies utopian planning as a solipsistic half turn from British narcissism into political oppression: 'Security first, and idealism afterwards' (*Y*, p. 202). The inversion of utopia into dystopia implies a politics wherein the external social and historical realities of an isolated England are held at bay by a dictator's fantasies of control. That such fantasies derive from and form a politics of protectionism, dependency, and domination is supported by Jameson's analysis of British politics. The year after Hitler came to power, she feared that Britain's 'aimless passions' undermined its moral energy.[52] The result rested on whether the British would 'choose to be governed despotically, or to govern ourselves in a condition of greater freedom and greater individual responsibility – dictatorship, or a society of self-respecting (because respected) men and women?' ('End', p. 219). Theoretically and fictionally, Jameson saw fascism taking over when the electorate yields 'in a moment of panic to a leader who promises to save us from our own weakness' ('End', p. 220).

Visiting Berlin in 1932, Jameson had trusted the moral force of 'cultured liberals', and her dystopia registers the results of feeling betrayed by their blindness and hers.[53] Her fictional, apathetic English populace chooses a weak leader who, like the real German Chancellor, Hindenburg, said '"You can trust me"'; in her dystopia such rhetoric leads to being deposed by the Hitleresque Hillier. The pervasiveness of this political betrayal in Jameson's writing of the thirties and forties testifies to the depth of her fears. Throughout the interwar scenes of *The Mirror of Darkness* and into her postwar novel, *The Black Laurel,* which dramatizes the question of Europe's future, appears the character of the billionaire industrialist, William Gary, who turns his own impotence and vendetta against Britain's aimlessness into plans for a utopian dictatorship of capitalist self-interest. *In the Second Year* warns that in its multiplicity and vulnerability, Britain can no longer view itself as an island. Isolation from its European allies will lead not only to Europe falling to the Nazis but to Britain yielding to a fascism derived from the insularity of an old order and the compliance of everyone else.

The novel's gestation in Spain and Norway substantiated Jameson's view that neither fascism nor democracy is the unique product of any nation or society. Reclaiming Britain's ties to Europe, she retraces her faith in 'freedom as the supreme good' and her 'tart sceptical northern humour' to the Storm family's Norwegian origins (*J* I, p. 335). In her dystopia, she plots a logical progression from a weakened democracy to fascism by tracking the consequences of Frank Hillier's promise to make England 'a self-sufficing and self-contained people again' (*Y*, p. 34). Ironically, though, what Hiller delivers is dependency – 'When the state is your father and mother, you are free again' (*Y*, p. 36). In their complicity with fascistic paternalism, Jameson shows the dangerous result of an electorate believing they can abrogate responsibility for their physical, psychological, and moral well being. The seductive power of dependency not only denies Britain's citizens their sexual lives but silences them.

Jameson's dystopic future, however, does not rest on 'a green world of the past'. Instead, it recalls Britain's puritanical past as sharing ideological aims with Hitler's present. Frank Hillier sees his regime rectifying a Britain 'going rotten with greed and looseness. . . . Men selling their manhood, and women losing their womanliness' (*Y*, p. 35). Echoing Oswald Mosley's rallying cry, 'We want men who are men and women who are women', Hillier's rhetoric creates rather than reflects the reality of Britain's moral decay. Jameson's fictive polemic warns that Hillier's platform, like Mosley's or Hitler's, appeals to people's fears of losing economic and social stability and both reinforces and assuages those fears by celebrating xenophobia and misogyny. In this way, the novel shows how Britain's decay emanates from Hillier's retrograde solution, the hallmark of which is a cartoon-like caveman rhetoric. In Hillier's language, sharply defined gender distinctions denote feminine weakness as a rationale for confirming masculine aggression as a leadership quality. Constructing this opposition, however, does not in itself lead to the downfall of democratic principles. Instead, Jameson shows how polarizing masculinity and femininity is a flourishing business in a fascistic Britain because it lay dormant all along in the psychological and social lives of her male characters. Awarded the trappings of power, Hillier and his henchman, Richard Sacker, institute what has been a social reality all along – that being estranged from each other in their domestic lives leads men and women to become politically isolated. Once Hillier is in power, such isolation makes it easy to legalize political oppression and sexual repression.

The dramatic analysis of this condition is verified by two narrative voices. Andrew Hillier, the Prime Minister's cousin who has been living in Norway, sees Britain as 'a country decaying', a view that critiques the dictator's platform (*Y*, p. 5). This critique is reinforced by the alternative voice of an unnamed but markedly male narrator. In effect, the two male narrators enact and connect Britain's isolation and 'regression' to oppressive dualities of sexual identity. Voicing both resistance and complacency, Andrew participates in a male-dominated political discourse that has no recourse to self-questioning or alternative voices: 'As most men in my circumstances would, I believed in the reality of the world I was born into, a world kept in order by a known compromise between force and goodwill' (*Y*, p. 260). His faith in the pragmatism that justifies a world of male constructed 'circumstances' allows him to assume a passive position as events explode around him and thus illustrates that political mindset which Jameson judges as leading from 'compromise' to 'inertia', and then to fascism. This is the same faith that Mitchison found in 'public-school spirit' and which occludes women's voices from public debate and denies them self-determination. Instead of dramatizing a woman's consciousness to illustrate this, Jameson dissects male dominance through their dominant narrative voices. Self-critical and ambivalent as always, Jameson's misgivings about sharing the authority of a male dominated public politics echo in Andrew's apologetics.

That she sees such authority sliding all too easily into 'autarchy' is illustrated by Frank Hillier's friendship with Sacker. Jameson imagined this relationship as the core of her novel while watching two men at a café in Spain. She sensed an extreme tension between them that suggested 'a homosexual relationship infinitely subtler and more powerful than the physical one, . . . [an] attachment and hostility, both a little dangerous. I had my English dictator and his friend, the man he would have murdered' (*J* I, p. 335). What turns out to be more than 'a little dangerous' is Hillier's attraction to Sacker's impulsive energy and Sacker's dependence on Hillier's inscrutable management style, the combination of which produces dramatic tension and a political explosion deriving from their equal mistrust of the other's power. Jameson's alternating narrative voices and the sexual politics of her rhetoric show how the men's bond represents and justifies a male-centred politics devoid of mutual support and nurturance, qualities she associates with the feminine.

Excluding women from the ideology that supports the body politic allows the men to see their interests as universal, and this model of thinking becomes the ideological basis for a revolution that will only replicate the old nation. Male supremacy thus collapses the dualistic thinking Jameson deplored, but only by subsuming its opposition. This political strategy, as one of the narrators observes, 'divorces words from realities, so that it is possible to forget that nations are made up of living human beings, with brains and hearts' (*Y*, p. 43). In the realpolitik of this dystopia, whether Sacker or Hillier rules, the experiential integrity of women's lives is denied except to be exploited for the regeneration of the country. In this way the subjugation of women coincides with an ideology that despite its language of parental concern, calls for sacrificing the lives of its subjects for a masculinist state. Through the enmeshed, exclusionary relationship of Hillier and Sacker, Jameson exposes the manipulation of gender distinctions as a sealed line of fascist defence. Any deviation from its rigidly enforced categories, as aggressive women and nurturing men would be, is politically threatening to the totalitarian state. Whatever resemblence this demarcation bears to Nazi Germany, Jameson sees it as emblematic of Britain's inert old order and its life denying consequences.

As in Mitchison's dystopia, the experience and consciousness of women's subjugation register the impact of a brutal past on a crisis-ridden present and dystopic future.[54] Set on the cusp between present and future, the novel dramatizes Jameson's anxiety that 'the next World War' will certainly arise from England's failure to 'remove the causes and occasions of [the last]'.[55] From Hervey Russell in the novels about the twenties to the women victimized by fascism in her dystopias of the thirties and forties, Jameson identifies women with history by having them feel dominated by and dependent on the ongoing self-interest of men. As embodiments of resistance, however, these women transmute themselves into moral sensors of their own generation's will to power. It is true, as Jennifer Birkett observes, that after Hervey Russell, Jameson's women 'live on the margins of men's violence', and they pay heavily, not just for what they see from there, but for what they say (p. 80).

It is thus no coincidence in this dystopia that a woman embodies consequences of fascism's cultural myths. And so Sacker's wife Lotte delivers a stillborn boy on the day the General Strike begins. Her suicide at the end of the novel is the result of a nation bent on self-destruction in its hopeless nostalgia for 'the idea of England becoming great again' (*Y*, p. 201). Jameson shows how the imperial drive behind this 'idea' is justified by language that naturalizes masculinist aggression as leadership. The fact that it is Lotte who thinks about 'naked forces tak[ing] charge' of the 'history' and future of England exposes woman's subjugation as embedded in its nationalist myths (*Y*, p. 214). Although we only hear about and do not witness Lotte's suicide, it achieves its emotional effect as we are given cause to reflect on the total lack of political and personal outlet for her intensely cogent analysis. In its neatly gendered symmetry, the new order, like the old, embeds its dangers in assuming women's dependency to be natural, to mark an essential female nature. Sacker's response to his mistress, Harriet English, is thus chilling because it is neither idiosyncratic nor merely rhetorical, but signals a cultural norm that issues in a conjunction of personal and political oppression:

> Clever though Harriet was, she had never realised that he despised women and was sentimental about them from the same impulse. He knew what they were made for and what all of them, even the clever ones, wanted. He had been very fortunate in not knowing a woman who would continue to despise him even if he had her flogged. (*Y*, p. 76–7).

A professional singer, Harriet, like Lotte, is useful only as a mindless body, a commodified object of amusement without recourse to self-determination. To bring home this point, Jameson positions these women in both literary and historical 'exile' (*Y*, p. 228). Lottie's sense that her life is 'taking place in the past' recalls a history of women's exploitation and violation, not romantic nostalgia (*Y*, p. 228). Unlike the trilogy of Hervey Russell's tortured love life, there are no romantic longings in this dystopia or, indeed, in any of Jameson's anti-fascist and World War II novels. It is as though once the inequities of domestic life explode into fascism and war, she deploys a male-identified public discourse in order to fight it on her own terms. She writes political novels which expunge any signs of conventional love stories, arguing, in effect, that the historical moment exposes such stories as smoke screens which obscure the correlation of private and public brutality. Jameson's dystopia does not revise such stories, but warns us of their political implications. Thus, Richard Sacker, a 'violent man, with strong physical passions' is not romanticized as a Byronic hero, but denounced as an 'opportunist and undertaker of

[Europe's] decay' (*Y*, p. 3). Like Mitchison, Jameson evokes witch burning to mark the oppression of women as a retrograde political solution: 'it only needed a few years of isolation for them to begin burning witches again' (*Y*, p. 6). But such a conflagration, like Hillier's paternalistic double talk, also proclaims the power of women's voices in its ritual destruction of them. The image of their burning bodies, both fantastic and real, prefigures the Nazi's conflation of misogyny, racial hatreds, and death camp technology, epitomizing Jameson's warnings about the cruelty derived from a mechanized masculinist state.[56]

Women's voices and bodies in this novel represent both dissent and its punishment. Sophie Burtt, a writer, whose 'bitter pen' expresses her incorruptible critical faculties, is interned at Winchell, a concentration camp for liberals and dissidents (Jameson is punning Winston Churchill, still in the proverbial wilderness in 1936). Sophie, like Lotte, has violated the Hillerian feminine ideal by taking 'too serious a view of life' instead of writing about the 'pleasant, good innocent, quiet things in the world' (*Y*, p. 58, 121).[57] This critique could easily have been written by any of the original reviewers of *In the Second Year*. Malcolm Cowley complained that in contrast with Sinclair Lewis's belief in the 'eventual triumph' of liberalism, 'Storm Jameson is so terrified by Hitlerism that she looks forward to a bleak world from which all the liberal virtues have been starved into exile'.[58] Other reviewers claimed: 'Miss Jameson's principal protagonists possess one grave defect – they are not English. One has the feeling throughout that a gang of outlanders has simply moved in and taken possession . . .'.[59] On the same wavelength, *The Manchester Guardian* reviewed the villains as 'plywood figures of German origin' while *The Times Literary Supplement* was appalled at the British leaders' 'lack of social sense' and bewildered by the 'shadowy' villains .[60]

In each of these reviews the woman writer is the villain by virtue of her suggestion that 'Hitlerism' could arise and derive strength from a 'liberal' society rather than be ignored as completely alien to it. Representing the menace as a 'shadowy' puppet makes it easy for a critic to dismiss, and thus only validates Jameson's characterization. She is, after all, portraying her fear that English villainy could be ignored and rationalized, especially if it passed the test of good 'social sense'. Conversely, these criticisms enact the xenophobia that relegates German national character and woman writer to the position of 'outlander'. Like Harriet English, whose voice is not taken seriously and like Sophie Burtt, Storm Jameson's pen is 'bitter' because she cannot tolerate the self-defensive denial that Britain could betray its ideals by fulfilling the insular and misogynist bylaws of its old boy network. Her pen also deploys an aggressive voice that is a character in its own right: it mocks not only the swaggering Sacker and despotic Hillier, but as though in anticipation, the critics.

In the Second Year reeks with the commitment of old and new guard alike to war as a solution to domestic and international crises. The formation of Sacker's 1 600 000 Volunteers not only solves the nation's unemployment crisis, but typifies a 'perfect instrument' of war (*Y*, p. 42). Jameson's apprehension about another European war is refracted here by figuring Germany as 'a man-eating tiger' meeting its match in Sacker, an English 'Goring,' who 'delight[s] in war' (*Y*, pp. 43, 73). Though such an analogy suggests the very despair she deplored, Jameson's dystopia can be read as hopeful because it registers a warning, not a dirge. As much as she condemned warmongering, she also empathized with men who found in war a 'sudden unlooked-for release' from the 'trail of half-fed children and men "economised" into misery' ('In the End', pp. 214, 215). Her version of a revolutionary solution would be to stop combatative competition for international power by revising Britain's 'unnatural social disorder', a condition that only produces a 'repressed' hostility whose expedient 'release' is war ('End', pp. 214, 217). In 1934, while predicting Hitler's European rampage, Jameson noted: 'It is precisely because I hope for social change that I fear war' ('End', p. 213). Much later, when she recalled the evolution of her hopefulness, she saw it solidify in response to those who found reasons to rebuild their 'humanity' after spending years in Nazi concentration camps ('Writer's Situation', p. 34). For Jameson, these survivors contrast starkly with H.G. Wells's belief that 'we have failed in the test nature imposes on all living creatures and are going to disappear from the universe as helplessly as have others before us' ('Writer's', p. 32).

Jameson's dystopia imagines an antidote to Wells's despair in the 'power of curiosity' and dissenting voices of Sophie Burrt and R.B. Tower, a Nobel Prize winning socialist economist, who recognizes that 'Repression is evil not only for its floggings and torturings, but because it makes people lie to themselves in the privacy of their hearts' ('Writer's', p. 35; *Y*, p. 90). These voices not only resist despotism, but question the faith in liberalism that invites 'decent' people to deny 'unpleasant things going on behind locked doors', a defensive measure that ensures the 'repression' they abhor (*Y*, p. 90). The significance of these voices lies in their combination of speech and action. In speaking out and paying the price, they engage political reality in contrast to those liberal compatriots whose ideals are only put to the test of their rhetoric. Jameson's dystopia thus also engages the reader not only through her own impassioned rhetoric, but through the emotional appeal for freedom that her heroes enact.

In contrast to Malcolm Cowley and his colleagues, Naomi Mitchison applauded Jameson's political vision for producing 'the creep of guilt for the years just before the last war' when those who needed to escape 'the grip of the Nazis' found 'so little help from us'.[61] Her review of Jameson's autobiography finds her friend's prewar vision relevant to the political morality of the 1980s:

> Are we so used to cruelty that it passes us by? In the Thirties political torture was still unusual, still shocking. Storm reacted to it and also watched the faces of politicians and publishers and ambassadors; also, of course, those of her fellow writers. . . . Whom can we forgive? Is forgiveness useful, does any good come of it? ('Eye', p. 25).

Even as every year of the thirties brought the possibility of war closer, Jameson balanced hopefulness with despair at 'the inflamed nationalism which divides the States of Europe politically, economically and . . . socially'.[62] For as she saw in Germany and Czechoslovakia, 'into a world made sufficiently unstable by economic rivalries, Fascism has brought a newly dangerous element of violence'.[63] Her concern that tied England to Europe was based on the interwar mix of historic and economic conditions and misguided, but not evil politicians: 'The triumph in Germany . . . was helped on by the coldness and weakness of the democratic leaders' who failed to arrange a just peace at Versailles and who in the intervening years also failed to reform 'the forced relation between debtor and creditor nations' and 'the authority of rich over poor' ('Twilight', pp. 6, 11, 9–10). As much as Jameson recognized and affirmed the capacity for caring that the maternal experience could encourage, she was never sanguine about women being more peaceloving than men. The danger, in her view, lies in both men and women being seduced by the power of 'the

Absolute National State' because it represents the capacity to console and 'exploit the irrational emotions of discontent, fear, and pride' ('Twilight', pp. 9, 13).

Jameson's next work combined dystopia with a parable based on the flood myth. *The World Ends*, published in 1937 under the name William Lamb, features a smug and stifled cosmopolitan, Richard Blake, who leaves London for a corner of Yorkshire where the prelude to regeneration is apocalypse. He is rescued from an earthquake by a farmer who then initiates him into the unadorned rhythms of his family's life. The novel's rhythm manoeuvres between Blake's struggle to make sense of his experience through writing, and the farming family's intuitive life. The interaction between the two narratives serves to vex storymaking as a heuristic guide to the world's history. Jameson merges the biblical stories of Noah, Cain and Abel, and Sodom and Lot and his daughters with that of Blake's struggle to write, and shows the dangerous practice of relying on myths to understand past and present. The problem for Jameson is that myths embed a sense of inevitability that makes it possible to rationalize our inability to take moral responsibility. In its occasionally strained passages, her own writing shows the painful struggle to avoid such rationalizing. Like a parable of Britain's identity politics, the novel depicts a farmer's daughter and two sons replaying the moral lapses of the past. Perceiving no love objects except themselves, they interpret all of their behaviour as following laws of necessity. Jameson's mythmaking, however, performs its own critical exegesis by showing that such laws of necessity subjugate the woman's regenerative powers to her brothers' competitive tyrannies. After one brother kills the other, their sister Miriam marries her killer brother in order to preserve the species.

Jameson's moral fable performs its critique through a cyclical and thus ominous pattern of repetition. Its apocalyptic vision is seen through the odyssey of Blake, who like his nineteenth-century namesake, discovers that in the conflation of the end of days and a new beginning, time-honoured moral dichotomies are vexed: 'He was afraid of some judgment – and that it would be heavier upon the innocent. And for that reason he was anxious to persuade – whom to persuade? – that all were guilty and all innocent.'[64] Blake can only imagine the rebirth of the world if it reconfigures the myths which explain the mistakes of the past. The narrative, however, presents the outcome as a historicist new testament, juxtaposing foundational biblical and romantic Blakean texts to suggest a critical commentary. *The World Ends* depicts men's violence, not as the inevitable result of a transcendent will, but as indebted to men's idea that God and nature are made in their image and therefore the world belongs to them.

The World Ends can easily be seen as Jameson's response to C. Day Lewis's political morality poem of the year before, *Noah and the Waters.* A very personal statement, the poem represents a moral and political working through of Day Lewis's 'feelings about political commitment' (quoted in Hynes, p. 200). According to Hynes, Lewis puts himself in the safe hands of creating 'a parable of obedience, not of choice', and therefore does not have to anticipate the consequences of choosing either revolutionary acts or bourgeois intellectual agonizing (Hynes, p. 201). Unlike Jameson's critical combination of myths and players, the Noah story gives us a protagonist who is chosen by God to survive and triumph over omnipotent and universal punishment. If Day Lewis identifies with Noah as being 'chosen by God for the small part of the ruling class that breaks away', Jameson identifies the issues and players lost to view in both Lewis's parable and the Noah myth (Hynes, p. 202). Her parable, structured by the gendered limits of choice, necessitates that a woman be sacrificed to God's plan for his people. Miriam, the powerful biblical prophetess who sets Moses free on Egyptian waters, is portrayed by Jameson as being engulfed by the flood waters representing overpowering patriarchal rule. Jameson's historical imagination synthesizes her critique of beliefs which she feared could lead to the world's end: contemporary utopian beliefs in technological progress and the lure of 'traditional knowledge, the wisdom and experience of our ancestors', which because it elided the power relationships embedded in mythic understanding could 'no longer save us from moral collapse'.[65]

It is in this spirit that in 1938 she wrote, under another pseudonym, James Hill, her novel of European civilization collapsing into the Spanish Civil War, *No Victory For the Soldier.*[66] Here ancestral knowledge is embodied in the character of John Knox who, as a child prodigy, has been force fed the highest culture of European classical music. Exhausted and disenchanted like Richard Blake, he too tries to escape, and while he finds purpose driving an ambulence for the Spanish Republicans, he is also destroyed in a crossfire between competing ideologies which mirror Jameson's view of English political disarray.

Although Jameson and Mitchison see the failures of British

capitalism, democracy, and imperialism as interrelated, they do not indict the structure and ideology of parliamentary democracy as responsible for the tragic conclusions in their dystopias. Instead, they show that despotism emerges when reform is thwarted by uncritical beliefs in nationalistic mythologies that romanticize an enduring past. In Mitchison's analysis, these myths can be as destructive as they are consoling, as 'the romantic archaism of the Nazis' reveals (*Moral*, p. 148). The 'association of blind obedience and cruelty with health, the deliberate suppression of scientific and historical truth . . . and, above all the refusal to admit other values' leads to abrogating individual and collective responsibility for positive change (*Moral*, p. 148). The result, according to Jameson, is that

> The Nazi crusade succeeded in gaining followers because with banners and trumpets it promised to do everything the existing rulers were only too clearly failing to achieve – it promised social justice to the workers, security to the other classes, and a future glorious victory to wash out the memory of defeat. It appealed to young men whom the doctrinaire weakness of the Left repelled or disappointed. . . . And it seasoned its promises with hate, a seasoning which intoxicates more quickly and furiously than any.[67]

Like Mitchison, Jameson dramatizes the relationship between women's social and political position, the stability of democracy, and the threat of fascism. Awarding women the moral energy to take responsibility for their complicity with oppressive power, Jameson illustrates how intoxication with masculinist political machinery can infect women. Their own weak position makes them vulnerable to the 'romantic archaism' that secures their power in traditional private roles with the alluring prestige of a privileged place. As supporters of the state's victimizing practices, women can rationalize their superior status. Jameson witnesses such a phenomenon in Berlin in 1932.

> At dinner I sit next to a gently-smiling old lady who says she is a follower of Hitler, and a member of the party. "You Hitlerites have a song," I say diffidently, "which begins something like: 'How fine to see the blood of the Jews spurting under the knife'" . . . Her face remains placid, smiling. "Yes. . . . It is a song.

> Like other songs." A little doubtfully I suggest that it is not very like other songs known to me. "No?" – a gleam of satisfaction comes in her eyes – "more lordly, no doubt." Much more lordly. . . . ('City', p. 49)

Jameson continued to use the dystopic form to file her complaint against mythologies that feed isolationist self-interest, supremacist ideologies, and their violence to alien voices. In her imagined worlds the dystopic future elsewhere becomes a consequence of the here and now because no changes in political process have considered how the omnipresent influence of old myths, even as they alienate men and women, create a community of shared rage against others.

3

Dystopic Visions of Hitler's Victory: 'The Future is Our Business'*

'FRAGMENTS OF A DISORDERED EUROPE'**: STORM JAMESON'S *THEN WE SHALL HEAR SINGING*

By the time England prepared for a German invasion in 1940, Storm Jameson was envisioning an unabridged, unrevised replay of the Great War. Her reading of continuous world war would not suffice, however, to explain her apocalyptic vision of high-tech escalations of terror compulsively repeating the savagery of the past. But as she foresaw it, a Second World War 'forces us to think about the catastrophes of the past, the destruction of cities, the collapse of empires, the return of poverty and barbarism', as a future that would meld 'London and Nineveh in the same breath' ('Crisis', p. 136). While she would build this eschatology into her speculative fiction of the forties, it would also be tempered by reconfiguring the universal icons of good and evil that were typically written into the heart of other dystopias. Jameson's aim was to deconstruct such icons because they all too often gave rise to the foundational and romantic myths which supported supremacist ideologies and politics. Although many other dystopias of the period drew upon the rise of Hitler and warned of international crisis, unlike Jameson's analysis of power politics, their focus on weapon technology would draw readers' attention away from the human consequences of Europe's current antagonisms.[1]

---

* Storm Jameson, *Journey From the North II.*
** Storm Jameson, *Then We Shall Hear Them Singing.*

Rather than imagine a war between inhuman forces, such as poisonous gases and supersonic planes, Jameson stressed the immediate effects of a Second World War on a nation's social fabric. Her rendering voiced the concern that 'the ideals of social justice, tolerance, freedom, are being ground to dust between the fragments of a disordered Europe' ('New Europe', p. 77). In despair, Jameson's dystopias warn that 'it is unlikely that Europe cannot now be saved .... It is unlikely that we shall be given another chance. Possibly we have not been given one this time'; with her incorrigible hopefulness, however, she added, 'We must assume we have' ('New Europe', pp. 68, 79). *Then We Shall Hear Singing* is Jameson's 1942 warning of what would happen if Britain lost its resolve to take that chance. Typically self-deprecating, she felt the novel was 'curious as a proof that even a minor writer is able, now and then, to overhear the future' (*J* II, p. 120).[2] The refrain that forms her vision is Hitler's domination of European culture and civilization.

Subtitled *Fantasy in C Major*, the novel is a moral fable cum dystopia, set in a Central European village occupied by the Nazis five years after their victory. Examining the consequences of the Nazis' racialist policies, Jameson imagines the destruction of undesirable cultures and their resident 'outlanders'. The novel brings apocalypse down to earth and into history by showing the impact of Nazi utopianism on the lives of the villagers. In a metafictional stroke, Jameson uses the villagers' lives to examine how the Nazis' supremacist vision requires a reordering of history. When the Nazis outlaw the local language, they reconstruct history by cutting the villagers 'off from the only past that is [their] own' (*Singing*, pp. 25, 56). As if this weren't enough to reduce the vanquished to 'a clown or servant', the men of the village are lobotomized, and so the history and culture embedded in their memories become the provenance of the victors, who rewrite it as a celebration of their supremacy in the past, present, and future (*Singing*, p. 56).

Jameson's inspiration for this vision was her fear for the fate of Czechoslovakia under German occupation. When she met President Beneš of Czechoslovakia in 1939, she saw that he posed a threat to 'powerful men in London and Paris' because his plea for help 'hinder[ed] them from coming quickly to terms with his would-be murderer ... they actually ... transferr[ed] to him the epithets that applied with complete accuracy to Hitler' (*J* II, p. 39). She foresaw the effects of this complicity in the Nazis' 'attack' on 'the intellectual life of a conquered country; there must be no minds left able to think against the German idea of the masterrace. Better if the others had no minds. God help their alien subjects on the day a German scientist discovers how to remove the brain and leave the body living and able to work'.[3] The dehumanizing process of mechanization that had worried Jameson since the twenties became a living nightmare, but not because its proportions under the Reich exceeded anything British industrialization or imperialism could imagine or produce. The difference lay in harnessing the goals of a triumphalist and racialist ideology. Under the Third Reich, technology would destroy other cultures in order to rewrite history as a myth of resurrected masculinist power.

Then We Shall Hear Singing was published in 1942, the same year the Germans brutalized the entire town of Lidice, Czechoslovakia, in retaliation for the assassination of SS commander, Reinhard Heydrich by Czech partisans. The punishment also served as a warning against further resistance. The novel and the historical event could easily script each other. In Lidice, the Nazis shot all 192 men, gassed 82 children, gave a few who looked Aryan to German families, and imprisoned all 196 women in Ravensbrück concentration camp. After they torched and dynamited the town, the Nazis completely altered the landscape so that new maps could show that Lidice never existed.[4]

In *Then We Shall Hear Singing* local history and culture are only sustained because the women are allowed to remain in their village; their individual and collective experience becomes the vehicle for continuity. The language of women's domestic lives is not only the novel's dramatic centre but an effective resistance movement since their lullabies, recipes, and needlework never become worthy of the Nazis' attention. Turned out of their homes, the women forge connections with their past and with each other through the essential 'gestures' of their daily work (*Singing*, p. 48). In its economic particularity, 'History, accurate history, is an affair of poor women.... Defeat and hope in their wombs, they scrape with their fingers a rim of dirt on the inside of a pan, and talk' (*Singing*, p. 91). This image, repeated ritually throughout Jameson's writing, deromanticizes the domestic model of the feminine. At the same time the image also celebrates women's activities as being antimechanistic and serves as the language through which women form an alliance and express their sense of necessity. Women's experience here represents a different kind of 'coherent theory' than that of fascism. It is a theory of continuity that is embedded in women's self-conscious efforts to sustain their community in the face of losing its primary cultural institutions.

Though they are named and particularized in their personal relationships, the women are also represented as a collective presence, prototypes of a communal life but in a typically historicist gesture, neither mythic nor heroicized. Instead, the women's communal character is formed by their reaction to the Nazis' oppressive presence. In concert with the ebb and flow of their shared isolation, the women draw in upon themselves and enact the rhythms of their domestic work to produce a shared politics of survival and a women's war narrative. Dominated by the Nazi ideology of 'kinder, kuchen, kirche', the women turn it to their advantage, using their prescribed nature – their position as mothers – to recreate culture.[5] As an old woman tells a young mother-to-be, 'A nation lives from mother to daughter' (*Singing*, p. 165). The power of this genealogy stands in stark contrast to the lobotomized men, whose helplessness is a chronic disorder, as though it were inherited from the entropy of the old guard in the 1936 *In the Second Year*. As Jameson observes about *Then We Shall Hear Singing*, 'it is not necessary to interfere physically with the brain to condition human beings to be apathetic or docile atomies in a dangerously overcrowded world, no nuisance to their betters . . .' (*J* II, p. 120). In contrast to the victimized men and to the Nazi oppressors, whose discourse is portrayed as self-cancelling empty abstraction, the village women are strengthened and come alive for the reader through the rebellious actions of their necessary work.

Jameson's portrait of the village women creates an anti-fascist argument as well as a proposal for the interdependency of democratic ideals among the world's nations. A primary step in forming this family of nations would be 'to persuade the English that we are responsible to Europe, and cannot out of indifference or modesty evade our responsibility. The responsibility is to the future of every child' ('Responsibilities', p. 172). In her 'Fantasy' women have the 'fire and faith' Malcolm Cowley found lacking in Jameson's earlier work; they assume responsibility for renewing the world by creating the relationships from which interdependence begins. Sustaining their individual identities through collaborative work, these female heroes redefine community. By deconstructing boundaries of hierarchical arrangements between self and other, they open the door to inclusion while resisting collaboration with the supremacist politics of the Nazis. Unlike the men in their village, the women possess a 'healthy scepticism', a state of mind Jameson claimed for herself as a politically engaged writer critical of the way her own nation's propaganda masked its xenophobia and its own supremacist self-image ('Foes', p. 571).

The women's scepticism saves them not only from the Nazis' propaganda, but from the slogans which are typical of both sides of the battle lines. For the women, the slogan, 'Victory at all costs' would ignore the human losses that accrue with each succeeding war ('Foes', p. 571). The denial of those losses for the purposes of maintaining morale leads to the loss of historic memory and the risk of losing moral responsibility. For Jameson, the euphoric slogans for 'Victory' reflected an equally irresponsible despair. 'The threat of a new dark age' lay in a romanticized pessimism that beset too many of Britain's intellectual old guard ('Writer's', p. 34). Writing against their grain with her 'healthy scepticism', Jameson berated one of them: 'It was because he had lost his belief in this divine power of curiosity in man that H.G. Wells died in despair' ('Writer's', p. 35). Her own stance was to fight despair because its arrogance makes it all too easy for writers to guard their 'solitude' and '"choke . . . in the officially induced fog' ('Foes', p. 571). In her double voice, Jameson inflects a patriarchal call to arms with that of a woman who will 'run the risks, in war time, of defending liberty of opinion and criticism' ('Foes', p. 571). Just as she struggled to rescue European refugees from Hitler, Jameson's fictional women achieve their dramatic power by rescuing themselves and others from becoming what a complacent old guard was calling the inevitable victims of history.

Once the war was into its third year and the uncertainty of allied victory combined with war weariness, it was no wonder that British women writers would continue to express their anxieties in dystopian fiction. But even years before, when the scars of the last victory against Germany had still not healed, there were those who expressed fears about waging another war against another version of German triumphalism. Two novels in particular, Vita Sackville-West's 1942 *Grand Canyon*, and Katharine Burdekin's 1937 *Swastika Night*, ask not only whether a Second World War could be declared and fought as a just war, but whether Britain's political culture contained the seeds of a defeat it might deserve. These dystopias pit Britain against Nazi Germany in an ideological war, the outcome of which is not only a military fight to the finish, but an open-ended trial of liberal democracy. Sackville-West and Burdekin test Britain's complicity with the ideological and political forces that allowed Hitler to gain power. Both writers dramatize the test as Britain's struggle to reevaluate its definition and commitment to liberal democracy.

With different conclusions, their dystopias assume that if peace is to be more than 'a prolongation of human suffering', Britain and its subjects must be held responsible.[6] *Grand Canyon* is haunted by the politics of appeasement, and as a result, argues that capitulation to 'the Nazi trap' will prolong a battle 'between darker forces than the warplane and the gun' (*GC* Author's Note, p. 302). Fear of these dark forces is already enunciated in Katharine Burdekin's 1937 dystopia, which exposes their presence in a triumphant Nazi Germany. The origins of its dark forces are not, however, confined to Nazi Germany. Instead, Burdekin locates their source in the male militarism which connects the ideologies and political culture on which both Britain and Germany stand. But in addition to its analysis of male militarism, Burdekin's dystopic warning also suggests that it is in the ideological and cultural differences between Britain and Germany that the possibility for change lies.

'DELUDED BY THE NAZIS': VITA SACKVILLE-WEST'S *GRAND CANYON*

Although Vita Sackville-West is often criticized for her nostalgic renderings of an aristocratic past, her dystopia weaves a powerful political critique into an elegy for the lost cohesiveness of a traditional society. *Grand Canyon* argues for international responsibility and cooperation stretching beyond the British-European alliance of Jameson's novels. Taking us to a newer but equally threatened world, Sackville-West sets her dystopia at a hotel on the rim of Arizona's Grand Canyon, where guests seek refuge from the Nazis' devastation of Europe. The Grand Canyon thus becomes a metaphorical bridge between the new world and the old – the last frontier of peace. As German planes attack the United States, it becomes clear that this outpost is no safe haven. The safety her characters expect from the pristine Grand Canyon is shown to be only a figment of their fantasies. By extension, the characters' faith in the physical isolation of the new world represents the political delusion that peaceful coexistence with the Nazis is possible. Over the course of the novel, the grandeur of the American landscape becomes paradoxical, imaged not lyrically, but like a natural monument to the follies of the Allies, who are shown to capitulate in perpetuating World War II. The idea of political and personal complicity is compressed and embodied in the figure of a fifth columnist, a hotel employee who sets the hotel on fire, turning it into a blazing target. The guests escape down the walls of the canyon, only to find that they have died in the fires of war. They now occupy an afterlife that is anything but spiritual. No escape from bombardment, it is dramatized as a limbo of never-ending war.

The novel was conceived in 1933 when Sackville-West visited the United States. She was enchanted by the California desert, the expanse of which reminded her of the timeless vistas she had seen years before in Persia. She imagined both as backdrops to a fantasy of death and transfiguration. By the time the novel was finished in March 1942, Sackville-West had material evidence that the rapid development of military technology had overwhelmed nature's gradual transformations. 'In spite of the mess mankind makes of mankind', she kept her abiding faith in 'the permanence and recurrence of Nature', for 'Nature' suggested a counterforce to the war machine that 'goes on' as a manmade threat.[7] In her dystopia, the hotel's blazing fire, the firepower of the air battles over the canyon, and the canyon's indestructible power over the moral imagination declare a symbolic conflict between our will to power and the human will to live cooperatively. In its connection to the immediate threats of World War II, this 'cautionary tale' satirizes the propaganda extolling the unified moral and military strength of the Allies, especially when the reality is composed of nations who deeply distrust the geopolitical designs of their friends (*GC*, p. AN). For Sackville-West, the myth of nature as a role model for harmony and regeneration cannot compete with the human propensity for deceiving ourselves and those on whom we rely for support.

The novel is set in 1945 following Germany's victory, an outcome facilitated by the war weary United States, which, after defeating Japan, has signed a peace accord with the Germans. Even more damning, however, is Sackville-West's indictment of

American smugness and egotism – '"the nation which, in its hour of victory, brought peace to the world"', and which therefore is 'deluded' by the Nazis (*GC*, p. AN). 'The terrible consequences of an incomplete conclusion or indeed of any peace signed by the Allies with an undefeated Germany are shown' (*GC*, p. AN)

Not 'intended as a prophesy', *Grand Canyon* instead presents a plea to the United States and Britain to maintain their victories over isolationism and appeasement, policies Sackville-West had considered 'wrong, foolish, and short-sighted'.[8] Though she agreed with pacifists in 1937 that 'we ought to retire from the competition, not merely for our own safety but to give a lead away from this insane barbarism', by the time Germany invaded Poland, she felt the war must be fought (Glendinning, p. 295). Her fears about the Allies' weak resolve materialize in her dystopia when the Grand Canyon is bombarded. In a fantasied second half, when the hotel guests emerge as the living dead, they meditate on whether peace can ever prevail over the 'mixture of madness and organization' that leaves 'no sanity . . . in the din and the speed and the destruction' (*GC*, p. 198).

The contrast between the wide-open American landscape and the insularity of American and English politics sets the stage for a dialogue between two English guests on war and peace aims in general and as they particularly apply to World War II. Lester Dale is a wartime misfit; first a pacifist and then an enlistee, he is tortured by 'not knowing where right lay, or wrong' (*GC*, p. 177). His ambivalences disguise an apathy Sackville-West locates in liberalism. In its language of progressivism, liberalism offers a false security by representing the belief that one need do nothing with 'useless out-of-date ideas' (*GC*, p. 174). As his name suggests, Dale represents a lowpoint in British political topography, more theory and structure than practice. In contrast, another English guest, Helen Temple, functions as therapist and activist. The combination of her empathetic comments and questions does not merely soothe, however, but suggests the spirit of mutually distrustful coalitions of the period. Although she accedes to the necessity of fighting, it is nonetheless 'a thing we hated even worse' (*GC*, p. 178). Whereas Dale abstracts the enemy into a symbolic order of 'spectral words', Helen Temple distinguishes between theories of 'Evil and Folly' and the material and human destructiveness of 'Nazi and Fuhrer' (*GC*, p. 178). Taken as a whole, their dialogue evinces Sackville-West's concerns with intellectual and ideological collaboration with 'darker forces'. To translate the actual events of war into metaphysical language represents a form of political identity and action that, in its denial of war's experiential costs, is a dangerous 'imitation' of the geo-politics of aggression (*GC*, p. 177).

The end of the novel offers a dystopic warning by putting the language of moral imagination into a critical relationship with the language of war's material realities. The fabulist fiction of the characters' living death and documentary style radio broadcasts of battles and strategies alternate, so that each perspective can be viewed in the light of the other. The tension between these narratives dramatizes the absurdity of ongoing mass murder 'when the obvious solution for all those millions of men sharing the same planet lay in co-operation, both economic and geographical' (*GC*, p. 195). As a synthesizing gesture, the narrator's voice overtakes those of the characters to present an argument similar to that offered by the Devil in George Bernard Shaw's epic dialogue on civilization's discontents, *Don Juan in Hell*. (Ironically, Sackville-West despised Shaw). Critiquing the scientific and technological progress so valued by H.G. Wells, the narrator ponders tensions between the drive to 'invent', the construction of 'a thing called "his enemies", and many means of destroying them' (*GC*, p. 196). The narrative consequence of this construction is an apocalyptic catastrophe like that in Jameson's *The World Ends*; here nature joins forces with human destructiveness to produce an earthquake that engulfs the manmade New York City. Destroying members of the Allies as well as the Axis powers, the impartial 'intervention of Providence' leaves a clean slate on which to conjecture a future built on trust, 'serenity and confidence' (*GC*, p. 205, 206).

Grand Canyon is like many dystopias, including Monica Curtis's 1934 *Landslide*, which also uses the motif of an isolated group of people to pose alternatives to the politics of appeasement and aggression. These novels, like Jameson's, rely more on dialogue and narration for their political and didactic purposes than dramatic plots. While such narratives can be accused of being 'talky' or even preachy, the dramatized debate also functions to question the plotting of progressivist ideas. Talking us through a journey from the rubble of war to possibilities for peace and harmony, these dystopias eschew much of the action-packed plotting of speculative fiction. In effect, these women authored dystopias perform a narrative and figurative rejection of the urge to find solutions in fabulist technology. These novels imply that to dramatize warfare as though the enemy is either a high tech robot or subhuman troglodyte dehumanizes the landscape of war. The effect of such technodrama is to convey the thrill of the chase so that victory is celebrated for its own sake, regardless of the fate of the actors or the political implications of a one-sided victory. Many dystopias legitimate hostile competition in general; they reduce technical knowledge and its machinery into conventional wisdom and figures, and creating hierarchies of human nature by reducing the enemies into conventional categories of good and evil. Their melodramatic effects then overwhelm the possibility of investigating the values of winners and losers. In the case of World War II, this problem has especially dramatic resonance; to abstract or reduce the particular evil of nazism into mechanical or primitive monsters would subsume the moral arguments of how to defeat it into a game. In turn, the focus on winning strategies elides investigation into the responsibilities for the war's origins and the maintainence of peace.

The narrative risk of sacrificing melodramatic suspense to the frustrations and tensions of inquiry and ambivalence is to lose audience appeal. It is thus no wonder that critics of *Grand Canyon* asked readers to 'agree that Mr Wells could have made it twice as solid and a dozen times as plausible'.[9] Sackville-West abjures Mr Welles's magical mystery rides to states of innocence and evil on time machines and rockets. Instead, she dramatizes the language of political confusion in order to expose the defensive strategies of those who turn out to be complicit with evil and therefore none too innocent.

Sackville-West also commits a breach of geo-political etiquette, according to another reviewer, who complained that her 'political warning ... can only rank in impudence and bad taste'.[10] Daring to criticize both the Americans and the British at a time when a unified Allied front was the only hope for Hitler's defeat was not a gesture to ensure a wide audience. Thus Leonard Woolf, who had published (with great financial profit) many of Sackville-West's earlier works, rejected *Grand Canyon*, probably agreeing with John Lehmann that it was '"profoundly defeatist" and would make "a bad impression"' (Glendinning, p. 318). That Vita Sackville-West was anything but defeatist is clear from her war efforts. Her propaganda pamphlet and work with the Woman's Land Army express her faith that women's physical and moral strength could preserve the civilization they have built from being defeated by Hitler. Thus a short piece entitled 'Apologia', from her 1940 *Country Notes in Wartime*:

> It is not easy to write these notes amidst the anguish and anxiety of Europe. The mother-fire of the garden becomes only too readily symbolical, and the destruction of harmless civilized cultivated plants equally symbolical. My only excuse can be that the determination to preserve such beauty as remains to us is also a form of courage. (p. 52).

Sackville-West's war work was consistent with her deepening commitment to aristocratic obligation, but her motivation also coincided with those on the Left like Leonard Woolf, who viewed a unified British front as progress towards social destratification. *Grand Canyon* represents an inquiry into the different ideologies that brought the likes of herself and Woolf to similar conclusions. Her dystopia asks questions about relationships between patriotism, liberalism, and the different ways they would be defined and enacted in a society that chooses to see itself as unified.

THE 'UNSHAKABLE, IMPREGNABLE EMPIRE': KATHARINE BURDEKIN'S *SWASTIKA NIGHT*

The dehumanizing effects of ideological domination at the expense of political pluralism and human diversity is the subject of Katharine Burdekin's 1937 *Swastika Night*. A year before the Munich agreement, Burdekin portrays a world 700 years in the future conquered by and divided between German feudal knights and Japanese warlords. The blueprint is 'Mein Kampf'; land has been reordered and whole species exterminated. Africa has been decimated, the Jews destroyed, and women are monstrous evocations of Hitler's racially correct female.[11] Burdekin's vision not only sums up all the dystopias I have discussed, but presents their concerns as both theory and practice. *Swastika Night* projects a fascist takeover of the world and traces its origination to supremacist ideologies that inspired not just the German empire, but the British. Its drama argues that these ideologies, spawned by masculinist aggression, nurtured such intense international jealousy and competition, that the only imaginable outcome is a dystopic vision of 'unshakable, impregnable Empire', and ultimately, a holocaust even more horrible than the actual.[12]

Like the dystopias of Sackville-West, Mitchison, and Jameson, Burdekin's embeds a critical debate about assuming responsibility for a dire future. Even more dramatically, the debate in *Swastika Night* shows how the rhetoric of historical narrative shapes historical events, and so the plot involves characters who learn that the unseen power behind their subjection is as textual as it is material. However Burdekin and Dorothy Sayers would disagree about the state of their nation and how to defeat nazism, they both recognized how the despotic power of Hitler's historical rhetoric cast a critical shadow over the relationship between words and action. Sayers's 15 June 1940 letter to *Time and Tide* would be a telling afterword to Burdekin's dystopia:

> The enemy knows all about the dynamism of words. We, in this country have grown too much accustomed to hearing words derided. Sneers at the poet and the highbrow and the booksey boys have diddled us into thinking that words do not matter. We paid no attention to Mein Kampf – it was only a book; it could not possibly mean deeds. We are seeing now that words can issue in deeds, and are painfully forced to the discovery that the deed is the word incarnate.[13]

At the centre of *Swastika Night*, its theoretical and dramatic hub, is a history book that decodes the deadly effects of the Reich's revisionist ethos. The book is a precious legacy, handed down from father to son in a family of aristocratic German knights. It figures not only as a text of secret knowledge, but as the only method by which knowledge can be recuperated from its status in the Reich as archaic myth and dogma. Like Jameson and Mitchison, Burdekin recognizes the dangers for any nation or people in romanticizing an enduring 'green' past, but her extended analysis suggests that the consequences are as unremitting as their origins. Written by Friedrich Von Hess 150 years after Hitler died, the book charts the brutal German conquest as 'the truth of history' (*SN*, p. 74). A prophetic icon of real history, the book's forbidden status haunts the modern reader with memories of Hitler's 1938 book burning. It also resonates with other forbidden books in earlier dystopias, such as those under lock and key in Huxley's *Brave New World* and in Zamiatin's *We*. That such a book inscribes historical change is suggested by its endurance and the ongoing rediscovery of its knowledge.

That ongoing rediscovery involves not only the novel's protagonists, but its readers as well. In its revelations of the secret origins of 'dark forces', the Von Hess chronicle represents and yet challenges the notion of narrative suspense. For the protagonists, each turn of the page exposes the past as a revisionary explanation of the present. Their efforts to alter the course of the future on the basis of this knowledge provide the novel's suspense. For readers in 1937, the novel's depiction of a disastrously static future also disturbs the experience of fictional suspense. As the turbulent fictional past unfolds, instead of offering a surprise, it resembles the actual present all too clearly. And instead of this knowledge providing a comforting hedge against the novel's dismal future, it works as a criticism and warning against the complacency that assumes the future could take care of itself. For readers today, though the novel's foresight may rest comfortably with our hindsight and we cheer the characters' heroic efforts, the historic past and its ideological determination of the novel's terrible present remain disturbingly unresolved. In all cases, the predictive and analytic capacity of the historical chronicle undermines the promise of fictional suspense to reorder past, present, and future.

The primary agent of Burdekin's historical and ideological analysis is Von Hess's descendent, an aging German knight. His dual legacy of leadership and resistance form his ambivalent relationship to the past, present, and future, and reflect back on his deadly empire as both indomitable and decaying. With no male heirs himself, the latter day Von Hess becomes the symbolic dead end of high German culture, its self-cancelling ironies embodied in the Von Hess duality. The sterility of empire and heir mark the impotence of a German enlightenment which, despite the rigorous questioning of its philosophical traditions, is swept away by 'a hysteria of rage and fear and desire to destroy' (*SN*, p. 83). Like the classical German music he loves, the knight cannot shake the romanticism that flavoured the timeless fantasy and self-absorption of Nazi supremacist myths. His more conscious attempts to critique and subvert those myths are overwhelmed as well. In order for his ancestor's book to survive, its anti-romantic, critical perspective must be kept secret, and so the historical understanding the knight inherited from his questing ancestor can have no impact on the prevailing political order.

Dramatizing the connection between political history and complicity with ideologies of power, Burdekin introduces another book; this one drives the Von Hess chronicle underground. This book, by a scholar knight, Von Wied, is clearly based on the pseudoscientific treatises of Otto Weininger and becomes the gospel of the real and fictional Reich. Its racialist theories feed the mobs' hysteria by inscribing the Germans' 'dark inside panic' and 'lunatic vanity' and testifying to Hitler's god-like birth and the protective appeal of omniscient power (*SN*, p. 83). The brutalities inspired by such unholy writ are made self-evident by another book of knowledge. In 1937 readers of a novel published by the Left Book Club would more than likely have been aware of what the real Hitler's gospel, *Mein Kampf*, contained, while readers today would view it retrospectively as a blueprint for the reordering of history and the destruction of all those deemed sub-human.

As Daphne Patai and others have observed, part of what is remarkable about *Swastika Night* is its pre-eminent analysis of masculinist aggression as the source of the Nazis' depreciation of life.[14] Burdekin's case in point is composed of the stooped and shrunken bodies of women under the Reich: 'with their small shaven ugly heads', women are signs of both the cause and effect of their abuse (*SN*, p. 9). By the last third of the thousand year Reich, Aryan mothers are literally bent out of shape from breeding. In their distorted bodies and consciousness, women represent a living death resulting from Nazi eugenics, the principles of which have caused those who conceive and bear life to regress to a primitive state of being. Robbed of any language by which to understand or question their state, women's only form of self-expression is the weeping that reverberates with their history of debasement. Unlike Jameson's women in *Then We Shall Hear Singing*, these have no access to women's culture and its arts of communication.

In Burdekin's novel, while the men take pleasure in disfiguring and then rejecting women, the narrative implies that this is linked to a self-cancelling ideology which results in a biological version of male masochism. The more women are degraded, the fewer female children they produce, an ominous sign of the beginning of the end of men. Burdekin's prescient depiction of women's protracted and brutal exploitation under nazism is imaginable through Rebecca West's analysis of their actual double bind in 1943. West notes that 'Hitler came to power largely on the votes of women', who were lured by his promises of 'a stable society' giving glory to marriage and motherhood with enhanced economic support.[15] But as West shows, Hitler 'lied' ('H'). Once the war took hold, the fate of German women was to leave their homes and children for work in heavy industry and in the very professions they gave up. West holds German women accountable for yielding the power of professional life and 'full political and social rights' granted by the Weimar Republic ('H'). She also argues, however, that the appeal of romanticized domestic myths was understandable in 1933 when economic and political instability had made young women and men frightened of marrying and having families; the marriage rate had dropped to 'a quarter of a million' and 'less than a million German babies were born' ('H'). Burdekin's imagined debasement of women's childbearing biology is parallel to West's observation that the war-dominated Reich would require 'decades' of women's 'frenzied effort' to sustain it ('H'). In the actuality of 1943, German women are driven by the ghosts of Hitler's romantic domestic myths; they must sustain their home front, for their husbands lie dead under 'the skies of England . . . in the African sands [and] in the snows of Russia' ('H').

Although women's debased state in *Swastika Night* would seem to have robbed them of the power of choosing or rejecting men, reproducing fewer women will save them from an indefinite future of sexual bondage. In this way, the women can also be said to embody the biological or material consequences of the Nazis' corruption of historical time and consciousness. Persecution has destroyed women's historical memory and therefore the living proof of a past that would nullify Nazi mythology. As predictive agents of a Nazi future, their biology demystifies the sense of an invincible Thousand Year Reich.[16]

The novel traces Nazi self-destruction to its ideology, as shown in the linkage between the Reich's masculinist war machine, its homoeroticism, and the degradation of women. Burdekin deconstructs the discourse of men's battlefield bonding by dramatizing their alienation, brutality, and death. Instead of mutual sympathy, this is the logical end of a political philosophy based on competition for supremacy rather than negotiation and cooperation. Similar to Jameson's point in *In the Second Year*, homosexuality in *Swastika Night* signals the origins of violence in exclusionary, masculinist codes of aggression. Hence a young Nazi,

Hermann, kills a young boy to whom he is attracted in an act of vengeance against the rejection of male supremacy. Since the boy had been lusting after a young, still radiant woman, the incident also illustrates the threat of difference women represent. In a world of Nazi absolutes, human attractiveness is constructed to validate a mythicized ideal of brute force and to deny empathy.

In their obliteration of so many Others, the wars for Aryan blood purity have led inexorably to a kind of narcissism, the condition of which is the Nazi destroying himself and his likeness as the result of being not only the one permissable love object, but the only legitimate contender for supremacy. It is in the process of this self-cancellation that Nazi Germany puts an end to history. The Thousand Year Reich, according to Burdekin, has collapsed the possibility for change as it has destroyed all vestiges of human difference and contingency. Because the Japanese empire figures in the novel as the Nazis' partner in crimes against humanity but is not dramatized, we can only assume that things are no different in their half of the globe. What came to be called the Axis can therefore be seen as a metaphor in this dystopia for the centripetal rotation of endless destruction and despair, never relieved, enlightened, or expanded by another perspective. The lack of additional perspective is exemplified by those remaining peoples who are enslaved and silenced as barely distinguishable *untermenschen*. Moreover, the inward turn of the Axis eliminates the value of difference between themselves. With no expression of human and political difference allowed, each of the partners' ideal of racial supremacism is subverted. Paradoxically, their competitive partnership and uneasy, stalemated peace ends the possibility of absolute superiority. Despite their own divergent cultures and histories, Japan and Germany eliminate any sign of distinctiveness as they mirror each other's ability to destroy all others.

Worse yet, the static and sterile condition into which these empires have evolved questions the power of aggressive masculinity that drives their political ethos and identity. Nowhere is this more apparent than in the absence of any dramatized heroic act or conquest; what fills the gap is the exposure of Nazi masculinity as nothing more or less than a ritualized expression of the fear of women. No matter how women are eliminated from the political and cultural identity of the Reich, one aspect of identity remains inescapable – that their physical and biological reality represents the baseline of difference. This fear, fact, and gap are graphically displayed in the form of a photograph of Adolph Hitler hidden in the book of Von Hess's ancestor. Instead of the mythic Nordic god worshipped by the Teutonic knights, the documented Hitler appears as we know him – an ordinary looking man, and one, moreover, who stands outflanked by a more physically powerful woman. Over 700 years of women's regression, their generative powers have been transposed onto a mythic Führer, who in reality represents the impotence and sterility of his masculinist empire.

The change from totalitarian entropy to historical change is made possible by transferring the Von Hess legacy to an Englishman. If Germany seven hundred years into the future represents the end of history, Britain, which has been denuded of its imperial past, is made by Burdekin to stand for history's restoration. Von Hess gives his book to Alfred, an English mechanic whose trustworthiness and talent have been rewarded with a trip to Germany's sacred places. Von Hess recognizes that Alfred's fearlessly critical questions make him the appropriate vehicle by which the history of mankind's backward march to dehumanization can be preserved and taught. At the end of the novel, however, despite his elaborate plans to conceal the book, Alfred's intelligence loses to Nazi brutality. Unbeknownst to Von Hess, Alfred returns to England only to be beaten to death by Nazi soldiers, but the book is passed on by his son to one of the few surviving Christians. Physically and intellectually debased by centuries of Nazi oppression, the Christian has only a corrupt understanding of his culture's history. This will be corrected only if the writing of a singularly inquiring German survives.

Burdekin's critique of supremacist ideologies is worked out through the relationship constructed by the Von Hess chronicle between Germany's rise to fascism and its envy of Britain as a model of imperial power. Her indictment of both nations, however, is not symmetrical. However misogynist and oppressive British imperialism is presented, *Swastika Night* sustains its hopefulness by supporting the living knight's appreciation of English intellectual ethics. For him, what is admirable about the English is

> . . . a toughness of moral fibre, an immovable attachment to what they believe, often in the face of large majorities, to be right. . . . They are sturdy heretics. The best of them are incapable

of spiritual panic, even the ordinary men among them are hard to move to dubiously moral courses by spiritual pressure' (*SN*, p. 114).

Von Hess's statement contains an implied criticism of the very ideology and cultural ethos that brought the German enlightenment to its Nazi apotheosis. It is, after all, the Germans who were swept away by 'spiritual pressures' to 'dubious moral courses'. This ironically stated contrast only highlights the Germans as the diminished ones, and all because of their policies of racial supremacy.

No one, of course, illustrates the qualities Von Hess attributes to the English more directly or more potently than Burdekin herself. By setting English and German political culture against each other's worst predelictions, she produces a heretically ironic history of their past and future. Speaking for Germany is a noble knight of the Hitlerian empire, whose admiration of the English echoes with an implied criticism of his own political history: the experiential and ethical self-destructiveness of the Nazi empire. The mere fact that a degraded people are to be admired admits not only to the oppressor's self-doubt, but to a vitality in the oppressed their debasement cannot conceal or destroy. In the complex arrangement of critique and appreciation lies the model for Burdekin's own persona as a British woman writing a narrative of resistance to her own nation's political history. In one facet, she puts on a German face to dramatize her recognition of a German enlightenment. Warning of a universal Nazi holocaust, this Janus face resists the possibility of universalizing or oversimplifying German guilt. Von Hess is certainly a cornerstone in the oppression he questions; his very nobility paradoxically legitimates the violence and oppression he both supervises and deplores. The figurehead of an ancient knightly clan, he stands for the stability of German supremacy.

It is only in relation to the Englishman that Von Hess reveals chinks in the Reich's armour and possibilities for viable resistance. As they read and argue over the Von Hess chronicle, German knight and English slave contest the Nazi myths which have identified them as types and species. Every time Alfred recognizes that 'There's something wrong somewhere', reading becomes a subversive act, exposing the manipulations of a seemingly impregnable text through the aggressive behaviour of responding critically (*SN*, p. 82). The text of Nazi history, which proclaims its own invincibility and inevitability, is threatened by the historical contingencies that shaped and aligned two individuals representing competing cultures and myths.[17] Alfred commemorates the medieval king hero of English national consciousness and survival, while the German knight represents the continuous struggle to maintain his own nation's self-consciousness and hegemony. Each one also stands in ironic relation to the continuity of his own and the other's national myths. Their combined scepticism shows England's decline to have started when national survival turned into imperialism; the Nazi future, figured as a rusty medieval relic, serves to comment on Britain's decline. In relation to each other and to the novel's ironies, Alfred and the knight undermine the mythic power of their medieval identities.

But it is their combined readership that ultimately carries the novel's resonance forward. As their joint quest calls attention to itself, it involves the reader of *Swastika Night* in the process of unravelling the relationship between its construction of the future and interpretation of the past. For the modern reader, this becomes even more thickly woven as we read the actual history of the Nazi past into the novel's projection of the future and gloss further on Alfred and Von Hess's cultural interpretations. We not only collude with their demystifications, but exercise our own resolve and resistance in relation to their defensiveness and ours.[18]

As we read their interpretive process our own historical and cultural positioning intersects with theirs, and the results can be as challenging as they are for Von Hess and Alfred. Burdekin's critique of masculinist militarism, as wide ranging as it is in this dystopia, is no more totalizing than her condemnation of German romanticism or English pragmatism. The Von Hess chronicle explores the complex conditions that enable these ideologies to be translated into nazism and imperialism. In so doing, this historical testament distinguishes between British and German cultural and political history and their individual manifestations as patriarchal societies. Especially significant are the uniquely horrific consequences Burdekin augurs for Nazi Germany. Her vision of a Thousand Year Reich historicizes the continuum of a masculinist ideology.[19] At the dramatic centre of the novel, women's oppression highlights but does not stand for the absence and silence of all those who have been exterminated by the Nazi creed of Aryan regeneration. The women's weeping testifies to the universal dangers Burdekin recognized in Hitler's policies, but her dystopia persistently gestures towards distinctions between these dangers as they had begun to occur in Germany in the early thirties and the safeguards in English culture and politics that could prevent it from lurching towards fascism.[20] While such characterization could too easily slip into essentializing national character and land in a pitfall of supremacist caricature and racism, Burdekin's personification of both Germany and Britain avoids this in the inconsistencies and contradictions, the glimmers of liberalism and clouds of misogyny, with which she invests the characters of Von Hess and Alfred. Each is ironically subject to the social arrangements of his own time and culture.

What saves the desire of these men to discover the political realities within these arrangements is their recognition of historical time and change. Alfred and Von Hess embody and articulate the political and ethical distinctions it is possible for human beings to make, no matter how much they have been robbed of their own distinctiveness. The only resistance to an endless fascist night in Burdekin's dystopia is the graphic projection of its universal but particular history into the future. In this projection, the narrative represents the logical consequences of nazism. At the same time, in the interpollated chronicle of the German knight, the novel reflects backward to ponder the origins of nazism in supremacist ideologies. The fact that the German knight ships the chronicle to England marks Burdekin's insistence on political distinctions. Despite Britain's complicity in its own decline and fall, it retains the promise of its tough 'moral fibre' and a stubborn belief in progressivism, the combination of which accounts for the development of Alfred's character. Against all pressures, he reaches out affectionately and respectfully to the woman who bore his child and to his daughter, gestures that can only bode well for resistance against fascism and change as it might originate in Britain.

The possibility for such change resonates in the crucial years of the novel's gestation and publication. Burdekin's reading of Nazi tyranny is so accurate and prescient that her critique of Britain and her pacifism must be considered in its light. For all of *Swastika Night*'s linkage of Britain to a universal masculinist militarism, its distinctions point to her acknowledgement that Britain had to defeat Nazi Germany in a second world war. Not to do so would lead to the monstrous absurdity of waiting 700 years into a Hitlerian nightmare for the Nazis to self-destruct. Alfred's death and the Christian inheritance of the Von Hess chronicle are signs that Burdekin did not totally despair of an intractible patriarchy, but that hope prevailed for her in the lessons of history as a pathway to political self-consciousness.

In her posthumously published novel, *The End of This Day's Business*, Burdekin is still reacting to the possibility that fascist oppression may overwhelm the drive to discover historical contingency and implement political change. Even though the novel features a feminist victory over patriarchal oppression, it proposes that the desire for revenge assumes its own ideology of aggression. And so the victorious women model their own security and hegemony on an endless cycle of dehumanization. That the victims are now men simply reverses and replicates the history of women's oppression. In this dystopia, nazism survives even in a feminist future because its principles of survival and supremacism are so deeply embedded in the consciousness of people divided by gendered, racial, cultural, and historical circumstances. Playing out the social consequences of plots generated by such divisions, both dystopias dramatize the dehumanizing effects of constructing and collapsing differences that do not allow the other self-definition.

Any attempt to interpret Burdekin's political philosophy at this point must be limited to her fiction, as very little is known about her life and political activity. It was not even known, until Patai rediscovered *Swastika Night*, that its author was Burdekin, and not Murray Constantine, the name affixed to the original Gollancz publication.[21] Burdekin did publish six novels under her own name in the twenties, some of them science fiction, and one, *Quiet Ways* (1930), with a decidedly pacifist theme. She began to use a male nom de plume with her novel *The Devil, Poor Devil!* (1934). *Proud Man* (1934) uses a dystopic method to question gender inequalities.

In all of the dystopic novels by British women I have read, such gender inequality may be endemic to all cults of masculinity, but fascism and nazism do not merely represent logical steps along the line from domination to oppression to psychological and physical death. As Maureen Duffy, who has written two retrospective novels about World War II, said to me, 'We must not forget that there is a vast difference between racist theories of domination and Hitler's unique racist exterminations'.[22] It is no accident of timing that Burdekin's *Swastika Night* links the horrific consequences of gender and racial politics to *Mein Kampf*. The interdependence for which Jameson and Sackville-West plead begins with the recognition that Hitler's genocidal plans were not lunatic rantings but a public policy that was to become a nightmare from which few would be exempt. Because Burdekin's dystopia clearly recognizes this nightmare as a real possibility and one distinct from Britain's patriarchal imperial history, her pacifist critique of fascist militarism cannot be taken to exclude the necessity of stopping Hitler before it was too late. The political critique and decisive action advocated by Jameson, Mitchison, and Sackville-West represent the only policy that could counter *Mein Kampf*. For each of these women writers, hope replaces the despair of Wells and others by first recognizing the dangers of complacency on the home front and then joining forces to keep Hitler from conquering the rest of the world.

Registering their dual visions, each of these writers forms an idea of interdependence that complicates any call for a unified struggle against fascism by analysing the ideological, social and economic assumptions of national identity and unity. If democracy as a political process is to be preserved, they argue, the prevailing British definition of democracy must be exposed as political rhetoric that conceals time honored but destructive ruptures among men and women and across social and economic classes. For these writers, the continuing economic crisis and the coming of a new world war are not separate events. Instead, they intersect when the problems that produced the foreign-born fascism turn out to be infecting Britain as well, and can no longer be avoided through the politics of denial. As Burdekin, Jameson, and so many others file their complaints across the political spectrum, from the radical margins of the left on through Torydom, they challenge prevailing definitions of progressive and conservative. By showing the inadequate responses of both political positions to the dangers at home and abroad, they imply that political responsibility defies political categories. At a time when it was becoming expedient to erase political differences so that national unity could be preserved, each of these writers is insisting on a redefinition of nation by asking what of the old Britain should be preserved and how must it change.

As so often happens with such criticism, its purveyers might be accused of exonerating themselves. But as their dystopias reveal, these women writers are only too happy to join the fray in order to redefine political identity. In so many different combinations, they explore the social and economic circumstances that not only produced themselves, but the political climate of Britain in the 1930s. In their dystopic mode, they could also be accused of not imagining an alternative, optimistic view of the future. But here again, alternative visions are embedded in the argumentative and polemical strategies of their dystopias. They posit a definition of nation and civilization as mediating and equalizing the different concerns of women and men across their social spheres. As a result of this redefinition, men and women are empowered to discover their own alternative future. The act of writing these dystopias therefore paradoxically represents a hope, in that even as they risk their professional lives to say what their critics and publishers do not want to hear, these women writers will have taken the necessary decisive action 'to take the bitter trouble to find hard ground under the disorder and decay of society – and stand on it to write . . . to keep our right to criticize and ask questions' (Jameson, 'Responsibilities', p. 178–9).

4

No Place Like Home: The British Home Front

'HER BROKEN HOUSE'

In her 1982 poem entitled 'Picture From the Blitz', Lois Clark commemorated the British women who suffered the loss of their homes while holding down the home front:

> After all these years
> I can still close my eyes and see
> her sitting there,
> in her big armchair,
> grotesque under an open sky,
> framed by the jagged lines of her broken house.[1]

The English domestic novel similarly survived the Battle of Britain, but its import was equally altered forever by the image of a woman who may have nowhere to go when her home is destroyed. The actual loss of one home in three and dislocation of 60 million people underlies the poetic image whose emotional power also suggests questions and possibilities unforseen before sky and home were blasted 'open' by enemy bombs. The war on the home front exposed relationships between the ideologies which informed domestic novels, the sexual politics which conditioned women's daily lives, and domestic politics of the wartime home front. Objectified as 'her', the woman in Clark's poem is 'grotesque', as though she is exposed as something Other without her home to define her, but the 'jagged lines of her broken house' offer possibilities for revising her image and role as angel of the house, and as a result, her definitions of home and homeland.

At a time when World War II was brought home by 'the terrifying whine, of Messerschmitts 110 and 109', as poet Elizabeth

Lister put it in her 1941 poem, many British women writers agonized not only about the targeted destruction of their own homes but about nazism's victims outside Britain.[2] This relationship between self and Other complicated their politics of home and nation. The domestic novels of the war not only address women's unequal status in their own homes; they also challenge the patriarchal state which made conflicting demands on them: to do war work, evacuate children, and 'stand firm' at home while coping with relocations, shortages, and deaths for a war effort which also classified young mothers and old women as 'immobile'.[3] Neither government policy nor its propaganda recognized the particularly embattled conditions of women on the home front; as Phyllis Bottome reminded her readers:

> . . . their work is just as hard, or harder than ever; and they must adjust to sudden changes and emergencies that have nothing to do with it. Sometimes they have to work in offices with glassless windows; sometimes in shelters during air raids . . . and above all those workers in crowded factories and workshops where precautions have to be postponed to the last moment (*Tyrants,* pp. 156–77).

Contrary to government labeling, however, even those women who did not serve in the Land Army, in other Auxiliary Services or work in the factories contributed to the war effort, albeit, on their own terms, as a 1940 woman's study reported. They did community work with evacuees, counselled lonely soldiers and other women, and kept community morale high through cooperative meetings.[4]

Such efforts transformed the home and community in both the cities and villages. At the start of the war, women's magazines exhorted women to keep the home fires burning for the returning men; being married to a soldier did not change the pressures on women.[5] Despite wartime restrictions, women were still expected to be helpmates and sexually available.[6] Women's ability to balance an increasingly complicated life was promoted throughout the forties by popular magazines. Articles, advertising, advice columns, and stories elevated homemaking 'to a science', like 'running a business, army, or a factory' (Beddoe, p. 19). Once the extent of women's war work and fortitude became clear, however, the magazines were pressed to reflect changes in women's attitudes and conditions.[7] These changes had not come easily, though, but instead, were highly charged, as reflected in the mostly ambivalent outcomes to feminist debates of the inter-war period on marital relationships.[8]

Women's ability to give coherence to their desires for reshaping these relationships was further vexed by double messages in social policies. Although a government survey of the nation's domestic health had deemed marriage a mutually fulfilling partnership, women were still viewed as the barometer of a family's emotional well being, and therefore its primary caretaker. Naomi Mitchison for one, felt 'netted by invisible rules of family and domestic life', and she had more freedom than most (*All Change,* p. 24). By the 1940s, as Jane Lewis notes, these rules added to women's burden by asking them to give even more attention to the emotional support of their husbands.[9] Even when women's political activities received community support, it was 'premised on the importance of their roles as wives and mothers' (Lewis, p. 19). In her memoir of the war, Barbara Kaye recalls the pressure to give up her writing from her 'middle-class upbringing with its built-in belief that standards must be kept up, as if to appease some domestic God'; likewise, Fay Inchfawn, magazine writer and author of the wartime *Salute to the Village,* remembers juggling the role of 'keeper-at-home' with the dilemma of whether writing or 'some vital task' were to be her wartime priorities.[10]

Once the Blitz rained havoc, however, its stresses and demands gave women a critical view of their political and conjugal rights. With the unsettling of domestic life, women were now questioning their own sexual expectations and behaviour as well as those of their absent husbands and erstwhile lovers. Although many women assumed that strict fidelity was incompatible with soldiering, their own participation on an embattled and turbulent home front showed them that the old double standards were no longer acceptable.[11] In running their own homes and assuming community responsibilities, in forming new kinds of communities in underground shelters or in the villages to which they were evacuated, women redefined family and collectivity according to a newly formed sense of their priorities (Minns, p. 66). In a larger sense, these experiences raised questions about sovereignty, boundaries of power, and gender roles that would resound in the postwar years. Not that these questions were resolved, however, for throughout the war women felt opposing pressures to maintain traditional political and social relations and to yield to their desire for change. Domesticity may have represented a permanent value system throughout the war years, but the wartime domestic fiction illustrates many forms of resistance to it.

BRITANNIA'S 'OAKEN HEART':[12] THE VILLAGE HOME FRONT OF ELIZABETH GOUDGE, VIRGINIA WOOLF AND OTHERS

One setting that could easily be imagined as sustaining domestic traditions and community stability, even under embattled skies, was the English village. Margery Allingham conveyed its unsettling reality in her 1941 book *The Oaken Heart* in order to explain wartime village life to an American audience: 'Living in Auburn was like following a quiet domestic film which had been accidently photographed on the negative of a sensational thriller' (*Oaken*, p. 67). Given the relative safety and insularity of many rural areas, bringing the village setting into wartime novels often became a matter of treating its unchanging qualities with bemused detachment.[13] This tonal quality produced an entertaining fiction for those readers who were in the thick of it, as was novelist G.B. Stern. Stern recalled 'That-Village-in-Wartime novel [as] my happiest form of escape fiction.... Very little sob-stuff, a little more snob-stuff, and perhaps rather too much amusing dialogue'.[14] Stern's irony was not lost on other writers, who found much to question, in this case, about the social structures embedded in the genre and in actual village life. Well within the bounds of escape fiction, there are several writers who incorporated their criticisms of domestic and international policies in the conventions of wartime village fiction. As a result, they produced revisions of the genre that raise not so amusing questions about 'snob-stuff', that is, the stuff of social class divisions and cultural identity. Elizabeth Goudge (1900–1984), popular writer of historical romance, converts one of its icons, the medieval castlehold of an old family, into a site of disenchantment about 'the greatness of England'.[15] Where her setting could easily have invoked the battle cry of 'our sceptred isle', Goudge instead appropriates the historic moment for revisionary purposes.

Published in 1942, *The Castle on the Hill* evokes the home front as Elizabeth Bowen saw it that year – a new 'generation of ruins' which, because 'they took their places as the norm of the scene', were 'insidious'.[16] For Goudge, this third year of the war is a time to reevaluate the antiquarian but still powerful social and political arrangements of village life – the older 'generation of ruins' in relation to the new. In so doing, she redefines homeland as a haven for outsiders – 'a fugitive Jew', Jo Isaacson, and a poor spinster, Miss Brown, who make their way to the west country village of Torhaven (*Hill,* p. 134). By dint of their position as marginalized Others in the past and current history depicted in the novel, the 'immobile' woman and the Jew represent a critical perspective on the village as haven. Imposing their turbulent lives on the village highlights how its traditional structures are designed to deny historical contingencies. On the one hand, in its image of timeless stability, the village typically represents a refuge. But in Goudge's vision, where the castle rules both politically and morally, the village haven also serves as a kind of feudal internment camp, keeping the outsiders destabilized, 'in an entirely different stratum of society' (*Hill,* p. 164).

Precisely because they are set apart from the indigenous village culture, Isaacson and Miss Brown represent an antithesis to its mythic embodiment of England as 'all that is gallant and beautiful' (*Hill,* p. 164). Individually powerless and strangers to each other, once they are thrown together this unlikely pair exposes the mythic England as 'A tired old country living on her past, a country so bankrupt of ideas that she could let her unemployed drift about her streets like grey-faced ghosts in hell and not be able in years to think what to do with them' (*Hill,* p. 107). These words are actually spoken by one of the castle heirs, but like the solution he proposes, to 'get [England's] face washed and her pants hitched up', they merely form the sentimental rhetoric of aristocratic noblesse (*Hill,* p. 108). Denied access to the privilege of sentimental reformist rhetoric, the woman and the Jew are instead given the moral agency to regenerate the moribund village. Merging the zeal of reformers with the docility of the oppressed, Goudge's odd couple opens the village gates that signify their nation's xenophobia and take in slum-bred evacuated children.

The combination of Goudge's social criticism and melodrama produces an ambivalence that in effect jettisons any nostalgia for a heroic 'olde' England. The enfeebled Jewish civilian, who could easily be typecast as effeminate and thus a threat to the nation's sense of its manly strength, ensures its future instead. Playing

Britannia as a Jewish mother, he nourishes her children. In an ironic juxtaposition, the Jew's nurturing presence and interpolated scenes of medieval violence validate the war effort by revising the myth of feudal harmony. The novel's single Jew not only embodies the history of Jewish persecution in England and elsewhere, but dramatizes a plea to England to make reparations and set a moral standard by continuing the fight against Nazi conquest. Through the figure of the nurturing Jew, Goudge transforms the cultural tradition of a feminized rural England protected by the phallic castle on the hill. As the woman and the Jew assume the role of nurturer protectors of the nation's children, they render the castle an anomalous relic, pacify the nation's militaristic image, and enlarge the war's just cause.

Goudge's transformative vision is based on her trust in England's inherent stability, a trust as we have seen in other women writers that is buttressed by Christian faith, here in the moral standards set by the lives of Christ and St Francis. Although belief in Britain's stability also generated the hope that underlay women's dystopias of the thirties, the fictional domestication of national stability in the forties provided an imaginary escape hatch from the war's destruction. And yet despite this shared trust, women's versions of England as domestic space differed markedly from each other. Unlike Goudge, whose occasional sentimental optimism is offset by her critique, other women's faith in Britain's indomitability justified their commitment to an idea of the nation as homogeneous village. Fay Inchfawn questions her own 'complacency' about facing the war in her 1943 memoir, *Salute to the Village* (p. 19). But she does so in language that locates stability in a feudal past that reconciles domestic serenity with military protection; hence her admission that she is 'too anxious to protect my small citadel of peace from disturbing thoughts' (*Salute,* p. 19). Her vision of homeland turns out to be threatened less by Hitler than by the London refugees, 'the strangers within our gates' out of synch with her feudal harmonies (*Salute,* p. 28). Unlike Goudge, who feels that the feudal relationship between the village and the castle weakens Britain's future, Inchfawn sees their feudal interdependence as a civilizing force, the hub of an idealized village community where the evacuees are lucky to have fallen 'on their feet' (*Salute,* p. 28). Unlike the internationalist sense of interdependence proferred by Rebecca West and Storm Jameson, Inchfawn envisions a gentrified hegemonic Britain.

Inchfawn's 'snob-stuff' may very well have comforted readers for whom 'sob-stuff' was the happy byproduct of dreaming of a victory that would restore the mythic harmonies of the past. Despite her professed compassion for the evacuees, the largesse of her cohesive village is easy proof of its moral superiority over the nation's own transient 'aliens ... who could not by any stretch of imagination be described as angels' (*Salute,* p. 28). Repeated again and again, images of village generosity become signs of insecurity rather than faith in its ability to absorb change. This insecurity is often expressed in village narratives as reflecting tensions that grew out of maintaining the hierarchical social relations of village life and the changing roles of its women. Positioning the evacuees as dependent and yet resistant to the charms of village life also suggests competing claims for national interests and identity. Margery Allingham expresses that competition as an invasion of Others escaping the Blitz in 1940–1941: 'We expected London to be razed in a week, and I know my own private fear was the idiotic notion that a terrorized city population would spread out like rings in a puddle all over the Home Counties, bring fear and quarrels and chaos with it' (*Oaken,* p. 40). The Irish novelist, Kate O'Brien, who sought creative inspiration as she travelled in English villages from Cornwall to the north, attributes the sense of village indomitability to the indifference, 'at [the village's] heart ... to all that comes in from outside'.[17] 'The village-character', for O'Brien, 'is static. ... Dullness is the essence' that produces 'the preservative and anaesthetic and sedative' that prevents even war from disturbing 'the slow, rich, wasteful, boring and valuable evolution of village existence' (pp. 580, 583).

Other writers of domestic literature used the unlikely setting of the 'static' village and its country houses to conduct heated debates about war aims and their connection to domestic social relations and cultural identity. Susan Ertz, whose reputation as a romance writer belies her social criticism, intensified her political analysis in her 1943 novel, *Anger in the Sky*. Here a country house is portrayed as 'a little community with its own laws, customs and traditions', but not in the least bit harmonious as Inchfawn would have it.[18] For Ertz, the country house is a microcosm of England's 'exclusive and self-conscious society which, possessing both humiliations and advantages, demanded from its members something special in the way of uprightness, simplicity and courage . . . cut off from the outside world' (*Sky*, pp. 8–9). The house represents a myth of continuity that allows its residents to feel 'the war was no more than a storm that lashed the windows and then passed' (*Sky* p. 14). What will not pass, however, is the novel's criticism of this myth in the voices of village women who rebut the manor's call for 'affection and mutual respect' with accusations of class exclusions and snobbery (*Sky*, p. 29). In its most critical move, the novel self-reflexively uses the convention of drawing room repartee (G.B. Stern's 'rather too much amusing dialogue') to question it as a hallmark of English civilization. Turned against itself in Ertz's novel, this often mocking conversation suggestively asks whether country house residents and their concerns are even relevant to wartime fiction.

The tensions that afflict Inchfawn's evacuees and villagers and Ertz's village and country house women also emerge when women of different social classes and regions are portrayed as actually working together and enacting new arrangements of power. Diana Gardner portrays this tension in her story about a smouldering clash between a farm woman and a land girl doing her bit after being expelled from boarding school. 'The Land Girl' captures the home front war as it spills over from the female-dominated house onto the male-dominated land. In its tragicomic form, the story exposes the power and myopia of upper class self-interest as manipulating the goals and meaning of defending and sustaining the homeland. Gardner herself manipulates both class and gender roles to show how each category receives its power at the expense of the other. The story's protagonist, 'Miss Una', deploys the power of her class as she lords her upper-class manners over the farm woman, Mrs Farrant, and underplays them to seduce Mr Farrant.[19] Enraged by Mrs Farrant's recalcitrance, Miss Una launches a retaliatory strike by laying a trap that will destroy the Farrants' marriage, and by implication, a sustaining ground of the home front. Una messes up Mr Farrant's bed and pretends to retrieve her brooch from his night stand just in time for Mrs Farrant to see it upon returning from an overnight trip. At the end, leaving Mr Farrant bewildered and abandoned by his wife, Una savours her victory and power.

If this were all, the story would be a savage indictment of class privilege and exploitation. Its subtle arrangements, however, point to a clash of cultures that reveals how the myopia of upper class self-interest is a fifth column of self-deception. With its wartime setting, the implied dangers not only have historic resonances, but are immediate. As narrated by Miss Una herself, the story shines light on her misreadings of the pertinent signs of the farm couple's relationship and cultural values. Taking her own social codes as normative, she concludes that the Farrants' marriage is in trouble because Mrs Farrant 'never calls him by his name or anything else, and refers to him as "Mr Farrant"' ('LG', p. 151). The alienation she assumes between the Farrants, however, reflects her own distance from the social realities of another culture, its own exclusive traditions, and their representation in gender roles. Because Miss Una is unable to acknowledge the integrity of another woman's home and the position of power Mrs Farrant has maintained to sustain it, she cannot see her own relation to it except as the legitimate usurper of domestic power.

The result is a guerilla war in which Miss Una only appears to be the winner. At the end, when she leaves the farmhouse, chilled and not knowing where she is going or what she will do next, her avowal that her 'life has only just begun' has the effect of being equally chilling ('LG', p. 158). Not only has she foreclosed on the legitimacy of her own ascendancy to power, but in driving Mrs Farrant out, she is responsible for destroying the delicate ecological balance of the land she was supposed to tend. Manipulated and then abandoned by both women, Mr Farrant is not just confused at the end, but has been feminized by the women's struggle. He has become increasingly passive, inexpressive, and helpless as the women use him as the symbolic goal of their fight for sovereignty. As he is slowly crushed in the process, his feminization mirrors women's subordination to the roles into which they have been conscripted. Gardner explores this power struggle from the perspective of a shepherd's wife in another wartime story, 'The Visitation'. Here, during an incendiary bombing, Mrs Lethbury is reconciled to the futility of challenging her husband's concern for his sheep over his children. Though his concern makes him 'like a woman: confident and tender', it also establishes him in a world 'apart' as though in competition with hers.[20] Again, a young woman's sympathy for him – this time the daughter – signals the man's power and her mother's impotence. In 'The Land Girl', Una's manipulations may look like resistance to subordination, but they only highlight how the assumptions of class privilege upset but intensify the traditional gender imbalances on which the wartime nation depends.

The ambiguities resulting from Miss Una's self-centred misreadings carry the reader along so that while her perspective seems authentic, it also feels disturbed and disturbing. With this strategy, Gardner implicates the reader in the power struggle for the ruling interpretation of home and homeland. Because the story was originally published in *Horizon* magazine in December 1940, its appeal was directed towards a specific segment of British society.[21] The largely upper-middle-class audience would at that time be concerned with the onset of the Blitz and its dangers to the culture and civilization celebrated by *Horizon*. This was an audience, moreover, that serves a critical position in relation to the gentry and farm classes depicted in 'The Land Girl'. The story embeds the expectation that readers will sort out the social conflicts it dramatizes and by implication their relationship and the characters' place in British culture. In calling upon readers to do this, the magazine and its story hold a combined position as arbiter of culture and cultural critic of the audience. In the combined domestic and external struggle for social and cultural sovereignty, the gendered, class, and regional identities of readers, writer, publishers, and characters form the authentically complex identity of the home front.

As the Blitz began, the identity of the home front as a village became an icon not only of the immediate present, but resonated to key moments in English history. Just as Dorothy Sayers could invoke 'Fenland' and Cornwall's 'cliffs of stone' in her patriotic poem, 'The English War', so, for Virginia Woolf, the country house and its residents are redolent with the history that led to a Second World War ('English War', p. 45). Published posthumously in 1941, *Between the Acts* represents the identity of the home front from a critical perspective that does not share space with either *Horizon* magazine or Dorothy Sayers. Woolf situates the coming of war in an epic drama of English history that is performed on the lawns of a country house. As planes fly overhead, the villagers and their hosts perform an interplay of rivalries and revelry that appears to end harmoniously but embeds an ongoing saga of violence. *Between the Acts* enacts the human and historical implications of Woolf's theories of war and male militarism that she had articulated in her 1938 polemic, *Three Guineas*. In her novel, the lineage of male militarism is drawn from old Bart Oliver to his son Giles, and when Giles squashes a snake caught in its own rash and instinctive gluttony, Woolf is arguing that civilizations are built on a history of violent extinction. In a novel much concerned with performance, nature's violence acts like a muse to cycles of creation and destruction of ancient and modern civilizations. Woolf began writing the novel as she saw another such cycle completing itself, in the spring of 1938, and she completed it on 23 November 1940. As she wrote and revised it at a time when Hitler's acts of aggression were escalating, her mockery and despair over the militarism of patriarchy's institutions became more intense.[22] Thus Woolf deromanticizes patriarchy's playing fields of Eton as ritualizing and therefore perpetuating nature's mindless violence.

It is but a short hop for Woolf from the rituals of men's games to Parliamentary debate to battle, for she sees war as not only continuous, but as violating boundaries of nature and culture. In *Between the Acts*, Giles's violent action is prefigured in the civilization whose imperialist ideologies rest on a history of reciprocal conquest, from the Romans to 'the scars made by the Britons' and borne by 'the Elizabethan manor house' which perpetuates the claims of patriarchal hegemony.[23]

Woolf's pacifism, as it reflected her growing ambivalences about a defensive war, rests on a critique of progressivism that she defines as theorized and practiced by British patriarchy. This critique was shared by other women writers, such as Storm Jameson and Naomi Mitchison, but they drew different conclusions about the relationship between progressivism, patriarchy, and the Second World War. As we have seen in their dystopias, even when men profess to progressivism, their plans to institute social change rely on old hierarchical and gendered arrangements of power, and so they recreate male-dominated political structures. As a result, progressivism becomes an ideological rationale by which solutions to social problems seem to demand that women are subordinated once more. Many women writers fully recognized that this would continue to be the case in a Second World War as the goal of victory would demand a coalition of male power both in the armed forces and in government. While they warned against the social effects of such all encompassing power, many of these writers still felt that another war would be necessary to defeat Hitler and male militarism would have to be its primary weapon. Margery Allingham, for example, also envisions the war as a regression into barbaric violence, but she attributes it differently: by 1940 she

> ... really saw the new German experiment for what it manifestly is: the plainest and most elementary attempt to gain the world by laboriously and meticulously backing the downward drive in the universal equilibrium ... (*Oaken*, p. 154).

For Woolf, victory over Hitler involved not only the violence of the battlefield and the wholesale destruction of civilians, but the official seal on women's subordination. She feared that the gap between fascism and British misogyny was closing as the war against Hitler would require the ultimate valorization of male domination in the fight for a just cause.

This perpetuation of male militarism is part of Woolf's reading of history and progressivism as cyclical and self-defeating. At the beginning of *Between the Acts*, Mrs Swithin is immersed in 'her favourite reading – an Outline of History'; this is clearly a reference to H.G. Wells's perennially popular work of 1919 which, in 1940, at the very moment the peace of 1918 has unravelled, inspires her to reconstruct the past as a descent from 'barking monsters' (*Acts*, p. 8). Woolf is spoofing Wells through Mrs Swithin's enthusiasm, for as domestic as well as epic battles are waged, reinscribed, and performed within and on the lawns of Pointz Hall, humans are seen to descend, not in a progressive march towards greater humanity, but around and down into a tar pit containing their prehistoric and barbaric origins. Collectively, all the players in *Between the Acts* are compulsively driven to retrace their steps from the carefully cultivated garden of the country house to the primordial forests which preceded it. It is thus no coincidence in Woolf's design that Pointz Hall was built 'in a hollow' and the parvenu Oliver men behave in some ways like caricatures of cave men. Old Bart Oliver, proud of the old manor as a monument to his nation's feudal history, combines the behaviour of 'barking monsters' and the commander of 'a regiment' (*Acts*, p. 12). He bawls at his grandchild and dog as if he were training his subordinates to obey like good soldiers.

Amidst such commitment to regimental violence, it is no wonder that Woolf concludes that progressivism, as theorized and practiced by men, leads to war; and that war leads not to peace, 'the third emotion' Woolf designated as mediating between love and hate (*Acts*, p. 92). Instead, war is a compulsive self-destructive habit. The image of Giles stomping on a snake which is choking on a toad belies the idea of progress, for it connotes violence begetting violence. Suggesting a Nazi stormtrooper, the image of Giles exposes the infamy of military victory even over a monster such as Hitler. For Woolf, the result will be 'birth the wrong way round – a monstrous inversion' of peace (*Acts,* p. 99).

In *Between the Acts,* war both leads to and is propelled by such rituals as the pageant at Pointz Hall. Like those on the playing fields of Eton, the Pointz Hall fête commemorates a history of Britannia's conquest and victory over domestic and foreign threats. In Woolf's construction, however, there is not much to celebrate, as the mixed messages of Miss La Trobe's production reveals. In both its domestic and public displays, violence is present in all relationships, whether overt acts of hostility or a more insidious coercion in private relations. In effect, Woolf is arguing, so long as militaristic victory remains the primary solution to political dispute, victors become victims in an endless cycle. In the persistent effort to guard 'respectability and prosperity, and the purity of Victoria's land', men must 'stand, truncheon in hand' (*Acts,* p. 172).

In response to the fragments of history which constitute the pageant's plot, the audience has presupposed coherent meaning, but the narrator teases them and us with reminders that along with 'harmony' and 'unity', 'Dispersed are we' (*Acts,* p. 196).[24] The pageant's conclusion illustrates Woolf's sentiments about the possibilities for conflict resolution at the historic moment of this novel's creation. The characters deliver fragments of their lines accompanied by a confused mix of musical recordings, while bits and pieces of mirroring objects are held up to the audience. The ensuing 'chaos and cacophony' mock the audience's expectations for harmony and coherence (*Acts,* p. 189). Not only is there no coherence in the triumphalist epic, but the pageant emphasizes that the greatest threat to harmony and peace is domestic, the very grounds on which they enjoy themselves. Fulfilling the multiple meanings of the word domestic – attached to home, tamed, intimate, indigenous – the land on which they stand and which is commemorated by the pageant as the foundations of the audience's sense of security, is by its very nature, unstable. As its own celebration implies, home and homeland have produced a history of discord.

The vexed meanings of home and homeland are portrayed in the movement of the fête from the manicured lawns of the estate to the old interior of the barn. Reflecting the nation's long history of discord and dispersion, this move also draws attention to the distances and tensions between Isa and Giles Oliver. As each is attracted to another and yet drawn back to each other, their love-hate relationship reflects not only the emotional nature of marital conflict but the struggles for power that afflict the nation. Husband and wife chafe against each other in a struggle for self-expression and against the controls embedded in the domestic responsibilities and duties each represents. They can only reunite at the end after a fight rekindles their attachment. Even if another child results from their embrace, Woolf's language of compulsion and inevitability – 'they must fight, as the dog fox fights with the vixen, in the heart of darkness, in the fields of night' – suggests that the drive for regeneration and unity here are aligned too comfortably with the brutal instincts of primordial nature (*Acts,* p. 219). But for Woolf, the personal meanings of domestic and family life also resonate with the political. The Olivers' 'fight' continues into the public sphere, recycled into the Pointz Hall pageant as a drama of wars between a male-dominated nation and the women and nations positioned as inferior Others. In Woolf's interpretation of celebrating English history as triumphal, the results of patriarchal victory are not regenerative, however, but enervating.

Despite its creative and performative energy, the affective tone of the Pointz Hall pageant suggests a funeral wake to an exhausted England. The language that commemorates England's isolation from the corruption and sieges of 'France and Germany' also represents England ironically as having 'died away', no different from the great but brutal civilizations of the ancient world, 'Babylon, Nineveh . . . Troy' (*Acts,* pp. 77, 140). For Woolf the political artist, it is as though the act of representing the violence of English history is as damaging as war itself, and so Miss La Trobe feels 'paralyzed' at the end of her play: 'Illusion had failed. "This is death", she murmured, "death"' (*Acts,* p. 140). Whether this sense of defeat is a prelude to Woolf's suicide in March 1941, before the novel was published, before the full extent of Hitler's brutality became known, and before he was defeated, we cannot know. Yet the yearning for hope and harmony that vies with despair in the novel could be said to inscribe the writer's internal war. Whatever the causes of Woolf's depression and suicide, her novel attests to her social analysis of war as an ongoing history, not of victory, but of oppression. In her last novel, her view of history as a continuous cycle is a recognition but also a resistance to arguments for change. On the one hand, her character Mrs Lynn Jones tries to convince herself that at least since Victoria's reign resistance has effectively led to change. But the 'maddening' tick of Woolf's fictional clocks insist that 'They were all caught and caged' by time's violent repetitions (*Acts,* p. 176).

Woolf's ambivalence about World War II moves her to declare that 'The present war is very different' because 'now the male has also considered his attributes in Hitler, & is fighting against them' (Holograph reading notes quoted in Silver, p. 271). At the same time, however, she was convinced that this war was coterminus with the first and that all wars are similarly oppressive operations. Her decision not to participate in any active support for the war was formed not only because she resisted the prevailing slogans and male-dominated political discourse. It was also because even as Hitler had to be defeated, it was not clear that this would change the course of a militaristic history. The title, *Between the Acts,* invokes two world wars, implying that history is both successive and regressive, and that intermissions dramatize the conflicts in personal and social relations that make war continuous. As the novel's historical critique shows, historical change from war to peace requires that authoritarian impulses and institutions be recognized as destructive. Reading Freud in 1939 confirmed her belief in 'subconscious Hitlerism', but also prompted her revisionary idea that 'though many instincts are held more or less in common by both sexes, to fight has always been the man's habit, not the woman's' ('Air-raid', p. 155, *TG,* p. 6). Woolf's political writing exposed the more insidious aggression sanctioned by social structures. But her 'pessimistic' historical vision, which did not foresee any change coming out of World War II also did not allow her to construct the England she loved as committed to reforming itself.[25]

That Woolf viewed World War II as both coterminus with the last and yet apocalyptic in its own right shook her belief in a struggle for change. With boundaries between past and present and war and peace dissolving, there can be no action, including writing, that will turn civilization away from its death instinct. Her conclusion agreed with Freud, as she recorded in her diary on 9 December 1939: 'If we're all instinct, the unconscious, what's all this about civilisation, the whole man, freedom &c?' (*Diary* V, p. 250). This transhistorical, pancultural view collapses distinct events into an epic battle with the barbarians within and at the gates, and disrupts belief in historical change. In 1940, when the Germans began their Blitz, she wrote 'Thoughts on Peace in an Air Raid', an essay in which she wrestled with the possibility that something of value could emerge from this dark moment. She did find hope, but only by defining victory as more than military and by calling for the redefinition of a 'fight for freedom' ('Air Raid', p. 154). Without redefinition this war seemed to Woolf like all other wars, as only the province of men, and therefore the struggle against Hitlerism would remain hopeless. To include women in the struggle for freedom could not only change the course of the war, but the course of peace: 'If [women] could free ourselves from slavery we should free men from tyranny. Hitlers are bred by slaves' ('Air Raid', p. 155). And yet despite this hopefulness, Woolf remained ambivalent. She could not reconcile herself to the purpose and outcome of a war which did distinguish Hitler's 'tyranny' from her nation's patriarchal oppression and which other women writers saw as freeing his victims from a fate worse than 'slavery'.

In that domestic wartime fiction represents war as an internal as well as external struggle, it reveals that there is no common purpose or unity among its women authors. Women's writing of the home front ranged from the deeply conservative to radical calls for change, but whatever their differences, these fictions show many British women forming their own reasons for 'fighting in the front-line trenches . . . for the first time in the world' out of their concerns for the relationship between the past and future and their definitions and location of home and homeland.[26] In much of their writing of the war, patriotic impulses are replaced by imaginative approaches to reconceiving the homeland. Women's varying definitions of homeland reflect their questions about the stability and viability of family life, their own roles within it, and the relationship between these roles and the nation. Their decision to participate in the war thus also exposed 'the tensions and contradictions between the needs of winning the war and the needs of maintaining the traditional gender order'.[27] This tension is evident in a 1940 magazine article by Willa Muir, 'What Should We Tell Our Children?'[28] Even as she assumes the traditional middle-class maternal guardianship of domestic responsibility for the child's moral development, Muir redefines home and nation and calls for change. She insists that the home 'ensure freedom . . . with a balanced relationship between the individual members of the family and the family as a whole' (p. 536) And as an extension of a democratic home, she rejects the idea of imperial Britain in favour of seeing it as one nation interdependent with others of equal sovereignty.

As home front and battleground merged with the actuality of the Blitz, the tensions that resulted spilled over onto the pages of home front fiction. Women writers not only filtered their experience and understanding of World War II through its literary conventions, but used them to question the political ideology of war and its relation to middle class domestic ideology. In these novels geo-political contexts are made social. Though the social frames of many of these novels would reflect the wartime mixing of people from different classes and places, their narrative perspectives and voices reflect the domestic ideologies of the middle classes. Vera Brittain dramatizes the gendered relationship between Britain's wartime ethos and middle class domestic ideology in her 1948 novel of the home front, *Born 1925*. By reversing traditional middle-class gender roles, she argues that war originates in the social pressures that subvert the capacity of educated men to nurture. Her protagonist, the Reverend Robert Carbury, combines her own wartime anguish with the pacifism of her mentor, Dick Sheppard, and agonizes over sending his children abroad and the public censure his anti-war work risks. In contrast, his wife's self-absorbed commitment to her successful acting career reflects on the politics of self-interest Brittain saw in the old guard.

Despite her critiques of narcissistic privilege, Brittain's narrative strategy also effects a disturbing distance from those who suffered most on the British home front. The Carburys see the bombs fall on London's East End, but while they despair over the results, neither fires nor victims encroach on the novel's centre stage, or affect the characters' or narrative consciousness. Brittain never saw her own privileged position as implicated in her decision to send her children to the United States; that this was a safeguard the East Enders could not afford. The novel thus does not relate Robert Carbury's altruism to upper-middle-class paternalism and its links to the old guard that knows only too well how to protect itself and its interests. For while the good reverend ministers to the poor and the feeble and his wife assumes the mantle of self-interest, the novel supports the traditional belief that the home and the nation suffer most when women follow their non-domestic interests.

Many domestic novels written during the war confront their own class and political biases. On the surface, they seem less radical than Brittain's gender reversal and anti-war arguments. For one, they appear to make a simple substitution to accommodate prewar illusions of harmony, homogeneity, and wartime disruptions: the familiar upper-middle-class household is transported to other people's homes in provincial towns which, in Josephine Bell's *Total War at Haverington*, adjust 'less by assimilating the foreigners than by a form of ingestion of them'.[29] In a way of life where change is tantamount to violent illness, a quiet revolution takes places during this domestic invasion. Bell (1897–1987), a practicing physician who also became a well-known writer of detective thrillers, is moved by the war to question some of the most hallowed conventions of genre fiction. The wartime period, according to Bell, instigated changes as though 'the spirit of democracy, expanding shyly under the compulsion of a common purpose, embraced all present. It had not yet grown into that state of rude health it was to attain during the next five years, but . . . [c]lass differences vanished, conventions lapsed' (*TW*, pp. 73–4). This statement could easily be taken for the nostalgia one expects in novels written from the perspective of postwar disillusionment. But that nostalgia is tinged with an irony so persistently ambivalent that it suggests as much call for change as women's dystopias of the thirties and forties.

What happens in these revisionary domestic novels is that in the face of a war on the home front, melancholy yields to a yearning for change, a development which has to be seen as revolutionary because it occurs in 'the class' that Elizabeth Bowen observed, 'in England changes least of all'.[30] *The House in Paris* shows how this upper-middle-class world had withstood 'the Boer War, the [Great] War and other fatigues and disasters [with] so many opportunities to behave well' (*HP*, p. 70). The gentle satire in this statement points to a conservatism which fits quite comfortably into the form of the domestic novel. Its model is the irony which drives the novels of Jane Austen. Set within an ideology which 'glorified the values of family and home', of village commonality and continuity, the ironic twist also shows a tempered resistance to 'duty, self-sacrifice, and endurance'.[31] Despite British losses in World War I and economic disaster, the interwar period was a time of rebuilding a society which still believed it had a shaping role in the world and at home.

With the actual bombing of the home front, however, gentle satire questions the ideological basis of the domestic novel. For Bowen and such writers as Betty Miller, Elizabeth Taylor, Marguerite Steen, and Lettice Cooper, the onslaught of World War II destroyed forever any assumption that the middle-class home was an inviolate sanctuary preserving universally held values. Death and evacuation forced women to confront disturbances in domestic life which earlier could be managed with humour. Without the stability that a secure empire had endowed with purpose and prestige, the roles of housewife and hostess became noticeably frustrating and constraining (Lewis, *Women and England* 116). With bombing and evacuations, as the discreetly ordered interior was blasted open or disrupted by the presence of strangers, women's roles and expectations reversed themselves. Private life, that bastion of middle-class value, could no longer be the retreat for an individuated, insulated self, as Alison Light shows interwar fiction depicting. Norah Hoult (1898–1984), whose novels and stories portray the difficult social and economic conditions of women's lives, wrote a wartime novel, *There Were No Windows*, which questions individualism as an upper class antiquarian privilege. It portrays an eldery woman living with her servant as though they are relics from a Victorian story.

For the woman writer of wartime Britain, a room of one's own is a nostalgic dream. The women in Susan Ertz's *Anger in the Sky* register how that dream has been bombed into a nightmare of exposure, loss, and exile: 'It's the combination of the horrors of war with ordinary, normal life that's so unbearable. . . . We haven't got private lives any longer. . . . the war has . . . destroyed the separateness of the worlds we live in' (*Sky*, pp. 97, 293). The smashing of private space also threatened the opportunity for self-expression that British women had found in writing. We can imagine what Isa Oliver in Woolf's *Between the Acts* would have suffered if the private space in which she did her poetry had been bombed. Rose Macaulay, whose books and papers burned in the Blitz, showed how the war publicly violated women's space in her story, 'Miss Anstruther's Letters'. As she frantically tries to rescue her lover's letters from her gaping apartment, Miss Anstruther feels their 'burning words' 'jabb[ing] at her heart like a twisting bayonet'.[32] As the material realities of men's fighting blasts through their private space, women find themselves isolated from the propaganda messages of the war ministries, and bitterly questioned them. On the one hand, the love letters in Macaulay's story jab at Miss Anstruther as though she is guilty for not being able to protect the artifacts of man's culture. Such guilt, however, ignores the woman's loss of a space in which to give expression to her own feelings, in which she could create a culture of her own. Paradoxically, it is in women's blitzed private space that her individual self-expression forms her definition of community. Unlike prewar Britain, this is a community inhabited by women reading and writing about their own home front wars.

Against the background of Britain's battle, domestic fiction hangs out the dirty laundry and exposes both the vulnerability and revisionary tactics of women for whom private space and middle class domestic ideology have been liberatory but imprisoning as well. The depiction of living in the open, on the move, exposes traditional domestic ideology as a negative force in women's lives; it questions the traditional view that a 'powerful and rewarding sense of community . . . and continuity' are 'necessary values of the nation in wartime' (Feathersone, p. 156). These values are now exposed as propaganda, pressuring women into believing that their best interests lay in reviving the 'angel in the house'; the underlying meaning of 'continuity' was to preserve the traditional domestic sanctuary for which their men were sacrificing their lives. Although domestic fiction had inculcated and perpetuated these values even in the quietest times, (even when it valorized women's interior lives), it took the war to expose the propagandist nature of its conventions – to suggest that the message of domestic novels could fit too easily with that of the Ministry of Information. In their revision of domestic plots, women writers discovered that representing the home front required confronting ideologies which characterized women as 'passive, weak and "naturally" inferior' and which they internalized as a mindset that Elizabeth Bowen identified as an 'unconscious sereneness behind their living and letting live' (Lewis, *Women in England*, p. 135; Bowen *HP*, p. 70).

A wartime short story, 'Tell it to a Stranger', by Elizabeth Berridge, illustrates how domestic ideology under the threat of wartime dispossession could 'dissolve' a woman 'into an understandable hysteria'.[33] Relocated to a seaside resort town, Mrs Hatfield visits her London home only to discover it has been 'ransacked' during an air raid ('Tell', p. 39). Though mildly annoyed by her material losses, her 'heart lift[s]' as she concocts a dramatic story of loss for the new friends who fill the emotional vacuum left by a husband she could never please ('Tell', p. 39). When she returns to her seaside hotel, however, she discovers it has been bombed and her friends are now either dead or wounded. Mrs Hatfield's reaction exposes the extent to which she has been shaped by her material privileges and the myth of continuity they represented. Tearing away at the rubble, she can only utter 'My lovely wineglasses' ('Tell', p. 42). Having been deprived of a space in which to develop a language of self-expression and human intimacy, her human losses have collapsed into the material possessions which have defined her. Like her wineglasses, she has fractured under the pressure of a collapsing myth.

'THIS SHUDDERING NIGHT'[34]: THE LONDON HOME FRONT OF ELIZABETH BOWEN, MARGUERITE STEEN AND LETTICE COOPER

Whoohoo go the goblins, coming back at nightfall,
Whoohoo go the witches, reaching out their hands for us,
Whoohoo goes the big bad wolf and bang go his teeth.
Are we sure we shall be the lucky ones, the princess, the youngest son,
The third pig evading the jaws? can we afford to laugh?
They have come back, we always knew they would, after the story ended.

Naomi Mitchison '1940'[35]

'It was a science fiction novel in action'.

Bryher. *The Days of Mars*

By the time the Blitz of 1940–41 came to a halt, one Londoner in six had experienced homelessness, and yet more people chose to stay than leave. Mollie Panter-Downes reported how this 'concourse of humanity' created a new underground city that at least momentarily, revolutionized the old: 'If history is being torn up by the roots in London, history is also being made'.[36] The city's new complexion, physically pockmarked by fires and blasts and psychologically recoiling from fears of death and invasion, became an imaginative and critical template for many women writers who remained. Its landscape is often remembered and evoked not as wreckage, lifeless and inert, but as shattered but sparkling pieces to be reassembled into tragic-comic collages. The novelist Marguerite Steen captures this imaginative process as always tinged with 'the squalor' and 'tough end of the war', but also as:

> . . . the beautiful, rather than the hideous and terrifying moments; and absurd rather than the tragic events? . . . mornings when we crawled up, blind as moles, from the shelter, to see the crescent moon and the morning star set like jewels in an aquamarine sky; the appalling beauty of nights rose-red with fires. . . . A night when the Hun scored a bull on one of the West End whore-houses, and half-way down the blasted facade was a double bed, with a madly embarrassed coupe, both without a stitch on them, wildly attempting to cover themselves with wooden slats and handfuls of rubble.[37]

For Rose Macaulay, Vera Brittain, and Lettice Cooper, London stood for the aggressive power they identified as a tool of war. But the blitzed city was also a woman-defined object of love. As Vera Brittain reported, its burning exposed it as a female 'companion' facing 'an ordeal' which called upon them 'to endure for her sake' (*EHour*, p. 118).

For so many women writers the besieged city also exposed the relationship between people's resolve, a tremulous social landscape, and their own shifting aims of war and peace. In the second month of the Blitz, after witnessing the death of women and children in a raid, Rose Macaulay analysed her renunciation of pacifism. Despite their different conclusions, her reasons recall Virginia Woolf's sentiments. It is not just the war on women that moves Macaulay but its being the 'sample corner of total war' in which 'Civilian war deaths are no worse than those of the young men in the fighting forces'.[38]

The shocking fusion of battleground and home front spurred many women writers to recognize distinctions that made the war both agonizing and easy to support. At one level, as Bryher recalled, 'Not all things in wartime were bad' because 'one of the taboos that the Blitz was breaking down was that it was wrong to speak to strangers' (*Mars*, p. 17). At another level, the war exposed painful distinctions between the economic conditions of men and women of different social classes. As if these differences were not enough, the lines of gender and class were crossed by the effects of wartime circumstances and historical consciousness on the personal and collective politics of self-interest and that of international responsibility.

Although London's sustained blows affected rich and poor alike, walls between classes did not simply dissolve; instead, they came to resemble Alice's looking glass. When underground shelters became public habitats, people who might otherwise have avoided eye contact became momentary friends. Bryher noted wryly that it was not the upper and lower classes who broke through their mutual suspicion, but 'the lower middles who consider it a status necessity "to keep themselves to themselves"' (*Mars*, p. 17). Ursula Bloom recalled, 'At that time the feeling of comradeship in London was tremendous, as standing side by side we fought the common enemy' (*WIW*, p. 82).[39] But her enthusiasm is dampened by a foreboding of loss: 'I did not know then that when the end came this would go, perhaps for ever. It was a lovely bond none of us could afford to break' (*WIW*, p. 82).

Such nostalgic yearning was in itself divided. The upper classes, like Alice, often found themselves in two realities at once. They suffered human losses, but their material dislocations were often temporary, and unlike the poor, they could escape to the country or to friends when their own homes were battered. The rich also had access to shelters that highighted the war's equalizing dangers as well as their distinct privileges; the basement shelter of the Dorchester Hotel offered the same amenities as its suites, except that room service was en masse. The privations of the rich could therefore afford mockery, as Marghanita Laski showed in her satire of the blitz, *Love On the Supertax*: 'This is not a story of that spring of 1944 as it came to strong vigorous citizens with an ample present and an assurance of the future, but of spring as it came to the needy and the dispirited, to the fallen and the dispossessed of Mayfair.'[40] Laski pokes fun at the gentry who mourn their damaged mansions and ignore the real home front victims, the working class who live 'between the gaps, among the rubble and the destruction' and who ironically, unlike their down-at-the-heels betters, sustain the belief that England's 'static' aristocracy is vibrant, not 'stagnant' (*Love*, p. 6).

If Laski could render the upside-down social morality of the London Blitz with comic élan, Elizabeth Bowen (1899–1973) depicted its psychological disorientation and ambiguities. Her response to World War II was shaped by her historical consciousness of war's desiccation. Born into an Anglo-Irish family, she inherited a history of imperial conquest and domination that led to a protracted struggle for national identity and political culture. The Irish Civil War had brutalized the Irish Catholics and dispossessed many of the Anglo-Irish, and when World War II came, Bowen was able to fuse her historical memory with an experience of heightened consciousness which brought new awareness of imaginative possibilities for her writing. Even as she experienced the bombing of her own home and as an ARP (air raid precautions) warden, the destruction of other homes and their occupants, she found creative impetus:

> Walking in the darkness of the nights of six years (darkness which transformed a capital city into a network of inscrutable canyons) one developed new bare alert senses, with their own savage warnings and notations. And by day one was always making one's own new maps of a landscape always convulsed by some new change. . . . through the particular, in wartime, I felt the high-voltage current of the general pass.[41]

She described how 'self-expression in small ways stopped. . . . One cannot take things in. What was happening was out of all proportion to our facilities for knowing, thinking, and checking up' (*DL*, 96). Her 1949 novel, *The Heat of the Day*, depicts the breakdown of fictional and experiential boundaries, where 'the wall between the living and the living became less solid as the wall between the living and the dead thinned' (*HD*, p. 92).

A story of wartime dispossession, *The Heat of the Day* turns domestic fiction inside out. Not only does it portray the end of private life at this historic moment, but its heroine's psychological divorce from domesticity shows how the war enabled women to resist its ideologies. Forty-year-old Stella Rodney finds that having 'come loose from her mooring' exposes traditional family structures as imprisoning, and so she welcomes dispossession (*HD*, p. 114). An appropriate position for her ambivalences, transience allows her to maneuver between two conventional plots which threaten to captivate her – a love story and a spy thriller. Living in a borrowed flat with a few token possessions parallels the unstable ground which threatens her personal and political commitments. Having discovered that her lover is spying for the Nazis, she is torn between defining her responsibility to their relationship and to her vulnerable country. Stella's ambivalences remain unresolved. Encircled by historic events she has no role in shaping, she is also subject to Bowen's reading of fictional possibilities for female character. Bowen marries Stella off at the end, but what remains most powerful for the reader is the sense that in her elusiveness, Stella has resisted the moral and literary categories so readily available to stabilize her.

The Heat of the Day suggests the mutability of women's character in a fleeting connection between two women of different classes. Working class Louie Louis envies Stella's elegance, fantasizing that it represents her character and life, but Stella's appearance turns out to be one more entrapping fiction. As Stella herself makes an ambiguous peace at the end, so must Louie. Stella seems to comply to a domestic plot by remarrying, but her disappearance from the end of the narrative suggests that Bowen has also wrenched her from any conventional reader expectations. Louie, on the other hand, seems to emerge as a more aggressively self-determining character. She takes charge by creating a self-defining fiction. Louie invents a hero husband whose death allows her to shape her character independent of its social and literary antecedents. And yet as the white birds fly overhead at the novel's conclusion, signalling peace and a new horizon, Louie is wheeling her baby's carriage, another domestic model of female character. Presenting Louie as a single mother, however, the novel positions itself in an interplay of self-questioning fiction and social reality. If the war has provided opportunities to imagine open-ended fates for female characters, as it ends, the fictive landscape is invaded once again, by the social and economic realities which British women's fiction has never sought to escape.

Social and historical realities have often lurked behind the scenes of Bowen's fiction, a narrative strategy that positions readers to focus on the more surreal surfaces of her imaginative topography. Her surreal mapping exposes her characters' 'unconscious, instinctive' 'hallucinations' as the 'saving resort' of wartime experience, and for this Bowen's short fiction has been rightly celebrated as capturing the disorienting experience of the blitzed cityscape (*DL*, p. 96). In 'Mysterious Kor' the 'war-climate' of London resembles that in a ghost story, registering not the traumatic event, such as an air raid, but its after shocks which produce a state of 'lucid abnormality' (*DL*, p. 95). The narrator's blueprint of the historic moment, when '[t]he Germans no longer came by the full moon', works in tandem with the story's focus on her heroine's psychological experience and imaginative reflections that connect this war with imperial destruction in the ancient world.[42] The combination produces a self-reflexive and self-questioning fiction that provides an interpretive strategy to this war. Bowen explains the appeal of such a strategy in her 1947 broadcast about the fiction which gave 'Mysterious Kor' its title – Rider Haggard's *She*. At the same time that she recalled the story's 'soaring unrealism' being 'ideally directed' to herself as a 'non-moral' 12-year-old reader, Bowen chooses to mention 'the thunder clouds which were to burst in 1914' as an event of which she had been unaware at the time.[43] The historical and psychological bridge between the child reader and adult writer and the two world wars is a compelling matter for Bowen, for what shapes the writer's creative figuration and her World War II characters is the historical omnipresence of war.

'Mysterious Kor' evokes both the desolated ancient imperial city of Rider Haggard's *She* and the threat of imperial conquest in the modern age. Acutely aware of military conflict as an imperial enterprise, in her broadcast Bowen invokes not only the 'vanished civilization' of Kor and two world wars, but the English Civil War and, more subtly but thus significantly, her own historical identity in the Irish struggles for independence from Britain ('She', p. 110). For Bowen, the imperialist impulse begins in the psychological 'wish for accession to full power', a problem she was to explore in so much of her fiction ('She', p. 107). With particular resonance, her phrase implicates her in the history of her family as part of the Anglo-Irish ascendancy, the emotional and political damage of which she traced in her chronicle, *Bowen's Court*. As an adult writer living in blitzed London she takes a critical stance in relation to imperial conquest and its appeal as an 'adventure' story to a 'non-moral' child ('She', p. 108). Lurking behind the scene of her story 'Mysterious Kor' is Haggard's story of Britain's self-defined claim to inherit the spoils of another empire. As Bowen interprets *She*, Britain justifies its imperial 'adventure' through its civilizing mission, which carries the self-proclaimed wisdom of 'quiet college rooms' to a 'savage tribe' on 'the Eastern shore of Central Africa – a perilous coast' ('She', p. 109).

The peril for Bowen is mutual, even universal, as empire confronts empire around the globe and across time. Thus, from Dublin to London and to Kor, she extracts 'the idea that life in any capital city must be ephemeral, and with a doom ahead' ('She', p. 111). Bringing her childhood memory of imagined Kor to blitzed London, the latter looks 'like the moon's capital – shallow, cratered, extinct' ('Kor', p. 728). The deadness that war brings destroys not only human lives but the sense that even for those who survive, the now barren ground on which they had depended for nurture is the result of a human propensity for domination. As a commentary on human evolution, the story's historicizing strategies resemble Virginia Woolf's *Between the Acts*. But where Woolf's characters are enervated by their unrelenting drive towards conflict, Bowen's are energized by their imaginative yearning for both power and reconciliation. Although the plot of 'Mysterious Kor' is about the stresses of wartime dispossession, it expresses the desire for something beyond being grounded either in a stable place or in human connectedness. Despite the frustrated relations between the lovers, Pepita and Arthur, and Pepita and her roommate, Callie, the story works towards keeping them apart. Going beyond the elusiveness of Stella's character in *The Heat of the Day*, Bowen here establishes Pepita's irritability as a mechanism separating her from others and giving her a psychological space in which to imagine a woman's power of self-determination.

For Pepita, restless and wary of the emotional and moral authority of both sexual intimacy and friendship, the desolate city of Kor suggests a 'disenchanted' world, a space that invites imaginative and critical play ('Kor', p. 730). Her reflections and dreams of Kor enact the implications of unleashed desire and power where sexual and imperial power intersect at the dangerous point of domination. That such power becomes a problem beyond the self is evident in the character of She-who-must-be-obeyed, the larger than life ruler of Kor. Lurking in the cracks and crannies of Bowen's story, the ancient city and its Queen are present in the World War II story and as its inspiration. Suggestive of both female sexual power and the power of empire, She, as Bowen concluded in her broadcast, 'with [h]er proud, ambitious spirit would be certain to break loose and avenge itself for the long centuries of solitude. In the end, I had little doubt, she would assume absolute rule over the British dominions, and probably the whole world. . . .' ('She', p. 112). Like Pepita, She is trapped in a space created for her by a past, present, and future history of political rivalry and conquest. But whereas She is also imprisoned by her author, that is, Haggard's male imagination of female destructiveness, Pepita is freed by the woman writer's critical imagination. The very 'finality' of Kor which represents the end of imperial solutions is for Pepita the beginning of a new kind of plotting for female character entrapped in war ('Kor', p. 740). Having fallen asleep at the end, drifted off, so to speak, from the romantic fiction which shaped her story, she also escapes into her own imaginative space. Her lover has been 'the password, but not the answer: it was to Kor's finality that she turned' ('Kor', p. 740).

Not all of Bowen's wartime fiction depicted the imaginative possession of place as a possibility for the construction of the female self. Particularly for her male characters, as in the story 'Ivy Gripped the Steps', the loss of a stable place and the failure of imagination to provide an alternative is very threatening.[44] Though sympathetic to such a plight, Bowen is also critical of the imperialist connotations of an identity attached to the idea of possessing a country. Like Virginia Woolf's refutation of 'My country', Bowen's critique embeds a fear of the desire for power that accompanies a sense of personal worth dependent upon a nationalist identity. She herself reveled in her dual nationality, and although she loved her Irish ancestral home, Bowen's Court, spending summers there whenever possible, she made her adult life in England. When the war broke out and her visits to Bowen's Court were curtailed, her historic memories of Anglo-Irish conflict became overlaid with tensions between the Republic of Ireland's neutrality and Britain's war with Nazi Germany. At peace with her dual identity, she accepted an assignment from the Ministry of Information to report on Irish attitudes towards the war. She was able to empathize with 'Eire's first major independent act' while questioning it from the moral perspective of what she called 'freedom's war'.[45]

It was her belief in the war as representing interest beyond national borders that led her to begin writing her Anglo-Irish family chronicle in 1939. The values she brought to *Bowen's Court* were based on 'taking the attachment of people to places as being generic to human life, at a time when the attachment was to be dreaded as a possible source of too much pain'.[46] The 'dreaded pain' reflects not only the possibility that a home might be lost but that home and homeland represent sites of oppressive power. Thus in so much of Bowen's writing throughout her career houses are haunted by histories of 'infatuation with the idea of power'

(*BC*, pp. 454–5). Through its trajectory of family and political history, *Bowen's Court* shows how these histories begin in 'the private cruelty' in family homes and then radiate outwards to shape national rivalries and 'world war' (*BC*, p. 455). Thus at the moment of World War II, the lives of her ancestors made Bowen 'conscious at almost every moment of nightmarish big analogies everywhere' (*BC*, p. 455).

If fantasies of power lead to conquest, domination, and, in World War II, mass extermination, Bowen sees this as a result of 'the outsize will' having no outlets for expression that are healthy for itself and those it affects (*BC*, p. 455). But in addition to those who would suffer in the wake of the frustrated giant, Bowen's victims are often women whose wills are undersize but who nonetheless crave expression for which their homes and homeland provide no outlets. Pepita's imaginative place, Stella's elusiveness and Louie's fictional family represent only one side of Bowen's story of women's oppression in their homes and homeland. 'The Demon Lover', by contrast, features a woman who is taken prisoner during the Blitz by the ghost of her World War I fiancé. His actions remind us that the tragic death of a nation's soldiers reverberates in its continuation in another world war. These wars, however, do not produce their tragedies only on the battlefield. The woman who cannot escape her ghostly lover must suffer the guilt for having survived the war he died for and for which he is now punishing her. In Bowen's story, tragedy begins in the domestic codes which situate the woman survivor as guardian of the soldier's well being. At the end of the story, having run out of her house to escape his haunting of it, Kathleen Drover finds herself a prisoner of the demon soldier in the taxi which she thought was her refuge. Like a military vehicle out of control, the taxi will drive her around its circular and destructive route to nowhere. That there is no context between the powerless woman and the 'outside will' of her demon lover is symbolized by the lack of a place in history to nurture her will. If her lover has been granted his 'outsize outlet' by the military action which renders him inhuman, he uses it to situate Kathleen Drover as his victim and victimizer (*BC*, p. 455). Finally, we can say, he drove her to his no man's land, the place where two world wars converge in perpetuity.

Bowen's analysis of women's historic and symbolic wartime roles as resistant and victimized is borne out by social realities.

Women's actual progress towards self-determination was complicated by wartime conditions and government policies, but many novels of the period show them using their prescribed roles as a mask which could conceal their search for alternative outlets. It is as though the absence or tenuous presence of men leaves a gap in which women redefine themselves in relation to each other. The psychological analysis of female character through introspection or narrative intervention is replaced by women speaking to and through each other, either directly, or in response to the other's character and behaviour. Conventional relationships between women competing for limited access to economic and social stability could be imagined to assume new dimensions once the men went off and women discovered the pleasures, pressures, and pains of living with each other.[47] So in Sylvia Townsend-Warner's wonderful story, 'Sweethearts and Wives', a crazy quilt mix of evacuated women learn through their growing comraderie that the men they long for are also an invasive presence in their new community.

Marguerite Steen (1894–1975), best known for her trilogy of the Bristol merchant Flood family and novels of Spain, produced a novel of the London Blitz that attends to the issue of class and personal conflict among women whose domestic space is made public and unstable. Published in 1941, *Shelter* was inspired by Steen's experiences and takes place in the fall of 1940 with the onset of mass bombing. Her prologue sets an atmosphere in which all assumptions about continuity and human connection are dashed. The loveliness of the 'sun-drugged' late summer signals the end of days for those manners and morals that marked stability for the middle classes. It is a summer so tropical that while it provides an illusion of 'peaceful squares' and 'happy parks', it also signals the shock brought home by that most intense period of the Blitz, when London was bombed every night – that England is not a self-sufficient, homogeneous island, home to the happy breed.[48]

Steen's novel focuses the shock of war on women whose emerging sense of being marginalized in the war effort urges them to question 'the Briton's conception of war: the stiff upper lip, keeping the home fires burning' (*S*, p. 11).[49] In this same light, Vera Brittain recalled how war propaganda not only 'conceal[ed] the chaos and distress caused by the air-raids', but 'threatened . . . humane values' by extolling the virtue of 'Taking it' (*T EX*, p. 274). This credo, a legacy from the Great War, struck Brittain as producing not heroism, but a denial of death and dehumanization, 'submitting our standards, our consciences, and our capacity for thought to progressive brutalisation' (*T EX*, p. 274). A related story by Sylvia Townsend-Warner, 'Rainbow Villa', shows women isolated from each other by the domesticated version of 'taking it' – where 'a nice cup of tea' will 'pull you together'.[50] For those women in Steen's novel, coping with every imaginable insecurity, the idea of patriotism, especially as its meaning derives from a prewar trust in continuity and stability, elides the war's dehumanizing economic fissures:

> . . . this was a war for the leisured classes. If you had a private income, a husband in a position to support you, or a relative in "high society", you cold be fairly sure of getting a salaried post of some kind, probably with a uniform thrown in. . . . If you needed to earn your living, you had a choice between something at thirty shillings or, in exceptional cases, two pounds ten, with fares, food, and personal upkeep to come out of it. It was difficult to be patriotic on these terms . . . (*S*, p. 20).

In these fictions of the London front, women already isolated by terror and loss of community are further divided by the social and economic codes implicated in expressions of traditional patriotism. Boundaries of class that survived one world war assume new trappings in *Shelter* with the 'smarter sorts of uniform' that mark differences between the 'cushy end of the war', paid, and volunteer war work (*S*, p. 48). Such social tension becomes the focus of celebrating the end of the war in Dorothy Scannell's comic memoir of the home front, *Dolly's War*, where the complaints of one woman are mocked by the economic plight of another: 'Amy had worked at various jobs, so that with Jimmy's full and increased pay from his reserved occupation, and Amy's salaries, the £78 Marjorie received for five years' separation and hardship was only cigarette money compared to Amy's affluence.'[51]

Despite available evidence of such inequities, it was difficult to squash the buoyancy produced by another reality – British steadfastness under fire. Equating heroism with progressivism, outsiders especially, saw the war as having had an equalizing effect on British society. Margaret Culkin Banning, an American novelist reporting on the war's effect on English women, was very optimistic about women being 'shaken loose from' their 'class-ridden' dependencies on parents and husbands, and saw wartime conditions 'making women less narrow in a social point of view'.[52] Steen's novel, however, exposes a different perspective. Women who don't fit into the War Ministries' categories for paid and volunteer work are isolated by a sense of irrelevancy, and therefore 'ashamed to get together, as they might have done, to make some form of mutual diversion – ashamed because they felt they also ought to be doing an active war job', (*S*, p. 120). This shame only added another layer to Britain's class consciousness. Rather than war work having an equalizing effect, its categories provided new ways of devaluing women's labour, as Naomi Jacob noted about 'the thousand and one small, uncounted jobs', which were distinguished from the more 'spectacular work of the war'.[53] Women themselves were ambivalent about all types of war work. Many women felt a great sense of independence from earning more money from war work than they had ever controlled. On the other hand, a 1941 survey concluded that 'Although most women publicly agreed that women should do their part in the war effort, in private many had strong reservations' about working conditions, pay, and whether they would have to leave home to work.[54] Steen argues that the problem arises structurally, because of the lack of government guidance: 'masses of [women's] potential energy' were 'wasting in shelters' (*S*, p. 120). Through a panorama of women's responses to the Blitz, *Shelter* shows how this waste is generated by social policies which rely on women's compliance with class and gender roles that formerly served their security.[55]

Steen's concentration on the first month of the Blitz becomes a dramatic metaphor for women's transformation. Portraying their experience as alternating moments of boredom and fear conveys the sense that the women's passivity is shaken into recognition of their social constraints by the bombs' relentless shockwaves.[56] Steen's women are energized paradoxically by the recognition that intransigent government policies have manipulated them from feeling merely vulnerable into paralysis. Her heroine, trapped in an unhappy marriage, jobless, and cynical about performing her duty or expressing patriotism, discovers that women's self-effacement, their sense that 'if we could not be a direct help, at least we need not be a hindrance . . . was failing us' (*S*, p. 12). Steen transforms Louise's entropy into a new kind of war aim:

> Women were, in fact showing themselves to an extraordinary degree independent of men and their opinions. It was as if

they were saying, "This is going to be our war, and we're showing you we're ready". Ready for what? Most of them did not know, but they seemed to have the dim idea that slacks and head scarfs helped towards it. (*S*, p. 23)

In one sense, this statement reflects a romantic wish that could all too easily be manipulated by propaganda, especially because of the double messages women were internalizing about trading in their dresses. Pants could symbolize strength and self-sufficiency, but women's magazine ads were urging readers 'to compensate' with make-up while there was also disdain for 'making themselves "cheap"' (*Cage*, p. 166). Steen's novel confronts the wartime double bind that undermined women's sense of agency; propaganda called upon women to fulfill their destinies by following orders. *Shelter* shows how those restraints were deeply embedded in the failure of wartime conditions and culture to erase traditional constructions of femininity as defined by their need for men's heroic protection: Even when Louise's 'feminism rose', 'she thrust it back. It wasn't the time for feministic flag-wagging, and, after all, the men were taking the tough end of it. What can a woman really do to be useful in the war? Not give trouble' (*S*, p. 152). As an alternative, the novel builds a plot that bonds Louise to other women, in particular, her husband's sister and his mistress. This plot not only subverts that of romance and loss, but creates a cultural vehicle for women to define what is 'really useful' to them in wartime.[57]

The expression of women's needs and the subversion of romance plots in novels of the Blitz had an impact on women writers' construction of masculinity. Male characters in these novels highlight the difficulties of negotiating the value of their home front service and their often antiromantic personae. Rather than emphasize the good fortune of being the only men available, many women writers depict men's home front work – as firefighters and bomb squads, air raid wardens and espionage agents – as essential but lacklustre compared to the tales of daredevil victories and losses in the skies above. Monica Dickens's 1943 novel, *The Fancy*, addresses the masculinist biases of wartime work as they emerge in the character of a munitions factory foreman, Edward Ledward. In a story where the lives and work of both men and women converge to build and defend against lethal weapons, Dickens explores heroic meaning through Ledward's private retreat into nurturing. In his spare time, he devotes himself to breeding rabbits in his backyard, an activity prone to community ridicule and scorn because its inconsequentiality and caregiving combine to suggest the maternal. For Dickens, this transformation of maleness provides the basis for building a lasting peace.

In *The Heat of the Day* Stella Rodney's preference for homelessness answers Bowen's question of whether 'all wartime writing is not resistance writing?' (*DL*, p. 97). For Stella represents a threat to the men who rely on her nurturing to motivate their war work. A critical commentary on the masculinist traditions that underwrite her nation's identity, Stella's resistance is a betrayal of England's male centred hold on stability at the very moment her lover is committing an act of treason by spying for the Nazis. Unwilling, in the final analysis, to provide succour for either her spy lover or the counterspy who enlists her support, this woman redefines her femininity by betraying masculine desires. For the men who came home from the battlefronts, these desires could be translated as comfort and renewed motivation to fight, and thus it is no surprise that propaganda campaigns conceived women as indispensible. One propaganda poster, entitled 'Embarkation leave', shows a soldier about to be restored to battle by his family's care, the orchestration of which is marked by 'Mother's chattering on and laughing / As if parting were just fun'. Commercial advertising appealed to women's acquiescence to self-sacrifice and the pressure women felt to do their bit by catering to their men. A wartime cartoon ad for Mrs Peek's puddings portrays a wife apologizing to her husband for not having prepared him a hot meal because of her air warden duties. The last square of the cartoon embeds his expectation that she can only do her real bit by resigning her job. The highlighted name of the product applauds the role of wife as the nation's saviour, and not her juggling of two jobs.[58]

As so many women writers of the home front show, however, women not only juggled escalating responsibilities, but did so with the kind of self-consciousness that questioned the gendered boundaries which denied the complexities of their lives. These writers argue that the femininity prized by middle-class women was threatened neither by holding down men's jobs nor by their own often aggressive critical questioning. Such fictive recognition highlights the masculinist theme of claiming supremacy. For despite the differences of the second world war from the first, the dualities of righteous power on the battlefield keep rising, like living dead, to serve gendered and cultural hierarchies once again. One of the more remarkable fictional efforts to dissolve such dualities is Lettice Cooper's very fine 1947 novel, *Black Bethlehem*. Already known as a writer and editor for *Time and Tide* and Labour Party activist, Cooper (1897–1994) made politics the centre of her fiction. The plot of her 1938 novel, *National Provincial*, sets a revisionist socialism against its older guard. During World War II, she worked for the Ministry of Food and wrote for *Time and Tide*, but did not write another novel until the war was over.

Her retrospective view in *Black Bethlehem* is panoramic and dialectic, juxtaposing the varying and competing perspectives of 'The Man', 'The Woman', and 'The Child': the primary players are Alan Marriot, a returning soldier, his mother, Lucy, a Women's Service Volunteer, Marta, a Czech refugee, and a small desperately frightened child. Using the period of 1944–1945 as a watershed of war and peace consciousness, Cooper focuses on the soldier's quest to understand the war in concert with the experiences and roles of those men and women who serve on the home front. Thus Alan's changing views are reflected in a spectrum of characters who identify themselves as pacifists, socialists, and pragmatists, as well as victims, cynics and activists. This panorama coincides with Cooper's own synthetic view, which she expressed in her political pieces in *Time and Tide*. On May 1, 1939, the day of Hitler's Reichstag speech, she surveyed her Lancashire compatriots, and identified with both their cynical dismissal of the führer's words and the pragmatic activism that would drive them to feel that 'we may have to take notice of what he does'.[59] At the same time that her 'we' expresses her allegiance with the idea of collectivity, the essay also endorses the development of an individual political and moral consciousness, both working together to produce a discursive system of checks and balances. Like Storm Jameson and Naomi Mitchison, Cooper was a participant observer in English politics and questioned her own allegiances and attitudes as they shifted in response to growing international crisis.

In *Black Bethlehem*, such a revision occurs in a woman's critical response to the soldier's quest. This is narrated in his mother's diary, going back to November 1940 as the moment when she notes that the privileges of upper middle class personal, social, and political life ended. As the war began, spilling into the streets and undergrounds of London, it made a sham of any coherent individual consciousness or collective political vision. It is this collision of public and personal that shapes the character of London into a smoking and smashed *Black Bethlehem*, an unholy place where the child at the end can represent a saviour only if a spirit of interdependence is born from the city's ashes to support him. Conversely, the novel insists that the meaning of the war itself, however broad its reach, can only be assessed by showing its impact on the individual lives and consciousness of men and women as they shape a complex and contradictory collective. Working dialectically, the novel shows both the absurdity of valuing one kind of individual or collective suffering over another while arguing for making distinctions. These distinctions include not only the complex social and political allegiances of the British, but the distinctiveness of historical consciousness.

One remarkable achievement of this novel is its relationship between prevailing gender stereotypes and attitudes towards the war. Recording different responses of men and women to the war's causes and aims, the novel registers a debate reminiscent of Virginia Woolf's *Between the Acts*: whether 'biological man' is a survivor constituted by brute force or 'one who can learn to live on a basis of good will', whether 'an aggressive spirit' is endemic to all men and whether women 'inwardly participate in wars to the same degree'.[60] Because of the particularity with which Cooper treats her characters' participation in the war, these terms question universal or essentialist levels of inquiry. 'Inwardly' motivated constitutions of men and women are complicated by their socially constructed responses to such political issues as letting those with brute force 'get away with things' as happened in Czechoslovakia (*BB*, p. 219). As a result of her complex gender characterizations, Cooper's analysis of war shows that the realms of feeling and pragmatics as well as differences between caring and aggression are not divided between women and men respectively but coalesce in the process of coming to terms with the 'universal guilty conscience' produced by the politics of appeasement and the brutalities even a just war necessitates (*BB*, p. 27).

The publication of that 'guilty conscience' comes in the form of Alan Marriot's broadcasts in the Spring of 1945 just before victory is declared. Deriving from an intensely personal experience of fearful, anguished, and grief stricken heroism, Marriot's battle narrative becomes public and universal over the air waves, inviting his diverse audience to share the recognition that the collective costs of victory include assuming individual moral responsibility for whatever deadly actions Hitler, the unambiguously evil enemy, incites. Like an air raid of peaceful means and ends, Alan's radio voice demolishes the separation between civilian and soldier and problematizes that between enemy soldier and the voices of men and women. Alternating between 'I' and 'we', as Cooper did in 'Politics in the Provinces', Alan shows the interdependence not only of individual and collective resolve and guilt, but that regardless of the different moral imperatives and political and military aims of each army, as they destroy each other, their distances dissolve, until, in death or grief, they occupy the same space.

Alan's broadcast is made in brief statements summarizing the events of a German counterattack on his platoon's advance on the Rhine in December 1944. His public language is glossed by the inclusion of his unspoken reactions alternating and interrupting the battle narrative for the reader but not, of course, for the radio audience. The public voice is stereotypically male – understated, objective, free of feeling and full of 'taking it'. Like a propaganda machine, it delivers the message of a uniquely British heroism, inherited from the language of forbearance that marketed the victories and masked the failures of the Great War. But the inclusion of Alan's emotional responses in the written text undermines the rhetoric of a masculinist war machine. His asides for readers reveal that if there is anything just about the second world war it is reflected in the empathy and caregiving that will make victory a lasting value. The focus of this empathy is on a German prisoner referred to in the broadcast only as a nameless wounded object for whom 'We did what we could' (*BB*, p. 32). The collective and casual voice masks the feelings in Alan's private reflections but expresses the political urgency Cooper attaches to the gendered discourse of the aims of war. After the broadcast, Alan's thoughts are revealed as obsessed with the German who has become an individual in his own right and part of the Englishman's emotional and political experience. The symbol of their connection is a photograph Alan finds of the German's daughter, representing the caregiving imperative of a family relationship, but also the hostilities of war. But rather than construct an essential split between feminist caring and masculinist aggression, the novel explores their interplay, the process by which men and women become, as Rose Macaulay observes, 'all part of the blind, maniac, primitive, stupid bestiality of ... total war' ('Notes', p. 981). For Alan, it 'seems absurd there should be different languages' when 'We're all in the same boat really' (*BB*, p. 32).

Lettice Cooper questions her own vehemently anti-war position by not offering Alan's universalist language as the last word. The private document of his mother's diary, like Alan's unspoken anguish, becomes part of a public debate on war aims as it repositions feminist categories of caring and conflict into the realm of the geo-political and is published in this novel to be engaged by readers. Although Lucy shares her son's private anguish about the war's brutalities, she is unambivalent about her war work and about Britain's war aims to defeat Hitler. Lucy's diary reveals her emotional identification with another war victim, but it also argues that similarities in individual suffering could not erase the differences between the war aims of Germany and Britain. She recounts the story of Marta, a Czech refugee whose husband was murdered by the Nazis. Witness to countless acts of Nazi terror, Marta can only conclude that 'the news that England and France had declared war on Germany ... was good news' (*BB*, p. 146). In its interpolated form, Marta's story comments on Lucy's and on Alan's narratives, and in her position as victim and involuntary exile, questions any universalist claims that deny 'a clear division ... between bad people and good ones', claims that all too easily rationalize malevolent acts: 'If you had lived in Europe in the last three years you would not have any doubt' (*BB*, p. 183). But even as her impassioned plea is supported by historical evidence, it is also not the novel's last word on individual and collective guilt and responsibility. When Marta is discovered to be having an affair with Lucy's lover, she is no longer simply an object of oppressive geo-politics, but the role of victimized Other has also made her an agent of her own oppressive personal politics, and thus undermines her distinctions between good and evil.

Working against the politically motivating forces Marta indicts as rationalization, Cooper positions her in a love triangle where each subject, male and female, is complicit and therefore responsible for the betrayal of the others. Inside the triangle are the personal relationships that are separated from the geo-political contexts which form the outside, and yet in sharing a boundary, impinge on each other. In this way men and women are both shaped by and responsible for the twin contexts of personal and geo-political structures.

The interdependence that Cooper imagines in her plotting is similar to that proferred by Storm Jameson, and in its linkage of personal and family relations to the nation, to Betty Miller and Elizabeth Taylor, as we shall see. Cooper ends her novel with a chapter whose title and subject privilege the perspective of 'The Child', but which connects individual and collective consciousness and responsibility. Looking backward to September 1935, the chapter presents a child's fear of abandonment to highlight the role of the family as moral and emotional basis of the nation. This same fear, which drove Cooper herself to abandon writing novels for the war's duration, is present in her poem 'New Year, 1939' in which she asks:

> How can I write a novel in the world today?
> . . . where the baby at the breast
> Is only safe for the next minute . . .[61]

The child in *Black Bethlehem* is soothed, ultimately, by an air raid warden who despite having been wounded himself, defines his work as nurturing the nation's next generation out of their fear. The future represented in his hopefulness is defined by Cooper in her poem 'New Year' as 'that decency', the 'something left that cannot die?'.

Like so many of her compatriots, Cooper's criticisms of Britain's misguided and oppressive social and political goals and policies are balanced by a narrative structure in which unrelated characters form an interdependent family of British society as the goal of peace. Thus, although Alan Marriot realizes that the war was not the one 'we really wanted to fight', what 'matters' is that 'England does stand for something that mustn't be lost' (*BB*, p. 118). Such a statement could easily seem to reflect either the exceptional nature of World War II or an aberration on the part of an avowed feminist social critic. As it coincides so powerfully with other women writers over the vast and complicated spectrum of war politics and ideologies, it must, however, be considered otherwise.

Across the divide of all fictional genres, from mass audience popular romance to less accessible experimental fiction, British women writers transformed the unsafe quiet and chaos of the home front into a living laboratory for the critique and creation of an imaginative empiricism. Ruthlessly and sometimes even comically, they explored and questioned 'that decency' and pragmatism that enabled them to live from one anxious moment to another but which were so taken for granted in British cultural ideology that they had also served to justify exploitative and oppressive domestic and class relations. It is in the hopefulness towards which so many of their creative and critical experiments yearn that we find alternative definitions of the cultural keywords that these women writers find at the hearth of British domestic relations. In the act of creating critical redefinition, at the moment war will strike, throughout its duration, and in their retrospective reflections, they exercise the resolve that keeps these women writers from allowing silence or the possibility of a 'lost war' to victimize them.

5

'Perpetual Civil War': Domestic Fictions of Britain's Fate[1]

'THE BORROWED HEARTH'[2]: BETTY MILLER AND ELIZABETH TAYLOR

British women writers represented the shattering social conditions of the home front; the bombing, however, usually provided only a backdrop to dramas instigated more by the social pressures driven by wartime domestic ideology. Many writers only found the emotional stability to write about women's wartime lives years after, while others felt compelled by the urgency of the moment to put pen to paper, even as paper was becoming a luxury. Noel Streatfeild, a successful children's author, wrote in her diary of the Blitz: 'Tried to write yesterday and couldn't. Repeated to myself over and over again all that anyone has ever said about carrying on as usual, but sat with my pen in my hand staring at a blank sheet'.[3] For some women writers the end of the war was therefore cause for many celebrations, not the least of which was the peaceful time to translate their wartime experiences into written narratives. One of the most successful examples is dramatized in the work and life of Betty Miller (1910–65), who was still struggling to become a serious writer when the war broke out. Having to uproot herself and her two children each time her psychiatrist husband was moved to a different army hospital made the act of writing impossible. But the experience also inspired her major novel, *On the Side of the Angels*, which resounds with the clashes of army and domestic life. She later said that in order for a wife and mother to become a writer, she would 'have to conform with . . . all the rituals of domesticity . . . but keep the true faith to yourself and hide every trace of it'.[4]

In her novel, *On the Side of the Angels*, the 'sereneness' of women's courageous resolve is tied to their entrapment in the domestic and romantic myths legitimized by total war. Honor Carmichael's relocation to a Cotswold town where her husband Colin will serve as army medical officer signals women's isolated status amidst the conflict between the family life established among the officer corps, the village community which keeps army wives at arm's length, and the expectations of the middle-class family home. The routines that unite these public and private worlds and yet keep them embattled are used by Miller to reflect how women became catalysts for change in the social morality of the British upper middle class and in the domestic novel. The novel opens with a section called 'Afternoon', evoking the sense that even though life and purpose 'flagg' and 'wilt' in an atmosphere of lassitude they also 'hissed with unavailing fury, like a kettle on the boil' (*Angels*, pp. 7, 9). The domestic metaphor is an appropriate bridge between the aimless, deflated home front of the 'phoney war' depicted in Evelyn Waugh's *Put Out More Flags* and the battles raging around the world. For it is the women, managing a domestic camp of British displaced persons, who will 'throw off the afternoon sloth, to seek again the direction, purpose, relinquished during these hours of inertia' (*Angels*, p. 9).

War, in *On the Side of the Angels*, is both an experience and the subject of debate for the two central female characters. Recalling Eliot's *Middlemarch*, Lawrence's *Women in Love*, and Elizabeth Bowen's *Friends and Relations*, Miller's novel works around two sisters who represent different responses to the power structures which drive the war machine, but which are now exposed as having primed the heart of British middle-class society. In a 'state of perpetual civil war', Claudia is a portrait of ambivalence (*Angels*, p. 99). She is 'irritated' by 'all this male pirouetting' and by her older sister's 'complacency, accepting everything' (*Angels*, p. 18). Yet despite the fact that she is a teacher of history, its lessons are lost on her when she is seduced into a romance starring a tall, dark commando, the enigmatic Neil Herriot. Claudia searches for her own point of view between two traditional tales which inscribe the constraint of women in both fictional and social conventions. Engaged to a young man with a damaged heart, she is expected to become part of his tradition bound and privileged family home, but in her vision of it as 'the future', she is already 'opposed' to the 'cherished past' of 'the temperate life at Honeybourne' (*Angels*, pp. 23, 72). Although some critics have argued that Miller supports Andrew's attitudes, the novel actually charts Claudia's unsteady course between two positions: Andrew's eloquent arguments about 'our own deepest inclinations and desires' as the basis of war and the life or death rhetoric of her imposter commando, Herriot (*Angels*, p. 78).[5] At the end, Claudia chooses Andrew, and as a result, tempers the two men's equally romantic if opposed views of war. This alliance between a man with a heart problem and a woman who is a 'potential source of unrest' reflects a feeling of 'affectionate irony' towards the future of their nation (*Angels*, pp. 40, 238).

Claudia and her sister struggle against men's stories about war. Unlike Claudia, however, Honor rarely speaks openly for herself, living only in the expectation that she will embroider herself into the texture of a man's world. In the merged society of a garrison town, the private space of the home is invaded by the military priority of mending injured men without compromising their public image of unbroken heroism. Whatever power had formerly been allocated to 'the angel in the house' is revealed, in this home front war, to rely on a myth of domestic separateness. Tending to their domestic duties, mindful of 'military secrets', women maintained this myth with self-effacement. Like the nurses who in turn wore the garb and title of religious 'sisters' and like the maidservants who had disappeared into memories of a stable past, army wives were expected to tuck any expression of individual need under their caps. Based on her own experience in the community built around the military hospital where her husband served, Miller unearths and dissects a conflict between the interests of domestic and army life. The effects of the military power hierarchy on ordinary men and women are evident in the scene where Colin Carmichael, out walking with his Colonel, is 'humiliated' by his wife's unexpected presence: 'A male world, without loyalties outside the rigid artifact of military life' confronts the housewife's 'complacent challenge' (*Angels*, pp. 38–9). Burning with shame, Honor becomes aware of her dishonour: her 'femininity: . . . the slipshod contours, of all that was inchoate, ununiformed about her: that which was capable of giving offense . . . to the men before her' (*Angels*, p. 39)

Even categorical distinctions that represent woman as anarchy or as mother can be dispensed with here, for the woman does not count; the object of male desire lies well outside the confines of the kitchen garden. As Colin vies with Herriot, the impostor hero, for the Colonel's attentions, it is clear that the family home is only a breeding station for male bonding. In Miller's construction, World War II provided a psychologically and morally justifiable outlet for the reification of a patriarchal society. Nurtured by the family home but free of its constraints, men thrive in the games of war. As Simon Featherstone observes, the community of men who

> ... protect "the sleeping English hills and fields and homesteads" ... is represented as and for England ... for a single purpose. The action of gathering together transforms the village community into the "wartime community," with the effect that traditional values are preserved and even heightened by a new singularity of social and hence national purpose (p. 156).

Miller's novel shows the casualties of that national purpose and women's redefinition of it. Like Virginia Woolf's angel, Honor is 'free' to help herself to scraps 'once everyone else was served' (*Angels*, p. 205). She cannot, however, follow Woolf's call in *Three Guineas* to join a Society of Outsiders. Miller's heroine is in the double bind of wanting to preserve her life with her children while suffering the deprivation and decentring it affords. She might therefore revise Woolf's famous declaration from: 'As a woman, I have no country. As a woman I want no country. As a woman my country is the whole world' to: 'As a woman I want a country. As a woman my country is my home front' (*TG*, p. 103).

Honor's performance on the home front, however, is not as compliant as her sister claims, for her 'lethargy and benevolence alike, seemed to sanction a certain fertile disorder' (*Angels*, p. 119). Drawn in opposition to Andrew's mother, who 'by instinct of class preservation' stands for old values in old domestic novels, Honor disrupts the elegant, carefully ordered house she rents (*Angels*, p. 70). As Honor recognizes the cost of her servitude, she begins to imagine what her country might be like, to feel her husband's absence as 'something positive: a leaden weight from the oppression of which she did not know how to escape' (*Angels*, p. 205). At the end of the novel, when Colin calls to say he will be having supper with his Colonel, the narrative focus turns to a child's lead soldier, a 'tiny Guardsman, faceless, shouldering resolutely his damaged rifle' (*Angels*, p. 237).

Nowhere is the self-destruction of male militarism more apparent than in an incident at the heart of the novel in which an enemy plane is shot down. As the townspeople bury the German pilot, the only reaction given expression is that of the Carmichael's nursemaid, Edith, for whom the pilot is as much a stranger as for anyone. But unlike any of the others, Edith, 'who knew no values, who, solitary, had nothing to lose or gain by the betrayal of her emotions ... unguardedly expressed, the very ecstasy of love itself' (*Angels*, p. 161). When Colin accuses her of feeling that 'the enemy is really her ally', that she has displaced the hate she must feel for 'us all', he exposes the unbridgeable gulf between his reliance on war to feel whole and the women's redefinition of unity. While Edith does not represent a universal or essential female empathy, her response highlights the polarity men depend on to justify war and male authority. Relying on old categories of them and us, Colin's analysis guarantees that women, like the enemy, are the Other. Despite the fact that so much propaganda was designed to make women feel that their nurturing capacities were holding the besieged nation intact, they were also cited for the dangerous possibility of extending their sensitivities beyond the pale of national interests.

Edith's empathy is similar to that of other women writers who discovered a 'politics of identification' that bridged the political gaps between England and Germany through the imagined shared experience of motherhood. In her memoir of wartime domestic life, *Where Stands a Winged Sentry,* Margaret Kennedy's fears for her children's lives and future led her to discover 'unsuspected passions and loyalties' that questioned the insularity of conventional patriotism.[6] 'We realized which things we valued most', and while that includes a protracted struggle against Hitler's absolutist racialist policies, the war's imminent dangers also radicalized the most conservative longings for continuity and community: 'Surely', Kennedy continues, '[i]t must . . . be all right to pray that both England and Germany may be delivered from the Nazis' (*Sentry,* p. 22). The boundaryless concern that Kennedy openly expresses represent the same values which Colin rejects and is therefore incapable of reading in Edith or in Honor. These are the values which portray Honor at the novel's end, alone, wanting to and having to protect her baby, but representing as well, an empathetic commitment to a relationship which defines family and homeland in opposition to her husband. Susan Suleiman sees such an opposing force as figured in terms of 'the mother's body... a place of dis-order and extreme singularity in relation to the collective order of culture'.[7] In this sense, Honor's 'absent and rapt' union with her baby does not serve patriarchal war but, in its expression of love and empathy, opposition to it (SS, p. 238). According to Suleiman, the mother's body must also be 'the link between nature and culture, and as such must play a conserving role' (SS, p. 368). Because the mothers in these domestic novels are confronted with a war on the home front, they are conserving only what they need in order to imagine a culture based on a mother's empathy.

Elizabeth Taylor (1912–1975), who reclaimed the novel of sensibility for the postwar period, uses her own wartime experience in her first novel to give it a critical edge. Like Betty Miller, Taylor moved around with two children to join her husband, who was an RAF officer. *At Mrs Lippincote's* shows how wartime domestic novels feminize the definition of homeland and nation. The protagonists, Julia and Roddy Davenant, with their son Oliver, have moved to a rented house in a provincial town near Roddy's army base. Like Colin Carmichael, Roddy finds the comraderie of army life more congenial than family intimacy. Like Honor, Julia discovers through the dislocation of war that the home front is besieged by irreconcilable differences in the middle class couple's expectations of each other and of marriage and family purpose. Julia too, 'leaves disorder' in her wake and is challenged by the different vision of another woman relative, Roddy's cousin Eleanor.[8]

As in Miller's novel, in *At Mrs Lippincote's,* the contiguous communities of home and army, village and military base, are seen to reflect an uneasy alliance, a cold war which questions the purpose of a nation. Through the expression of power and patriotism represented by army life, women are shown to be manipulated into believing that they must repress their needs for individuation and submit to the higher and more public purpose of protecting the nation. Cynthia Enloe shows that women are integrated into the army base community by feeling pressured to comply with an institutional authority which portrays itself as a family and thus appeals to their priorities (p. 47). Being a military wife, however, isolates Taylor's heroine from female support in the outside, less controlled world, and so if, like Julia or Honor, she cannot regiment herself to serve her husband's new family, she risks the only purpose and support available to her in her military marriage.

At Mrs Lippincote's shows the process whereby Julia awakens to her individuality and typicality by testing herself against women's traditional roles, as they are intensified by the army community and as the army sees itself as representing the nation. A wife and mother, she has 'no life of her own, all she could hope for would be a bit of Roddy's – (*Mrs L*, p. 20). Moreover, she is responsible for weaning her son from the intimacy they share and grooming him for the higher purposes of the world she cannot enter: 'Could [Julia] have taken for granted a few of those generalizations invented by men and largely acquiesced in by women (that women live by their hearts, men by their heads, that love is woman's whole existence and especially that sons should respect their fathers), she would have eased her own life and other people's' (*Mrs L*, p. 27). Julia's lot is not an easy one because she makes a revolutionary discovery, that 'I love myself' (*Mrs L*, p. 26).

Taylor dramatizes Julia's redefinition of herself and of family and nation by having her read earlier women's novels. In order to assess the governing conventions of her life, Julia must become a critical reader, reinterpreting the conventions of romance and realist fiction. At first, Julia acquiesces in her reading by responding to *Jane Eyre* as romance. Feeling oppressed and in need of rescue, she identifies the Wing Commander who befriends her as Mr Rochester. Only when she decides to leave her house for a walk by herself does she recognize the potentially transformative aspects of Bronte's text. Like Jane Eyre, who answers the question 'Who cares?' with 'I do', Julia almost a century later still risks criticism by announcing her own agency in the face of the commands which both the Wing Commander and Mr Rochester represent.[9] Thus when Julia and the Wing Commander compare recipes from favourite novels, Julia is able to express her preference for the boeuf en daube from *To the Lighthouse*, a text which he finds too modern, controlled by revisions of traditional social and linguistic conventions which threaten the hegemony of his own. Similarly just as she comes to see the tropes of rescue tales as self-imprisoning, so she later rejects the moral of Flaubert's realist fable: 'I never wanted to be a Madame Bovary. That way for ever – literature teaches us as much, if life doesn't – lies disillusion and destruction. I would rather be a good mother, a fairly good wife, and at peace' (*Mrs L*, p. 204).

Such an alternative, recalling Jane Eyre's final acquiescence to domestic ideology, must be viewed as equally self-defeating, however. In the light of Taylor's depiction of the war's complex material realities, the wounds that make Rochester fit to live with are pure wish fulfillment fantasy. Unlike Andrew, in Betty Miller's novel, whose impairment inspires his philosophical reflection, Rochester is not capable of assuming any responsibility for 'the anti-social impulse within the social framework' (*Angels*, p. 133). And even if he were, as does the Wing Commander, such an 'anti-social impulse' undermines Jane Eyre's early self-assertiveness and Julia's later and milder strike for independence. Reminding us only too well of the domineering Rochester, the all too healthy Roddy exposes men's 'anti-social impulse' as the aggression leading to war on the home front. By implication, it positions women's resistances to the tight controls and expectations of wartime domestic life as 'anti-social' and therefore against the war effort.

Taylor's novel suggests that domestic fiction is a successful form of those chapbooks that prescribe the formation of female character according to traditional codes of conduct. Domestic fiction appeals to women readers in a self-justifying way: it inscribes a romance that conforms to beliefs women are socially pressured to internalize – about needing 'to be brave and competent, look their best and stand by – or possibly behind – their men. Family life must be held together...' (Waller and Vaughan-Rees, p. 13). In wartime, such messages in women's magazines were as loud and clear as posters proclaiming 'Your courage / Your cheerfulness / Your resolution / WILL BRING US VICTORY' or the Queen's tribute to women's 'readiness to serve... the State in a work of great value' (Minns, pp. 11, 28). This propaganda turns out to be just as deadly as either accepting or rejecting Madame Bovary's romantic fantasies and interpreting Jane Eyre's quest for selfhood as a rescue by Mr Rochester. As Julia corrects her reading, she forms a consciousness that heals what some feminist critics describe as the split personality of many female characters imagined by woman writers. Unable to reconcile the tensions between domestic imperatives and their desires for self-expression, many women writers, especially in the nineteenth century, created such a split as a defensive strategy.[10] Julia's reaction to her nineteenth-century reading is informed by the specifically marked historic contingencies that shape and distinguish her own narrative from the earlier ones and that vexes the idea that for women writers and characters the significance of the war was its more technologically advanced masculinist attack on women – the combination of propaganda and bombing of civilians.

Paradoxically, it is the totality of this war that provides the pressure for Julia to transform her consciousness into a critical and therefore safe space. At the same time that she rejects the Wing Commander's copy of *Wuthering Heights* as the gift of 'an incurable sentimentalist', she also tears up all her letters from Roddy (*Mrs L*, p. 206). Having discovered her husband's infidelity, Julia must face the connection between a sexual double standard and the romantic fictions whose claims for undying love support women's self-abnegation and set the stage for their wartime roles. The 'borrowed hearth' has shown her that to be its angel, accepting 'the little rules' which are supposed to keep the nation safe, has been like 'skat[ing] on thin ice' (*Mrs L*, pp. 214, 105, 213).

Julia's refusal to acquiesce to 'the little rules' that unify the life of a house signals the breakdown of the power of domestic ideology (*Mrs L*, p. 105). Seeing through the myths of home and hearth gives her the critical language to dissect the romantic legends which seduce women into feeling nourished by their private space. Written at the end of the war, the novel marks an important rupture in an ideology which had assumed immense power over women's lives. Jane Lewis describes the contradictory message for middle-class women in their having won more mobility, legal freedom and increased expectations of sexual pleasure by World War II, but also having to yield to 'staunchly defended strict separation of spheres' (*Women*, pp. 35–6).[11] As in Miller's novel, however, the maternal sphere here is also a saving grace. Only Julia can save her son from the lingering illness which like Andrew's damaged heart in Miller's novel, is a symptom of war. If it turns out that Oliver is not 'good at games', or 'even that he would want to be', it is because his mother's tutelage has intervened in the war games he was supposed to inherit from his father (*Mrs L*, p. 31).

If Julia, like Honor, cannot begin to imagine alternatives for herself outside the domestic sphere, it is because in a total war these women rebel enough to recognize a newly developed sense of themselves, but not enough to threaten the fabric of a nation that they would like to save for their children. Thus they might resist the patriarchal nation state while protecting it. In their unhappiness and self-recognition, the war also assumes a different meaning for these women. Despite the fact that many British women subscribed to lingering notions of Empire along with men, an overwhelming mass of women's writing is no longer about global domination, but about the sharing of power which begins in the family home. These domestic fictions present ambivalence as a first step toward the possibilities for change in British domestic society. Basically this ambivalence takes the form of juxtaposing mothers who recognize their exploitation but adhere quietly to their family responsibilities. In Miller's novel, Claudia is 'a potential threat to that emotional control that was the basis and governing factor of the temperate life . . . perhaps, a Trojan horse' (*Angels*, p. 72). Ambivalence is also portrayed in mothers, who at each novel's end are seen managing their domestic duties, but their blunted sense of self is abetted by the urgent need to save their children from the very real horrors Storm Jameson called 'artificial hells' (*J* II, p. 21) and Audrey Beecham images in her retrospective poem, 'Eichmann':

> . . . incense of Belsen is stench in the nostrils of heaven
> Ashes of Ravensbruck idly drift over the air
> Lightly touch down in the teacups of innocent parties
> Dusting with grey the blondest of teenage-dyed hair.[12]

Far from indicating traditional maternal selflessness, the concern with war's victims in this writing is a sign of agency.

In these novels, motherhood is not a separate sphere, but invaded by war, and mothers act on several fronts at once. They hold down the home front in order to protect their children, but like Betty Miller's Honor, they also protest the war by redefining domestic priorities as a commitment to an interdependent love they hope will reshape the core of their nation: 'It was if the focus of peace that was Honor with the child at her breast, deepening, permeated the whole house: as if from her body there radiated a beneficent influence which . . . was detected by senses that were incapable at the same time of recognizing its source' (*Angels*, p. 232). This is not a 'Mother who is overly invested in her child, powerless in the world', the figure who some contemporary feminists worry about.[13] This is a woman whose definition of family and nation represents both an alternative to war and her own reasons for 'doing their bit'. Such revision incorporates the assumption that the war against Hitler must be fought, for to ignore his designs for conquest, enslavement, and extermination would destroy the grounds on which change could take place. Rosamond Lehmann's World War II story, 'When the Waters Came', dramatizes the way motherhood provides the initiative to reimagine a nation's fate. Unlike Storm Jameson's dystopic flood epic, *The World Ends*, Lehmann's is a domestic tale of a woman transforming natural and geo-political disaster into a vision of regeneration. When the earth thaws after an ice storm which deadens the earth, a mother saves her drowning daughter and in so doing, saves her world.

Only through the emotion which Susan Suleiman calls 'the physical and emotional experience of motherhood and of maternal love' do the women in the above novels realize that they have been exploited by a patriarchal order which must be reimagined in order to save what they value (SS, p. 370). In her agony over the war she insists must be fought, Margaret Kennedy embeds her protest against Hitler's unique terror in an expression of maternal love: 'The future of all these children, of all the children in the world perhaps, is in the balance.... There has never been any moment quite like this before in the whole of history... and we have no power, no power, to save them from a most hideous fate. We can only wait for tomorrow' (*Sentry*, p. 104). To wait may seem passive and compliant, but as a position which holds the ground supporting the lives of children, it holds fast against domestic as well as external dangers.

Ambivalent and complex, the women in these novels interrogate what feminist critics point to as 'the essentialist assumptions' of the conventional war text (Cooper *et al.*, p. XV). In their redefinitions of the home front and the purpose of this second world war, they cannot be reduced to either apolitical nurturing figures or politically compliant victims of culture. These women struggle to distinguish their idea of home and family from that which they inherited or married. They represent the construction of female character in the course of an historical crisis their writers recognized as threatening to the lives of women and their children who are both keys to change.

PENNY HEARTBREAKS: RESISTING ROMANCE FICTIONS

Women's popular fiction of World War II, especially that written afterwards, could easily have ridden the wave of victory, and many women writers did use the wartime home front as a nostalgic setting for reviving conventions of irresistible passion, lost love, self-sacrifice, and domestic reconciliation. A Gothic imagination was unnecessary, however, since the Battle of Britain and the Blitz offered treasure troves of gory and glamorous images for romantic melodramas fusing turbulence in the air and on the ground. Because of its spectacular victories and tragic losses, the Battle of Britain is easily exploited as a set piece of young RAF flyers annointing local ingénues with the passion of risk. With a backdrop of village resolve, the war produced a romance of national regeneration even at moments of fiery death.

And yet despite this dramatic opportunity, an interesting sample of women writers used wartime social realities to provide dramatic checks on romantic melodrama. The invitation to escape into passion is supplanted by the opportunity to test women's choices for this duration and their lasting impact. In these fictions the appearance of a modern swashbuckling hero in silk scarf and bomber jacket is no cause for celebration, but a reminder that women's lives were costumed by the mundane necessities of their own war work, and that passionate longings are subdued by the need to cope with the rationing of food, fuel, and clothing, and other privations that made hunger and fatigue more powerful emotions than lust. In these novels, the war on civilians was a catalyst for revisionary thinking about war. These novels reflect the hardships of women leaving the sheltered bastions of middle class homes for paid and volunteer wartime work, but instead of romanticizing the freedom and constraints of juggling private and public spheres, they use the conventions of romance to question relationships between the heightened emotions of war's constant crisis and the easy emotionalism of their own genre.

This revisionism did not spring whole cloth from the shock of a home front war, but was already developing in the interwar period. As Alison Light shows, while many interwar writers rejected sensationalism as the price for being considered serious and progressive, others deployed it to appeal to readers 'who imagined they were above that sort of thing, and [their] unhappy endings both prolonged the passion and provided a cynical comment on the impossibility of romantic love' (p. 164). These interwar novels privilege the individual female self while questioning both middle-class domesticity and romantic rebellion as satisfying destinies.

When both romantic rebellion and domestic stability are undermined by the realities of wartime contingency, popular romance can find itself questioning women's roles and attitudes to the war, not as ornaments to melodrama, but as a resistance to the social and emotional codes the genre represents. *The Lonely Road*, by Mills and Boon writer, Elizabeth Carfrae, is a conventional romance in which a woman's war convictions question pacifism and militarism as they define the romance and marriage plots that seem to be her destiny. Instead of the skyborne thrills available to a novel of 1942 or the melodramatic misunderstandings of the genre, the romance of Linda Wantage and Lawrence Holt is propelled by their opposing political views. Lawrence, a reflective and passionate teacher, clings to his pacifist principles at the cost of professional and personal happiness. Linda, a spoiled debutante, challenges Lawrence with politically pragmatic questions charged by her belief in personal happiness. Their relationship withstands their differences, and they marry to live happily ever after, until Lawrence takes a job in the United States where in 1939 he can still find a strong pacifist and isolationist community. Linda decides to stay in England where she will be supported by family and nation.

In a novel paced by the unfolding of crisis-ridden events, what becomes exciting is the imagined political and moral development of Linda's character. Despite Linda's romantic view of losing part of herself when Lawrence leaves, her character will continue to develop out of the process of critical questioning she began with him. This is not a magical or melodramatic operation. The separation necessitated by their political differences also highlights the dynamic quality of Linda's character present from the beginning, deriving in part from her class-bound confidence but also from Carfrae's confidence in a woman's political thinking. Given the chance to maintain domestic stability, Linda instead becomes an agent of disruption when Lawrence refuses to give up teaching pacifism to boys who are expected to fill the nation's seats of military and political power. Though her support for the war also upholds the patriarchal institution that Virginia Woolf so powerfully denounced, Linda's reasons are neither traditional nor conventional. Instead, she analyses the political and moral implications of the specific historic moment for the home front and beyond – the Munich crisis and then the Nazi sieges. Her later decision to join the Women's Auxiliary Services and leave her baby daughter with her family is the novel's final blow to expectations for her submission to traditional arrangements of domestic power.

Giving due respect to Lawrence's pacifism, Carfrae also examines linkages between his transhistorical view of war and his reliance on patriarchal hierarchies of power. His dismissal of Linda's historically based arguments is expressed with the same insistent air his assumption of domestic power has allowed him, and so he expects her to support and follow him. He couches his principles in the language of a universal maxim, as though it were a given not to be questioned, especially by a woman who cannot abstract the meaning of war from the concrete experience of 'now': 'If long ago we and other countries had taught their youth not to fight there would be no wars threatening us now'.[14] Linda resists his assumptions by validating his 'lonely road' while recognizing the integrity of others: 'But when it means taking others with you, then it's another matter' (*Road*, 143–4). Her insistence on the integrity of a chosen Otherness then becomes a validation of her own struggle for self-determination.

Lawrence is made to find his way home the moment war becomes his own experience. Responding to the death of their daughter in an air raid, Lawrence falls from the lofty position of his universal principles into a hell of guilt and revenge:

> My ideals aren't any good.... I can't live up to them. When the war touches me personally, I crack. It is humiliating, because I was so sure of myself. So sure that I had in me the power to make a better world. And now I want nothing – nothing but the ability to kill... (*Road*, p. 195).

A popular romance like this could easily romanticize Lawrence's transformation by sending him into battle to save the pleasant green land invoked so often in the novel. To rehearse another meaning, while he heroically rescues his pilot from their burning fighter plane, Lawrence catches fire himself, burning out the arrogant narcissism of his pacifism, his desire for revenge, and his self-doubt. Rescued by his ordeal by fire, his feeling of loss for his child can be nurtured into empathy for the war's victims and bring him closer to Linda's reasons for supporting the war. When he accepts an offer to return to the English boys' school his pacifism forced him to leave, the novel affirms conservative gender and political attitudes. It is easy to see how Carfrae's 1942 readers would find the novel a rallying and reasonable support for both a war whose end was nowhere in sight and for the victory that would regenerate myths of shared national values. At the same time, however, the challenges implied by Lawrence's transformation and Linda's questioning affirm the possibility that a consciousness of empathy, of tolerable differences will be introduced into the curriculum.

Another novel by Carfrae, published in 1946, is a conventional war romance which also questions assumptions about domestic relations, its village ethos, and 'the People's war'. A combination *bildungsroman* and novel of manners, *Penny Wise* is shaped by the heroine's time honoured conflict between passion and stability, but now undercut by a self-conscious narrative which has its heroine proclaim: Sentimental novels 'only go to prove what trash people write'.[15] As though written against its own grain, Miranda Kenyon's character is shaped by a quest for alternatives to sentimental romance. As the daughter of renegade aristocrats who have abandoned the manor for the stage and family responsibility for their self-absorbed passion, Miranda has romance in her blood. At first, her choices seem limited to her parents' example or the more conventional domain of middle class security. She can marry dependable but sexually uninspiring Roger Marsh or succumb to the mercurial Bill Dawson's sex appeal.

Miranda becomes engaged to Roger but marries Bill after one night of bliss. Sexual ecstasy, however, leads only to despair, and Bill's anger, which erupts when she tells him she is pregnant, ensures the divorce of romance and domestic fiction. Carfrae offers one resolution when Bill is reported killed in action and Miranda is rescued from the instability of a romance plot by marrying Roger. When Miranda learns that Bill is alive, melodrama threatens, but recommitment to Roger assures victory for the traditional renunciation and marriage plot. And yet, through the destabilized presence/absence of Bill, Carfrae's plotting also manages to question itself. Like Taylor and Miller, Carfrae assesses the condition of marriage in light of propaganda about the wartime relationship between family and nation. Recalling Miller's dualistic portraits of the invalided soldier and imposter commando, the two men in Carfrae's novel also show how the home front and battlefield are opposed even as they support each other. Like Claudia, Miranda's choice between passion or stability enfolds an opposition between 'the beautiful warrior' and the plain noncombatant. Bill, unlike Miller's Neil Herriot, is an authentic commando, but his romantic daring is tied to restlessness and extravagance, qualities which must subvert domestic imperatives, and by implication, the home front. Roger, like the real Herriot, works rather than fights, and cannot arouse Miranda's passion. His munitions work supports both home front and battlefield, but as Miller's Claudia implies, the worker, no longer sufficiently masculine, cannot compete with 'the fiction . . . of the hero: the killer, tough, unscrupulous; outside the bounds of ordinary convention' (*Angels*, p. 232).

Miranda chooses Roger on the basis of values embedded in debates on England's war aims, and thus implicates romantic fiction and domestic ideology in geo-politics. Early in the novel, in 1939, Miranda and the narrator reflect on how 'broken promises and scrapped agreements' made the war inevitable (*PW* p. 63). Such causes reflect back not only on Miranda's rejection of Bill's fitful loyalties, but even further, on her parents' break with the covenants of traditional family life and by implication the stability of domestic political ideology. Roger's attitude towards the war makes him the ideal candidate to save the home front from a double perfidy, from errant parents and lover and from Chamberlain's appeasement policies: 'But when war comes – and mind you, it will come . . . – we'll lose it unless we realize that it's no good trusting a man who wouldn't recognize truth if it was handed to him on a plate' (*PW*, p. 66).

Roger's reasoning connects the acting careers of Miranda's parents and their flight from both aristocratic and middle-class social codes to the self-deceived romanticized self-interest that threatens home and nation. Thus Chamberlain's 'scrapped agreements' can be said to originate in the aristocratic code of noblesse oblige, which in the guise of beneficence, sacrifices its dependents to the upkeep of its own power. These codes make their way into domestic ideology masked as an equally misleading arrangement of power called paternalism. If, as with the Kenyons and Bill, rejecting these codes leads to no more than betrayal, then there appears to be no way out of a home front threatened by the illusions of its governing polity. The determining, indeed governing power of both Chamberlain's good intentions and the Kenyons' hollow performances is derived from the same value system that Betty Miller criticized as leading to passivity and dependency for both men and women. Andrew, invalided out of he war, observes: 'We create a fiction out of our own desires. . . . A fiction so attractive to the law-abiding that we chose in its favour to ignore the reality' and thus choose to see in the soldier's 'fancy dress . . . the brass buttons, the tin hat, the revolver – the paraphernalia of power' (*Angels*, pp. 232, 30). Andrew, the counterpart to Roger in Carfrae's novel, recognizes that

> . . . you've got to have a war to show where people's real values lie. A war turns us inside out, shows the lining: pacifists become war-mongers, intellectuals worship the man with the tommy-gun. . . . Gives us a chance to discover the lie we were all living, during the so-called peace years" (*Angels*, pp. 30–1).

The epistemology of denials and lies by individual men and women and in nations' collective polities questions both the justice of fighting a second world war and saving the domestic front. Miranda's choice of Roger rejects a politics of self-interest that like her parents, opposes an interdependent family life. By extension, such a choice represents a geo-political strike, one that implicates the interdependence of nations, where the 'pacts' that insure reciprocal regard for each other's security and well-being originate as concepts of mutual family concern. Thus, while these domestic novels express powerful criticisms of all misuses of individual and collective power on all fronts, of all wars, they recognize as 'truth' that to ignore or deny the universal threat posed by the armies of National Socialism is, as Andrew points out, tantamount to exposing Britain's values as the mirror image of Hitler's.

Penny Wise views the home front war as clarifying the values by which Britain distinguishes itself. In both peace and war, Britain is unified by a rhetoric of individualism in the service of motivating a collective spirit of enterprise. As a militant noncombatant producing munitions, Roger represents both a cooperative war effort and postwar competition as antidotes to the government's 'take-it-or-leave-it' neglect of its people (*PW*, p. 88). Miranda's choice of Roger tests such rhetoric as it is enacted in different marriages. In her parents' marriage, both individualism and the collective are subsumed by the narcissism that makes their passion an exclusively self-interested enterprise. Another marriage, by contrast, dramatizes how interdependence without respect for autonomy elides individual identity. Miranda's cousin Phillipa and her husband are passionately attached to each other, recalling the Kenyon's marriage and questioning Miranda's experiences with Bill and Roger. Miranda's conclusion could be considered sour grapes were it not for its correspondence to the novel's critique of the politics of family and nation. She sees Phillipa's marriage as one of blended identities reflecting a 'possessiveness . . . which resulted in their grudging to each other even the privilege of an individual thought' (*PW*, p. 90). Miranda's lack of passion for Roger questions whether marriage as a governing institution can support both autonomy and collectivity. Opting for the security of boundaries, Miranda is only too happy that 'Roger liked her to think for herself and encouraged her to live a life that was her own' (*PW*, p. 90).

At the end of the novel, Miranda, like her Shakespearean namesake, will be domesticated, but with a hope for change in the power relations of the home front. Like Shakespeare's move from a fantasied island to one that is war torn, Carfrae moves her characters from a surreal wartime romance to postwar domesticity. The postwar is now safe, not only because Hitler's armies have been defeated, but because war has exposed the domestic front as harbouring illusions of romance and masculine power that cannot accommodate the complex interplay of individual desire and collective need. Instead of the happy ending readers would expect from this 'penny' novel, there is a subdued sense of resistance that leaves Miranda happy with a decision to construct a domestic space subject to change.

This novel is all the more remarkable when compared to another wartime romance, Maysie Greig's *Heartbreak For Two*, which situates its glamorous upper-class ATS (Auxiliary Territorial Services) heroine in a class and sex war between an aristocratic (and therefore dashing) Squadron Leader and an upstart Major who, because of the war has been able to rise from his status as chauffeur's son.[16] Even while Grieg criticizes snobbery and traditional sex roles as flighty, especially in a time of national emergency, she also reaffirms them. When the Major is blinded in an accident, readers are reminded that it was his questionable social status that denied him a more heroic fate on the front lines. Moreover, whatever sympathy the narrative grants him is undercut by his oppressive demand that our heroine 'be his eyes', taking his directions and serving his purposes because his life is more important than hers (*H* p. 175). His victory, however, is dubious. As he commands the woman in the driver's seat, the chauffer's son reminds us once again of our last view of Bronte's Mr Rochester.

Narrative defences against the expectation that war brought

unsettling social change also produced a kind of fictional ambivalence marked by a wish for romantic release and fear of instability. In *Total War at Haverington*, Josephine Bell (1897–1987) departed from her more typical mystery writing to dramatize the wartime fear of change as it would affect the ethos of English village life. Published in 1947, the novel takes place in a Thames valley town blundering through its absorption of evacuees in 1942. Hester Dearsly, the Evacuation Centre Organizer for the local Women's Volunteer Service, is distinguished from the 'universal mixture of apathy and impatience' by her devotion to her work, but she is also criticized by the town and by the narrator for not being domesticated (*TW*, p. 166). Her mistake is to work around rather than with Haverington's social and political codes, and this marks her as a sign of war's unsettling effect on traditional institutions, including marriage. In this respect, Hester's war work also functions as her resistance to an otherwise unfulfilling domestic life, but Haverington's traditional values prevail as a counter-reformation. Her commitment to the evacuees' welfare is thwarted not only by an intransigent bureaucracy and the town's petty jealousies, but by her relationship with her husband. Neither passionate nor capable of intimacy, Julian's poetic nature coincides with his need to 'escape involvement', but his complacency is respected by Haverington as reflecting its own wisdom and stability (*TW*, p. 150).

Although privileged by the narrator, this compatibility signals the novel's ambivalence towards the social and moral codes of Haverington. The wartime setting exposes such compatibility as making the poet complicit with the town's 'indifference' to the plights of the evacuees or any others noted as different (*TW*, p. 279). However much Hester's war work is valued, the novel devalues her energy and drive by supporting her husband's attempts to dominate her, as when he gets away with misdirecting her report on inadequate evacuee housing. In undermining her ability to act, he subverts a humane war aim – rescuing alien victims – instead, the 'all-pervading importance of the war' turns out to be protecting the social and political hierarchies that keep Haverington an island within the island nation (*TW*, 179). The village must defend itself against the threat of change, embodied by Hester and the evacuees.

Within the tension between the narrator's allegiance to Haverington is a threat that predates the war. The pressures of war on the home front expose a marital breach that was only held together by the prewar stability of a provincial town. Thus Julian is given cause to reflect that Hester never 'had really thought and worked directly for his comfort' (*TW*, p. 170). Her domestic infamy is highlighted by the character of the woman who wins Julian at the end. An evacuee, Margaret Sheldon arrives in Haverington with a two-year-old orphan and an air of mystery. Portrayed as a chaste madonna, she becomes the avatar of the narrator's moral judgement against the childless Hester, whose frustrations have led her into an affair with an unsavoury real estate speculator. For the contemporary reader, the two women represent a conflict between one whose aggression and goals defy her prescribed roles and one whose maternal devotion and reticence typecast her as a Mrs Miniver. Nonetheless, although Margaret's perspective is privileged by the narrator, it emerges as the other side of Hester's, and thus ironically vindicates her rival. Margaret's 'inner loneliness of spirit . . . in a shallow stream through barren land' matches Hester's experience with the town and with Julian (*TW*, p. 267). When Margaret realizes that Julian's inattention is tantamount to 'indifference', she begins 'to despise herself for her compliance' to his conventional morality which 'had assumed an equal sacrifice of personal satisfaction to patriotic needs. . . . Who was she to imagine she had any power to alter that constant rule?' (*TW*, p. 279).

'That constant rule' reflects the double bind to which the narrative confines both Margaret and Hester. Hester's attraction to Bob Manders is an escape from one kind of male domination to another. Attracted to his energy and drive, just as Miller's and Carfrae's women resonate to military energy, Hester is ultimately repelled by the way 'all their encounters seemed to lead to a situation in which she lost the initiative and he took it; in which she was led, commanded, arranged for' (*TW*, p. 192). Margaret, by contrast, is ultimately coopted by the narrator to help Haverington regain its sense of stability; but her words speak louder than her actions, especially as they subvert the narrator's final condemnation of Hester, whose death in the London Blitz is enacted as a macabre farce. (Hester and Manders are crushed by their bed!) The only 'personal sacrifice' in this novel turns out to be the fates of Hester and Margaret, while 'patriotic needs' emerge as the narrator's faith in traditional social and narrative structures, the force of which is expressed in the eleventh chapter.

The chapter begins with a summary of the war's events between 1938 and 1942 and their meaning in relation to Bell's creation of Haverington: 'That unbreakable faith in the future that had been born two summers before' reveals a nostalgia for a past undisturbed by domestic or geo-political wars (*TW*, p. 165).

The universalist voice in the narrator's formulation of history and prophesy testifies to the sustaining power of a myth of national unity. Such 'faith' in a 'People's War' is activated by Bell's endorsement of domestic ideology in a plot shaped by women finding homes for evacuees. But the novel's overriding ambivalence exposes such work and its validating ideology as a traditional trap for women. This is not surprising considering Bell's own career, in which after graduating from Newnham College, Cambridge, she studied medicine and then practiced it full time with her husband–partner. In *Total War*, Hester's plans to improve the evacuees' housing are foiled ultimately by her female adversaries, who fear she will upset the power hierarchy that supports them. Ironically, women's infighting sustains the unified stability of Haverington; totally dependent on the myth of common goals for their prestige, the women uphold it by aggressively competing for its leadership. And this commonality all depends on the xenophobia that rejects both Hester and the evacuees as alien.

The fifth column in Haverington, however, turns out to be its own concept of citizenship. Despite the novel's adherence to the codes of domestic ideology, the rebel of the hearth is not completely buried – the fate arranged for the errant Hester – nor is her angelic counterpart resurrected in her romanticized rival. The representative voices of Haverington are too shrill, patriarchal power as represented by Julian, too deflated, not to be felt as a feeble defence against the novel's most eloquent voices: the discontents of women. To have 'ingested' its evacuees, 'in the manner of an amoeba with a particle of indian ink', suggests that the community and this domestic novel are sufficiently strong to accept a foreign substance as nourishment and remain undisturbed and unchanged by war (*TW*, p. 62).

Nowhere is such stability so reified as in the wartime trilogy of Angela Thirkell's Barsetshire novels, *Cheerfulness Breaks In* (1940), *Northbridge Rectory* (1941), and *Marling Hall* (1942).[17] Never dropping a stitch from her previous country house romances, Thirkell shows village life adjusting itself to the advent of war only ever so slightly. Her endless roster of courtship and marriage plots changes its venue only to be complemented by comedies of evacuation and bumbling war work. Thirkell's time honoured targets of county satire are now marked by exiled icons from besieged Central Europe. These gypsy-like aristocrats not only add relish to Barsetshire's basically indolent xenophobia, but they provide a critical edge that complicates Thirkell's comic élan and our laughter. Her mockery of profiteering refugees and their epic celebrations of Transylvanian blood lust highlight the reasonable ethics of Britain's core. But the joke is then offset by her satire of Britain's perfidious responses to the fall of Czechoslovakia and Poland. And while it is clear that Thirkell's own war aims valorize Britain's political and social hegemony, she also parodies the slogans of both patriotism and pacifism.

As the war progresses and its losses are integrated into Thirkell's plots, her comedies are infused with a more sombre tone, even sadness. Marling Hall is thus not just the seat of an isolated and anomalous minor nobility, but integrated into the theatre of war by a daughter whose husband has been killed at Dunkirk. The conventional courtship plot is no longer a laughing matter when it stars a war widow with two small children. Angela Thirkell never failed to charm middle-class readers by reassuring them that nostalgia for harmony and continuity could also be a blueprint for the least disruptive if inevitable change. *Marling Hall*'s melancholy also marks the recognition that the war had become the blueprint for unpredictability, a sign of contingency that did not accord with the conventions of the comic manor house novel.

The stability of the village and domestic life and women's resistant voices form a comic conflict in the gently satiric domestic literature that was serialized in women's magazines throughout the war. Appealing to generational, social, and regional differences, writers such as Joyce Dennys, E.M. Delafield, and Dorothy Una Ratcliffe chronicled the domestic lives of provincial 'married women [who] still feel that the part we have to play in this war is mundane, unromantic, and monotonous'.[18] A consequential role played by these comic writers was to build a coalition of support to reassure women that their complaints were not idle. In *Henrietta's War* and *Henrietta Sees It Through*, fictionalized accounts of her own wartime life, Joyce Dennys bemoaned with good humour how 'It's not much fun . . . being a middle-aged woman, safe and protected, on a roof, thinking of other people in danger' (*HW*, p. 49). Such self-deprecating humour also allowed these writers to deromanticize the village as an enviable haven. E.M. Delafield's provincial lady reports how despite the anticipated invasion of 1939, 'evacuees from all parts of the country are hastening back to the danger zone as rapidly as possible, as being infinitely preferable to rural hospitality'.[19]

Joyce Dennys, like Betty Miller, was a doctor's wife who dramatized the pressures related to their husbands' increasingly indispensable position, a major consequence of which was 'practicing the negative virtues of the wartime house-keeper'.[20] For Dennys, resistance takes the form of mocking her husband's authority in its larger relation to government propaganda and policies. She can assume her readers recognize her no-win situation, and going public with it offers a solidarity of mutual understanding. But Dennys is not offering complacency and a stiff upper-lip as a solution. In *Henrietta Sees It Through*, the women mock the government's edicts and double standards about women's service and compensation by confronting two military officers with their links to domestic ideology:

> " . . . one day women are being told that their place is the Home, and the next minute they have to man the guns."
>
> "And if they get their legs blown off, it's supposed to matter less to them than it does to a man," [Henrietta] said. (*HT*, p. 57)

Although these complaints were registered by women of all classes in the 1942 campaign for equal work injury compensation, Dennys's voices are middle and upper class. Dennys assumes the privilege of social authority that comes with having access to a public voice that in print builds bridges with women's private, domestic concerns in various parts of the nation. Dorothy Una Ratcliffe used her access to various Yorkshire newspapers to publish her correspondence with a Yorkshire neighbour, whose protestations of having 'no book-learning' would otherwise have guaranteed that her astute wartime observations would have been ignored.[21] Mrs Buffey's reports connect women of regional and social differences by addressing their domestic concerns in relation to both the larger war aims and to the national hierarchies of authority and power. She is bemused by 'archbishops telling us what miserable sinners we are', and snarls at the BBC's condescension, instructing women how to make their homes safe while omitting news of the war (*Mrs B*, p. 11). Using juxtaposition for both comic and critical effect, she registers sympathy for all women involved with evacuation policies: 'It's nobbut Bachelors at the London School of Economics . . . would think of asking two women to share one kitchen, especially two women bred in different parts, having very different ideas about most things' (*Mrs B*, p. 16). As homeless women invaded the private space of middle-class home-bodies, domestic fiction of the war represented them as forming a domestic nation that defied myths of a homogeneous people.

Even in their tamest forms, women's domestic fiction of the Second World War highlights women's struggles with the male authority that so often constituted their relationships with other women. When they resist their designated wartime social positions, these fictional women represent an Other in relation to the social norm propagated by government policies and home front military installations. But as we have seen even in the most conventional fictions, when ambivalence about women's wartime roles seeps through the seams binding narrative voices and plotting, the fiction can expose its own ideological tensions and thus create a different kind of dialogue with readers. As all of these diverse fictions show, the wartime domestic novel leads a quiet revolution against what had heretofore been considered a normative tradition. Whether they enact resistance or suggest it between the lines, they express a yearning for change in both the defining terms and social acts that constituted their lives at home and in their nation. Against the grain of government policies, myths of chivalry and national unity, as well as the rhetoric of resolve and rationality, women writers and fictional characters represent women's domestic experience as the defining testimony and evidence of a war too much historical narrative has ignored. As we shall see, women's critique and quiet revolution of domestic ideology and experience did not stop at the island boundaries of Britain, but became a vigorous form of resistance against Nazi oppression on the European home front.

6

Fictions of the European Home Front: Keeping Faith with the Conquered

We are in history to our necks . . .

Storm Jameson, *The Black Laurel*[1]

But years ago the glass was turned,
Glass balls with its image of a peaceful scene
Turned upside down, and the snowflake fugitives
Whirling, darkening the shape of Europe,
Blot out the lights and the village green.
Because of our parting, yes, but also
Because of those who endure far worse –
Jews and Gentiles, guilty or gentle,
Martyrs or mere sufferers – because of heartbreak
And the falling tower,
Falling now, and now rebuilt
by the future in the present, with perpetual tedious pain,
And because it seems in vain – dear as this day is,
I must wish you many returns, happier than this.

Anne Ridler, 'Poem For a Birthday', 1942[2]

Before World War II, Europe was easy prey for English fictions of foreign intrigue. Stories of the Continent's political revolutions and sexual excesses and its history of ethnic and political rivalries fueled plots of ill-fated love, dynastic intrigue, and feudal conflict. Staging these plots required little imagination, for Europe's baroque facades and labyrinthine passageways could all too easily be made to symbolize the elaborate manners that lent mystery to stories of romantic and political betrayal. These fictions often revolve around highly principled if politically pragmatic English characters who become deeply invested in saving the Europeans from their already compromised political morality. Whether they succeed in saving the Europeans from their own worst tendencies, the English characters confirm the moral and political superiority of British democracy. By contrast, European protagonists and antagonists in these political romances are portrayed as incorrigable Others, heirs to internecine conflicts they replicate from gothic and byzantine pasts, albeit with the benefit of modern technology.

In the self-congratulatory rhetoric of these fictions, English heroes and heroines are put to work exposing the barbaric origins and violent nature of such conflicts. In plots of political and sometimes romantic intrigue, the English decode the elaborate manners and morals which appear to represent a civilized order, but which instead turn out to conceal a barbarism that is seen not as a product of historic circumstances, but as inherent, as though the Continent suffers from a congenital moral drift. At the finale of such fictions, whether the European nation yields to the superior influence of British culture or resists it, the English return home to reassert their moral hegemony from the site of their more moderate clime.[3]

In effect, these fictional relationships emphasize Britain's political position as utterly distant from the Continent. This is true even as the fictional Britain intervenes, playing a paternalistic role so that Europe can achieve a political order resembling democracy. These fictions can thus be seen to enact a psychological conflict of approach and avoidance, mirroring not only the nature of diplomatic relations, but Britain's political debates about its role in Europe's affairs, especially in the thirties. As the rise of nazism confirmed Britain's worst suspicions about Europe's tendency towards political extremes, defining and situating Britain's role in Hitler's takeovers and conquests was sharply debated in the press and in Parliament. Both appeasers and their opponents argued the merits of negotiation with Hitler or waging war against him as ways of upholding beliefs in Britain's aims for peace. As these debates became more intense, their reflection in the fiction of the European home front became more polemical and didactic, especially as it also resonated with ambivalences towards British domestic politics.

For many women writers, what was happening in Central Europe was no longer a matter of debate. Emotional ties that had been forged in travel and living on the Continent were intensified by the politically charged events of the twenties and thirties. For Rebecca West, Storm Jameson, Phyllis Bottome, Stevie Smith, Olivia Manning, and Ann Bridge, Central Europe seemed to move closer to England as their anguish about the fall of Yugoslavia, Austria, Czechoslovakia, and Hungary to the Nazis became a mirror of feeling about their own nation, a response that would develop into a political critique of Britain's domestic and international policies.[4] Their prewar and wartime fictions depict Central Europe, not as the unregenerate Other, but as a member of their own political and cultural family. For these writers, this family tie mediates geographical, cultural, and ethnic tensions to produce an ethos of political interdependence they would propose as a model for peace. As Anne Ridler expresses in her 'Poem For a Birthday', precisely because British women could 'count considerable happiness, Even good fortune', in being so removed from Europe's battlegrounds and being able to 'cherish our child' and 'live', they felt they could not forget the war on 'those who endure far worse –' (p. 83).

At the moment when the home front was being invaded as a 'sample corner of total war', Rose Macaulay redefined it as a bond between Britain and Europe. To appease Hitler in order to vouch for Britain's safety, was tantamount to

> . . . surrendering to the still more blind, maniac, primitive, stupid bestiality of Nazi rule over Europe, which would be to spit at and rout civilization even more earnestly. Not even the most pacific pacifist can see (so far as I can discover) any third way. It is a choice of bestialities: let the foul scene proceed, or let it give place to one fouler, while we abandon Europe to a cruel and malignant enslavement, breaking faith with the conquered countries which look to us for freedom, handing over to their torturers those who have sought safety with us, as did so unprotestingly the Fascist and anti-Semite old French Marshal, canting meanwhile of a regenerated France. A disgusting dilemma, and one which agonizes many pacifists ('Notes', p. 982).

If, as Rose Macaulay feared in 1940, England was becoming 'a sample corner of total war', it was also fertile ground for defining this specific war as defensive and liberatory. More pragmatist than theorist, Macaulay stands for a liberalism responsive to social and political reform rather than committed to a radical overhaul based on ideology. Like other women writers, she became a pacifist after World War I, but by 1940 she felt that holding to pacifist principles, especially that of self-sacrifice, would only succeed in sacrificing the lives of Others who could not afford such principles. The aggressive tone of her statement reflects the depth of her anguish, and even more, her conviction that 'freedom' was no mere abstraction to be manipulated rhetorically but a material state of being which had been entrusted to Britain by those Others.

Macaulay's fierce sense of responsibility is matched by her blunt condemnation of any European nation that sacrificed their Others to their 'torturers'. Other women writers, equally critical of Britain's imperialist aims and refugee and internment policies, also came to see that the feudal legacies of Central Europe could lead to an all too easy absorption of nazism. Olivia Manning's *Balkan Trilogy* registers despair but not surprise at Rumania's acquiescence to the Iron Guard. If her Central Europe is a tragicomedy of political corruption, British political integrity is depicted as farcical. Britain's secular missionaries, the British Council team, crosses swords with fascism by purveying Shakespeare's mythic power struggles. If British cultural imperialism is no match for the Iron Guard and the Nazi troops at the Rumanian border, Manning's British characters embody a counterforce. Despite all odds, they sustain belief in the reformist tendencies they attribute to their own pragmatically charged liberal heritage.[5] It is this heritage that drives them to implicate themselves in the fate of Europe's Others.

The rise of European fascism and its assault on the Other moved Virginia Woolf to acknowledge a difference between 1938 and the past. Where she had viewed patriarchal domination and the fascist state as coterminus, she now found differences in their justifications of aggression. Now the 'Tyrant, Dictator' has 'widened his scope' to make 'distinctions not merely between the sexes, but between the races' (*TG*, pp. 102–3). Among those she singles out who are now . . . being shut out' and 'shut up' are Jews, but this recognition of a new kind of political terror only reinforces her global condemnation of masculinist oppression. As a woman who has also been 'shut out' and 'shut up', she identifies with the Jew, but instead of struggling as British Jews had, to become an insider as well as to remain an outsider, she will use her status as outsider to end oppression (*TG*, p. 103). She will not work to end all tyranny by joining forces with her British oppressors, but will use her writing to revise their historical ethos. For Macaulay, Manning, and so many others, to avoid the war effort in protest of masculinist self-destruction would mean to 'abandon' the victims most clearly in the wake of the new fascist machine. Macaulay's seemingly offhand 1940 reference to 'the Fascist and anti-Semite old French Marshal' invokes a victim who represents a significant reason to join the war. To rescue the Jew means the rescue and regeneration of their own 'civilization'. To not even try means that Britain would deserve the fate to which it left Hitler's victims.

For these women writers, the figure of the Jew serves as moral template of the future of English and European civilization. Whether the Jew is worth saving is the question that addresses whether European civilization is worth saving, and the fate of both reflects Britain's ambivalent relations with the Continent and how this ambivalence defines Britain as a democracy. That these writers should look to Europe's treatment of the Jews as a gauge of British democracy is not surprising in light of their own position in a society that remained unresolved about its ambivalences towards Jews. The all too open persecution of European Jews reflected back on England's treatment of its own Others. After all, while England allowed the Jews to return after a 374-year expulsion, it continued to bear their presence with as little sufferance as it could muster and yet still congratulate itself on its liberal tolerance. As David Feldman observes, the Jewish presence in British history had the political significance of a debate beginning in the nineteenth century and, as we shall see, was going strong throughout the Second World War; the debate concerned a conception of the nation based on relations between 'institutions of state which guaranteed individual freedoms' and 'conceptions of national identity'.[6]

By the twentieth century, British law and social institutions tolerated Jewish separatist observances and local Jewish community institutions. But the Jews' insistence on their difference was also troubling in a society that activated its ideology of national unity all too often by denying its peoples their own cultural differences.[7] Compounding this tension was the fact that even if the Jews wished to assimilate, they were 'shut out' from those clubs and circles which made and marked English identity. In her study of ambivalent literary representations of the Jews in the interwar period, Andrea Loewenstein speaks of 'the British liberal tradition, which I had previously seen as a force which served and protected the Jews of Britain', but which she discovers through her research to be 'instead consistently used as an enforcer of this hypocrisy'.[8] Bryan Cheyette has pungently summed up British ambivalence towards the Jews as the 'antisemitism of tolerance', a cultural attitude that viewed prejudice as the Jews' own problem because they refused to alleviate it by assimilating.[9]

By the time fascism was a European threat, there were already laws in place that restricted the presence of Jews in England. Since 1919, with the passage of the Aliens Act, Jewish immigrants could be deported without cause. And yet the Jews were also protected by British laws against inciting or enacting violent actions towards minorities. It was a consequence of such laws that the threat of Oswald Mosley and his British Union of Fascists ended with his imprisonment in 1940. Official punishment, however, did not dissolve British antisemitism, which continued to thrive in more genteel fashion as befit British reserve.[10] Thus Virginia Woolf could share the antisemitic snobbery of men whose politics she otherwise deplored. Well into the thirties, when atrocities against Jews in Europe were reported in English newspapers, she was moved not only to invoke the Jews as victims, but to write a disdainful and only thinly disguised portrait of a Jew, 'The Duchess and the Jeweller'.[11]

Such ambivalence characterized both official and popular British treatment of Jews who were trying to escape extermination by fleeing to England. As many have observed, class-based prejudice against the Jews' presence continued into this period unchanged from the past. Jews were considered ill bred and therefore unfit for genteel society. Among leftists and the labouring classes, however, efforts were organized to sign petitions and protest actively against Mosley and European fascism. It was up to the Jews themselves, however, to shoulder the economic cost of the government's decision to allow German Jews to immigrate. British writers and intellectuals were as divided in their responses to the plight of the Jews as the general populace and government. As Andrea Loewenstein reports, some who remained absolutely pacifist also supported an appeasement policy with Germany which would have included 'nonintervention' with 'Germany's right to dispose of its Jews as it saw fit' (p. 30). Other pacifists advocated stopping Hitler through non-aggressive strategies and would accommodate none of his domestic policies, including racialist persecution. Loewenstein cites Maude Royden as an example of 'private efforts to denounce Nazism and to rescue European Jews' as 'attempts which had no influence on government policy' (p. 30). Royden also illustrates the mindset that found reason to abandon pacifism because '"there had come into the world something worse than war"' – that something being '"what Hitler was doing to the Jews"' (Loewenstein, p. 30). This attitude contrasted sharply with the mostly negative ambivalences towards the Jews Loewenstein traces in such writers as T.S. Eliot, Wyndham Lewis, Charles Williams, and Graham Greene.[12]

THE 'SENSITIVE CONSCIENCES' OF STEVIE SMITH, ELIZABETH BOWEN AND STORM JAMESON

Sharing Royden's views were those of other women writers who not only used their writing to protest fascism but engaged actively and relentlessly on behalf of the Jews. In the same period that Virginia Woolf published 'The Duchess and the Jeweller' and her anti-fascist polemic, *Three Guineas*, Stevie Smith published her monologic anti-fascist novels, *Novel on Yellow Paper* and *Over the Frontier*, polemical narratives which enact a personal confrontation with the political implications of polite antisemitism. Letting neither herself nor the reader off the hook, Smith indicts all 'goys' who cling to a sense of their superiority with intolerance of Jews (*NYP*, p. 11). In Smith's meandering but relentless musings, fascism and antisemitism are linked not only to masculinist militarism, but to women's struggle for self-determination. In *Over the Frontier*, Smith's heroine, Pompey Casmilus, travels to Germany on a journey of recovery and self-discovery only to be seduced by the temptation that war is an empowering experience.[13] Named for military heroes, Pompey joins their ranks when she is dressed by her lover in a military uniform. Despite her conflicted response of passivity and protest, she quickly enough takes the reins of war into her own hands and rides across a besieged no man's land to commit her own act of violence. It is all too easy to kill a 'rat-faced monster' whom she sees as the personification of 'hostility . . . the backside of the world' (*OF*, p. 252). Despite the German setting and its ominous overtones of feudal militarism, this enemy is not identified as German and yet Pompey's intrigues and meditations call attention to a Second World War which at the time of writing is on the horizon. The rat monster is a figure that crosses the boundaries of war, embodying 'the cruelty' of which 'We are so many' from 'London' to 'New York' (*OF*, p. 252).[14]

In her conflicted efforts to resist aggression and to defeat it, protesting her soldier's uniform and yet adapting quickly to war, Smith's anti-heroine dons the very emotion that fuels the masculinist war machine. Smith constructs Pompey's response as driven by a 'swift tide of hatred' that derives not from the circumstances of war, but from a political ideology: a 'liberalistic world-conscience, that is still persisting in Opposition' (*OF*, p. 252). Whatever its reformist and egalitarian intentions, the result of 'persisting in Opposition' makes Smith's female characters here and elsewhere conceive of themselves as alienated and anxious in relation to an Other. In this relationship, the Other, for Smith, can only be situated as an enemy, in peacetime as well as in war, and therefore subject to the aggressively defensive outbursts of her female protagonists. It is thus no coincidence that the eruption of Pompey's hatred in *Over the Frontier* resembles her earlier outburst in *Novel on Yellow Paper*, in which she confessed her 'elation' at outsmarting 'a clever Jew' (*NYP*, p. 11). Growing with intensity in its repetition, these outbursts are consistent with Smith's elaboration of Pompey's odyssey into embattlement. The 'Opposition' of self and other thus overwhelms Pompey's 'sensitive conscience' with its origins in 'the racial hatred that is running in me in a sudden swift current' (*OF*, pp. 158, 159). Stripping Pompey and her male compatriots of all their liberal and democratic English intentions and actions, Smith bares their most hostile and aggressive fantasies as both the basis and justification of oppressive political systems and manoeuvres.

Narrated ambiguously as either an extended dream or fantasy, or even the logical progress of the inward turning historical narrative, Pompey's transformation into militarism enacts a drive for power and control. But because she becomes both subject and object of military power, she is depicted as not only a victim, but a victimizer, and the end result is more imprisoning than liberating. When Pompey is captured near the end of *Over the Frontier*, the regulations and purposes of her military prison are hidden from her, and it appears that all constructions of 'Opposition' and fantasies of aggression in the novel have converged as a force which cannot be understood as rational. The result is to produce, at ever escalating levels, the violation of self and Other. But Smith does not disembody such violence as some kind of force independent of human intention and action. Pompey's self-accusations and aggressive fantasies fit all too well with her self-conscious reflections on the cruelty of British imperialism. In effect, she implicates herself in the oppressive consequences of British racism and imperial power. She may be overwhelmed by male militarism, but she also acts as its agent when she assumes the language and acts of conquest.

Within her critique of aggressive fantasies and their translation into conquest and oppression, Smith creates distinctions that complicate her conclusions about war. Even as Pompey concludes that aggressive fantasies lead to the collapse of boundaries between a defensive and offensive war, she engages in an historical analysis of the differences that prevail between the political culture and ideologies that shape the drives of Britain and Germany towards expansion and war. Even as she indicts her own liberal construction of oppositions as resulting in racism and tyranny, she constructs the history of Jewish persecution as a reason for defeating Germany in war. Woven throughout, like a refrain connecting the two novels, are various European Jewish figures who represent destabilizing and affirming responses to the positioning and identification of Otherness. Though they suffer in their social role of Other, in Britain as well as in Germany, Smith's Jews emerge as a model that authorizes an authentic selfhood embedded in an affiliative but distinct national and cultural identity. In her fiction, Jews have developed their selfhood out of a persistently uncertain relation to whatever nation they inhabit. When these Jews are rejected, it is because they hold onto an identity which sets them apart; in their unstable relation to the dominant culture, they appear to be a destabilizing presence. Their presence thus casts a threatening shadow of doubt on the nation which is exercising its dominance as a sign of its own authentic identity. When, as in one case in *Over the Frontier*, the Jew appears to be accepted, he still casts an ironic shadow on the security of his position and that of the nation. He is accepted because genetics and national identity luckily converge; thus the blond good looks of Pompey's actor friend, Igor Torfeldt, resemble European icons of an Aryan Christ. In his embodiment of reassuring sameness and threatening difference, he thrills his gentile audience.

Smith links this ironic connection to her most powerful argument for waging war with Hitler. If Britain is to keep her promise of fulfilling a democratic destiny, she must begin by defeating fascism in disavowing any expression of 'Opposition' and antisemitism. Acts of expression in these novels cover not only words and deeds, but the assignment of value to only those faces and figures which reflect the eradication of difference. The Jew's difference does not, therefore, represent 'Opposition', but a relationship between the selfhood of a nation and the myriad identities of its people. Not to tolerate difference nails the coffin not only on the Jews but on Britain's claims to democracy, a just war, and a national identity that embraces the complexly differentiated peoples of its island.

Stevie Smith made two trips to Germany, in 1929 and in 1931. Although Hitler's racialist policies had not yet consolidated into political power, she witnessed the growth of antisemitic expression, especially as it affected her Jewish friends. And so even at this early date, 'she felt "awfully nervous" and, on leaving, as if she were taking the last train from Berlin' (Spalding, p. 84). So repelled was she at the rise of German racialist emotion, that it continued to haunt her as late as 1955, when she published a short story about a young German whose antisemitism marks him as a Nazi and a war criminal. Most significantly, Maxi's character reflects the consistency of Smith's views of what went wrong with 'that beloved Germany' whose 'dream change[d]' (*NYP*, p. 49). For its 'idea of sleeping, dreaming, Germany', as embodied in 'her gentle women', changes to reflect the violent subordination of women as a sign of the coming persecution of Jews (*NYP*, p. 49). As her Englishwoman protagonist recalls her teenage year in Germany with Maxi and his family, his antisemitism merges with his violent behaviour towards her, and the Jew and the woman become mirror images of unbridled hatred of the Other. Both the Englishwoman and the Jew are Other in the political philosophy of the German male, and therefore subject to the violent assertion of his rightful claim to dominance. Although by the postwar period the attitude of the young Englishwoman is one of forgiveness, and she 'hate[s] this "holier than thou" situation we are all in now', she is reminded by her English companion that compared to Maxi, '"We ARE holier than him".'[15] The distinction between English democracy and nazism is maintained only through an English politics of identification with the fate of the Jew.

Smith had already linked her anger at Nazi masculinist supremacism and antisemitism to her view of the war in a 1939 essay, 'Mosaic'. Here she finds British equivocation and indifference about Central Europe and its Jews 'a record of dead leaves before a wind that is blowing up storm-strong'.[16] The 'dead leaves' represent Smith's assessment not only of British arguments 'for an insecure peace', but of such self-serving tales as the following ('Mosaic', p. 106):

> . . . of two Austrian Nazis who helped their Jewish friend to escape. Yes, he was forced to scrub the pavement of Vienna, but he laughed while he did it; he took it in the right spirit. Some old Jews begged not to be made to do it; they were forced to. They did not laugh; you see they did not take it in the right spirit.

This tale confirms both Nazi oppression and the need to defeat it by highlighting the condition of the Jews. Dependents in a dominant culture and polity, the Jews can validate Aryan superiority through their self-deprecating behaviour, and so must be 'forced'. The tale of escape, however, also bears relation to Britain, which historically may stand as a rescuing power, but can also be interpreted as a dominating and oppressive polity. In this regard, the 'right spirit' suggests questions about an uneasy historical and fictional relationship between any national identity and the status of its subjects/characters who define themselves as different.

In 1942, when the outcome and human costs of the war were still unclear, Smith was still creating arguments for its just cause based on the status of the Jew. Her story, 'In the Beginning of the War', looks back to the moment when there was still resistance to the war, and registers anger at those pacifists who insist that the battle for 'ideals' must be against 'the unrighteousness of war'.[17] Smith challenges the pacifists' position by arguing that their mocking dismissal of Nazi terror implicates them in Germany's 'unrighteousness': 'They knew how strong Germany was in the strength of a lie, and how a lie is strong because it can be so much simpler than the truth' ('War', p. 29). The lie these war resisters share with Germany turns out to be the claim that Nazi Germany is unjustly demonized, that there is a German political reality that refutes 'The bogey of nazi-ism, the bogey of atrocity stories, the bogey of war sacrifices' ('War', p. 29). Each of these claims (and here we are reminded of Ethel Mannin's refusal to believe atrocity stories) is rebutted in a poem a young woman recites in the story:

'For every blow they inflict on Jewry,
And other victims of their fury,
They ask for death on bended knee,
And we will give them death and we,
Will give them death to three times three' ('War', p. 29).

While the pronouns establish an opposition between 'we' and 'they', the violent actions they both perform destroys the moral and lexical distance and difference between villains and heroes. Moreover, typical of Smith, the nursery rhyme allusion, 'three times three', becomes a self-mocking critique of elevating heroic action from the childlike but dangerous aggression it suggests. And yet despite this critique, Smith is calling for British retaliatory aggression against the Nazis, and at the centre of that rallying cry, caught in the vise of hostility is the Jewish woman who must be rescued from it. She might wish 'Nazi-ism' were only a 'bogey'.

Smith's prescience and concern for the Jews in the 1930s is shared by another writer who negotiates her marginal identity with the uniquely threatened status of the Other in the coming war. Elizabeth Bowen's 1935 novel, *The House in Paris,* is shaped by her Anglo-Irish identity politics, an historical consciousness which locates moral and political responsibility in the tense relationship between two peoples asserting their identity through nationhood. As the conflict involves not just nations but victims, it would enter her fiction as a wider scene of political responsibility – Europe. Bowen draws our attention to the moral topography of the historical moment by having the illusory quiet of the novel's interwar setting invaded by two Jewish characters – Max Ebhart and his son Leopold. The political terrain of World War II begins in this novel with our first sight of the nine-year-old Leopold, about whom we are given nothing more or less important to know than that he is a 'very slight little boy who looked either French or Jewish' (*HP*, p. 27). An identity of either or, or even half and half, as Bowen defines her identity politics, is always to be perceived as historically and not just geographically marked Other – as she said of herself, she was English in Ireland and Irish in England. That Bowen endows the child with a 'nervous, susceptible temperament' may be a matter of the poor psychological coping skills he inherits from his parents (*HP*, p. 40). But he also has much more to be nervous about. Within the narration of his suffering the effects of his parents' ill-fated romance, and outside the ill effects of his inherited identity lies another plot.

Leopold's only claim to Jewish identity can be measured as a dubious one-third, coming through his English-French Jewish father – and therefore marginal at best. And yet the novel marks him as indelibly as history will mark the European Jew. The novel embraces and yet tosses about the Jew already caught in the historical moment. The literary plot shunts Leopold about a continent on the brink of disaster, beginning with his birth in Germany, where one year before the novel's publication the Nuremberg Laws would have marked him a full-fledged Jew. He is then treated to long train rides; like a displaced person he is moved from one temporary encampment to another, from Italy, where his adoptive parents raise him, to a stopover in Paris to meet his birth mother, and then only maybe to stay in London. These are travels frought with many risks, not the least of which is that it is unclear and uncertain that the indelibly marked Jewish child will ever find solid ground on which to determine his own identity or that of a defining community.

Leopold's place in the novel is that of exile. He can not fit into the belief of his English mother's people in a steady state of historical quiet. He cannot even claim to be part of the historically threatened cultural heritage of his father. This exile is so beautifully captured in Paris, where Leopold is shunted upstairs and downstairs at Mme Fisher's, torn between his mother's unexplained broken promises and the mystery of his father's life and death. The plot lines of Leopold's movements in claustrophobic and unfathomable spaces are not so much gothic or modernist as they follow the trajectory of European Jews in the 1930s.

This plotting of the historical moment is nowhere more apparent than in Bowen's portrait of Max Ebhard, Leopold's father. Although a wonderful brew of French-English-Jew, he is tolerated neither by the English nor the French. The mothers of his lover and fiancé, Mrs Michaelis and Mme Fisher, are all too prepared to exploit him but keep him in the unsteady space of exile as they construct him to fulfil conveniently negative Jewish stereotypes. These stereotypes, moreover, are not dissimilar from the warrants by which the Nuremberg Laws condemned the Jews. Examples: Mme Fisher describes Max as having 'a darting womanish quality, enforced by a manly steadiness of will' (*HP*, p. 106). For Mrs Michaelis, 'he is a touch Jewish perhaps – of womanishness' (*HP*, p. 110). Mme Fisher concedes that he has 'the ability of his race but' then she worries about his interest in her daughter's money, whereas Mrs Michaelis observes that 'No Jew is unastute' and thinks Max is after her daughter's money and her social position as well (*HP*, pp. 130, 143). All things to all accusers, the feminized Jewish cad is a fitting father for Leopold. Max is a genetic guarantor of the child's Otherness in a world where even a narrow little house in Paris squashed in a space of nebulous social status clings to its cultural stability at all costs.

Max's character is destabilized and threatened more by external historical forces than by his own psychological and moral queasiness. He confirms his own sense of where his decentredness will lead. He tells his beloved Karen:

> I looked back at my humiliations, my ridiculousness.... You do not know what it is to be suspect and know why. What it is to have no wall to put your back against.... My lack of a home, of any place to return to, had not only deprived me, it chagrined me constantly (*HP*, 162–3).

Max's problem is neither universal nor personal; that is, it is the product of an historical condition that is already exploding outside and inside this novel at the time of its writing and publication. Max's suicide, a blood-bath, is about having no place to realize his fate among those who cling to a deluded and xenophobic sense of cultural stability. What the house in Paris and the house in London share more than anything else is their refusal to grant asylum to Max as Other. In their last stand against his invasion, they are primed for war. Max conveniently and literally exterminates himself. Running out of Mme Fisher's house while bleeding to death, he removes himself from a historic scene and plot which Bowen recognizes has already eliminated him.

On the basis of this inherited destiny it is no wonder that Leopold is such a nervous child. In her unsettling combination of empathy and incapacity, his mother knows the burden of Leopold's inherited character: 'But if he is like Max and me he would hate ... exile, hate being nowhere, hate being unexplained, hate having no place of his own' (*HP*, p. 188). In the novel's most emotionally powerful scene, when Leopold learns his mother is not coming and bursts into tears, the narrator works as an empathetic stand-in: 'He is weeping because he is not going to

England; because he has been adopted; because he has nowhere to go' (*HP*, pp. 196–7). At the end, Leopold may be saved by a substitute father: the Englishman who bursts through the moral paralysis of London and Paris with his passion for critical questions.

Other writers were equally repelled by Hitler's eugenics and Britain's disregard, and until war broke out, kept returning to Central Europe if only to offer support to those who had fallen to Hitler's henchmen. As President of British PEN, Storm Jameson attended the 1938 international PEN conference in Prague, but instead of going directly home like most of her compatriots, she chose to go on to Vienna to see for herself what could be expected if Hitler were to conquer all of Europe and England as well. It was at the British Consulate that she recognized the import of appeasing the führer:

> [The Courtyard] was filled to suffocation by men and women, Jews, hoping for visas: they stood, pressed closely together, some patiently, others angry and scolding; there were even children, gripping the skirts of mothers they hardly knew any longer, so changed were they by waiting and fear. . . . The instant the door opened, an eddy set towards it, like the dead eddying and whirling about the blood poured out by Odysseus. I was ashamed to have thought this, What right had literature, even the greatest, here? And even more ashamed, after hesitating for a long time, of holding up my English passport when the door opened again, so that I was let in at once. (*J*, I p. 383).

For Jameson, what ultimately justified bearing literary witness on this threshold to tragedy was the necessity to politicize her writing and her PEN office, which she continued to do throughout the late thirties and into the forties. Too impatient to consider changing men's consciousness through her art, she felt an urgent need to affect their political actions. And so in novels, essays, and letters, Jameson argued that Britain's fate as a democratic nation rested on its interdependence with Europe, and as a sign of that, in its response to Jewish refugees. Although she insists that the reasons she stayed in office were not political, she began her presidency 'by writing a long letter to the *Manchester Guardian*' on 'the duty of writers to abhor racial intolerance', and followed this with relentless pleas for money and political intervention to save persecuted writers, especially Jews, from 'Hitler's bloody harrow' (*J*, II p. 18).

Britain's official response to Jewish refugees was punitive. In addition to curtailing the numbers of Jews it would absorb to 'nil', and using its imperial power to prevent immigration to Palestine and elsewhere, Foreign and Colonial Service officers passively resisted the rescue efforts of Churchill and others (Loewenstein, p. 55).[18] In 1943, after facts of the Jewish extermination had been acknowledged by Anthony Eden's 'famous Declaration', Eleanor Rathbone wrote a pamphlet on behalf of the National Committee for Rescue From Nazi Terror entitled *Rescue the Perishing: A summary of the Position regarding the Nazi Massacres of Jewish and other victims and of proposals for their rescue: An Appeal, A Programme and a Challenge.*[19]

After reporting 'The Facts of the Massacres', the pamphlet suggests 'Measures of Rescue' and goes on to reply to objections and cite 'Examples of the Harsh Working of Home Office Regulations' (*Rescue*, p. 1). For Rathbone, the rescue of Hitler's victims was central to the war effort and therefore of an entirely different perspective than the government's, which in her view, promised 'practical measures' for the purpose of 'retribution' (*Rescue* p. 3). A year later, when the final solution was escalating, Rathbone published another pamphlet, this time responding not only to the British Home Office, which continued to obstruct Jewish rescue, but to ordinary 'Jew haters who continued their 'spiteful stories' about the 'evil of the Jews'.[20] *Falsehoods and Facts About the Jews* argues that as it is translated into political policy, British antisemitism mirrors Hitler's use of it as 'an almost indespensible medium' (*F&F*, p. 4):

> The Home Secretary himself, who mainly controls the entry of immigrants to this country, when pressed in 1942 by a weighty deputation to admit Jewish refugees more freely at a time when the Hitler policy of total extermination of European Jews was beginning to be implemented, mentioned the danger of provoking Anti-Semitism as one reason for refusing the modest concessions asked for. The same argument is frequently used by lesser politicians. (*F&F*, p. 4).

In the early thirties, Storm Jameson and Naomi Mitchison had feared that liberal complacency could lead to a British fascist state, with a total crackdown on minorities and dissent. Now in the midst of war, many women writers mistrusted the coalition of liberals and conservatives even though it made a full offensive against fascism possible. Jameson, Rathbone, and others felt that the new government was complicit with fascism in failing to recognize the urgent, perhaps radical measures required to save the Jews. By extension, they concluded, this meant the failure of will to save Europe and Britain. They would no doubt agree with Andrea Loewenstein's assessment that 'The English liberal ideology prevented overt violence against Jews in England but encouraged less open, more passive forms of prejudice which were in the end equally lethal' (pp. 42–3).

ENGLAND
By Anna

A Will against my country,
A will against my land,
A will that is so terrible,
A will I can not stand.
And merry merry England is all I'm praying for,
That Hitler gives up for ever more.
That merry merry England has not got Germany,
And sorrow comes great on to Italy,
Let merry merry England become a happy land,
And that the Will will be gone,
The Will I can not stand.[21]

The poet Lilian Bowes Lyon reprinted this poem by a Jewish 'victim of Nazi oppression aged nine' as part of a letter to *Time and Tide* in 1940. For Lyon, the poem expressed 'so clear-cut and spontaneous an expression of what thousands of her fellow aliens feel about this country, even though the home it offered them has now for many of these natural Allies become a "home" behind barbed wire' (*T&T*, p. 821). Lyon is addressing the fact that of the relatively few European Jews Britain admitted, many were interned as potential fifth columnists. Despite the persistent debates of war aims and wartime social and political policies in British newspapers and magazines, this issue seemed to touch more sensitive government chords than others.

Storm Jameson, who was already blacklisted by the Nazis for reporting their brutality, now risked British censure. Her mistake was not only to press British agencies with the cause of Jewish refugees, but to protest the British internment policy. Worse, she compared Britain's policy to the Nazis' concentration camps: 'Very often I could only think that the jailing of these helpless refugees opened a crack into an abyss of dull meanness like the final disgusting irrelevance of Dostoevsky's cockroach' (*J*, II p. 78). She attributed 'dull meanness' to a kind of self-congratulatory liberalism that prides itself on celebrating the self-sacrifice of Others while hiding their xenophobia behind their own self-interest. Thus she quotes an Englishman defending his internee friend: 'And suppose he is, in fact, innocent, what a splendid chance for him to show his gratitude to this country by refusing to complain about a few months of comfortable internment!' (*J*, II p. 78).

It was on the European home front that writers like Jameson found the conditions from which they created metaphoric mirrors of Britain's supremacist and antagonistic ideologies. Jameson's novel, *Europe to Let: The Memoirs of an Obscure Man*, published in 1940, is an historical epic of the present. It recounts the odyssey of a young Englishman, a writer who fought in World War I, who travels across Central Europe from 1923 in Germany, to Hungary in 1936, and to Prague and Vienna in 1938. A barely concealed self-portrait, her narrator doesn't bother to disguise his rage at the German brutality no historic contingencies can sufficiently explain. Ambivalent about the defeated and punished nation, he 'had chosen to come to Germany because I thought that Germany, starving, bankrupt, must have removed some, at least, of its filthy rags from truth'.[22] The historical 'truth' this novel investigates is the political language and behavioural psychology of Germany's internal moral responsibility. But in addition to her analysis of local German political culture, Jameson investigates the failure of the Allies to support the growth of Germany's democratic institutions during the Weimar era. The search for 'truth', as embodied by Jameson's 'obscure man', examines Britain's image of itself as arbiter of democracy in Europe and the relationship between the two civilizations. Sorting out this relationship, however, only proves that its 'truth' remains elusive; what becomes apparant, however, in Jameson's exploration is that she metaphorizes 'truth' as responsibility for the Jews.

Europe to Let depicts the Jews as individuals and then more globally, shows how they are demonized by being held responsible for their own rejection and persecution. Jameson's Englishman notices 'the faces of the Jews gathered, like guests who do not know when to remove themselves.... Added one with another they formed a map of Europe with its rivers of uselessly spilled blood, scourges set up in the market-places, the towns hostile and the country yielding a harvest of deaths' (*Europe*, p. 275). The description of the present 'map' recalls Elizabeth Goudge's scene in *Castle on the Hill* of a medieval English pogrom. Jameson's novel 'maps' the Jewish presence in Europe but she clearly fears for them in Britain as well. The map of the Jews' form is threatening and must be destroyed because their presence fuses boundaries between discrete ethnic and national identities, thereby robbing towns and nations alike of the possibility for creating a writ of superiority. Moreover, as with those interned in Britain, the Jews' map must be superceded by the barbed wired boundaries that shut off the Jews' destabilizing presence from the threatened nation.

Exercising his nation's democratic spirit, the Englishman in *Europe to Let* then asks a Jew why he doesn't leave for England, all the while 'hop[ing] he would turn this idea down:

> 'There are still too many refugees, although it is made as hard for them to get into England as if England were a raft and Europe going under. It would be less embarrassing to sensitive people if they would die peaceably and dumbly, and not try to escape (*Europe*, p. 275).

Recognizing his own complicity in the fate of the Jews who 'made me feel responsible for all the cruelty in the world', the Englishman is from beginning to the end of the novel also passive, impotent, and incapable of intimacy (*Europe* p. 260). As his train leaves the platform at Budapest and he sees his Jewish journalist friend for the last time, the Englishman's 'burden of love and respect dropped off. Tihaneth's features became smudged; he was smaller; drawn swiftly backwards, he disappeared', and as Jameson's polemical novel argues, the Jew can thus disappear from Britain's conscience all too easily (*Europe*, p. 282).

Jameson has been criticized for adopting male personae and voices in her fiction, but as befits her thematic focus on moral responsibility, we can see this as her recognition of women's active implication in male-dominated political forces. To show that women must take responsibility for their participation, Jameson embeds a sense of her own guilt in her Englishmen.[23] Like Stevie Smith, Jameson will not let herself or her readers off the hook for their own ambivalent politics, and the test case is always the condition of the Jews, who are so easily made to seem culpable for their own fate. Because they choose to be different in such visible ways, the Jews lend themselves to be considered a mutative affront to the dominant culture: 'Yes, his forehead was ugly. There was the Jew, the man with too much intellect, the man to be envied, despised, stoned' (*Europe*, p. 69).

At the end of the war, in a novel that is also part diary and transposed autobiography, Jameson assumed a woman's voice to meditate on moral connections between the two world wars. *The Journal of Mary Hervey Russell* is no private matter, but an interaction with the fates of the war's victims. Mary Hervey Russell becomes an actor in historic crisis as she presents the story of a Jewish woman to represent war's 'vileness and cruelty spreading its stain in the clear air'.[24] Using reflections and reminiscences from her diaries that she would later transpose into her autobiography, Jameson interprets Mary Hervey's journey through Central Europe as uncovering the brutal 'secrets' behind its romantic charms – 'from the days when children were sacrificed to [the Danube] as a god until now when last night's suicide disappears as quickly as all those Jewish bodies, old and young, tumbled into it a few years ago' (*JMHR*, p. 109). The method which exposes these 'secrets' is to revise the tales that comprise a culture's mythology. Jameson transposes the terrors and happy endings of such tales into plots that show how their illusions of hopefulness end in terrifying ambiguity. Her sample tale within a tale concerns a princess who wanders into an alien place where she is offered a marriage arrangement against which she rebels. The princess manages to escape to her own garden, but when she falls asleep smiling and weeping, her tear reflects the marriage plot and her status as Other from which there may be no escape.

In this revisionary folktale, Jameson conflates a domestic plot with an alien setting in order to expose deep seated myths that supported the wartime behaviour of both Europe and Britain. Consistent with her most pointed concerns about the war, the tale inscribes the Jews' problematic assumptions that Europe was their home and Britain could be their refuge. Like the princess, the Jews were easily deceived into thinking that the familiar charms of places they called home and the alien but charming England were resistant to plots of their captivity. Jameson's female narrator, in conjunction with other women characters, enacts connections between freedom and captivity and between domestic and antisemitic plotting. These women share the historically symbolic meaning carried by the domestic objects signifying women's role in the continuity of their cultures. In one instance, when the British narrator visits the home of Jewish friends in Vienna, she learns that despite its modesty and the 'great number of years' they have lived there, they will be evicted simply because they are Jews (*JMHR*, p. 96). Much of the shock comes from the depth of the family's attachment to Vienna itself; generations of continuity are personified in 'the voices of old cups, of chairs polished during a lifetime, of worn fine linen' (*JMHR*, p. 96). When these people leave, Jameson argues, the loss will be Vienna's: 'What, when she goes, will happen to the things in her house which she has served carefully all her life because it was a way of serving her parents, who also had used them, and her children? . . . Who will drink from [her mother's cup] in future – and what, in Nazi Vienna, will he drink?' (*JMHR*, p. 97).

The traditions Jewish women follow in their kitchens, like those in Jameson's dystopia, *Then We Shall Hear Singing*, are the language of cultural preservation. As a gloss on that work of 1942, this Englishwoman's wartime journal commemorates women's work as the record of Nazi tyranny and victimization. The linkage of this language to the fate of the Jews suggests resistance to any argument that either women or Jews are passive subjects of war. The Englishwoman, moreover, is not positioned merely as an innocent observer. Her presence and questions about the Jewish woman's kitchen implicate her in her nation's responsibility towards those they knew were being excised from their home grounds.

That Jameson held other Allies responsible for the war is evident in her 1941 novel of interwar Alsace, *Cousin Honoré*. Separating and yet joining France and Germany, Alsace stands on contested borders and for Jameson, represents 'something that became Alsace and might become Europe. It is a tree that sends roots down on both sides of a frontier but puts out leaves in its own air'.[25] On national margins, Alsace is always in the position of subject and Other, for she has opportunities to be complicit with the politics of either nation or to develop its own hybrid culture. For Jameson, the benefits of a hybrid culture would be its critical stance in relation to the mutual enemies on either side. By extension, the relation of Alsace to her neighbours suggests Britain's critical position in international politics, especially as the novel is dominated by men manoeuvring for power and supremacy. Despite their individualized characters, the men's collective actions reveal their almost undifferentiated and unquestioning complicity with the horrors of war.

In this way, too, the novel implies that the ideology of island individualism on which Britain's national identity hinges is tainted by the supremacist policies of self-interest against which it defines itself as a reason for going to war. Nowhere in the novel is this more evident than in the section, '1936', where Edward Berthelin, an outsider brought in to run the great iron works of the ancient Alsatian Burckheim family, expresses alarm at 'the invalidism of France' in ways that resemble Jameson's critique of Britain's interwar politics (*CH*, p. 150). It is the 'malevolent blindness' of the 'old men' in office which makes lies of their pious talk 'about their horror of war and the sacrifice of young lives. What they dread, he thought, is the loss of their power . . . to defend it they will in the end . . . [be] making the usual speeches and calling up the usual words, honour, liberty, courage, and the rest' (*CH*, p. 150).

By 1939, such words have become lethal to Berthelin. The possibility that the iron factory may survive only if it accepts loans from the German branch of the Burckheim family would implicate it in Germany's war machine because by now, 'the usual words' have become disguises for deadly acts:

> 'Justice, which means concentration camps. . . . Pacification, which means forced labour, the murder of unarmed opponents, torturing of prisoners. . . . Before long, to know the exact meaning an official German attaches to such words as peace, decency, kindness, truth, it will be enough to reverse their meaning in other countries – and speak of war, indecency, bestiality, lies. No body of men has ever put abroad so many lies as, since 1933, responsible German statesman. Except' – a look of bitter grief altered his face – 'except those Frenchmen who pretend that what happened at Munich in September was not a fearful defeat for France.' (*CH*, p. 172).

For Jameson, similarities between Germany, France, and Britain represent the rhetorical danger points where the ideology of common good slips into acts which betray self-interest, self-delusion, and public deceit and terror. In 1941, the year of this novel's publication, Jameson is still hopeful enough to issue this analysis as a warning to maintain a safe distance from Germany's lapse into a state of self-congratulatory terror. Britain and France must therefore take joint responsibility for the future by recognizing their complicity in 'not having managed to set Europe off on a different path in 1919' (*CH*, p. 253). Whatever historically contingent differences she finds between the two world wars and ideological distinctions she identifies between the players, Jameson fears that the self-interest and xenophobia that drives the politics of both sides may collapse their differences and make fighting a second world war an exercise in futility.

By 1944, when it was too late to issue warnings, Jameson created a fictional French provincial society to analyse the relationship between its cultural history and its wartime behaviour. *Cloudless May* explores how internal social collapse leads to the defeat of a fiercely independent and democratic nation. The novel takes place in a Loire valley town between 5 May and 19 June 1940 when German tanks cross the bridge to Seuilly on their way to conquer France. Although defeat is at the hands of an external enemy, like Jameson's earlier dystopia, *In the Second Year*, this novel indicts 'a diseased society' which crumbles at the first sign of an outside threat.[26] One sign of an outside threat is the Jew Sadinsky, a Rumanian emigré trying to buy his way into the centre from the margins. More than willing to exploit 'the dangers that threaten France' for his own safety and reward, Sadinsky joins forces with a woman who plays a minor but crucial role in sharing the margins with the Jew (*CM*, p. 37). Subjected to a position which guarantees that they cannot be agents of their own fate, the Jew and the woman construct a defensive strategy of manipulating events for the other characters from behind the scenes. The result, not surprisingly, backfires, and they are marginalized further by being diagnosed as carrying the symptoms of each other's 'disease'. Accusations of self-interest combined with a wily disregard for social and legal conventions mark the woman and the Jew with qualities that exacerbate the Otherness of each. But as Jameson plots their course, the behaviour of the woman and Jew merely represent symptoms of 'a diseased society'.

Interestingly, the novel positions another Jew, Louis Mathieu, as the muckraker of this 'diseased society'. Mathieu is editor of a newspaper which is 'too uncompromising' in criticizing the Right 'as mercilessly' as the socialists (*CM* p. 20). In his role as both fated and self-determined outsider, Mathieu signifies the external threat. He embodies 'the advance of violence' in his 'obsession with death which springs too quickly in the memory of his people, even in the young' because 'the Jews have to face death in its least bearable shape, the cruelty of human beings. . . . His memory, his instincts, his old alliance with history, warned him that the new time of sorrow would be darker than any in the past' (*CM*, p. 359). Mathieu's grim vision, like that of his creator, leads him to judge everyone harshly, even himself, and especially France, which Jameson dearly loved. What distinguishes Mathieu from France's leaders is his ability to make political judgements based on a responsibility that extends beyond the town walls. The target of his condemnation and Jameson's is the mayor, Labenne, who represents the dilemma that Jameson constructed as the means by which to judge France as it fell to Germany in 1940. Torn between love for the land and seeing all morality in terms of its 'costs', Labenne stands for his nation's losses as he explains to Mathieu why 'we can't defend ourselves any longer'. (*CM*, p. 377, 376). In the face of the Jew's fate, the cost of France's surrender is measured as selling out its Jews, a move that proves self-destructive. The Jew, in his 'disobliging austerity', is as France prefers to see its moral self, but as the execution of Mathieu demonstrates, the nation has sold itself into slavery to protect its extravagant self-centredness (*CM*, p. 484).

In a short novel written between October 1940 and February 1941, *The Fort*, Jameson portrays a French scene without Jews, but it is haunted by a voice condemning 'All those Jews and Jewish blackmailers who wanted a war . . . the Jew squatting everywhere'.[27] The scene is a farmhouse cellar hideout where English soldiers debate with their French hosts on the war's merits and plan their return to battle. This all takes place as Paris falls to the Germans. Every turn of argument and action is connected by the antisemitic utterances which represent France as threatened internally if it yields 'its different minds, voices' and 'many words for freedom' to the single voice of Germany which 'has silenced all its voices except one that Goethe wouldn't have understood' (*Fort*, p. 32). In the company of the British and French allies, whose decency signals Jameson's hopefulness more than her assessment of national character, such a warning might seem gratuitous. But even at the end, when the Allied soldiers jointly defeat a German incursion, and the antisemite has cleared off, his voice echoes as a reminder that it is not France alone which is endangered by its resemblence to Nazi Germany, but Britain, too, which suffers from 'the same hardness, you'd think it was indestructible' (*Fort*, p. 158).

Of course, as we have seen from the survey of Jameson's dystopias, she felt that England's trust in its indestructibility is more myopic than clearsighted. Her position fictionally encapsulates both the myopia and an attempt to gaze critically and historically through its distortions. In this way she is both insider and outsider, a position that invites her empathy with the fate of European Jews as well as encouraging a self-directed guilt and recrimination. In every work that features a male-centred plot and/or male narrator or protagonist, Jameson is present in her identification with Britain's patriarchal history. She holds herself accountable for being complicit in her love for the nation whose politics she questions. As both insider and outsider, she assesses Britain's conflicted embrace of those it would rule but not grant equal economic, political or social status. It is from this position that she serves as both guide and accomplice to the male characters she sends on the European odyssey she herself took in the thirties. Her European fictions then track her own critical awakening through that of these men to the collective consciouness of civilizations that are not only distinct from Britain, but who need Britain's support to keep the integrity of their differences. In this sense, Europe also figures as the presence of the Other in Britain itself. For as the world both shrinks and splits apart with the coming of the Second World War, Jameson redefines Britain's international role in her own empire. Questioning and then dismissing mythologies of an essential Englishness as supporting supremacism and imperialism, she nonetheless locates its centre in the halls of political power where its mythologies reign as determining policies of independence and hegemony.

7

Defending Europe's Others

THE BATTLEGROUNDS OF PHYLLIS BOTTOME AND OLIVIA MANNING

Like Storm Jameson, Phyllis Bottome (1882–1963) created a series of fictions that analyse Britain's historic relationship to Europe. A prolific and popular author in her own day, Bottome combined her interest in the psychology of social responsibility and women's self-determination in several novels, including the 1934 *Private Worlds*, whose central character is a woman psychologist torn between the professional pressures of forging a place in a male-dominated hospital, her work with patients, and her love for a male colleague. Bottome also lectured and wrote about international relations and political responsibility from the perspective of having lived in Vienna in the early twenties and then in Munich from 1931 to 1933. Her European fiction was based on her experiences there and the force of her social and political involvement led her to create plots that predict the fate of European civilization through the plight of its Jews. She and her husband, Ernan Forbes Dennis, a British passport officer, left Munich in May 1933, 'when it was no longer possible to live there without witnessing the cruel persecution of our Jewish friends, or ourselves refusing to make terms, however passively, with the controlling gangsters'.[1]

This decision occurred after years of forging deep professional ties and friendships. Among her many humanitarian commitments, Bottome helped organize and run soup kitchens to feed 600 people a day in the wake of Austrian economic collapse after World War I. Her belief in the nurturing possibilities of education led her and her husband to found a school for the disadvantaged at Kitzbühl, an experience reinforced by meeting Alfred Adler, whose moral psychology of individual and collective responsibility she admired so much. Through him Bottome came to believe that Britain's best interests lay in a moral obligation to restore Europe to its own political well-being.

Bottome's conviction that psychological health was inseparable from its social and ethical contexts led her to assess the ideological and political alternatives at the end of World War I as 'static'.[2] She felt that

> Communism promised all that Christianity had once offered; but.... The theory of salvation through the fallacy of 'economic man' became strangely bloodless by the time Bolshevism had done with it. Dictatorship of the Left had a far better programme than dictatorship of the Right, but it rested upon the lie which is the foundation of all dictatorships – that authority can take the place of personal responsibility. (*Mansion*, p. 186).

Bottome was also not sanguine that British democracy in its present form could infuse personal responsibility into political morality. Although she did not subscribe to the concept of 'class war', she identified a primary flaw in British democracy as its economic and social inequities. She felt that even if World War II saved the world for democracy, Britain's 'unfair privileges which lead direct to dictatorships ... might make Great Britain – after the war is over – precisely such a slave State as the dictators we are now fighting made of Germany and Italy' (*Mansion*, p. 201). The victims she had in mind were not only the economically and socially oppressed of Britain, but those alien to the British political imagination – the Jews, for as she wrote to *Time and Tide* from Paris in March, 1938, 'To our everlasting shame we too, who are responsible for this débâcle [the Anschlüss], are also tightening up our frontiers against those people whom we have given to the wolves'.[3] In this same letter, Bottome warns that unless Britain is shamed 'into doing her duty ... [e]ventually we shall have to pay for so long having enjoyed immunity from personal suffering at the expense of others' (*T&T*, p. 453).

On her return to Britain, Bottome acted upon her definition of political responsibility by campaigning tirelessly for Jewish refugees. In the process, she implicated her own nation in the fate of the Jews as much as she did the Nazis. Reminding her readers of 'what the Jewish people have done for us and for our culture for more than a thousand years', she implores 'England and America to find homes for [those] trodden into the mire by an empty transitory fanaticism that carries within it the seeds of its own death' (*T&T*, p. 453). By 1941, when the war was in its third year and appeasement was but a bitter memory, she continued to argue for a war against 'universal State Slavery' (*Mansion*, p. 187). For Bottome this was not only a war that carried the democratic banner against Italy and Germany, but, recalling the failed outcome of World War I, she mocked the rallying cry of democracy with her own 'aim of fighting to keep democracy safe for the world' (*Mansion*, p. 188). This fight would include keeping her own nation on its ethical toes lest its brand of democracy fall into the same political pit as Nazi Germany; for Bottome, the potential was already there in Britain's exclusionary and dangerous hierarchies. Refusing to accept the arguments that cast Jewish refugees as an economic threat and potential fifth column, she excoriated government policies of severely limited Jewish immigration as xenophobic.

For Bottome, British and European culture and history are not only inseparable from that of the Jews, but dependent on and responsible for those very people who, she argued tirelessly, created the moral foundations of the culture that would now exclude them. Furious at Europe's rejection of the Jews, she wrote a letter that was published in the American magazine, *The New Republic*. With calculated resonance, the letter is entitled 'I Accuse'; it begins by finding the Archbishop of Canterbury 'culpable' for his 'joy over the German military occupation of Austria'.[4] What is at stake for Bottome here is a Christian culture and eschatology interestingly different from that of Ethel Mannin, Dorothy Sayers, or even Vera Brittain: the fate of 'the race from which the Founder of his own religion sprang' ('Accuse', p. 232). She asks the Archbishop: 'Can any Christian accept lightly the fate of the 200 000 Jews in Vienna who are being systematically pillaged and tortured . . .?' ('Accuse', p. 232). The Primate, however, is not alone in his guilt. She also accuses the Prime Minister, the 'Cliveden set', and the press; for Bottome, all those institutions that represent the power 'to juggle with the conscience of England' are complicit in a 'gentleman's agreement' with 'forces inimical to our birthright of freedom' ('Accuse', p. 232). Bottome's letter had been written the previous spring in response to Germany's takeover of Austria, but had 'been refused with regret' by 'several liberal-minded weeklies in Great Britain' ('Accuse', p. 232). By the time it was published in *The New Republic*, on 28 December 1938, the letter's accusations pointed to the escalating violence that had issued from the 'gentleman's agreement': on 9 November Kristallnacht had exploded in Berlin.

It is more than likely that a driving force of Bottome's wartime fiction was the rejection of her letter in Britain, especially as she saw it as an ominous sign of her nation's 'shame'. The rejection coincided with her observation that there were too few who expressed concern for the Jews. Among the silent voices were the liberal press, government ministries, and the workers who feared Jewish refugees would take their jobs, not to mention the gentry who sympathized with Germany and found fascism a bulwark against their dissolution.[5] That Bottome's fiction fills the silence is not a new development, however; her wartime fiction merely shifts the grounds for her ongoing concerns. Her fiction of the twenties had already begun to explore relationships between the Jewish origins of Christianity and the rejection and persecution of the Jews. How these themes were relevant to the fate of Central Europe was the subject of *Old Wine*, her 1924 novel of the fall of the Austro-Hungarian Empire at the end of World War I. Startingly prescient, *Old Wine* traces the increasingly systematic persecution of Jews to the destabilized populace of Central Europe. This includes not only the now anomalous but irresolute aristocracy, but the new regime, as well as ordinary people.

In rhetoric and behaviour that cut across class and gender lines, Bottome saw that the supremacism to which old Europe clung for its power was threatened by the Jews' will to survive and prosper. For Bottome, old Central Europe constituted a society driven by 'blind arrogance' ('Accuse', p. 232). But if Central Europe's trappings and social codes appear alien and feudal compared to the more moderate climes of Britain, Bottome makes it abundantly clear that moderation and restraint only mask the failure of moral and political responsibility.

By 1937, Bottome had launched her crusade for Europe and its Jews on both a British and American audience. Her novel, *The Mortal Storm*, a blockbuster on both sides of the Atlantic, dramatizes the rise and consequences of nazism with trenchant psychological, social, and historical analysis. Her psychological analysis of political events was the outgrowth of applying the principles of Alfred Adler's moral psychology to individual and political behaviour. During the twenties, when Bottome met Adler in Germany, she was particularly taken with his view that people's political behaviour was shaped by their particular historical and social circumstances. What made *The Mortal Storm* so popular as a novel and an American star-studded movie, was not Bottome's political analysis, however, but its treatment of nazism in a romance and adventure plot.[6] Through the daring of its heroine, Freya Toller, the novel's anti-fascist and specifically anti-Nazi analysis focuses on the fate of the Jews at the moment of the Reichstag fire and Hitler's consolidation of power.

The novel expresses Bottome's despair that Germany would turn to nazism for salvation, but it also enacts her deep love for its people. She dramatizes the Nazis' takeover by depicting a family torn apart not only by divided identities and responses, but by terror and persecution. The family, half Toller and half Von Rohn, is composed of a Jewish father, two stepsons who have joined the Nazi party, an aristocratic mother, a daughter whose ambitions betray the Nazis' presciptions for women, and a son too young to leave the fold. Together, they enact Bottome's concerns about the fate of Germany, the nature of collective responsibility, and the role of the individual.

The novel constructs Germany's fate through that of its Jews, embodied specifically in the characters of a Jewish Nobel scientist, Johann Toller, and his daughter Freya. Bottome portrays the Nazis' *realpolitik* as a travesty of individual and cultural identity. According to Hitler's Nuremberg laws, because her mother is a German aristocrat, Freya can save herself by identifying as a German; but shaped by Bottome's politics, she assumes her father's Jewish identity. Freya's choice of this identity tests not only her personal fate, but that of the future of Europe. Bottome creates an irony in Freya's choice by juxtaposing Jewish law and Hitler's belief in racial purity. Jewish law prescribes that Jewish identity passes through the mother, while Nazi policy identified Jews through more inclusive channels. For the Nazis, the Jews of Europe would include not only those who claimed their inherited identities, but those who chose to assimilate, as well as children and grandchildren of Jews married to Germans and other European citizens. Freya's assumption of her father's Jewish identity represents a choice that defies Nazi racialist ideology at the moment antisemitism becomes political action in Germany. Instead of destroying her, however, as it probably would have in reality, Freya's Jewish identity activates her will to survive. At the novel's end, Freya escapes the Germany that in history as much as in Bottome's fiction would destroy her Jewish father.

Bottome's 1937 prediction of the Final Solution serves to comment on the Allies' political responsibility as well. Together with Freya's passage to the West as a Jewish woman, Bottome's prediction represents a rite of passage into geo-political maturity for Europe, Britain, and the United States. The targeting of an American audience stemmed not only from her political judgement that the United States was needed to help fight the Nazis, but from her deep attachment to the country where she had spent years of her childhood.[7] As Freya skis across mountain passes that have historically marked national and cultural distinctions, rivalries, and antipathies, Bottome translates her reading of Jewish history into the shaping of a moral character that could save the west: 'to be wise against ignorance, honest against piracy, harmless against cruelty, industrious against idleness, kind against cruelty'.[8] Unlike the nations that cling to the survival strategy of conquest and insularity, Bottome's Jews wish to live in the world and serve it while serving their distinctive beliefs.

The Mortal Storm was published at a time, Bottome notes, when 'the fate of six million Jews was in the balance' and dismissal of a Nazi threat inspired her to ask if 'England had gone Nazi in its sleep?' (*Goal*, pp. 258, 9). Her political purposes were clear to reviewers in Britain and in the US, one of whom found them an artistic limitation:

> ... the writer's own horror of what she conceives to be the fanatical worship of false gods, blunts her sympathies for the individual characters she has created.... Our lasting impression of this book is that we have been reading pages and pages of unadulterated political argument. Moving as it is in part, we do not consider this a great novel, because it is more a tract than a fictional masterpiece.[9]

Other reviewers found the novel 'not a tract, but a rapidly moving story' in which Bottome 'writes with so burning a conviction that the most precious thing in life is liberty of mind and conscience, that one is inclined to overlook what is weak in the narrative itself'.[10] Eric Duthie in *The Left Review* found Bottome's 'liberal sentiments genuinely held', and while no distraction from the novel's artistry, also found that her commitment critically highlighted her lack of 'need to question her premises'.[11]

The Nazi threat in *The Mortal Storm* is elaborated through Freya's character as she becomes aware of her status not only as a Jew, but as a woman. Having just passed her first year in medical school the winter before Hitler's election, 'She was conscious suddenly, and once and for all, that her womanhood was a disability', for the Reich 'threatened to turn back Freya's advancing sex into the mere production of cannon fodder' (*MS*, pp. 11, 9). The concerns expressed here by connecting the Nazi war machine and its biological determination of women's fate recall Katharine Burdekin's predictions in *Swastika Night*, also published in 1937. Rather than postdating her inquiry as does Burdekin and therefore dramatizing the effects of victimizing ideologies, Bottome allows her victims to debate these ideologies and to understand their political consequences even as they begin to explode. Unlike Burdekin's dystopia, where the future remains tenuous at best, Bottome's novel is more hopeful, especially as she engineers it in the form of a woman's escape.

Bottome's hope for Jewish survival and the value of European civilization rests not in government policies, but in a woman's critical capacity. Amongst all the men who dominate personal and political domains in this novel only Freya develops a political wisdom that is translated into action at the very moment when the fate of Europe passes into 'too late'. In assuming her father's identity, Freya does not reject her mother either as an individual or as representative of German culture. In fact, even as she identifies with her father, Freya incorporates her mother's critique of German androcentric culture. To become a professional woman, a doctor like her father, defies the fate the Nazis have designed for women and for which Freya's mother fears: 'Another girl is to be tortured – to have the life of her soul frozen . . . I thought we had escaped from the world where women were at a man's mercy – considered only as his tools or his toys!' (*MS*, p. 245). If Freya were to remain in Germany she would be destroyed twice over – as a Jew and as a woman, seeking not just to live, but how to live. Bottome thus identifies the Jewish woman as a doubly damned Other, but in addition to Jewish victimization, she locates salvation in the infusion of the Jews' talents and the woman's in each other.

Although their narrative perspectives and degrees of optimism differ, Bottome and Burdekin share the basis of their hopes for undoing the possibility of a thousand year Reich. Even as they locate their own nation's worst inequities in the Nazi's masculinist political culture, they also discover possibilities for positive change in their construction of English national character. Resembling the views of the English held by Burdekin's Teutonic knight, Johann Toller urges his daughter to escape to 'an Anglo-Saxon country' because 'The English have always been practical, and ruled themselves and each other with common-sense. They have a love of freedom for themselves which makes them – occasionally – fair to others' (*MS*, p. 385). In full recognition of Britain's history of oppressing women and aliens, Bottome insists that the nation is something more than its public institutions. These, which are 'known and given, like the Britain to which Churchill's rhetoric appealed' are also 'in a state of becoming', that is, unlike the intractible Nazi polity, Britain is malleable, subject to the liberal pressures of a commonsense decency (*Gervais*, p. 178).[12] If this sounds suspiciously like a Whigish belief in progressivism, Bottome's embrace of Others is far too radical in its insistence on immediate action.

Freya's escape represents decisive and even romantic action, but it does not lead her to total freedom, for it involves personal and collective sacrifices that Bottome herself would see as viable political compromises. Freya's identification with her father as a scientist is both enriched and undermined by his lessons about Jewish history. She has learned to value her Jewish identity as part of the Jews' contributions to European culture as well as its internal 'strength that has outlived persecutions' (*MS*, p. 89). But Johann Roth also characterizes Jewish identity as bound up with Judaism as a religion, the importance of which lies primarily in its relation to Christianity. Thus he speaks to his 12-year-old son of the Jewish 'coming-of-age' as marking the moment when Jesus left his parents to found the religion ultimately embraced by Europeans (*MS*, p. 231). Toller is of course referring to the Bar Mitzvah, which is the ceremony marking the 13-year-old Jewish male's passage into fulfilling Jewish laws and practices. In Bottome's politics of identification, however, the event signifies a transition out of Judaism, not merely within it. It marks the moment when Jesus leaves his parent religion to fulfil and teach, but also to revise the moral precepts on which Jewish laws and practices rest.

Bottome's view of Jesus's teaching is not transcendent, however. Instead it reflects the history of the Jews in Christian Europe where Christian behaviour was often at odds with the moral basis of Christianity. In Bottome's historical interpretation, rather than promulgating the best intentions of Christian Europe, the new religion became 'a very dangerous idea' because it backfired (*MS*, p. 231). Bottome's writing argues that Christianity led to persecuting the Jews as a scapegoat for the moral failures of Christians; the Jews were viewed as the source of a moral code Europeans 'failed to practice' (*MS*, p. 231).

If the story of Jesus foretells the historic persecution of the Jews, it also transcends it, and *The Mortal Storm* becomes a parable about the sacrifice of modern Jews. Johann Toller is ultimately killed by the Nazis, but Freya becomes his apostle, representing his ideas and identity 'to the world that he had left too soon' (*MS*, p. 231). Freya will save herself by becoming a noble Jewish scientist, but what will save Europe is not the presence of the Jewish moral character she embodies. Instead, she leaves her otherwise illegitimate child to be raised by and identify with good Christian peasants; their home, in which she has birthed her son, is envisioned as 'a stable' surrounded by 'two-thousand-year-old shepherds' (*MS*, p. 412). The new saviour will regenerate a decaying Christian civilization, just as the infant Jesus in a crèche scene early in the novel represents the New Testament regenerating the Old. Bottome emphasizes the child's Jewish blood and heritage, but as also having been refreshed by the undefensive and therefore untarnished simplicity of his peasant family.

Bottome's ambivalences about the status of Jewish identity and religion never interfered with her belief that Jewish moral, intellectual, and cultural contributions were the foundations of Christian Europe's best intentions. Even more compelling, she never viewed Jews as anything but human and so was immune to and indeed, starkly critical of any efforts to stereotype or demonize their differences even as she relegates their irremedial status to Other. Years after World War II, when attention to the victims of Nazi Germany was supplanted by the Cold War, Bottome found it necessary to show that antisemitism had not been extinguished in Hitler's death camps, but flourished in the outposts of the British Empire. Her short story, 'The Oblation', published in her 1958 collection, *Walls of Glass*, treats the fate of a Jewish couple with sympathetic irony. August and Lisa Meissener, who 'had the sense to leave Germany in 1933' and the luck to land on an island in the British West Indies when war breaks out, are 'looked on as Hitler's chosen victims, and therefore the strongest of allies'[13]

Years after the war, despite their secure position, the Meisseners feel marginalized, even threatened by the coming of Christmas, the celebration of which they can only face by asking, as they might have of the coming of Hitler, 'Isn't there any escape?' ('O', p. 178). With no escape from their condition as Jews in a Christian world, the Meisseners revive a solution from their past, one that melds the ideals of Jewish and Christian goodwill. No panacea, this solution is tinged with a kind of self-mocking irony endemic to a fatalism that is the bitter fruit of their having made too many correct dire predictions. They decide to bring a gift to the British Colonel Ferguson, an unabashed racist and antisemite. Offering the gift is an unpleasant but necessary act for the Meisseners, an 'oblation', that will 'make sure of everything else going right' ('O', p. 181). By the story's end, the Meisseners reconceive their meaning of 'oblation', not to reflect their positive effect on the Colonel, but to affirm both their Jewish identity and its transcendence in Christian feeling.

Throughout the story, each time August Meissener confronts the Colonel's antisemitic disdain, he is moved to defend the uncertain state of his Jewish identity by explaining it in relation to the moral primacy of Jesus. Although the immediate cause of his uncertainty is, as readers might expect, the residual effects of the war, he focuses on the more remote event of the crucifixion of Jesus. But Meissener is not concerned about the persecutions of the Jews that are based on the belief that they killed Christ. Instead, he questions the separate beliefs of Judaism by bemoaning the fact that the Jews did not support Jesus, 'for he was an enlightened human being – the best kind of a Jew' ('O', p. 183). At the end, Meissener constructs 'the best kind of Jew' as a universalist or, one might say, catholic image of melding one's religious and cultural identity into 'a great fellowship' in which 'people's hearts and lives . . . melted' into 'the same songs, and . . . whose spirits and whose bodies' cohabit 'without enmity!' ('O', p. 190). Such an image, however, in the light of the story's implication in its own historical contexts and its own rhetorical structure, works ironically against itself. Thus Meissener's Jewish identity denies the very universality he claims above and still later. At the end, he redefines the meaning of 'oblation' as the 'pouring away of something precious, in order to show gratitude for what is still in the cup' ('O', pp. 191–2). What his revision relies on, what he feels cannot be taken away and includes him in 'brotherhood', is his identification with Europe ('O', p. 189).

But of course this continent of tightly bound national identities has not allowed him to forget his own specifically marked identity, much less 'melt' into theirs.

Bottome highlights Meissener's self-deluded buoyancy by situating his denial of historically determined differences in an exchange with the Colonel, one that expresses but does not recognize the gender differences they create. The Colonel and Meissener manage to achieve a kind of 'sympathy and fellow feeling' over their nostalgia for skiing in the Bavarian Alps, the value of which turns on a 'code as sportsmen' ('O', p. 190). This code had affirmed their manhood by accepting and protecting women as objects of natural beauty, like the mountains themselves. Bottome's irony here draws attention to the same masculinist ideology that she condemns as fascist in *The Mortal Storm* and, as we shall see, in all her other writing. Deeply implicated in the racialist policies that destroyed European Jews, such 'fellow feeling' also justified dehumanizing Jewish men by feminizing them – Jewish men cannot, by dint of their racial construction, ever be good sportsmen. They are therefore outcasts not only in the Nazi sphere, but in the empire represented by the Colonel himself. Meissener's final 'oblation' condemns the European history of Jewish alienation and destruction by affirming that 'We are Europe!' because 'its rich inheritance, its long acted upon traditions', were made possible by the presence of the Jews ('O', p. 191).

Bottome's 1943 novel, *Within the Cup*, combines her concerns about the place of the Jews in Europe and in Britain. Set primarily in an English village, the novel expresses Bottome's fear that English insularity would lead the nation to dismiss the moral and political lessons of Nazi-dominated Europe. The plot is propelled by an English couple who rescue a German-Jewish psychiatrist. Bringing Rudolph von Ritterhaus to Britain will not only save him from the Nazis, but rescue Britain from its failure to enact the moral precepts it claims. The nation's internal weaknesses are represented by three Englishwomen whom Ritterhaus restores to moral and psychological health – the neurasthenic Lady Wendover, her spoiled daughter, Gillian, and the young American wife who, the doctor says, has 'not learned to belong to herself.[14] These women find what the good doctor calls their 'aggressive will' by accepting his lessons and integrating him into English civilization (*Cup*, p. 149). Von Ritterhaus's diagnosis of the women's problems is analogous to Bottome's analysis of

Britain's weaknesses and her fear that they mirrored Nazi Germany. As a gloss on this fear, also in 1943, Bottome spoke of 'Hitler's Order' in her speech to the Austrian Youth Association in London.[15] Just as she enjoins these young people to use their moral strength to identify with the values of 'brotherhood' and selflessness, so Von Ritterhaus convinces Lady Wendover that her weak heart can be strengthened by giving up her emotional and moral isolation.

The psychiatrist does not, however, blame his women patients for their ills; instead he sees their problems as a double bind: they are ensnared by a social structure which reminds him of a statue of the Laocoon in classical mythology. This monument to the father 'struggling with terrific and hopeless valour in order to free his sons' renders women invisible; in their absence, women are figured as already crushed (*Cup*, p. 150). The doctor views the Laocoon as a neurotic family system which, in its allusion to the ancient Trojan War and to a myth of heroic masculinity, is a trope for this world war, 'an evil phantom in the mind of man' (*Cup*, p. 151). The family and social structure which has made women 'captive balloon[s]' squeezes the life out of people, like the concentration camps made possible, von Ritterhaus argues, only by a 'top-dog world – out of which murder springs' (*Cup*, pp. 65, 281).

The analogy here between this English family system and the system that produced death camps is neither gratuitous nor does it elide their differences. The 'orgy of selfish wish-dreams' that 'blotted out the conscience of [Hitler's] people', that encouraged them to think themselves 'superior' to everyone else is part of the three-tiered logic Bottome ascribes to the formation of the Nazi Order ('Austria', p. 9). The isolationism that denies others' needs creates 'the top dog', that is, the person who 'feels so superior to other people' that he or she feels justified in becoming the 'exploiter' of the other who has no choice but to be the 'under dog' ('Austria', pp. 16, 15). Bottome's novel also shows that such feelings as they apply equally to people and to nations also mask the fear of losing the hegemony that outwardly marks superiority and ensures it. Von Ritterhaus, as much prophet as psychiatrist, recognizes from his exiled position that these 'top dog' qualities are psychological and moral dangers to the internal politics of Britain. And so his medical efforts are also moral and political, designed to save Britain from yielding to 'selfish' isolationism.

This policy, which the novel translates as a moral/political position, includes hegemony not only over Britain's empire but over any of its subjects who define themselves according to different social or cultural codes. The good doctor thus directs his energies towards the exploited and weakened Other as a way of building Britain's resolve to fight the Nazi Order. In his diagnosis, women's vulnerability signifies Britain's moral weakness as well as its consequences. The novel shows women developing the defensive need to become exploiters in order to prove their own strength, not always for self-determination, but to retaliate for their condition.

By implication, the doctor's cure for the women can also save the world; for women will use their 'aggressive will' to lead men and thus to 'prove ourselves the spiritual enemies of the Nazis' (*Cup*, pp. 149, 281). We must 'fight . . . side by side . . . to win a world that belongs equally to all of us', but this is possible only if we love our enemies (*Cup*, p. 281). Unfortunately, however, the rhetorical implications of the doctor's cure produces another disorder, for von Ritterhaus restores the women's faith in the ideology which supports the very system that enfeebled them. His prescription for a Christian campaign may vanquish the master race by love, but it will also restore the hegemony of a patriarchal family system. Thus one of the doctor's patients, the American wife, is doomed to spend the rest of her life with her sadistic Christian minister husband. Inspired by von Ritterhaus's sermons, she exercises her 'aggressive will', and after being crippled in a heroic act during a Nazi air attack, is not only dependent on her husband, but made to understand that she must believe in his good intentions. She will be protected by the same masculinist code Bottome questioned in her story, 'The Oblation', in which women 'were treated with chivalry for their womanhood', by being protected from their own independence ('O', p. 190).

The possibility that Bottome's novel reinscribes the same double bind she laments is politically and morally complicated by the fate she designs for her noble Jewish doctor. Von Ritterhaus says: 'To a Jew, what is important is that God should be immortal . . . but to-night I thought that perhaps immortality is just as certain as mortality' (*Cup*, p. 184). The Christian eschatology to which von Ritterhaus refers will save him from a Nazi Götterdämmerung but as it also supercedes the Jewish emphasis on a mortal/moral life it prophesies a salvation that bears an uncanny resemblance to the very destruction that Bottome's text protests. In transforming the Jewish psychiatrist into a Christian healer, the novel converts him and therefore inscribes the disappearance of the Jew in the Jewish doctor.

Like all of Bottome's noble doctors, von Ritterhaus is based on Jewish doctors she knew, particularly Alfred Adler, whom she met in 1927. Her biography of Adler, *Apostle of Freedom*, transcribes his complex moral lessons, including those about Jewish enrichment of European culture as well as about those conditions that produced the same kind of defensive postures and isolation in Jews that she ascribes to women. In turn, she uses this history to construct Adler's biographical character as a model for her fictional Jewish doctors. She writes that he converted to Christianity in order to 'escape . . . the isolating qualities thrust upon his race by persecution. He was at once more courageous and more modest than those who have had to face constant rebuffs and are sometimes forced to try to get the better of their opponents by flattery or through undue persistance'.[16] Though his conversion allows the good doctor to escape the historic circumstances that would diminish and probably destroy him, it paradoxically serves as a reminder of a continuous history of Jewish persecution and a call to escape the character produced by persecution. The qualities of nurture, selflessness, and self-effacement may constitute the Christian healer as derived from the pacific character of Jesus, but because these same qualities are also associated with the passive character of women, they mark him as a problematic alien – an unChristian, demasculinized Jewish man. This feminization stigmatizes the good doctor not only as an unassimilable Other, but ironically, as a carrier of disease, especially as the effeminate, decadent Jew is a conventional feature of antisemitic cartoons.[17]

Bottome's apostle is saved from his own racial character and from having to be a victim of Jewish history by converting to a different subjectivity and to another historical narrative. This is nowhere more apparent than in the form of *Within the Cup*, which consists of Rudi's journal recording his disillusionment with Germany, his escape, and his experiences in England, all narrated in English. Like the narrative of the New Testament, according to Sander Gilman, Rudi's story parallels that of the Jews 'as a preamble to the coming of Christ' (*JB*, p. 18). Just as the original language of his testament is lost, Rudi's Jewishness is validated only as it becomes invisible. His loss, however, restores his masculinity and gains him access to English culture; assimilated into its literary plotting, he can marry the heiress to the manor at the end.

By the middle of the war, Bottome's fiction fully condemned not only Nazi Germany, but aspects of German and Austrian culture and historical consciousness she felt had nurtured self-destructive means of restoring their power. Her 1946 novel *The Lifeline*, set in 1938, finds Austria complicit and self-deluded in its Anschlüss and as a corrective, sets a heroic Jewish doctor against the policies and practices of nazism. The Nazi occupation of Europe is portrayed as the logical result of failing to recognize 'a suffocating masked horror' within its own culture.[18] In this novel the good psychiatrist is a woman, but still a Jew. With a Jewish grandmother 'tucked away', Ida Eichorn cannot escape the identity which for the Nazis competes with her aristocratic lineage (*Lifeline*, p. 24). It is in the fusion of this racial and class politics that Bottome locates the destructive power of Nazi ideology. Hidden away in Ida's schloss – now a mental hospital – is a figure embodying the monstrous aggression of old Austria and the new Germany. In a room of majestic proportions, below a heroic portrait of Archduke Michel Salvator, is a cage; inside, paces a creature who appears to be half man half animal. This is the living Michel Salvator, who has transmuted into a werewolf-like alter ego of Hitler. Unlike the horrible creature of Mary Shelley's Dr Frankenstein, Michel Salvator harbours no vestige of yearning for humane feeling. Instead, he is ruled solely by his desire 'to rule omnipotently by getting rid of all moral restraints' (*Lifeline*, p. 283). His cage protects him from self-destruction while protecting the victims of his omnipotent rule, including those like Ida who would be identified as Jewish.

Salvator represents the psychopathology that produced the alliance of the old order and the new, whose 'dreams are incurably dangerous' (*Lifeline*, p. 285). The Archduke may not be *compos mentis*, but that is the result of twisting his leadership responsibility to sacrifice others to his omnivorous urges. With Salvator as her test case, the woman psychiatrist cures her nation by treating him as an amalgam of individual and collective psychology. Her methods suggest a feminist incarnation of Tennyson's Princess Ida and Dr Frankenstein; Ida Eichorn is an altruistic warrior–academic who restores her nation's political health by re-educating and rehumanizing its men. Assuming political responsibility for her nation's destiny, Ida invents a holistic psychiatric strike against the devouring narcissism of Salvator and the Nazis. As much curriculum as treatment, Ida's medicine is designed to redirect men's 'incurably dangerous' dreams so that they do not succumb to the Nazi 'logic' that turns men into beasts (*Lifeline*, p. 286).

Bottome's novel takes the historic present further into the retrogressive pit Virginia Woolf imagined as the logical consequence of male militarism in *Between the Acts*. Salvator's aggression, linked to that of the Nazis, shares the same political means and ends as militarism, but the novel also distinguishes it from the defensive warfare of Ida and the Allies she helps. The success of Ida's experiment depends on rehabilitating those men self-consumed by nazism by modelling them on her empathetic character, emphasizing caring principles of the feminine. Her heroism however, reveals another political and cultural danger, for it depends on diffusing her character. Thus certain aspects of Ida's character protect others: as a Jewish woman, she is protected by being a Christian, aristocratic doctor. Her aristocratic lineage protects her womanhood; her healing skills make her indispensable to the Nazis, and her Christian goodness attracts protectors. Though such a dense texture enriches the complexity of her character, it also destabilizes that part of her identity which Bottome inserts in order to defend. In the metamorphosis of this female hero, only one characteristic is really lost. As a Jewish 'princess', Bottome's Ida can be heroic only if her Christian and aristocratic identities conceal her Jewishness and allow her, like von Ritterhaus, to be protected by an English marriage plot. The Jew in Ida is protected by disappearing into the margins of the text. In this novel, the Jew is saved, but has no place, either in this historical romance or in the story of a nation's regeneration.

Bottome's sympathy for the Jews throughout the Nazi threat never wavered, but she shared Alfred Adler's concern that their defensive character had been formed too indelibly by continuous persecution. She also believed that conversion to Christianity did not indicate the disappearance of the Jew, but rather a realization of Judaism's highest moral code. At a time when the material consequences of being different were punishable by either incarceration or death, Bottome's idea that equality necessitated assimilation was connected to her definitions of liberal democracy and feminism. And so Bottome's crusade for Jews, women, and European civilization collapses an ideology of opposition into a new kind of trinity. In her apocalyptic vision, the Jewish son, betrayed to the anti-Christ, Hitler, leaves his earthly kingdom to the daughters who carry Jewish history within them. But these daughters transform that history only by giving birth to a new Christian saviour who will defeat what Bottome calls 'the religion of cruelty and death' (*MS*, p. 27). An internationalist politically, she valued cultural difference but in the service of a 'brotherhood' that would mitigate the exlusionary qualities she attributed to ethnic and religious separatism. As the character of Freya Toller demonstrates, persecution of Jewish Others ends only as a result of locating oneself in their fate.

Like Bottome's novels, the World War II epic of Olivia Manning (1908–80) collapses oppositions between the fates of Britain and Europe as it intertwines a woman's war odyssey and the fate of the Jew. *The Balkan Trilogy*, written after the war, along with its sequel, *The Levant Trilogy*, was inspired by Manning's own experiences.[19] In Bucharest when the Nazis took over, Manning and her husband fled to Athens and then to Cairo and Jerusalem. Many years later, she fulfilled her authobiographical sense of creative process: as she told Kay Dick, 'I write out of experience. I have no fantasy. I don't think anything I've experienced has ever been wasted'.[20] And so she transformed her own odyssey into the fictional one of Harriet Pringle. Entwined in a panoramic representation of the home front on two continents, Manning's heroine becomes a rootless cosmopolitan after a whirlwind marriage to Guy Pringle, who, like Manning's husband, Reginald Smith, was a British Council lecturer in Bucharest in 1939. Manning's novels contrast the positions and perspectives of Harriet and Guy to emphasize relationships between the social and emotional marriage contract and the political contracts and dislocations of war.

Despite Guy Pringle's charismatic largesse, his avowed love for his wife and for the world's oppressed, Guy suffers from chronic detachment; he is never happier than when directing people and actions from behind the scenes, whether an English play on the European stage or supplying the rhetoric for the political actions of others. His nervous energy and political theorizing are better suited to the classroom and café than to sustained human and political commitments. Relegated to the edge of Guy's world, including their marriage, Harriet is always an innocent bystander to events that shape her life. Poised on her Bucharest balcony, she can only watch helplessly while European civilization and its traditional forms of security are destroyed. Among the ruins are the romance and marriage plots in which an English heroine's search for self-determination takes the form of resisting and yet falling for the fatal charms of an elusive brooding knight until her love demystifies him and he is domesticated. Like Elizabeth Taylor, who revised the fate of Jane Eyre in the consciousness of Julia Davenant, and Elizabeth Bowen, whose Stella Rodney rejects domestication and finds only betrayal in mystery men, Manning questions the stability of English civilization in the character of the man who represents it. Harriet follows her lecturer husband across Europe and the Middle East, barely keeping their lives intact as one after the other his lesson plans to redeem the fallen fail. In its revelations of her struggle to decide how to survive, her narrative implicates the hollowness of a male-defined courage in the war's tragedies.

As a result of being marginalized by her husband's play-acting, the forces of war, and the literary marriage plot, Harriet's point of view becomes increasingly depressed, reflecting not only her own position, but the unremitting necessity of fighting a war whose sweep and horrors so often obscure its goals. Manning herself was in a perfect position to make this determination as she worked throughout the war as press officer wherever she and her husband landed. In her story, 'Last Civilian Ship', depicting the flight from the German siege of Greece, she notes that 'There was no getting at the truth. The stop on news set everyone on edge'.[21] Through Manning's precision lens and reflective memory, we see Harriet struggle to identify the social reality of women's marginalized position in the mysterious ways of men's wars. Within the epic's intricate cast of characters, fictional plotting, and historically grounded events, Harriet Pringle dominates Manning's vast canvas with an ironically dramatic refusal of agency, appearing to sleepwalk through personal and political upheaval. Though her complacency parodies British reserve and stiff upper lip, especially Guy's Mr Chips's optimism, it also highlights the sense of a woman's redundancy in a male-dominated war zone.

Harriet is allowed no space in the theatre of world war in which to construct her identity or expression. Instead, Manning builds Harriet's character throughout the six volumes of *The Balkan and Levant Trilogies* as dependent on her identification with the fate of another marginalized Other, the Jew. Until she saves her young

Jewish friend, Sasha Drucker, from the Rumanian Iron Guard, Harriet's passivity marks the sufferance of a traditional English heroine waiting to be rescued either from or into a domestic or romance plot. But unlike the First World War, World War II will destroy the sanctity of civilian space and collapse differences between rescue from or into domesticity or romance. Focusing her historical interpretation on a woman's place in the Second World War, Manning's constructs her female character to show how she is subject to the imperatives of home front and battleground as they are now combined. The result is that Harriet emerges as a sign of both the oppressed and oppressor.

Figured as a space deep within Central Europe, this home front battleground is both threatening and a threatened place – a little shed perched on the roof of the Pringles' Bucharest apartment where Harriet hides Sasha. The vulnerable and yet easily overlooked shelter replicates the construction and constriction of Jew and woman as dependent and yet subversive Others. Conflating playhouse and prison cell, the shed is a likely candidate to signify either fantasy or nightmare. Such a confining space also reflects social and historical realities, however – the domestic space that infantilizes the woman by overprotecting her, and the ghetto that feminizes the Jew by keeping him powerless. Constructed and constricted as dependent and inessential Others, they are treated like pets, just like the homeless kitten Harriet adopts and whose loss she mourns as though it were her own life. By turns nonconformist and needy, amusing and annoying, Sasha earns the affectionate tolerance from Harriet that she endures from her husband and his colleagues. Playing games and teasing form the activities defining the childlike nature of their relationship, marked as distinctly nonsexual from beginning to end. Their identification as playthings, however, while rendering them harmless, also suggests that both Sasha and Harriet represent a threat to the very political systems that marginalize them. Thus Manning narrates their relationship as a counterdiscourse, both in relation to the fascist takeover which threatens their lives, and to the rhetorical force of the war stories playing out around them.

The combined perspectives of the hopeless Jew and the empathetic and depressed woman deconstruct and mock the war epic as it is implicated in the historical movements of fascism. To use Rose Macaulay's phrase, in their 'sample corner of the war' there can be no heroic acts; instead, their games enact a kind of passive resistance to subplots of hidden documents and clandestine anti-Nazi manoeuvres. In the end, such resistance works in their favour; their perspectives are discredited by their enemies as irrational and perverse, and as a result, the Jew and the woman are able to survive the war. In this light we can see how Manning constructs their stories so as to suggest that critical questions about the machinery of war depend on the survival of the silenced Other.

Manning's trilogies twin the Jew and the woman, but also distinguish them. Despite their near fusion as infantilized, feminized Other, despite their joint tenancy on the margins, the Jew and the woman are subject to different historical and literary fates. The narrative structure which links their historical and literary condition also reinscribes the hierarchies that earmark the politics of war and victimization. Harriet's efforts to save Sasha spotlight her oppression but also show that the Jew's victimization is an inescapable condition to which her own contributes. Harriet's only empowerment is to offer Sasha a shelter that caricatures her insularity but accurately portrays his captive state. Harriet's empowerment is thus construed as the transformation of passivity into passive-aggression. The rooftop shed becomes a site of resistance for her that both saves and imprisons the Jew.

Unlike the woman, whose resistance will fail and return her to the protective custody of British historical and literary narratives, the helpless, feminized Jewish man is ghettoized as an aberration in the culture that makes him what he is. Considered an unnatural presence, he is therefore marked as decadent and guilty of subverting the codes of masculinity by which the dominant culture defines itself. Being a Jew exoticizes him but also marks him as threatening. Unlike a pet or child with whom his captivity is compared and whose dependency undermines rebellious behaviour, the Jew represents irremedial defiance of the power that tolerates his presence. Moreover, a pet or child's defiance is acceptable not only because it is doomed to fail, but because in cultures ordered by hierarchical principles of masculine/feminine, it is construed as 'naturally' childlike, and programmed to evolve into either the passive female or the dominant male. In this context, the Jew's resistance is unnatural because his relegation to the position of child is supposed to have declawed and neutered him, removing any possibility for him to develop into an adult male. Sasha's behaviour, however, reflects the failure of this dehumanizing policy. Most significantly, his feminization and passive-resistance reflect an ironic interpretation of the hostile manoeuvres of a fascist culture. In Manning's view, fascism's brutal commitment to validating its own masculinity derives from its fear of an inherent weakness, perhaps a recessive desire to submit.

In this critique of masculinist hierarchies, Harriet is positioned not only as sharing the margins with the Jew, but in opposition to his fate. Harriet is saved by her inability to escape her condition as protected English heroine. Indeed, she leaves Bucharest almost against her will, and then only at the last moment, when the Iron Guard awards the key to the city to Hitler's legions. History as rendered in this fiction refuses her the fate of the victim. As the twin trilogies track her odyssey from Rumania to Athens and then to Cairo and Damascus, she is endangered only by the lack of a site in which to constitute herself as capable of risk and independence. When she discovers that Sasha has been taken by the Iron Guard, she loses the reflection of herself either as passive victim or as agent of rescue. Sasha's unexpected appearance months later in Athens registers as the anti-climactic turning point in her development. As a result of seeing him she ends the possibility of a love affair she was about to begin, and when he responds indifferently to her, she loses all desire for desire or for change.

The historical moment of the narrative spotlights the depressing consequences of traditional literary plots for English heroines; at the same time, this historical epic cannot avoid the more dismal ending for the history of European Jews in World War II. This is especially consequential for a contemporary reading of the trilogies because Manning wrote it years after the war when issues of difference were already being debated as the colonial empires of the Allies were being dismantled, formerly colonized peoples were emigrating to imperial European capitals, and Rumania was now deep within the Soviet bloc. Manning paints the difference between Harriet and Sasha as neither universal nor essential, but as between two culturally and historically constructed ideologies of the Other. In their relationship, they remain, in Levinas's construction of Otherness, 'absolutely foreign' to each other.

Enacting a critique and revision of literary modes of self-determination, the English heroine constructs herself as Other by resisting the fate prescribed by both romantic plots and historical epic. The Jew is granted a literary Otherness to spur the passive resistance of our English heroine, but his lack of opportunity to critique or revise his plight replicates his historical Otherness. Sasha is a Jew whose lack of agency in the wartime period offers him only the role of victim or wanderer.

In its rendering of World War II, Manning's historical fiction complicates the categories of oppressor and oppressed as they intertwine with those of gender and culture. The depiction of a reluctant English heroine and the feminized Jewish wanderer works in concert with portraits of Sasha's noble father and unfortunate aunts. In Manning's retrospective narrative, neither the power of wealth nor the moral integrity of character can save Sasha's father, Emmanuel Drucker, from being driven from the margins of European civilization to its centre of destruction. History, however, is shaped by a literary plot when it comes to the destiny of Sasha's aunts. We never learn what happens to them, but their grossly stereotypical representation reflects only too painfully the process of dehumanization which made the Jews the irremedial alien. Harriet's reluctance to call on the Drucker sisters is substantiated by the narrator's description of their chubby, bejewelled hands stuffing their heavily made-up faces with what their nauseated guest sees as an endless stream of rich cakes. Set in contrast to Harriet's reserved English femininity, the aunts are a cultural gloss on the feminized Jewish man and on Manning's representation of European antisemitism. But as Manning presents them through Harriet's sympathetically portrayed political consciousness, the aunts also raise questions about whether we are to take them as reflections of Harriet's flawed sensibilities or of Manning's. Portrayed as caricatures of both bourgeois consumerism and feminine excess and uselessness, in terms of literary history, they can appeal neither to marriage plots nor tragedy to rescue them, and in terms of this reader's response today, they present a serious critical problem in an otherwise masterly epic of the war.[22]

Such lack of literary sympathy casts ironic shadows over the otherwise empathetic portrait of Sasha, of whom the narrator comments: 'He would be at home nowhere except here, in the midst of his family' (*Balkan*, p. 97). Emmanuel Drucker registers a complaint that reflects as much on his historic oppressors as it does on literary representation: 'we did not cause the war. We must live.... Why do they hate us?' (*Balkan*, pp. 101, 102). The fate of Emmanuel Drucker is determined by historical events: he is seized and then murdered by the Iron Guard. His son and sisters are victims of a literary plot: they disappear from a text that marks itself as historical epic.

So much a part of British literary history, ambivalence towards the Jew is in danger of becoming clichéd analysis. Despite its repetition of the problem, Manning's linkage of the Jew to Harriet Pringle refreshes such analysis.[23] The depression that marks Harriet's position and perspective as a woman also makes her barely noticeable. This marginality positions her in full critical view of the often unconscious complicity of personal and political history.[24] When read as a narrative in itself, Harriet's depressed view of Hitler's war and her response to both Sasha and his aunts combine her anger at the ideologies that have created them and her as necessary Others. The narrator's view of the Drucker sisters is, after all, only an exaggeration and conflation of Harriet's role of hostess to Guy's parasitic cronies. Equally telling is the allusion to that part of Nazi ideology which viewed women strictly as nurturing mothers to the fatherland.[25] Harriet's disgusted response to the sisters could therefore be seen as the projection of loathing towards both herself and those traditional social and cultural roles she feels unable to resist. In her nurturant identification with Sasha, the female becomes the powerful purveyer of life to an enfeebled and endangered male. The only time Harriet is angry with Sasha is when he refuses to help himself; his inaction reflects too pointedly the self-indulgent complacency she shares with his aunts. The last time Sasha and Harriet see each other, in the hall of a hotel in Cairo, it is clear that neither one has found refuge from the exile that defines their alterity. There is no symmetry, however, in their self-reflecting but mutually exclusive states of exile.

In the end, Harriet chooses her tepid marriage as a safe haven in a world on the edge of destruction. Given what we know happens to the Druckers, her choice in the context of total war on the Other is founded on a politics of survival, and suggests that in Manning's construction, marriage may be a malleable structure in which Harriet can survive. Despite the effort to conserve a traditional form of marriage, with a woman's dependency at its base, *The Balkan and Levant Trilogies* comprise a revisionary epic that heroicizes a woman's point of view. Instead of complying with her economic and emotional dependency, Harriet's pervasively depressed perspective questions not only her marriage, but the grand operatic register of the traditional war epic. This combined critique is characterized most pointedly when she returns to Damascus after a brief escape from Guy and the theatre of war in *The Levant Trilogy*. Her resilience highlights the tragic fall of those who never had a chance to participate in a heroic struggle. The point of view of this survivor thus deconstructs the mythos of traditional epics by constructing a marginal tale of the European Jew whose history cannot be resisted by literary tradition.

In Manning's historic epic, unlike Bottome's European war fiction, there is neither crusade nor transformation, only continuous decay. Continuous decay actually marks a succession of Manning's writing about the war which we can see in her 1951 novel of wartime Jerusalem, *School for Love*. In a city already divided between Arabs and Jews, the war exposes antipathies even among those who share a common culture and history. With a Dickensian kind of implosive characterization, Manning portrays an expatriot Englishwoman, Ethel Bohun, as the embodiment of ideological and emotional terrorism, an evocation of 'memories of horror stories about houses as dark and cold as this'.[26] Miss Bohun's presence in her house represents the encampment of colonial power, not as the British would pride themselves, as a civilizing administration, but as coercive and destructive of civil relations and society. So Miss Bohun has taken over the home of Polish Jews who are now reduced to living in the kitchen and maintaining her household, and so she uses her apocalyptic religious group, 'The Ever-Readies', to manipulate the frail and homeless into feeling saved. The downward slide of the novel's emotional and political clashes ends with Manning's ambivalent vision of the English homeland. The young boy whose consciousness shapes the novel returns to England, orphaned and alone, in the wake of betrayal and death.

Whatever their differences, Bottome's romances and Manning's epics confront us with the same conundrum. For both writers, despite terrible costs and a 'precarious peace' (*LT* Coda), World War II was a just and necessary campaign to save the world from being engulfed by Hitler's armies and death camps. Neither complicit nor patriotic, they construct a second world war based on their ambivalent identification with another Other. To dramatize this point, Manning creates the following exchange between two Englishmen about a Polish refugee in her 1941 story, 'In a Winter Landscape':

'What did he expect from us?'
I said: . . . 'He thought we had something to give'.
. . . 'Well, it's too late now', said Jake at last, and we're only worrying because it's too late. So let's be thankful we can go and eat in peace'.
We never saw the Pole again.[27]

Manning's wartime world recalls Storm Jameson's portrait of the English in her novel, *Europe to Let*. For both writers, the English are omnipresent but impotent in the impossible and misguided task motivated by their self-appointed moral responsibility as empire builders. Ultimately, they are always hindered from moral resolution by their combined attraction and revulsion to Others. In such fashion, Manning depicts a detached but committed journalist in her story, 'A Journey'. Mary Martin involves herself deeply in the geo-political intrigues of wartime Rumania, but when faced with its refugees scrambling to get on her train, she is 'gentle and humble with relief' not only 'at her escape', but at the difference and political distance that separate her from them.[28]

Unlike Virginia Woolf's woman who rejects the idea of country in favour of a free world, Bottome's and Manning's exiles have no secure point of origin to reject or transform. As Harriet Pringle, Freya Toller, and their other female protagonists wander an imperfect world, they highlight the fate of those who, having wandered from a particular historic moment into the worlds of these novels, have disappeared. It is in their absence that these novels of World War II deconstruct our definitions of the Other.

'DANGEROUS UNHAPPY REALITY'[29]: WOMEN'S FOREIGN INTRIGUES

In popular novels of foreign intrigue, exile is usually the condition of an English scholar-adventurer or diplomat on a mission to locate the political faultlines of a disaster-bound Europe. Suspicious but fearless, he goes off primed by the foreknowledge that this shadowy and shaky Europe is an affront to his sense of decency and fair play. In the late thirties, however, there are women writers of the genre who discovered for themselves that exile could mean something else entirely. Living in Central Europe, they witnessed the displacement of Europeans who found themselves either on the wrong side of destabilized national boundaries or in an occupied land seeking help from other nations.

Two popular novelists, Ann Bridge and Helen MacInnes, had formed ties to Europe in the twenties and thirties that led them to romanticize its people and culture. Though the rise of Hitler and outbreak of World War II produced ready-made icons of evil villains and besieged victims, their novels took an unexpected turn. If they depict the war itself conventionally, as a labyrinthine melodramatic tale of feudal rivalries and heroics, they do not depict Hitler as a generic descendent of gothic evil. Indeed, he rarely figures at all because he is upstaged by their narrative focus on struggles to subvert and survive his conquest. For these writers, it is Nazi racialist ideology that make the difference.

Observing at close hand how this ideology became policies that were implemented all too easily, MacInnes and Bridge reset the timeless lapses of romance adventure. What emerges instead are thrillers driven less by plot manoeuvres than by the fateful historic moments of Europe about to collapse as Hitler threatens it and Britain stands by. In the case of Ann Bridge, this revisionary move coincided with her sympathy and sense of political responsibility for people threatened by the Nazis, responses that grew out of her role as wife of a diplomat. In one example, instead of gothicizing the 'unbelievable horror' of Nazi terror or the travails of escape, her novel, *A Place to Stand,* uses the the heroine's arrest by the gestapo to remind readers that 'the new twentieth century diabolism' was historically specific: 'In 1941 the world at large knew nothing of Buchenwald or Belsen, Katyn or Oswieczim' (*Place,* p. 189).

Ann Bridge (1889–1974) was the pen name of Mary Dolling (Sanders), Lady O'Mally, who wrote many popular spy and travel-adventure novels based on her experiences in diplomatic posts in China, and then in the late thirties in Budapest. Two of these, which she wrote after the war, are about her experiences in Budapest in 1940–41 just before the Germans took over and the British Legation had to leave. *A Place to Stand,* published in 1952, and *The Tightening String,* 1962, translate the novel of exotic European politics into polemical reflections on Britain's commitment to Central Europe. Inspiration for the novels came not from her previous writing, but from a meeting with the Hungarian Regent, Horthy, who implored her to write a novel about '"the real Hungary;

not only night-clubs and paprika-chicken!"', which was his complaint about other English writers.[30] Bridge, however, does not construct the 'real' Hungary as a stage on which to celebrate a distinctive Central European culture. Instead, in both novels, she dramatizes rapidly changing scenes which represent a nation destabilized by the historical moment. As it tries to remain intact, Hungary's capital veers between accommodation to the Germans and neutrality, each based on the history of a small state in the heart of Europe, vulnerable, according to one patriot, to being 'crushed between contending forces, great rich Powers who can do as they choose – cut our country in two, and give half to others, as they did last time' (*Place*, p. 8).

Instead of stock figures battling a monolithic evil force, the Hungarians are represented as voices which struggle to be heard. Their dramatic force in the novels derives from their struggle, not their effect, for if Hitler's tanks and sealed trains don't create enough din, the voices of the Hungarians are drowned out by their political ambivalences. As a result of Hitler's co-optations and conquests, as well as their own conflicted allegiances, the Hungarians are now Others who share a state of exile with the refugees pouring into Budapest.

As she confirmed in her memoirs, Bridge valued Hungarian culture and respected its difficult history, but as the title suggests, *A Place to Stand* also calls for a commitment to restabilize Europe, and as her narrative dramatizes it, this could have only been accomplished by cooperative efforts to defeat Hitler. Otherwise, as *The Tightening String* shows, Central Europe is squeezed lifeless. As with so many other British women writers of the war, Bridge developed her commitment to Germany's defeat out of sympathy for its victims; in *A Place to Stand*, she rewards a like-minded commitment by giving the most powerful voice and decisive actions to a young man on his way to England to fight with the Polish Free Forces, Stefan Moranski.

In her memoir, Bridge describes *A Place to Stand* as 'not only pure history, but a first-hand account of events as they happened' (*FF*, p. 81). This historical interpretation is narrated as 'a tense novel of love and intrigue', in conventionally rapid plot movements and terse dialogue, but its perspective from the account of a young woman, while conforming to that of the genre's prototypical plucky ingénue, is also revisionary.[31] Hope Kirkland, 19-year-old daughter of an American businessman, joins forces with Stefan Moranski, but her adventures take her beyond ballroom and coffee house intrigues to political awareness and empathy. In the process of manoeuvring between social and political pressures, Hope becomes a heroic figure. Recognizing her privileged and protected position – 'we have passports and dollars, we can go anywhere!'– she uses her American currency to help those who would resist oppression rather than accommodate it (*Place*, p. 142). Her attraction to Stefan Moranski thus leads her to identify with his nation's struggle for independence. When Hope and Stefan part indeterminedly at the end, she is sustained by the awareness that she 'must have become to some extent European . . . to care about Europe's things for Europe's sake, and for the sake of justice and freedom' (*Place*, p. 182). If such a statement is attributable to the naïvety of a young woman in her romantic position, it also becomes political critique as the novel has tracked her political identification with the Others of Eastern and Central Europe.

Through Hope's position, the novel argues that the war is only worth fighting if the 'great rich Powers' recognize their responsibility for the sovereignty of the small nations of Europe. Functioning as a corrective to her divided adopted city, Hope builds political coalitions where deep and abiding mistrust and cynicism have reigned as political policy. The novel builds its case for political identification on its formal use of doubling and division, highlighting it through Hope's relation to a Euopean woman, Stefan Moranski's sister, Litka. Different in every respect except an uncanny physical resemblence, the American woman and the Pole both realize that their political and historical differences can be neither bridged nor reversed. And yet it is the indelible mark of this difference that creates the possibility for Hope's heroic actions, and so she gives Litka her passport and coat to be able to escape the Nazis, while risking her own arrest.

While melodramatic in effect, Hope's heroic actions are only made possible by intertwining her easy familiarity with Budapest's linguistic collage with her growing sense of the political dimensions of social relationships. Her linguistic facility, valuable as a ticket to rebellious but safe partying with young Hungarians, becomes a password to political and emotional risk. Feeling empathy for the exiled Poles motivates her actions, but she must also learn that such empathy can neither be disinterested nor unambivalent. Setting scenes of diplomatic security against those of political and personal risk highlights Hope's journey into the politics of identification. Involved in both scenes, Hope learns that the language of social bantering at embassy parties inscribes a political hierarchy which retains the power of one speaker over another, while the language of her Polish friends is a sign of their total powerlessness. As long as their nation is occupied by the Germans, the Poles are not allowed to read or to speak Polish. And yet just as Storm Jameson portrayed in her dystopia, *Then We Shall Hear Singing*, only women can overcome the silence imposed by nazism. So Stefan and Litka have learned Polish from their mother despite the threat of severe punishment. The novel further demonstrates that language is a political instrument when Hope gives Litka her American passport. She helps her friend to freedom, but in the process, Litka will have lost her birthright identity and joined a state of exile.

Bridge actually based the novel on a book her daughter had begun but later destroyed. Like her fictional counterpart, Kate O'Mally was 19 when she instigated herself in the political affairs of her adopted nation while her parents 'thought she was amusing herself with her Hungarian friends' (*FF*, p. 81). It was she who supplied the novel's plot and together, after the war, when the consequences of political risk became all too clear, mother and daughter worked out its progression and details. One also senses the reflective process of this collaboration in the novel's politicization. The story of lost love and lost identity is not rescued at the end by its conventional affirmation of English good cheer. What prevails instead, is

> Hope's own interior story [which] was really one of escape, quite as much as that of the friends who had, thanks to her, physically escaped from Hungary; escape from a foggy happy unreality into a sharp-edged, dangerous, unhappy reality, which even in this short time had brought her something of the fulfillment that suffering always brings (*Place*, p. 259).

Based on Bridge's own experiences, *The Tightening String* charts the political risks of a diplomatic wife as she manipulates her assigned roles, her own nation's bureaucratic policies, and the conflicted allegiances of Hungary, Bulgaria, and Turkey, the stations of her adventure. The novel's primary consciousness, Rosina Eynsham exploits her roles as diplomatic hostess and lady of good works as well as the diplomatic immunity known as 'laissez passer' to arrange for the surreptitious purchase and shipment of supplies to British prisoners of war in Germany.[32] Her enemies in this war effort are not the Germans, however, but 'British officialdom' and the British Red Cross (*FF*, p. 85). As the narrator comments only half in jest, the problem is that misguided policies of both 'the old gentlemen in Grosvenor Crescent' and the British Red Cross produce a 'dottiness' that can only be compared to Dickens's 'Great Circumlocution Office' (*TS*, pp. 126, 192, 138). In addition to their obstructionist management style, the British Red Cross hides its politics under the cloak of neutrality while 'the old gentlemen' suffer from historical myopia: as Bridge recalled in her memoir, they 'mistook World War II for World War I where there was an open frontier to an Allied country – Italy' (*FF*, p. 86). Tied to the historic moment, the novel's critique extends beyond its genre's melodramatic conventions and dark comedy and even beyond its own fictionality. As Bridge recalled, her publisher warned that her novel risked libel actions.

As in *A Place to Stand*, Bridge plunges headlong into the political criticism and politics of personal relations that diplomatic life works so hard to avoid. Tied to her repudiation of neutrality, *The Tightening String* subverts British reserve. Rosina Eynsham expresses both deeply felt sympathy and irritation at the Hungarians' 'ambivalent attitude in a conflict where – to her it seemed so simple – human freedom was at stake!' (*TS*, p. 9). Their ambivalence, she feels, will lead not only to their own dissolution, but offers 'a glimpse of what the Nazi attitude meant to the Jews of Central Europe' (*TS*, p. 116). In Bridge's critical reading the Catholic Jews of Hungary are a sign of the dangerous instability of their intersecting and overlapping Central European Otherness. Despite their religious conversion and contributions to the economic and social development of Hungary, their cultural assimilation remains suspect as they also cling to their Jewish identity. Bridge portrays the Hungarian Jews as Others twice over. At the moment war begins, they work behind the scenes to expedite the production of goods for the British prisoners' relief. Then, the novel's 1962 retrospective view casts the shadow of the Jews' fate after the close of the novel.[33]

All of this history is depicted and foreshadowed in the character of Hugo Weissberger, scion of a noble Hungarian Jewish family to whom Lucilla Eynsham, Rosina's daughter, becomes engaged.

Like Stefan and Hope in *A Place to Stand*, Hugo and Lucilla's fictional plotting, as it works in tandem with history, cannot promise a happy romantic ending. Unlike Stefan, however, Hugo has no Free Army to fight with, either for his life or for any kind of self-determination. Rather, like Olivia Manning's Balkan epic, the narrative trajectory of the second world war determines the disappearance of Sasha Drucker and Hugo Weissburger from any saving plot available to the Jews. As Rosina and her family leave Budapest for an arduous journey back to Britain, they will be saved by the historical fact of diplomatic immunity and by Bridge's mission to expose the critical disregard of war on Europe's Others.

I can think of no more emphatic way to demonstrate the serious purpose and didactic art of Bridge's novel than to link it to Storm Jameson's 1947 novel about the fate of European civilization at the very moment the war ends, *The Black Laurel.* Like Bridge, Jameson argued that novels of foreign intrigue and Allied politics of international relations drew blackout curtains over the glare of war atrocities and moral dilemmas of victory. Even at that moment when the destruction seemed to be over, Jameson 'felt horror at each fresh evidence of the ruin begun in the War, and finished in the Peace' (*No Time*, p. 101). Among the questions still open for Jameson 'in the Peace' was how Europe was going to deal with its responsibility for its Jews. And so in *The Black Laurel*, the fate of a bumbling Jewish profiteer becomes the template of the Allied powers' moral force and of the moral fate of western civilization. Unaccountably paradoxical, the Jew in this novel brings out the best and the worst of Western civilization. As Jameson weaves him in and out of the cracked ruins of Allied-occupied Berlin and he is objectified in the perceptions of military and diplomatic functionaries, he comes to represent a kind of Rorschach test, an amorphous figure to be filled in with ink blot silhouettes of the geo-political and personal self-interests of his friends and enemies. His craggy and ill-defined outlines, suggesting a strange amalgam of man, beast, and Jameson's previous references to 'Dostoevsky's cockroach', always produce disturbing responses, as though he represents some evolutionary mistake that calls into question other people's most basic sense of what it means to be human and civilized.

In *Before the Crossing*, the novel which is really a prologue to *The Black Laurel*, a conversation illustrates how responses to Jews begin in the notion that a civilization is worth more than the lives which built it:

> 'Isn't their crime just that they infected the deliciously egotistical civilization of Greece and the vulgar egoism of Rome with the idea, so corrosive, too, of individuality?' 'They did something infinitely worse, they exalted the individual.'[34]

It is the idea of a coherently satisfying culture and civilization that casts the Jew as alien so that everyone else can feel secure in their own citizenship, especially at a time when national borders were being redrawn in Europe and Britain began to cope with the end of empire and the status of its post-colonized. The Jew also mirrors our fear of being ostracized or merely left out simply by dint of being ourselves and being, as we feel ourselves, to be different. In so much of Jameson's work, as in Stevie Smith's and Phyllis Bottome's, it is not the Rorschach image that is grotesque and terrifying, but the hatred and aggression which defend us from seeing ourselves reflected in it, feelings which lead to war.

The Black Laurel argues that the ethos of the victors will be tested not only as it decides the fate of the enemy, but as it responds to the face of the victim. As a military and political delegation convenes in Germany, its determination of truth and justice depends on discovering the relationship between self and Other as it is embodied in the figure of the Jew. Living on the margins of European civilization, neither a bad man nor good, serving all his masters, Heinrich Kalb survives so long as no nation has to claim him as theirs. Once the victors become the judges, however, he is sacrificed to the frustrated need to make distinctions between 'murderers and blackguards', especially at a time when the equally strong need for order makes expediency so necessary. (While they do not figure in the novel, the Nuremberg war crimes trials cast a very large shadow.) The refugee, despite his status as one of few Holocaust survivors, is, as one character points out, by definition, a 'bad citizen'. Stateless for the last 12 years and a displaced person in the postwar scene of victory, he is nonetheless easy to dispense with (*BL*, p. 316). He typifies what Colin Holmes reports came to be known in Britain as 'a race without a country' and is reviled as a 'sojourner and deficient therefore in patriotism' (p. 171). With no stable national identity, he defies the order of a civil society.

But when Kalb is sacrificed, so is justice. Bringing each of the major characters into contact with Kalb reveals the misalliance of justice and order even as this was being prosecuted at Nuremberg. Taking the same risk as Stevie Smith, Jameson deploys antisemitism, not as a problem of history but as symptomatic of the problematic relationship between artistic representation and moral responsibility. Jameson begins by dramatizing how the need for order begins as a defence against one's own chaotic and contradictory feelings about the identity and stability of the self. Kalb, who has become involved as a petty go-between in a scheme to steal and distribute art works from a Nazi abandoned cache, is composed entirely of Jewish stereotypes. Small and frail, his eyes nervously 'frisking behind' thick glasses, he is also obsequious, secretive, and self-incriminating (*BL*, p. 191). He uses his knowledge of art, not to disseminate learning, but to make deals and ingratiate himself into circles otherwise closed to him. Like Sadinsky, in Jameson's *Cloudless May*, he incurs the wrath of his customers by offering the opportunity to indulge and therefore confront their vanity and greed.

But in another sense, it is less important what the Jew is than how others react to and then represent him.[35] Basically inept and pathetic, Kalb arouses only revulsion, never compassion. One character finds that Kalb irritates him because he 'resented the little creature's friendliness, and yes, his innocence. Who in this world has an excuse for being so simple-minded, so resolute in believing in goodness. In its way it was a provocation' (*BL*, p. 107). One of the novel's most sympathetic characters, Colonel Brett, sees Kalb as 'a friendly insect', while the noble German philosopher, Lucius Gerlach, acting as Kalb's defence lawyer, cannot bring himself to touch his client, repelled by the Jew's grimy and shaking hand (*BL*, p. 191).

As the novel is shaped, when no one can find reason enough to save the Jew, the fate of Europe is sealed in its past and the future of democratic justice is cloudy at best.[36] Failing to see onself in the Other, despite their irrevocable differences as enemy or as victim, threatens to perpetuate an endless cycle of war. Near the end of the novel, a woman who supervises a displaced persons camp in Czechoslovakia speaks from the heart of Europe:

> What has happened to Europe is so terrible that no one believes it.... It's all our faults, not only the Germans', and especially your English fault – you wouldn't believe that horror was being born in Germany.... We are in history to our necks ... from crime to punishment, and from punishment to vengeance for it. Yet there must be punishment for Terezin. There must be

justice. The wounds made by justice are frightful. I know it, and I consent to them. And they will be avenged . . . the next war, is the end. It doesn't matter, I tell you. We shall smile at it in its face. Until the last minute – until we are all dying of remorse for being ourselves – we can live! (*BL*, pp. 300–1)

For Storm Jameson, as for Stevie Smith and Ann Bridge, among others, seeing the Other in ourselves means recognizing war's ruthlessness in English best intentions and that political responsibility is both individual and collective. Thus in *Over the Frontier*, Pompey tries to locate herself as she examines her cultural history through the lens of a German military memoir about a battle with Britain. In her last novel, *The Holiday*, Smith shows how Germany is not the only nation that invokes universal forces of nature to justify an instinct for violence:

> What is the dog within us that . . . tears and howls. . . . It is the desire to tear out this animal, to have our heart free of him . . . and for the innocent happiness, that makes us cry out against life, and cry for death. For this animal is kennelled close within, and tearing out this animal we tear out also the life with it.[37]

Smith's own experience shows how deep within lies the tearing dog. In 1949 – the same year that *The Holiday* was published and years after the horrors of the Holocaust – Smith lost her friendship with Betty Miller because she failed to understand the Jews' lasting anxiety about being outsiders. Smith had published a story, 'Beside the Seaside: a Holiday with Children', whose main characters are easily recognized as the Miller family. The Betty Miller character expresses 'profound uncertainty' over 'a strong growing anti-Jewish feeling in England' and then asks about her children: 'when they get a little older, will they also be in a concentration camp in England?'[38] However powerfully her novels confront antisemitism, Smith's use of the Millers' anxieties is blatantly unsympathetic – testament to the recalcitrant antipathy she admits is potentially dangerous.

The wartime history of the Jews and its characterization by British women writers complicates debates about the justness of World War II. When Phyllis Bottome and Storm Jameson gloss their fiction with anguished letters and public appearances about the fate of the Jews, they argue for the war on grounds that even many of those who otherwise supported it, then and now, would often reject or find problematic. Moreover, even in the sympathetic renderings of Stevie Smith and Storm Jameson, the Jew remains an unassimilable Other whose separateness represents a test of English moral and literary imagination and therefore an uncomfortable presence for which no narrative space can be found. For Storm Jameson, who castigated herself as much as she did an indifferent audience, mourning the failure to save the Jews marks the apocalyptic moment when a new beginning is imagined for western civilization. In Jameson's novel, *The Black Laurel*, at the moment the Jew is executed, the English political policeman, Renn, adopts a child: 'With something between self-mockery and a painful joy, unexpected, he understood that he had attached himself again to the world by this child . . . [t]o begin to learn existence from the beginning' (*BL*, p. 349). Stevie Smith locates her own moral and historical responsibility as a British woman writer in the character of Pompey Casmilus, who performs simultaneously as historian of male militarism, female victim, warrior, and uncomfortable wielder of the scales of justice. At the end of *Over the Frontier*, Pompey identifies a just equilibrium by facing two enemies, those masked as friends and those within herself: 'Power and cruelty are the strength of our life, and in its weakness only is there the sweetness of love' (*OF*, p. 278).

Years after the war, Stevie Smith and Storm Jameson still debated the merits of the devastating tactics which brought victory to the Allies. Jameson's novel, *The Green Man*, depicts the years 1930–47 from the perspective of progressive leaders, intellectuals, artists, industrial barons, and a Jewish survivor, and concludes that antisemitism and cultural supremacy are too deeply rooted in European history to have led to anything but indifference to the Holocaust. This is not to say that either writer justifies the war solely to save the Jews, but rather that they saw the prevailing antisemitism in England as symptomatic of cultural values which depend on a mission of superiority and dominance that all nations and all their men and women share to some degree. Antisemitism for these writers, representing such a visceral, violent response to an Other, is more than the sum of economic deprivation, social inequity, or oppressive power. Women, they argue, already Other, must see themselves as holding the power to participate or not in the events that issue from racist and supremacist language.

As Pompey sits out her imprisonment at the end of *Over the Frontier*, she confronts not only her complicity with her captors but the source of it in their shared will to violence:

> But you see it is my fault I am in this galère . . . I may say I was shanghaied into this adventure, forced into a uniform I intuitively hated. But if there had been nothing in me of it . . . should I not now be playing, in . . . boredom, but safely and sanely enough, with those who seem to me now beyond the frontier of a separate life (*OF*, p. 272).

If Pompey is guilty of a defensive contempt and a warring spirit, she is also vindicated. She understands her role in a culture where, as Colin Holmes reports, 'hostile literary stereotypes of Jews were unlikely to have been presented if readers were unable to identify with them' (p. 219).[39] Like the debates Jameson's novels dramatize, Smith gives Pompey the courage to violate the deadly silences of a passive aggression which make war and destruction seem like the evil that others do. No matter who the victimized Others are in any war, they reflect the politics of identification we use to justify our constructions of war resistance. Jameson reminds us:

> Our enemies are not the men and women of another country. They are ourselves . . . they are the interested persons . . . they are the 'realists' who accept a disorder which exists; they are the romantically-minded . . . they are the women who commit the indecency of assenting to wars which others will fight; they are all of us in those moments when, losing faith, we think of a war as something other than it is – the blasphemous betrayal of the future of man ('The Twilight of Reason', pp. 19–20).

The resistance to racism and supremacism enacted by the war writing of Storm Jameson and many other women is a victory of war for a new kind of peace. It may not have felt like victory to Eleanor Rathbone who wore herself out trying to rescue Hitler's victims. It is also true that after the first waves of relief, disenchantment set in for many who felt that the use of atomic weapons and the onset of the Cold War could easily mean more of the same. And more of the same, as feminist studies has shown, also meant a postwar return to an often stifling domestic hearth.

And while we cannot read any literature as isolated from its wider historical contexts, the World War II writing of British women does constitute a distinct tradition. As these women's postwar writing shows, World War II not only continues to haunt their creative imaginations, it stands as a defining moment in a literature of political and moral discovery. This literature engages a specific historic crisis by enacting debates about the aims, conditions, and aftermath of a war even many pacifists came to realize was necessary. As the war drew on and news of Nazi atrocities came home, it became clear to many that there was no other way to save people's lives and the right to live as self-defined Others. Even for those like Vera Brittain and Ethel Mannin, who sustained their pacifist beliefs in full view of Nazi atrocities, World War II never ceases to be a productive creative ground, the fruits of which are necessary complications to our study of women's responses to war.

So much women's war writing expresses their power to confront the 'howling dog', not only in the enemy and even the victims, but in themselves. With intense and, as we have seen, often ambivalent identification with or reconstruction of the victim, as well as with detached irony and on occasion with humour, these writers used their pens to assert their own power of self-expression and moral responsibility. With critical and imaginative responses, many of these women assert their presence in the war, not as victims, but rather as identifying the possibility for action that distinguishes them from the war's panopoly of victims. These British women writers fully understood the political conditions that enabled them to question the conventions, policies, and laws that shaped their lives. Many wrote that understanding into their representations of the powerlessness of the war's victims and of women who struggle for responsible action. Even as it is painful to acknowledge that some women translated that understanding and agency into a problematic politics, without their inclusion, we cannot fully appreciate the heroism of those like Storm Jameson and Phyllis Bottome. In recognition of the breadth and complex depths of British women writers of World War II, this book commemorates the moral and political victory enacted by the individual and collective voice of so many.

Notes

Introduction

1. Quoted in Michiko Kakutani, 'Novelists Are News Again', *The New York Times Book Review* (14 August 1983) 23.
2. Tom Harrisson, 'War Books', *Horizon* (Dec. 1941) 417. Harrisson also dismisses much British war literature for its antisemitism and jingoism. For discussion of the enormous demand but short supply of books during the war, see Robert Hewison, *Under Siege: Literary Life in London 1939–45* (NY: Oxford University Press, 1977), p. 76.
3. Arthur Calder-Marshall, Cyril Connolly, Bonamy Dobree, Tom Harrisson, Arthur Koestler, Alun Lewis, George Orwell, Stephen Spender, 'Why Not War Writers', *Horizon* (Oct. 1941) 236–9. Cited in text as 'Why Not'.
4. Typical of surveys which give only token space to British women writers of the thirties and forties is Randall Stevenson's *The British Novel Since the Thirties* (Athens: University of Georgia Press, 1986), which sees Ivy Compton-Burnett, Rosamond Lehmann, and Elizabeth Bowen adopting modernist techniques rather than questioning them and developing their own. Valentine Cunningham's compendious *British Writers of the Thirties* (Oxford: Oxford University Press, 1989) discusses Bowen, Lehmann, and Naomi Mitchison, with brief mention of Storm Jameson and Rose Macaulay, but always within extant categories, in league with Orwell's belief that 'on the whole, literary forms proved widely resistant to change', p. 319. Samuel Hynes's *The Auden Generation* (London: The Bodley Head, 1976), discusses literary theories of Rosamund Lehmann and Storm Jameson, but not their imaginative literature.

   Holger Klein purports to rescue *The Second World War in Fiction* from neglect (Houndmills: Macmillan, 1984) but leaves women writers to Mary Cadogan's and Patricia Craig's *Women and Children First* (London: Gollancz, 1978). Klein claims that World War II literature produced no 'formula', but in arguing that its structure positions 'the action . . . within the overall action of the war' elides women's English and European homefront fictions, p. 25. Alan Munton's *English Fiction of the Second World* (London: Faber & Faber, 1989) questions 'the representation of women in war fiction', but his claim that it 'scarcely recognizes . . . changes', fails to grasp the extent of women's writing about change and the dangers of stagnation, p. 3. Andrew Sinclair's recreation of London's Fitzrovia, *War Like a Wasp: The Lost Decade of the Forties* (London: Hamish Hamilton, 1989), succeeds in mostly losing women writers, except for honorable mention of Bowen and Lehmann. For a similar gesture, see Sebastian D.G. Knowles, *A Purgatorial Flame: Seven British Writers in the Second*

World War (Philadelphia: University of Pennsylvania Press, 1990). Samuel Hynes observes that 'The center of horror in the second world war was on no front at all', but omits women's treatment of this horror, 'War Stories: Myths of World War II', *Sewanee Review* (Spring/Summer 1992), p. 103. Bernard Bergonzi's *Wartime and Aftermath: English Literature and its Background 1939–1960* (Oxford: Oxford University Press, 1993) applauds Arthur Koestler's *Darkness at Noon* for bringing an insider's view to the plight of Hitler's European victims, but ignores the work of Storm Jameson and other women who warned of such tragedy.

5. David Smith dismisses Naomi Mitchison's *We Have Been Warned*, as 'silly solemnity', *Socialist Propaganda in the Twentieth-Century British Novel* (London: Macmillan, 1978), p. 80. Cadogan and Craig's pioneering study of British women writers of the two world wars rescued many from not so benign neglect. Gill Plain's interesting readings of some women's wartime fiction provides historical context, but her emphasis on the coping strategies of fictional narratives adumbrates women's political differences and allows her to interpret war as a victimizing experience for women. We shall see.
6. Storm Jameson, *Journey From the North II*, p. 21.
7. Elizabeth Bowen, Preface to *The Demon Lover*, p. 97.
8. See Margaret Higonnet, Sonya Michel, *et al.*, *Behind the Lines: Gender and the Two World Wars* (New Haven: Yale University Press, 1987) (cited in text as *Behind the Lines*); Cooper, Munich, and Squier, *Arms and the Woman: War, Gender, and Literary Representation* (Chapel Hill: University of North Carolina Press, 1989); Miriam Cooke and Angela Woollacott, *Gendering War Talk* (Princeton: Princeton University Press, 1993); and Sandra Gilbert and Susan Gubar's three volume *No Man's Land* (New Haven: Yale University Press, 1986–94). While my study follows Claire Tylee's important restoration of World War I women writers, *The Great War and Women's Consciousness* (Iowa City: University of Iowa Press, 1990), and even traces some of the same who continued to write through the later war, I find their responses to warfare shaped more by particular geo-politics than by the horrors of war itself.
9. Carole Snee, 'Working-Class Literature or Proletarian Writing?' in *Culture and Crisis in Britain in the Thirties*, Jon Clark, Margot Heinemann, David Margolies and Carole Snee (eds) (London: Lawrence and Wishart, 1979), p. 166.
10. The recent canon wars have created new limits that exclude writers even as claims are made for inclusion. Laura Marcus questions valuing one literary category over another, such as modernism and realism, because this is an oppositional strategy that serves exclusion, 'Feminist Aesthetics and the New Realism', *New Feminist Discourses: Critical Essays on Theories and Texts*, Isobel Armstrong (ed.) (London: Routledge, 1992), pp. 11–25. Exclusion results from expanding definitions of modernism as well. As modernism now includes experiments with speculative fiction and fantasy, as well as with realism, it embraces writers who might not identify with modernism as they

knew it in the twenties and thirties. Keith Alldritt, *Modernism in the Second World War* (NY: Peter Lang, 1989), argues that Eliot and Pound found modernist renewal and war images in 'push[ing] language and syntax to their limits and [in] the rhythms and forms normally associated with discursive writing', Preface 1. So many British women writers distrusted the transformative ends of discursive writing as being manipulated all too easily for propaganda, and linguistic experiment for its dislocation from the war's everyday traumas. Forming a feminist war literary canon has also led to problematic interpretations.

11. Liberal humanism is generally taken for granted as being a unified political philosophy with a universal liberal subject, without socially constructed gendered and cultural identities. In her otherwise cogent study, *Postmodernism and Feminism*, Patricia Waugh falls into step with many poststructuralist critics who assume that there is a 'dominant liberal view of subjectivity, with its belief in the unified self and a universal human nature' (NY: Routledge, 1989), p. 23. Such formulation elides the theoretical, political, and literary debates that shaped the varied liberal humanist thinking among many women writers of the thirties and forties. As their construction of fragmented and decentred male and female characters show, they saw political and historical events challenging notions of wholeness and self-direction. On the other hand, they did sustain belief in 'a potentially free' self, that is, one that could fight for their idea of freedom against the certain destruction of the self at Hitler's hands and for a changed world (Waugh, p. 25).
12. In the holistic model of women's war writing in *No Man's Land*, Gubar links American and British women writers of World War II to Gilbert's treatment of World War I writers, eschewing all differences among wars and writers.
13. Jean B. Elshtain, *Women and War* (NY: Basic Books, 1987), p. 3.
14. Micaela Di Leonardo, 'Morals, Mothers, and Militarism: Antimilitarism and Feminist Theory', *Feminist Studies* 11 (Fall 1985), p. 602.
15. Sara Ruddick, 'Notes Towards a Feminist Peace Politics', *Gendering War Talk*, p. 119.
16. Cooper, Munich, and Squier argue that 'as an object of discourse, war has no more self-evident a significance than does gender: its meaning also changes as culture codifies that meaning differently', 'Arms and the Woman: Con[tra]ception of the War Text', *Arms and the Woman*, p. 19. Their transhistorical approach, however, ignores cultural and historical distinctiveness.
17. Jane Marcus, 'The Asylums of Antaeus: Women, War and Madness: Is there a feminist fetishism?' *The Difference Within: Feminism and Critical Theory* Ed. Elizabeth Meese and Alice Parker (Philadelphia: John Benjamins, 1989). Cited in text as 'Antaeus'.
18. Lynne Hanley, *Writing War: Fiction, Gender and Memory* (Amherst: University of Massachusetts Press, 1991), p. 34.
19. Simon Featherstone, *War Poetry: An Introductory Reader* (London: Routledge, 1995), p. 99.

20. Jana Thompson, 'Women and War', *Women's Studies International Forum* 14:1, 2 (1991) 63; Lois Scharf and Angela Woollacott, Book review in *Signs* (Spring 1992), p. 663.
21. Judy Barrett Litoff and David C. Smith, 'Women at War with Militarism II: The Experience of Two World Wars', *Women's Studies Association Journal* 4 (Spring 1992), p. 103.
22. Ruth Roach Pierson, 'Beautiful Soul or Just Warrior: Gender and War', *Gender and History* 1 (Spring 1989), p. 80. In her influential essay 'Rewriting History', in *Behind the Lines,* Joan W. Scott argues that socially embedded metaphoric representations of gender are exploited in wartime to influence social relations and political and social policy. Her emphasis on victimization, however, does not allow for women's critical responses.
23. In his new study, *The Myth of the Blitz* (London: Cape, 1991), Angus Calder criticizes many assumptions in his earlier work, *The People's War,* especially issues of wartime national unity (London: Cape, 1969, 1986). And yet the harder he tries, the more apparent it is that however disunited England would always be, because of government manipulation, economic, gender and class inequality, this war against Nazi Germany produced a sense of common cause in which the home front siege rallied people towards equality. See Julian Symons's review of *The Myth of the Blitz, London Review of Books* (12 Sept. 1991) 9. As regards these myths and realities, Andrew Davies asks, 'How could the majority of the population be mobilized into fighting to preserve the inequalities and injustices of the interwar years?' He answers: 'In a whole number of areas – evacuation and the blitzes, the campaigns for war aims and postwar reconstruction, the alliance with the Soviet Union, the voracious interest of both civilians and troops in discussing and exploring social and political questions the effects of the war had a democratizing and radicalizing tendency', *Where Did the Forties Go?* (London: Pluto Press, 1984), pp. 26, 27. Ian McLaine discusses home front morale in relation to the propaganda campaigns and administration of the Ministry of Information in *Ministry of Morale* (London: Allen & Unwin, 1979). McLaine argues that despite bungled efforts to propagate the Ministry's 'basic themes: the justice of the British cause, Britain's strength, and the commitment of the whole community to the war effort', despite mishandling such issues as 'the prospect of post-war reform, the nature of the Soviet regime, and press freedom', the British public read through the most noxious rhetoric and rallied most favourably to the facts of the war's progress, pp. 30, 3.
24. Melissa Hall, 'Military, Gender and the Imagery of the First World War', *Phoebe* 3 (Fall 1991) 26.
25. Martin Pugh argues that social pressures on women after 1918 'to replace the manpower lost in the First World War pointed unambiguously to a return to marriage and motherhood'; feminists were caught between disparaging domesticity and supporting the housewife, 'Domesticity and the Decline of Feminism, 1930–1950', *British Feminism in the Twentieth Century*, Harold L. Smith (ed.) (Amherst: University of Massachusetts Press, 1990), p. 149.

26. Alison Light, *Forever England: Femininity, Literature and Conservatism Between the Wars* (London: Routledge, 1991), p. 2.
27. Deborah Gorham, '"Have We Really Rounded Seraglio Point?": Vera Brittain and Inter-War Feminism', p. 96.
28. Susan K. Kent, *Making Peace: The Reconstruction of Gender in Interwar Britain* (Princeton: Princeton University Press, 1993) discusses how the postwar anti-feminist backlash stressed gender differences, p. 115, but so did some feminists, whose views may have been too easily co-opted.
29. Storm Jameson, *In the Second Year* (1936), p. 111. Cited in text as *Year*.
30. Henry Louis Gates, Jr., 'A Liberalism of Heart and Spine', *The New York Times* (27 March 1994), p. 22.
31. Dennis Smith, 'English and the Liberal Inheritance After 1886', *Englishness: Politics and Culture 1880–1920* Ed. Robert Colls and Philip Dodd (London: Croom Helm, 1986), p. 256.
32. Virginia Woolf, *Three Guineas* (1938), p. 103. Cited in text as *TG*.
33. Betty Miller, *On the Side of the Angels* (1945), p. 9. Cited in text as *Angels*.
34. Emmanuel Levinas, *Totality and Infinity* Trans. Alphonso Lingis (Pittsburgh: Duquesne University Press, 1969), pp. 214, 39, 195. Cited in text as *T&I*. Feminists disagree about Levinas's gendering of 'otherness'. Tina Chanter defends him against the charge of subordinating the feminine: he 'is upsetting, not accepting, the traditional values which identify the egoism of male dominance as superior to female sufferance', 'Feminism and the Other', in *The Provocation of Levinas*, Robert Bernasconi and David Wood (eds) (London: Routledge, 1988), p. 36.
35. Emmanuel Levinas, 'Useless Suffering', in *The Provocation of Levinas*, p. 162.
36. Emmanuel Levinas, 'Apropos of Buber: Some Notes', *Outside the Subject* (Stanford: Stanford University Press, 1993), p. 45; Theodore De Boer, 'An Ethical Transcendental Philosophy', *Face to Face with Levinas*, Richard A. Cohen (ed.) (Albany: State University New York Press, 1986), pp. 102–3.
37. Tamra Wright, Peter Hughes, Alison Ainley, 'The Paradox of Morality: Interview with Levinas', *Provocation*, p. 176.
38. Paul Ricoeur, 'On Interpretation', *From Text to Actions: Essays in Hermeneutics* II Trans. Kathleen McLaughlin and David Pellauer (Chicago: University of Chicago Press, 1991), pp. 2, 7.
39. See Hayden White's challenges to historical narrative in *The Content of the Form: Narrative Discourse and Historical Representation* (Baltimore: Johns Hopkins University Press, 1987).

1 'Differences that Divide and Bind'

1. Elizabeth Bowen, 'Portrait of the Artist', p. 286.
2. Rebecca West (1942), 'Differences that Divide and Bind', p. 562.
3. Phyllis Bottome, *Formidable to Tyrants* (1941), p. 12. Cited in text as *Tyrants*.

4. Ethel Mannin, *Christianity – or Chaos* (1940), p. 189. Cited in text as *CorC*.
5. Phyllis Bottome, Letter to *Time and Tide*, p. 1116.
6. Rebecca West, 'I Believe', p. 388.
7. Pamela Frankau, 'Anything's Realer than War', p. 517. Frankau, a close friend of Rebecca West, was a successful novelist. *The Willow Cabin*, reprinted by Virago, has a very compelling section about the Blitz. Her full-fledged World War II novel, *Over the Mountain*, is out of print.
8. In *Death of the Moth*, p. 155.
9. Quentin Bell, *Virginia Woolf: A Biography* Vol. 2, pp. 258–9.
10. *Letters of Virginia Woolf* Vol. 2, pp. 348, 582; Vol. 1, p. 441. Roger Poole criticizes yet exalts Woolf's 'intolerable oversimplification' in her claim that 'the origins of war' are traceable only to men's need for glory, 'We All Put Up With You Virginia', in *Virginia Woolf and War*, p. 99. In her cross-cultural study of *Women Writers and Fascism*, Marie-Louise Gattens points out 'the dangers of an inflationary use of the term *fascism*, which not only erases the historical specificity of political systems such as National Socialism in Germany but also mitigates the particular oppression and brutality of that regime', p. 2. Gattens defends Woolf's use of fascism as questioning ties between 'historical discourse', 'nationalism', and 'the social subject', p. 2. A trenchant gloss on Woolf's use of fascism is Umberto Eco's essay, 'Ur-Fascism', *New York Review of Books* (22 June 1995) which counters the totalistic fascism of his youth with an analysis of its distinctive ideology and political culture. In 'Ur-Fascism', '*the cult of tradition*' rejects the 'advancement of learning', modernity and 'the critical spirit', as derived from the Enlightenment; it 'doubts the legitimacy of a parliament', and instead, prefers to feel 'humiliated by the ostentatious wealth and force of their enemies [Englishmen and Jews]', to 'advocate a *popular elitism*', and is '*obsess[ed] with a plot* against the nation which reinforces its nationalistic identity', pp. 14, 15.
11. For Woolf as the foundational anti-war feminist, see *Arms and the Woman*, *Gendering War Talk*, and *Behind the Lines*. Johanna Alberti traces feminists' different views of fascism to their generations and forms of political activity and resistance, but her approach is shaped by Woolf as the basis of her theory, 'British Feminists and Anti-Fascism in the 1930s', *This Working-Day World: Women's Lives and Culture(s) in Britain 1914–1945*, Sybil Oldfield (ed.) (London: Taylor & Francis, 1994), pp. 111–22.
12. Jacqueline Rose, *Why War?* (Oxford: Blackwell, 1993), p. 32.
13. Rachel Bowlby's suggestive reading of Woolf's ellipses replicates their critical method, with no indication of their 'hidden meaning', of women's alternative peace platform, p. 165.
14. Brenda Silver surveys women readers who correct Woolf's factual errors and confusion about 'rearmament-for-defense with a desire for war', but is uncritical of Woolf's belief that only a woman perceives 'the destructiveness inherent in her culture'; she thus fails to note the thinking of women who supported Hitler, pp. 267, 272.

15. Leonard admits this social insecurity in his autobiographies, *Sowing* (NY: Harcourt, 1969) and *The Journey Not the Arrival Matters* (London: Hogarth, 1970) and in his novel, *Wise Virgins. The Letters of Virginia Woolf* Vol. 6, p. 379.
16. Virginia Woolf, *A Writer's Diary* (1954), p. 313. Cited in text as *WD*.
17. Schneider' s complex analysis is necessary to any discussion of Woolf's responses to war, and is cited too seldom, p. 100. She also uses these quotations from Woolf's *Writer's Diary*.
18. *The Diary of Virginia Woolf* Vol. 5, pp. 142, 169. *Letters* Vol. 6, p. 379.
19. Paul Berry and Mark Bostridge. *Vera Brittain: A Life*, p. 359. Cited in text as *VB: Life*. Brittain's daughter, Shirley Williams, describes her mother's belief that World War II was 'a personal Calvary and a personal redemption', p. 2. Studies of women and war rarely mention religious faith as a feature of cultural and personal identity and politics.
20. Vera Brittain, *Testament of Experience* (1957), p. 170. Cited in text as *TE*.
21. Vera Brittain, 'Peace and the Public Mind' (1934), p. 60. Cited in text as 'Peace'.
22. Vera Brittain, *Wartime Chronicle* (1989), p. 49. Cited in text as *Wartime*.
23. Vera Brittain, *Born 1925* (1948, 1982) . Cited in text as *Born*.
24. Stevie Smith, 'Brittain and the British' (1941, 1983), p. 176. Cited in text as 'Brittain'.
25. Lorna Lewis, *Time and Tide* (1 March 1941) 170.
26. Vera Brittain, *Humiliation with Honour* (1943), p. 9. Yvonne A. Bennett sees Brittain mediating her own class biases through her belief that the transcendent power of love could overcome class, sexual, and political distinctions.
27. E.M. Delafield, 'Sentimental Journey', p. 153.
28. Vera Brittain, *Testament of a Peace Lover* (1988), p. 21. Cited in text as *Peace Lover*.
29. Stevie Smith, *Novel on Yellow Paper* (1936), p. 118. Cited in text as *NYP*.
30. Stevie Smith, *Over the Frontier* (1938), p. 89. Cited in text as *OF*.
31. Dorothy L. Sayers, *Begin Here* (1940), p. 141. Cited in text as *Begin*.
32. Dorothy L. Sayers, 'Notes on the Way', (15 June 1940), p. 633. Cited in text as 'Notes'.
33. Dorothy L. Sayers, 'The English War' (1940), p. 45. Cited in text as 'EW'.
34. Ralph Hone, *Dorothy L. Sayers: A Literary Biography*, p. 115.
35. Dorothy L. Sayers, 'Aerial Reconnaissance', p. 270. Cited in text as 'Aerial'.
36. Dorothy L. Sayers, *Creed or Chaos?* (1940), p. 7. Cited in text as *Creed*. Sayers never questioned her racist use of 'Jewboys' and 'niggers'; as Nancy-Lou Patterson notes, what makes Sayers' slurs 'culpable' are their 'casualness . . . if we assign moral responsibility, we cannot say, "but everybody did it"', pp. 17, 23.
37. James Brabazon, *Dorothy L. Sayers*, p. 212.
38. Dorothy L. Sayers, *The Mysterious English* (1941), pp. 8, 16.
39. Andy Croft, 'Ethel Mannin: The Red Rose of Love and the Red Flower of Liberty', p. 206.

40. Ethel Mannin, *Privileged Spectator* (1939), p. 297. Cited in text as *Spectator*.
41. See Sander Gilman's groundbreaking study of the Nazi construction of the Jew as black and a disease eating away at the heart of Europe, *The Jew's Body* (NY: Routledge, 1991).
42. Ethel Mannin, *Brief Voices* (1959), p. 50. Cited in text as *Voices*.
43. Storm Jameson, *No Time Like the Present* (1933), pp. 237–8. Cited in text as *No Time*.
44. Martin Ceadel, *Pacifism in Britain 1914–1945: The Defining of a Faith* (Oxford: Clarendon Press, 1980), defines activists and sympathizers as the relationship between public support and 'the psychological and social pressures implied by activism', p. 225. Overall, British women activists received little or no support for their internationalist views.
45. Storm Jameson, *Journey From the North* Vol. 1 (1969), p. 326. Cited in text as *J* I.
46. 'In the End', *Challenge to Death* (1934), p. 328. Raphael Samuels explores the ideological, historical, and cultural manifestations of British identity politics in his three volume work: *Patriotism: The Making and Unmaking of British National Identity* (London: Routledge, 1989). 'Little Englandism', in his introduction to Volume I: *History and Politics* is defined as isolationist and xenophobic.
47. Constance Babington Smith, *Rose Macaulay*, p. 140.
48. 'Moral Indignation', *The English Genius* (1939), p. 176. Cited in text as 'Moral'.
49. Rose Macaulay, 'Consolations of the War' (1941), p. 75.
50. Storm Jameson, Letter to Vera Brittain, 6 August 1940. Berry and Bostwick offer a balanced view of Jameson's and Brittain's friendship, conceding that Brittain's dependence on the unequivocal support of her close friends led to expectations that made the already reticent Jameson withhold the fact that she had retreated from pacifism earlier in the thirties.
51. Storm Jameson, Letter to Vera Brittain, 4 Sept. 1941.
52. Vera Brittain, *England's Hour* (1941), p. 197. Cited in text as *E Hour*.
53. Simon Featherstone, 'The Nation as Pastoral in British Literature of the Second World War', *Journal of European Studies* xvi (1986), p. 156.
54. David Gervais, *Literary Englands: Versions of 'Englishness' in Modern Writing* (Cambridge: Cambridge University Press, 1993), p. 81. Raphael Samuel finds World War II countryside images celebrated as 'nationalist ideology', wherein 'Englishness was an essence residing in a race... found in its purest form in the country... an intensely personal' haven from destruction and from 'crass materialism', *Patriotism* III: *National Fictions* (London: Routledge, 1989), pp. 162–4.
55. Frances Partridge, *A Pacifist's War* (1983), p. 55. Cited in text as *PW*.
56. Nancy Huston, 'The Matrix of War: Mothers and Heroes', *The Female Body in Western Culture*, Susan R. Suleiman (ed.) (Cambridge: Harvard University Press, 1986), p. 119.
57. Storm Jameson, 'In Courage Keep Your Heart', p. 15.
58. Naomi Mitchison, Letter to *Time and Tide*, p. 1436.

59. Rebecca West, 'War Aims', p. 1520.
60. Naomi Mitchison, 'I Have 5 Children', pp. 17–20.
61. Rebecca West, 'The Necessity and Grandeur of the International Idea', p. 51. Cited in text as 'Necessity'.
62. Mary Agnes Hamilton, 'No Peace Apart from International Security', pp. 269, 270. Cited in text as 'Peace'.
63. Naomi Jacob, *Wind on the Heath*, p. 151.
64. Bryher, *The Days of Mars* (1972), p. 4. Cited in text as *Mars*.
65. Bryher, 'Third Year' (1941), p. 19. Cited in text as 'Third'.
66. Ursula Bloom, *War Isn't Wonderful* (1961), p. 55.
67. Ursula Bloom, *The Fourth Cedar* (1945), p. 56.

2 From Fascism in Britain to World War

1. Stephen Spender. *The Thirties and After: Poetry, Politics, People (1933–75)* (London: Macmillan, 1978), p. 13. Andy Croft notes of the thirties: 'on the whole novelists . . . were now turning to political subjects, rather than political writers turning to fictional forms,' *Red Letter Days*, p. 122.
2. See George Watson's 'The Myth of Catastrophe' in his *Politics and Literature in Modern Britain* (Totowa, NJ: Rowman and Littlefield, 1977). A.J.P. Taylor finds the interwar writers puzzling for their ahistorical lack of regard for enormous gains in social welfare, *English History 1914–1945* (Oxford: Oxford University Press, 1965), p. 180. Andy Croft argues that novels' realistic detail prevented 'the sort of generalized political hectoring' in poetry, *Red Letter Days*, pp. 199, 25.
3. According to Andy Croft, the most popular writers of the thirties, such as Frank Swinnerton, Warwick Deeping, Dorothy Sayers, P.G. Wodehouse, and Agatha Christie, did not deal with political issues, *Red Letter Days*, p. 27.
4. Recently released papers reveal that while Mosley's supporters 'came from all social classes', funding for his Fascists came from overseas, paid into a London bank in dollars, French and Swiss francs, and German marks; 'he was aware that to attract British support he had to conceal such connections', *The Times* (1 Oct. 1996), p. 4. Mosley was imprisoned at Holloway from May 1940 until the end of 1944, but unrepentent, he disseminated Fascist propaganda after the war.
5. Iain Wright, 'F.R. Leavis, the Scrutiny Movement and the Crisis', *Culture and Crisis in Britain in the Thirties*, p. 41.
6. Peter Widdowson. 'Between the Acts? English Fiction in the Thirties', in *Culture and Crisis*, p. 135.
7. Valentine Cunningham, *British Writers of the Thirties*. Also see Cunningham's essay, 'Neutral?: 1930s Writers and Taking Sides', in *Class, Culture and Social Change*, Frank Gloversmith (ed.) (Sussex: Harvester, 1980), pp. 45–70. Janet Montefiore's *Men and Women Writers of the 1930s* (London: Routledge, 1996) studies many British women writers absent from other surveys and makes the significant point that 'the only political issues in the women's writing of the 1930s much discussed by feminist literary historians are gender equality

and the sexual politics of representation'; this of course ignores 'the political role' these writers played in their lives and writing, p. 20.

8. See Andy Croft's study in *Red Letter Days*, p. 225.
9. Calin Andrei Mihailescu traces dystopias from philosophy of science and religion and the fiction of Dostoevsky through Zamiatin's *We*, the precedent for Orwell's *1984*, 'Mind the Gap: Dystopia as Fiction', *Style* 25 (Summer 1991) pp. 211–20.
10. Patricia Koster, 'Dystopia: An Eighteenth-Century Appearance', *Notes and Queries* 30 (February 1983) pp. 65–6.
11. Gordon Beauchamp questions technology in dystopias as a tool in totalitarian rule or a determining force in its own right, 'Technology in the Dystopian Novel', *Modern Fiction Studies* 32 (Spring 1986) pp. 53–63. Andy Croft argues that 'political science fiction in the 1930s' is 'transformed' from a 'reactionary, chauvinistic and anti-semitic' genre to being 'anti-fascist and optimistic', worrying more 'about the likely end of democracy' than the 'likely end of the world', *RLD*, p. 222.

    For literary historical surveys of dystopias, see Eric Rabkin, 'Atavism and Utopia,' *No Place Else: Explorations in Utopian and Dystopian Fiction*, Eric S. Rabkin, Martin H. Greenberg, and Joseph D. Olander (eds) (Carbondale: Southern Illinois University Press, 1983), pp. 3, 4; Lyman Tower Sargent, *British and American Utopian Literature 1516–1975: an annotated bibliography*, 1st edn (Boston: G.K. Hall, 1979) p. XI. Nan B. Albinski discusses the narrative differences, histories, and purposes of utopian fiction in her important study, *Women's Utopias in British and American Fiction* (London: Routledge, 1988). Gary Saul Morson distinguishes between the 'unqualified, absolute truths about morality and society that constantly occur in utopias [but] have no place in novels', p. 77, *The Boundaries of Genre: Dostoevsky's Diary of a Writer and the Traditions of Literary Utopia* (Austin: University of Texas Press, 1981).
12. Ken Davis, 'The Shape of Things to Come: H.G. Wells and the Rhetoric of Proteus', *No Place Else*, pp. 110–24, 113.
13. See Sargent's historical overview of British utopian fiction using scientific technology to propose solutions to social problems, 'Ambiguous Legacy: The Role and Position of Women in the English Eutopia', *Extrapolation* (19) pp. 39–49.
14. For Huxley's and Orwell's place in dystopic fictions, see I.F. Clarke, *Voices Prophesying War: 1763–1984* (London: Oxford University Press, 1966) and Chad Walsh, *From Utopia to Nightmare* (NY: Harper & Row, 1962).
15. John Rodden, 'Reputation, Canon-Formation, Pedagogy: George Orwell in the Classroom', *College English* (Sept. 1991) pp. 503–30. Orwell's disclaimer is quoted in Bernard Crick, *George Orwell* (London: Secker & Warburg, 1980), p. 398.
16. Orwell's views have been both appropriated and vilified by left and right. See 'The Legacy of Orwell: A Discussion', *Salmagundi* pp. 70–1 (Spring-Summer 1986); *Inside the Whale: Orwell: Views From the Left*, Christopher Norris (ed.) (London: Lawrence and Wishart, 1984), and

Daphne Patai, *The Orwell Mystique: A Study in Male Ideology* (Amherst: University of Massachusetts Press, 1984).

17. In his otherwise trenchant discussion of thirties British speculative fiction, Widdowson omits women writers. Joanna Russ shows how utopian fiction allows women writers to flourish outside conventional forms, *How to Suppress Women's Writing* (Austin: University of Texas Press, 1983). Daphne Patai's annotated bibliography provides a basis for research on women writers: 'British and American Utopias by Women: 1836–1979', *Alternative Futures* 4 (Spring-Summer 1981). An exception is Andy Croft's survey, 'Worlds Without End Foisted Upon the Future – Some Antecedents of Nineteen Eighty-Four' in Norris, pp. 183–216.
18. Martin Ceadel argues that the major interwar literature treated 'international affairs' 'as an advance warning of the intensifying struggle between extreme Right and Left which Britain might itself undergo' and not 'the unprecedented and all-pervasive fear of war. . . . Fascism was treated as an internal disease rather than as an external military danger,' 'Popular Fiction and the Next War, 1918–39' in *Class, Culture and Social Change*, p. 161. In his neglect of women writers, he cannot see that they combine these fears.
19. David Smith, p. 48. Arthur Marwick argues that by 1931, with 'no universal recovery from [World War I's] economic dislocations, [b]rash complacency was . . . replaced by feverish panic', *Britain in the Century of Total War* (Boston: Little Brown 1968), pp. 204, 205.
20. John Coombs, 'British Intellectuals and the Popular Front', in Gloversmith, p. 73.
21. Jane Lewis provides the historical context for this phenomenon by showing how policies left over from the nineteenth century still governed women's lives in the thirties. These policies 'assumed the existence of the bourgeois family model' and thus fostered women's dependency on their husbands' household contributions, *Women in England 1870–1950* (Bloomington: Indiana University Press, 1984), p. 48.
22. Naomi Mitchison, 'The Reluctant Feminists' (1934), pp. 93–4. Cited in text as 'Reluctant'.
23. Storm Jameson, 'Documents' (1937), p. 10.
24. 'Man the Helpmate', *Man, Proud Man* (1934), pp. 109, 112. Other contributors include Susan Ertz, Sylvia Townsend Warner, and Rebecca West. Susan K. Kent blames feminists' ambivalence in the interwar period on discourses that promised both 'sexual "liberation" and a new identity for women', yet highlighted 'the threat of discord and, ultimately, war', which 'led feminists to compromise their earlier egalitarianism', 'Gender Reconstruction After the First World War', *British Feminism in the Twentieth Century* (Amherst: University of Massachusetts Press, 1990), p. 67. This claim does not apply to Mitchison and Jameson.
25. 'Women On The Spot', p. 169–76.
26. Storm Jameson, 'Silchester', p. 525.
27. Storm Jameson, 'Cloud Form', p. 370.

28. Jill Benton, *Naomi Mitchison: A Biography*, p. 3. Cited in text as Benton.
29. *The Moral Basis of Politics* (1938), p. 84. Cited in text as *Moral*.
30. See *The Blood of the Martyrs*, which uses Nero's reign of terror to analyze the rise of European fascism; *You May Well Ask: A Memoir 1920–1940* and *Among You Taking Notes . . . The Wartime Diary of Naomi Mitchison 1939–1945*. Recently, Mitchison said that she did not want *We Have Been Warned* reprinted because 'It's got such a lot of thick bits, which seem to me like unstirred soup. . . . But I think there are some good bits in it . . . I've still got the original bits that were cut out and they were important', 'Naomi Mitchison talking with Alison Hennegan', p. 173.
31. *Naomi Mitchison's Vienna Diary* (1934), pp. viii–ix.
32. *We Have Been Warned* (1935), p. 46. Cited in text as *Warned*. Johanna Alberti quotes from Mitchison's letters to show how her 'political philosophy based on "love and awareness"' combined women's private and public lives, 'putting "danger and beauty, conversion and re-birth" together with "lots of small, ordinary things – more dustbins and bathrooms for people who haven't got them, more leisure and more education for people who need them desperately', 'Keeping the Candle Burning', p. 306. Janet Montefiore's discussion of the novel shows Mitchison's sense of herself as 'historic subject', p. 20.
33. Q.D. Leavis, 'Lady Novelists and the Lower Orders', p. 112. Cited in text as 'Lady'.
34. Interestingly, Leavis compared Mitchison's 'reporting of trivial conversations' and 'observation of the district-visiting kind' to Storm Jameson's 'stubborn honesty, humility' and sensitive observations, but Mitchison's self-questioning enfolds the socialist aesthetics Jameson developed in 'Documents'. Leavis never questions the authority she assumes as the wife of a Cambridge don and on behalf of a magazine the working class probably did not read.
35. *All Change Here: Girlhood and Marriage*, p. 60.
36. Beth Dickson criticizes Mitchison's mythic optimism in the early novels as well as her later unresolved conflict.
37. Benton reports that Mitchison wrote the rape scene first and built the rest of the novel around it, p. 105.
38. *The Home and A Changing Civilization*; 'The Home' (1934), p. 631.
39. *Time and Tide* (4 May 1935) p. 656.
40. *Times Literary Supplement* (25 April 1935) p. 270.
41. Quoting Victor Gollancz in *You May Well Ask*, pp. 176–7. David Smith admits Mitchison's painfully honest examination of her own attitudes; he dismisses the novel by focusing on Dione's sexual experience and interpreting her rape as 'allow[ing] him to make love to her', p. 80. Alison Smith applauds Mitchison's 'unbreakable openmindedness . . . valuable frankness, and wisdom', p. 17. Andy Croft sees the novel as having 'clear pro-communist sympathies', but as the abortion scene testifies, Mitchison is also very critical, *RLD*, p. 229.
42. Gloversmith's analysis of Orwell's 'accommodation of socialism' 'to the ethic of decency and respectability' is pertinent to this discus-

sion because in contrast, Mitchison's critique is relentlessly politicized, especially as she implicates herself and her class. See 'Changing Things: Orwell and Auden' in *Class, Culture and Social Change*, pp. 101–41.

43. 'The Fourth Pig: A Fable of Europe 1935', pp. 1395–6.
44. As Douglas Robillard observes, Jameson refashions scenes from her memoirs and fiction, 'often word for word', creating a 'kind of non-fiction novel', pp. 63–73.
45. Storm Jameson. 'To a Labour Party Official' (1934), p. 29. Cited in text as 'Labour'.
46. Storm Jameson, 'Crisis' (1936), p. 156. Cited in text as 'Crisis'.
47. Valentine Cunningham insists that Jameson was a 'sterner Marxist', but her autobiography, memoirs, and essays insist on her identity as a Labour socialist, *British Writers of the Thirties*, p. 263.
48. Jameson, 'The Responsibilities of a Writer' (1941), p. 170. Cited in text as 'Responsibilities'. Stuart Laing shows Jameson's theories coinciding with the development of Mass Observation, but his analysis of 30s fiction which also elevated 'fact over fiction' does not include Jameson's, p. 144.
49. 'The Writer's Situation', in *The Writer's Situation* (1947), p. 2. Cited in text as 'Writer's'.
50. Andy Croft shows how Jameson connects the British Union of Fascists, the National Government, and continental events to direct attention to 'the elements of latent fascism in British society', *RLD* p. 231. The model for both Mitchison and Jameson was probably Oswald Mosley, who turned from progressive ideas of the early thirties to fascism.
51. Although pessimistic about the Labour Party's 'narrow oligarchy of Trade Union leaders . . . out of touch with their rank and file' and 'rehearsing its funeral obsequies', Jameson finds hope in the possibility of an alliance of 'progressive Liberals, I.L.P. and Communist Party'; 'A Popular Front', p. 811.
52. Jameson, 'In the End' in *Civil Journey* (1939), p. 219; originally in *Challenge to Death* (1934). Cited in text as 'End'.
53. Jameson, 'City to Let – Berlin 1932' in *Civil Journey*, p. 35. Cited in text as 'City'.
54. Jennifer Birkett views Jameson's double voice as incisive, but conservative and male-identified. I see Jameson revising such categories with her historical consciousness.
55. Jameson, *No Time Like the Present* (1933), pp. 187, 185. Cited in text as *No Time*.
56. Such conflations are debated as 'the ambiguous relation between thought and action in fascism', Robert Paxton, 'Radicals', review of Zeev Sternhell, Mario Sznajder and Maia Asheri, *The Birth of Fascist Ideology* (Princeton: Princeton University Press, 1994), *New York Review of Books* (23 June 1994) p. 51.
57. Birkett sees oppressive sexual politics reflecting the political bleakness of the thirties, but claiming that 'women are almost entirely absent' from *In the Second Year*, ignores their resistant presence, pp. 80–1.

Nan B. Albinski relates the novel's events to British politics of the 1930s; see 'Thomas and Peter'.

58. *The New Republic* (29 January 1936) p. 85.
59. *Forum* 95 (April 1936) p. vii.
60. *The Manchester Guardian* (7 Feb. 1936) 7; *Times Literary Supplement* (1 Feb. 1936) p. 92.
61. Naomi Mitchison, 'Eye Opener', p. 25. Cited in text as 'Eye'.
62. Jameson, 'The New Europe' (1940), p. 69. Cited in text as 'Europe'.
63. Jameson, 'The Twilight of Reason' (1934), p. 16. Cited in text as 'Twilight'.
64. William Lamb, *The World Ends* (1937), p. 194. Cited in text as *World.*
65. Jameson, 'A Crisis of the Spirit' (1941), p. 138. Cited in text as 'Spirit'.
66. Andy Croft sees this as 'The only British novel that dealt at any length with the Civil war', *RLD*, p. 318.
67. 'The Youngest Brother', in *Civil Journey*, pp. 143–4.

3 Dystopic Visions of Hitler's Victory

1. Martin Ceadel's 'Popular Fiction and the Next War: 1918–1939' shows how in 'next war' fiction science is depicted as dangerous, propelling international competition for weaponry, and often became so extreme in portraying battle technology, it acquired an apocalyptic tone that 'could serve as a modern morality play's secular hellfire', in Gloversmith, p. 170. Most of the genre was formulaic.
2. *Then We Shall Hear Singing: A Fantasy in C Major* (1942), pp. 25, 26. Cited in text as *Singing*. In her 7 Oct. 1939 *TLS* essay, 'Fighting the Foes of Civilization', Jameson refers to the Jews' persecution to predict how complacency about the Nazis could bring the end to civilization, which she defined as 'the growth of justice and tolerance', p. 571. Cited in text as 'Foes'.
3. *The End of this War* (1941), p. 15. Cited in text as *End of War*.
4. See Jameson's story 'The Last Night' in *Lidice,* the PEN tribute to the village.
5. For analyses of the Nazis' application of their ideology to women's lives, see Renate Bridental, Atina Grossmann, and Marion Kaplan, Eds. *When Biology Becomes Destiny: Women in Weimar and Nazi Germany* (NY: Monthly Review Press, 1984).
6. Vita Sackville-West. *Grand Canyon* (1943), Author's Note. Cited in text as *GC.*
7. Vita Sackville-West, 'July 1940', p. 71. Cited in text as 'July'.
8. Victoria Glendinning. *Vita: A Biography,* p. 295. Cited in text as Glendinning.
9. J.H. Jackson. *Books* (1 Nov 1942) p. 14.
10. *Nation* (2 Jan. 1943) p. 31.
11. Sargent finds *Swastika Night* a powerful critique of Hitler, but anti-fascist dystopias quite conventional, ignoring Burdekin's gender analysis as well as the fact that unlike the split he attributes to concerns for scientific oppression and anti-nazism, British women writers often combined them, 'The War Years'.

12. Katharine Burdekin, *Swastika Night* (1937), p. 78. Cited in text as *SN*.
13. Dorothy L. Sayers, 'Notes on the Way' p. 634.
14. See Daphne Patai's Introduction and 'Orwell's Despair, Burdekin's Hope: Gender and Power in Dystopia'. Carlo Pagetti, 'In the Year of Our Lord Hitler 720: Katharine Burdekin's *Swastika Night*'.
15. Rebecca West, 'Hitler Promised Them Husbands' (1943), p. 143 only. Cited in text as 'H'.
16. Pagetti argues that *Swastika Night* is more complex than Huxley's and Orwell's canonical dystopias because it connects persecuted women as repositories of the past to the ambiguous confrontation between 'the historical present and the imaginary future', p. 364.
17. For a comparison of the impact of individuals on dystopia's concern with the control of history and time, see Renata Galtseva and Irina Rodnyanskaya, 'The Obstacle: The Human Being, or the Twentieth Century in the Mirror of Dystopia'. *The South Atlantic Quarterly* 90 (Spring 1991) pp. 293–322.
18. Anne Cranny-Francis shows how utopian fiction 'positions the reader as an active subject, or as one with the intelligence and wisdom to contribute to the reorganization of English society', *Feminist Fiction: Feminist Uses of Generic Fiction* (NY: St. Martin's, 1990), p. 111.
19. Patai asserts that fascism festers under all societies which subscribe to cults of masculinity. Her introduction emphasizes *Swastika Night*'s 'transcendence of the specifics of Nazi ideology' vii, but Burdekin's historically grounded critique insists on those specifics.
20. Paul Rich discusses differences between European fascists' efforts to radically regenerate society 'through notions of race and Volk' and British commitment to 'a more traditional Victorian idea of status and gentility' whose nostalgia for a mythic 'homogeneous' and rustic England 'could partly make up for the loss of the imperial adventurer tradition' and 'the horrors of the First World War', 'Imperial Decline and the Resurgence of English National Identity, 1918–1979', *Traditions of Intolerance: Historical Perspectives on Fascism and Race Discourses in Britain* Ed. Tony Kushner and Kenn Lunn (Manchester: Manchester University Press, 1989), pp. 33–51. Kushner shows that 'the British state, although opposed to the anti-democratic and law-and-order threat of the fascists, opposed what it regarded as the fascists' major weapon, antisemitism. It must be suggested, therefore, that fascism failed in the 1930s and 40s not because of its antisemitism, but because of the stability of the British political structure', 'The Paradox of Prejudice: The Impact of Organized Antisemitism in Britain During an Anti-Nazi War', in *Traditions of Intolerance,* pp. 72–90.
21. See Daphne Patai's recent work on Burdekin, 'Imagining Reality: The Utopian Fiction of Katharine Burdekin'.
22. Personal interview, July 1991.

4 No Place Like Home: The British Home Front

1. Lois Clark, 'Picture From the Blitz', p. 27.
2. Elizabeth Lister, 'Goering and Beethoven', p. 403.
3. Raynes Minns, *Bombers & Mash: The Domestic Front 1939–45* (London: Virago, 1980), pp. 7, 10. See Susan Briggs's study of wartime posters and advertising, *The Home Front: War Years in Britain 1939–1945* (London: Weidenfeld and Nicolson, 1975); Brian Braithwaite, Noelle Walsh, and Glyn Davies, *The Home Front: The Best of Good Housekeeping 1939–45* (London: Ebury Press, 1987); and Margaret Allen, 'The Domestic Ideal and the Mobilization of Woman Power in World War II', *Women's Studies International Forum* 6 (1983) pp. 401–12.
4. Peggy Scott, *British Women in War* (London: Hutchinson, 1940), p. 297.
5. See Deirdre Beddoe's study of interwar women's magazines and advertising *Back to Home & Duty: Women Between the Wars, 1918–1939* (London: Pandora, 1989). Mirabel Cecil shows wartime magazine fiction depicting marriage as a 'patrotic duty', *Heroines in Love 1750–1974* (London: Michael Joseph, 1974), p. 174.
6. Cynthia Enloe, *Does Khaki Become You? The Militarization of Women's Lives* (London: Pluto Press, 1983), p. 46.
7. Jane Waller and Michael Vaughan-Rees, *Women in Wartime: The Role of Women's Magazines 1939–1945* (London: Optima, 1987), p. 127.
8. Carol Dyhouse, *Feminism and the Family in England 1880–1939* (Oxford: Basil Blackwell, 1989), p. 13.
9. Jane Lewis, 'Reconstructing Women's Experience of Home and Family', *Labour and Love: Women's Experience of Home and Family, 1850–1940* (Oxford: Blackwell, 1985), p. 5.
10. Barbara Kaye, *The Company We Kept* (1986), p. 93; Fay Inchfawn, *Salute to the Village* (1943), p. 49. Cited in text as *Salute*. Harold L. Smith's *War and Social Change: British Society in the Second World War* (Manchester: Manchester University Press, 1986) debates whether the war brought real and lasting change. Penny Summerfield argues that despite 'challenge and expectation of change . . . continuity with pre-war attitudes and practices towards women was considerable in the areas of both domestic work and paid employment', *Women Workers in The Second World War* (London: Routledge, 1984), p. 1. Braybon and Summerfield note that in 1944 there was childcare provision for working mothers for only a quarter of all children under five, *Out of the Cage: Women's Experiences in Two World Wars* (London: Pandora, 1987), p. 239. Cited in text as *Cage*.
11. John Costello, *Sex and War: Changing Values 1939–45* (London: Collins, 1985), p. 22. *Out of the Cage* shows that rising divorce rates between 1939–45, for which women were blamed, could be attributed in part to the 1937 liberalization of divorce laws, but women also reported that wartime separation made them realize their marital dissatisfaction, pp. 212–14.
12. Margery Allingham, *The Oaken Heart* (1941). Cited in text as *Oaken*.
13. Throughout the war women adapted to constant changes dictated not only by domestic social policy, but by the pattern of German

air attacks, which as Tom Harrisson reports, was 'erratic' with 'senseless variants', but after London and the Baedecker raids on historic cities such as Coventry, the Blitz focused mainly on the coastal ports and cities, *Living Through the Blitz* (London: Penguin, 1990), pp. 143, 210.

14. G.B. Stern, *Trumpet Voluntary* (1944), pp. 70, 71.
15. Elizabeth Goude, *The Castle on the Hill* (1942), p. 107. Cited in text as *Hill*. Goudge is best known for her 1944 historical romance, *Green Dolphin Country*, translated into the Hollywood movie, *Green Dolphin Street*, starring Lana Turner.
16. Elizabeth Bowen, *The Heat of the Day* (1949), p. 92. Cited in text as *HD*.
17. Kate O'Brien, 'The Village and the War', p. 579. Judy Giles shows how the 'always fragile and uneasy relationship between middle-class women and "the poor" became 'publicly visible' in the 1939–40 evacuation of women and children 'in the most private arena, and in becoming so contested the compassionate and philanthropic public accounts of welfare workers', *Women, Identity and Private Life in Britain* (NY: St. Martin's Press, 1995), p. 106.
18. Susan Ertz, *Anger in the Sky* (1943), p. 8. Cited in text as *Sky*. In Ertz's 1934 feminist anti-utopian novel, *Woman Alive*, the only woman left after a nuclear world war resists the role of queen bee. I discuss this in '"A New World Indeed!": Feminist Critique and Power Relations in British Anti-Utopian Literature of the 1930s', *Extrapolation* (Fall 1995) pp. 259–72.
19. Diana Gardner, 'The Land Girl' (1940), p. 151. Cited in text as 'LG'.
20. Diana Gardner, 'The Visitation' (1942), p. 36.
21. David Smith's point that *Horizon* emphasized artistry rather than politics belies how Gardner's social and cultural critique extends the definition of both, *Socialist Propaganda*, p. 131. See Robert Hewison, *Under Siege: Literary Life in London: 1935–45* (NY: Oxford UP, 1977) for a literary social history of wartime London writers and poets. Aside from Elizabeth Bowen, Hewison's wartime literary scene is a male bastion.
22. Knowles dates the stages of writing *Between the Acts* according to Hitler's successive invations of eastern and western Europe, 'The Looking-Glass War: Warping the Contemporary Record in *Between the Acts*', pp. 36–7.
23. Virginia Woolf, *Between the Acts* (1941). Cited in text as *Acts*.
24. Debates continue about the novel's optimism or pessimism, regarding possibilities for change and progress. See for example, Nancy Topping Bazin and Jane Lauter and Karen Schneider's discussion.
25. Judith L. Johnston, 'The Remediable Flaw: Revisioning Cultural History in *Between the Acts*', p. 260.
26. Ursula Bloom, 'Courage', p. 33.
27. Di Parkin, 'Women in the Armed Services, 1940–5', *Patriotism: The Making and Unmaking of British National Identity*: Vol. II: *Minorities and Outsiders*, Raphael Samuel (ed.) (London: Routledge, 1984), pp. 158, 160.

28. Willa Muir, 'What Should We Tell the Children?', pp. 535–6.
29. Josephine Bell. *Total War at Haverington* (1947), p. 62. Cited in text as *TW.* Bell is a pseudonym for Doris Bell Ball.
30. Elizabeth Bowen. *The House in Paris* (1935), p. 70. Cited in text as *HP*.
31. Monica C. Fryckstedt's 'Defining the Domestic Genre: English Women Novelists of the 1850s', *Tulsa Studies in Women's Literature* 6 (1987), p. 9, applies to World War II era middle class women, especially in light of Margaret Allen's study, showing women's wartime paid work was based on policies defining home and gender roles according to 'the domestic ideal', p. 411.
32. Rose Macaulay, 'Miss Anstruther's Letters' (1942), pp. 45, 46.
33. Elizabeth Berridge, 'Tell It to a Stranger' (1943), p. 77. Cited in text as 'Tell'.
34. Mary Desirée Anderson, 'The Black-Out', in *Chaos of the Night*, p. 7.
35. Naomi Mitchison, '1940', reprinted in Tom Harrisson, *Living Through the Blitz*, p. 44.
36. Mollie Panter-Downes, *London War Notes 1939–45*, p. 112. For information on home losses, see Caroline Lang, *Keep Smiling Through: Women in the Second World War* (Cambridge: Cambridge University Press, 1989), pp. 18–19. See David Johnson for a topographical study of the Blitz, *The London Blitz* (Chelsea, MI: Scarborough House, 1990), and Constantine FitzGibbon's personal reportage, *The Blitz* (London: Macdonald, 1970).
37. Marguerite Steen, *Pier Glass* (1968), p. 6.
38. Rose Macaulay, 'Notes Along the Way', p. 981. Cited in text as 'Notes'.
39. Tom Harrisson's Mass Observation Studies in *Living Through the Blitz* argues for 'this enormous diversity which continually frustrates generalization about the civilian mass', but as other researchers and the novelists studied here show, much psychological strength on the part of the populace derived from a yearning for unity.
40. Marghanita Laski, *Love on the Supertax* (1944), p. 5. Cited in text as *Love.* Out of print and hard to find, this pungent satire is one of several comic novels of the war. See my essay '"Between the Gaps"'.
41. Elizabeth Bowen. 'Preface', *The Demon Lover*, p. 99. Cited in text as *DL*.
42. Elizabeth Bowen, 'Mysterious Kor', p. 728. The story's inspiration is both Rider Haggard's novel, *She*, and his dedication to Andrew Lang, the source for Bowen's title and the poetry Pepita refers to. Cited in text as 'Kor'.
43. Elizabeth Bowen, 'She', originally a 1947 radio talk, pp. 109, 107. Cited in text as 'She'.
44. For discussion of all of Bowen's World War II short fiction, see my *Elizabeth Bowen: A Study of the Short Fiction.*
45. Elizabeth Bowen, 'Eire', pp. 31, 30.
46. Elizabeth Bowen, *Bowen's Court* (1942), p. 454. Cited in text as *BC*.
47. Braybon and Summerfield note that social mixing took place mostly among the 'middle class and above who had spent their teens in

relatively restricted social circles', while most factory workers were only elementary school educated, pp. 199–200, 197.

48. Marguerite Steen, *Shelter* (1942), p. 12. Cited in text as *S*.
49. Alison Light discusses how these qualities, encoding 'self-control' in 'a language of reticence' had been accepted as masculine until they were incorporated into women's 'writing selves' between the wars, p. 210. This was also the language of propaganda. Despite critical attention to posters, radio broadcasting was far more influential in World War II, more 'immediate', 'easier to control and direct centrally than 'newspapers, leaflets, posters, and even films', Zbnek Zeman, *Selling the War: Art and Propaganda in World War II* (NY: Exeter Books, 1982), p. 21.
50. Sylvia Townsend-Warner, 'Rainbow Villa', p. 42.
51. Dorothy Scannell, *Dolly's War* (1975), p. 146. Caroline Lang reports that many wives of poorly paid servicemen desperately needed paid work, p. 38.
52. Margaret Culkin Banning, *Letters From England: Summer 1942*, p. 140.
53. Naomi Jacob, *Me In Wartime* (1941), p. 214.
54. Harold L. Smith, 'The Effect of the War on the Status of Women' in *War and Social Change*, p. 213.
55. Braybon and Summerfield discuss how policies to convert textile factories to munitions left many working women unemployed. When the Home Guard was formed under the threat of invasion, women 'were not allowed to join, so strong was both the ideology of the male defender of women and children and the antipathy to women bearing arms', pp. 156–57. Only during the Blitz in 1941 did the government conclude that it needed women, and as Dorothy Sheridan reports, England became the only country in World War II to conscript women into the war effort, *Wartime Women: A Mass-Observation Anthology* (London: Heinemann, 1990), p. 2.
56. Sheridan reprints the statement of eight independent women consultants to the Ministry of Labour which appeared on the front page of the *Daily Express* on 20 March 1941, to 'tell Parliament that they do not approve of the way [the Minister of Labour] has approached the women of this country to take part in the war effort', p. 128.
57. For samples of women workers' statements, see *War Factory: Mass-Observation* (London: Cresset, 1987).
58. Reprinted in Susan Briggs, pp. 23, 45. Di Parkin discusses how in the war between 'Patriarchy and patriotism', 'women's place was that of servicing the men', p. 158. Braybon and Summerfield show men bemoaning the compulsory war service of women because of the threat to conjugal relations, p. 161.
59. Lettice Cooper, 'Politics in the Provinces', p. 573.
60. Lettice Cooper, *Black Bethlehem* (1947), pp. 218, 219, 204. Cited in text as *BB*. Although Cooper's milder novel of the interwar years, *The New House*, has been reprintd, the more powerful war novel has been ignored.
61. Lettice Cooper, 'New Year, 1939', p. 72.

5 'Perpetual Civil War': Domestic Fictions

1. Betty Miller, *On the Side of the Angels* (1945), p. 99. Cited in text as *Angels*.
2. Elizabeth Taylor, *At Mrs Lippincote's* (1949), p. 6. Cited in text as *Mrs L.* Virago has reprinted this and other Taylor fiction.
3. Noel Streatfeild, 'From My Diary', pp. 36–7.
4. Sarah Miller, 'Introduction' to Betty Miller, *On the Side of the Angels* xviii.
5. Cooper, Munich, and Squier devote one page to this novel, subsuming it in a universalist war text which elides women's particular experiences and representations of World War II.
6. Margaret Kennedy, *Where Stands a Winged Sentry* (1941), p. 22. Cited in text as *Sentry*.
7. Susan R. Suleiman, 'Writing and Motherhood', *The (M)other Tongue: Essays in Feminist Psychoanalytic Interpretation*, Shirley N. Garner, 'Claire Kahane and Madelon Sprengnether (eds) (Ithaca: Cornell University Press, 1985), p. 368. Cited in text as SS.
8. I would like to thank Joan Perkin for her questions and insights on this subject.
9. Jane Brown Gillette sees Julia's flirtation with the Wing Commander as signalling Taylor's critique of the dangers of imagination for women, 'What a Something Web We Weave: The Novels of Elizabeth Taylor', p. 96. Florence Leclercq sees 'Julia's [ambivalent] feminism' coinciding with Taylor resisting the more turbulent social changes of her time, *Elizabeth Taylor*, pp. 13, 6. Despite the novel's wartime subject, Leclercq sees it 'as a definite postwar statement', p. 10.
10. Sandra M. Gilbert and Susan Gubar, *The Madwoman in the Attic: The Woman Writer and the Nineteenth-Century Literary Imagination* (New Haven: Yale University Press, 1979), p. 16.
11. Of course, in World War II women actually became more involved in warfare than ever before, flying planes and commanding gun batteries against invading air attacks.
12. Audrey Beecham. 'Eichmann', *Chaos of the Night*, p. 17.
13. Gayle Greene, 'Family Plots', *Women's Review of Books* 7 (1990) pp. 8–9.
14. Elizabeth Carfrae, *The Lonely Road* (1942), p. 100. Cited in text as *Road*.
15. Elizabeth Carfrae, *Penny Wise* (1946), p. 134. Cited in text as *PW*.
16. Maysie Grieg, *Heartbreak For Two* (1945).
17. All three novels have been reprinted and their back cover blurbs applaud their gently satiric treatment of hard times infused with 'the steady beacon light of courage' which marks their traditional setting. As with the comic novels of Dennys and Delafield, which have also been reprinted, readers can keep their distance from the war's harsher realities through the invocation of 'timeless olde England'.
18. Joyce Dennys, *Henrietta's War: News From the Home Front 1939–1942*, p. 53. Cited in text as *HW*.
19. E.M. Delafield. *The Provincial Lady in Wartime* (1940, 1986), p. 26. Cited in text as *PLW*.

20. Joyce Dennys, *Henrietta Sees It Through: More News From the Home Front 1942–1945* (1985), p. 19. Cited in text as *HT*.
21. Dorothy Una Ratcliffe, *Mrs Buffey in Wartime* (1942), p. 10. Cited in text as *Mrs B*.

6 Fictions of the European Home Front

1. Storm Jameson, *The Black Laurel* (1947), p. 316. Cited in text as *BL*.
2. Anne Ridler, 'Poem For a Birthday', p. 83.
3. Fictions of foreign intrigue echoed the suspicions of alien enemies erupting in World War I. In John Buchan's 1915 *Thirty-Nine Steps* British fears of invasion materialize as German agents, but other writers combined suspicious ethnicities – Irish-Spanish-Jew – who infect the English landscape with images of their presumed amoral otherness. Somerset Maugham's 1928 *Ashenden* took Britain's paragon of decent diplomacy into the European maelstrom, while in Eric Ambler and Graham Greene, the rise of European fascism is mirrored in an internal British threat; see John Cawelti and Bruce Rosenberg, *The Spy Story* (Chicago: University of Chicago Press, 1987), p. 47. Ambler's 1939 *Mask of Dimitrios* played off stereotypes of a byzantine Balkans. For analyses of female spy stories, see Patricia Craig and Mary Cadogan, *The Lady Investigates: Women Detectives and Spies in Fiction* (London: Gollancz, 1981), who note that in the early thirties, the enemy 'was usually a megalomaniac middle-eastern potentate or the ruthless dictator of an unspecified European state', p. 208. With Helen MacInnes's 1941 *Above Suspicion*, British innocents abroad must outwit a Nazi cabal through the twisting alleys and murky country lodges of Austria.
4. Rebecca West's historical/political travel chronicle of Yugoslavia, *Black Lamb and Grey Falcon*, is a masterpiece of cultural analysis. Space does not allow treatment here.
5. David Smith argues that events of 1936–40, peaking with Russia joining the Allies, led to writers' political reorientation and 'critical hostility towards political writing', as with the magazine *Horizon*, p. 130. It may be that pragmatism derived from disappointment with radicalism and political turnabouts, not to mention 'betrayals', which 'had rendered all political optimism childish or at best irrelevant', p. 130. Orwell, for example, said 'that the disenchanted communist of the thirties would now vote Labour', p. 130.
6. David Feldman, *Englishmen and Jews: Social Relations and Political Culture 1840–1914* (New Haven: Yale University Press, 1994), discusses connections between British liberalism, national identity, and anti-Jewish immigrant feeling, all related to the class system and changing ideas of Englishness. On the Jews' social and political position in Britain and economic pressures to assimilate, see Todd Endelman, *Radical Assimilation in English Jewish History, 1656–1945* (Bloomington: Indiana University Press, 1990). Tony Kushner's *The Persistence of Prejudice: Antisemitism in British Society During the Second World War* (Manchester: Manchester University Press, 1989) analyses popular attitudes and

government policies towards British and European Jews, especially how prevailing stereotypes and myths shaped both.

7. On British intolerance of cultural difference and national identity, see Raphael's *Patriotism: The Making and Unmaking of British National Identity* Vol. II: *Minorities and Outsiders*.
8. Andrea Loewenstein, *Loathsome Jews and Engulfing Women* (NY: New York University Press, 1993).
9. Bryan Cheyette, *Constructions of 'The Jew' in English Literature and Society: Racial Representations, 1875–1945* (Cambridge: Cambridge University Press, 1993).
10. Claims for a harmless genteel antisemitism are debated by Colin Holmes, *Anti-Semitism in British Society 1876–1939* (NY: Holmes and Meier, 1979). Its persistence even after the war is recalled by Philip Norman as part of war discourse which remained dominent: 'In the whole flood of war-oriented films and comic books I remember not one word about Jewish suffering in concentration camps', p. 19. Instead, there were 'Jewish jokes, told in nasal, supposedly Jewish accents, with index fingers crooked to burlesque the counting of money: "Q. Why was Israel so poor after the war? A. Because the Germans sent them a gas bill". A cosy British dose of the same old anti-Semitic poison', *The Independent on Sunday* (25 August 1991) p. 19.
11. Woolf records the Jews' persecution in her diary 14 November 1938, but identified with it only as 'a faint heat under us, like potatoes frying', *The Diary of Virginia Woolf*. Vol. V, p. 186.
12. The list reflects writers' political spectrum of the era, but among the noteworthy are Agatha Christie, T.S. Eliot, and John Buchan.
13. Frances Spalding shows how Smith's trips to Germany in 1929–31 filled her with dread about German antisemitism and 'idolization of German culture' even though this was before Hitler's accession to power, *Stevie Smith*, p. 84. Montefiore importantly shows that unlike Woolf's pacifist anti-fascist argument in *Three Guineas*, the response of 'Smith's autobiographical heroine' is 'clearly not of someone alienated from the institutions of British power; but neither is it the speech of someone who expects to make things happen', p. 67. I disagree however with her emphasis on Smith's depiction of a 'timeless' war since the historic markers are too pronounced, p. 70.
14. Also published in 1938, Auden and Isherwood's 'melodrama in three acts', *On the Frontier*, debates the possibility of war as a struggle between two national stereotypes, 'decadent, anarchical Ostnia and our own dear Westland – that paradise of solvency and order', and Westland's internal struggle between a fascist polity and well-meaning but misguided oppositions (London: Faber & Faber, 1938), p. 28. In sharp contrast to Stevie Smith, Auden and Isherwood's female characters are stereotyped as 'violently repressed', 'the butterfly type', and 'embittered by poverty and household responsibilities', p. 11.
15. 'To School in Germany' (1955), p. 38.
16. 'Mosaic' (1939), p. 106.
17. 'In the Beginning of the War' (1942), p. 29.
18. See Bernard Wasserstein, *Britain and the Jews of Europe 1939–1945*

(Oxford: Clarendon Press, 1979) on British policy towards the plight of European Jews as well as Tony Kushner, *The Holocaust and the Liberal Imagination* (London: Blackwell, 1994).

19. Eleanor Rathbone, *Rescue the Perishing* (1943), p. 2. Committee members included aristocrats, clergy, members of parliament, and prominent English Jews. Recent archival research shows that Britain knew of Jewish exterminations in 1942.
20. Eleanor Rathbone, *Falsehoods and Facts About the Jews* (1944), p. 4.
21. Lilian Bowes Lyon, 'England. By Anna', p. 821.
22. Storm Jameson, *Europe to Let* (1940), p. 4. Cited in text as *Europe*.
23. See Jennifer Birkett.
24. Storm Jameson, *The Journal of Mary Hervey Russell* (1945), p. 136. Cited in text as *JMHR*.
25. Storm Jameson, *Cousin Honore* (1941), p. 41. Cited in text as *CH*.
26. Storm Jameson, *Cloudless May* (1944), p. 16. Cited in text as *CM*.
27. Storm Jameson, *The Fort* (1941), pp. 103, 33.

7 Defending Europe's Others

1. Phyllis Bottome, *The Goal* (1962), p. 207. See Marilyn Hoder-Salmon's biographical essay, 'Phyllis Bottome'.
2. Phyllis Bottome, *Mansion House of Liberty* (1941), p. 199. Cited in text as *Mansion*. (Published as *Formidable to Tyrants* in UK.)
3. Phyllis Bottome, 'Austrian Refugees', p. 453. For historical context, see Todd Endelman, 'Anti-Semitism in Wartime Britain'. *Michael* (Tel Aviv: Diaspora Research) X (1986) and Tony Kushner, 'The Paradox of Prejudice: The Import of Organized Anti-Semitism in Britain During an Anti-Nazi War', *Traditions of Intolerance*, pp. 82–9.
4. Phyllis Bottome, 'J'Accuse', p. 232. See Tony Kushner, 'Ambivalence or Anti-Semitism? Christian Attitudes and Responses in Britain to the Crisis of European Jewry During the Second World War', *Holocaust and Genocide Studies*, V (1990) pp. 175–89.
5. See Richard Griffiths, *Fellow Travellers of the Right: British Enthusiasts for Nazi Germany 1933–39* (London: Constable, 1980) for the waxing and waning of fascist sympathies as well as post-war disclaimers of those sympathies.
6. The 1940 MGM film, *The Mortal Storm*, glamourizes and thus deheroicizes Freya. Margaret Sullavan skiing in a silk blouse marks Freya as too fragile to carry out her escape and so Jimmy Stewart, playing her bereft but stalwart lover, carries her dead body to safety. Bottome nonetheless felt that the movie succeeded as 'our final message to the hearts and minds of America; by it we had hoped, not to drag them into the war, but to awaken them in time to what must happen to humanity, if the Swastika took the place of the Cross' (*Mansion*, p. 5).
7. See Bottome's autobiography of her early life, *Search for a Soul: Fragment of an Autobiography*.
8. Phyllis Bottome, *The Mortal Storm* (1937), p. 89. Cited in text as *MS*. In her incisive constrast of British women's anti-fascist fiction with

such male authors as Graham Greene and Evelyn Waugh, Barbara Brothers shows how the British reception of *The Mortal Storm* revealed antisemitism and 'indifferen[ce] to, if not approv[al] of, German persecution of the Jews', 'British Women Write the Story of the Nazis: A Conspiracy of Silence', in *Rediscovering Forgotten Radicals*, p. 258. Andy Croft sees the novel 'casting Nazism as the enemy of love', with 'an important emotional appeal to universal human values, traditionally potent against the equally timeless forces of evil and cruelty', p. 326. In the US edition, Toller becomes Roth.

9. Olga Owens, *Boston Transcript* 4 (4 Sept. 1938) 1.
10. S.N. *Saturday Review of Literature* (2 April 1938) 36; *Times Literary Supplement* (9 Oct. 1937) 734. Kate O'Brien found Bottome's method 'laborious in places, and a shade sentimental; her dialogue is often windy and untrue; but she has a marked sense of character and of values, and she knows Germany'. *The Spectator* (22 Oct. 1937) p. 700.
11. Eric Duthie, *The Left Review* (4 Dec. 1937) p. 695.
12. Gervais is describing Orwell's brand of British liberalism, with which Bottome would agree, p. 178.
13. Phyllis Bottome, 'The Oblation' (1958), p. 169. Cited in text as 'O'.
14. Phyllis Bottome, *Within the Cup* (1943), p. 124. Cited in text as *Cup*.
15. Phyllis Bottome, 'Austria's Contribution Towards Our New Order', p. 5.
16. Phyllis Bottome, *Apostle of Freedom* (1939), p. 25.
17. Sander Gilman, *The Jew's Body*, p. 18. While discussions of difference and the Other are basic to cultural studies today, Jews are rarely mentioned, questioning whether the history and representation of Jewish persecution fits the ideology or paradigm of cultural critics; studies of Jews are still conducted mostly by Jewish scholars and critics. Particularly relevant to Bottome is Michael Ragussis's study of authorial conversion of Jewish characters in Victorian novels; he traces the threat of Jewish Otherness to a cohesive Englishness, but also identifies a positive change in attitude, *Figures of Conversion: 'The Jewish Question' and English National Identity* (Durham, NC: Duke University Press, 1995). That Bottome, an ardent defender of the Jews would convert them in the light of their World War II jeopardy challenges Ragussis's idea of progression.
18. Phyllis Bottome, *The Lifeline* (1946), p. 14. Cited in text as *Lifeline*.
19. Olivia Manning, *The Balkan Trilogy, The Levant Trilogy* (1960–69). Cited in text as *Balkan* and *Levant*.
20. Kay Dick, *Friends & Friendship*, p. 31. Gyde C. Martin traces Manning's career and critical neglect, 'Olivia Manning: A Bibliography'. See also 'Olivia Manning on the Perils of the Female Writer'. Walter Allen finds the trilogies 'remarkable', not only as 'recreation of history', but in its depiction of the Pringles and their relationship, *Tradition and Dream* (London: Hogarth, 1986), p. 261. Robert K. Morris sees their theme as a clash between historical contingency and the Pringles' romantic vision of permanence. Helen MacNeil sees the trilogy as 'that modern rarity, a philosophical novel formed entirely out of fragments of felt life'. Alan Munton compares them to postwar epics

by Evelyn Waugh and Anthony Powell and finds that despite its 'very wide range of diverse experience' it 'suppress[es] or limit[s] all those hopeful political expectations and personal freedoms that the war years made possible', p. 74.

21. Olivia Manning, 'Last Civilian Ship' (1945), p. 117.
22. Harry J. Mooney applauds Manning's evenhanded treatment of Jewish characters in that they 'in part betray themselves' and Harriet is both 'dismayed by and fearful for them', p. 43. Cheyette sees 'binary stereotypes' judging Jews who assimilate and those who retain their cultural difference.
23. Jewish women in earlier English literature are valorized as nurturing victims, such as Scott's Rebecca, or in Daniel Deronda, polarized as Mirah, the passive helpmate or Alcharisi, a more ambivalent version of Elisabeth Bleileben in Bottome's *Old Wine*, choosing ambition over motherhood, but in her eloquent self-defence, also charistmatic.
24. A stunning example of this complicity and a gloss on Manning and Bottome's novels is Gregor von Rezzori's *Memoirs of an Anti-Semite*, which traces the narrator's prejudices as emblematic of the cultural consciousness of his Rumanian and Austrian homelands after the collapse of the Austro-Hungarian Empire.
25. See Renate Bridenthal et al., *When Biology Becomes Destiny: Women in Weimar and Nazi Germany* (NY: Monthly Review Press, 1984).
26. Olivia Manning, *School for Love* (1951), p. 11. Cited in text as *School*.
27. Olivia Manning, 'In a Winter Landscape' (1941), p. 104.
28. Olivia Manning, 'The Journey' (1948), p. 72.
29. Ann Bridge, *A Place to Stand* (1953), p. 259. Cited in text as *Place*.
30. Ann Bridge, *Facts and Fictions* (1968), pp. 73–4. Cited in text as *Facts*.
31. Jacket cover blurb, *A Place to Stand*.
32. Ann Bridge, *The Tightening String* (1962), p. 65. Cited in text as *TS*.
33. The Hungarian Jews were among the last to be rounded up by the Nazis, for despite his antisemitism, the Regent Horthy considered the Jews his subjects and would not turn them over until the Nazis took over in 1944.
34. Storm Jameson, *Before the Crossing* (1947), pp. 98–9.
35. Balakian sees 'the helpless, gullible Jew' not as ironic use of a stereotype, but as 'the distilled essences of Miss Jameson's clear and humane reasoning', p. 16.
36. Harrison Smith's view of the novel as 'haunted with . . . the sense that civilization is in peril' is confirmed by Jameson's fear of an evil even greater than Belsen – 'Megadeath', 'Berlin Tragedy', pp. 22–3; Jameson, *J* II, p. 313.
37. Stevie Smith, *The Holiday* (1949), pp. 57–8.
38. Stevie Smith, 'Beside the Seaside: A Holiday with Children' (1949), pp. 12–26.
39. Colin Holmes shows that British antisemitism in fascist and professional circles did not lead to serious volence and Jews were not targeted for discriminatory legislation, p. 219.

Primary Sources

Allingham, Margery. *The Oaken Heart*. London: Michael Joseph, 1941.

Anderson, Mary Desirée. 'The Black-Out'. *Chaos of the Night: Women's Poetry and Verse of the Second World War*. Catherine Reilly (ed.). London: Virago, 1984, pp. 6–7.

Banning, Margaret Culkin. *Letters From England: Summer 1942*. NY: Harper, 1943.

Beecham, Audrey, 'Eichmann'. *Chaos of the Night*, p. 17.

Bell, Josephine, *Total War At Haverington*. London: Longmans, Green, 1947.

Berridge, Elizabeth. 'Tell It to a Stranger'. *Life and Letters Today* (July 1943) p. 37.

Bloom, Ursula. 'Courage'. *Woman's Own* (January 1941) Reprinted in *Women in Wartime: The Role of Women's Magazines 1939–1945*. Jane Waller and Michael Vaughan-Rees (eds). London: Optima, 1987, p. 33.

—— *The Fourth Cedar*. London: The Book Club, 1945.

—— *War Isn't Wonderful*. London: Hutchinson, 1961.

Bottome, Phyllis. *Alfred Adler: Apostle of Freedom*. NY: Putnam's, 1939.

—— 'Austria's Contribution Towards Our New Order'. London: Austrian Youth Association, 1944.

—— 'Austrian Refugees'. *Time and Tide* (2 April 1938) p. 453.

—— *Formidable to Tyrants*. London: Faber & Faber, 1941.

—— *The Goal*. NY: Vanguard Press, 1962.

—— *The Heart of a Child*. NY: Putnam's, 1940.

—— 'J'Accuse'. *The New Republic* (28 Dec. 1938) p. 232.

—— Letter to *Time and Tide* (19 August 1939) p. 1116.

—— *The Lifeline*. London: Faber & Faber, 1946.

—— *London Pride*. Boston: Little, Brown, 1941.

—— *Mansion House of Liberty*. Boston: Little, Brown, 1941.

—— *The Mortal Storm*. London: Faber & Faber, 1937.

—— 'The Oblation'. *Walls of Glass*. London: Faber & Faber, 1958, pp. 169–92.

—— *Old Wine*. London: Faber & Faber, 1924.

—— *Search for a Soul: Fragment of an Autobiography*. London: Faber & Faber, 1947.

—— *Within the Cup*. London: Faber, 1943. Published as *Survival*. Boston: Little, Brown, 1943.

Bowen, Elizabeth. *Bowen's Court*. NY: The Ecco Press, 1979.

—— 'The Demon Lover'. *The Collected Stories of Elizabeth Bowen*. NY: Knopf, 1983.

—— 'Eire'. *The Mulberry Tree* Ed. Hermione Lee. NY: Harcourt Brace, 1986, pp. 30–4.

—— *The Heat of the Day*. NY: Knopf, 1949. Penguin, 1986.

—— *The House in Paris*. NY: Knopf, 1935. Penguin, 1975.

—— 'Mysterious Kor'. *Collected Stories.*
—— 'Portrait of the Artist'. Review of *James Joyce: A Definitive Biography* by Herbert Gorman. *Spectator* (14 March 1941) p. 286.
—— Preface. *The Demon Lover. The Mulberry Tree,* pp. 94–99.
—— 'She'. *Afterthought.* London: Longmans, 1962, pp. 107–13.
Bridge, Ann. *Facts and Fictions: Some Literary Recollections.* NY: McGraw-Hill, 1968.
—— *A Place to Stand.* NY: Macmillan, 1953.
—— *The Tightening String.* London: Chatto & Windus, 1962.
Brittain, Vera. *Born 1925.* NY: Macmillan, 1948.
—— *England's Hour.* NY: Macmillan, 1941.
—— *Humiliation With Honour.* NY: Fellowship Publications, 1943.
—— 'Peace and the Public Mind'. *Challenge to Death.* Storm Jameson (ed.). London: Constable, 1934, pp. 40–66.
—— *Testament of Experience.* NY: Seaview Books, 1981.
—— *Testament of a Peace Lover: Letters from Vera Brittain.* Winifred and Alan Eden-Green (eds). London: Virago, 1988.
—— *Testament of Youth.* London: Gollancz, 1933.
—— *Wartime Chronicle: 1939–45.* Ed. Alan Bishop and Y. Aleksandra Bennet. London: Gollancz, 1989.
Bryher. *The Days of Mars: A Memoir 1940–1946.* NY: Harcourt Brace, 1972.
—— 'Third Year'. *Life and Letters* 32 (January 1942) pp. 19–24.
Burdekin, Katharine. *The Devil, Poor Devil!* London: Gollancz, 1934.
—— *The End of This Year's Business.* NY: The Feminist Press, 1986.
—— *Proud Man.* London: Gollancz, 1934.
—— *Quiet Ways.* London: Gollancz, 1930.
—— *Swastika Night.* London: Gollancz, 1937; NY: The Feminist Press, 1985.
Carfrae, Elizabeth. *The Lonely Road.* London: Hutchinson, 1942.
—— *Penny Wise.* NY: Putnam's 1946.
Clark, Lois. 'Picture From the Blitz'. *Chaos of the Night.* p. 27.
Cooper, Lettice. *Black Bethlehem.* London: Gollancz, 1947.
—— *National Provincial.* NY: Macmillan, 1938.
—— 'New Year, 1939'. *Time and Tide* (21 Jan. 1939) p. 72.
—— 'Politics in the Provinces'. *Time and Tide* (6 May 1939) p. 573.
Delafield, E.M. *The Provincial Lady in Wartime.* Chicago: Academy Chicago, 1986.
—— 'Sentimental Journey'. *Time and Tide* (23 Feb. 1941) p. 153.
Dennys, Joyce. *Henrietta's War: News From the Home Front 1939–1942.* London: Andre Deutsch, 1985.
—— *Henrietta Sees It Through: More News From the Home Front 1942–1945.* London: Andre Deutsch, 1985.
Dickens, Monica. *The Fancy.* London: The Book Club, 1945.
Ertz, Susan. *Anger in the Sky.* London: Hodder & Stoughton, 1948.
—— *Woman Alive.* London: Appleton, 1934.
Frankau, Pamela. 'Anything's Realer Than War'. *The Listener* (10 April 1941) p. 517.
—— *The Willow Cabin.* London: Virago, 1986.
—— *Over the Mountain.* London: Heinemann, 1967.

Gardner, Diana. 'The Land Girl'. *Wave Me Goodbye: Stories of the Second World War*. Anne Boston (ed.). London: Virago, 1988, pp. 151–8.
—— 'The Visitation'. *Life and Letters Today* (Oct. 1942) pp. 35–9.
Goudge, Elizabeth. *Castle on the Hill*. London: Duckworth, 1975.
Grieg, Maysie. *Heartbreak for Two*. NY: Doubleday, Doran, 1941.
Hamilton, Mary Agnes. 'No Peace Apart from International Security: An Answer to Extreme Pacifists'. *Challenge to Death*, pp. 261–74.
Hoult, Nora. *There Were No Windows*. London: Heinemann, 1944.
Inchfawn, Fay. *Salute to the Village*. London: Lutterworth, 1943.
Jacob, Naomi. *Me in Wartime*. London: Hutchinson, 1941.
—— *Wind on the Heath*. London: Hurst and Blackett, 1956.
Jameson, Storm (Margaret). *Before the Crossing*. London: Macmillan, 1947.
—— *The Black Laurel*. London: Macmillan, 1947.
—— *City to Let*. London: Cassell, 1932.
—— *Civil Journey*. London: Cassell, 1939.
—— 'Cloud Form'. *Times Literary Supplement* (29 July 1944) p. 370.
—— *Cloudless May*. NY: Macmillan, 1944.
—— *Cousin Honore*. NY: Macmillan, 1941.
—— 'Crisis'. *Left Review* 4 (January 1936) pp. 156–9.
—— 'A Crisis of the Spirit'. *The Writer's Situation*. London: Macmillan, 1950, pp. 136–63.
—— 'Documents'. *Fact* 4 (July 1937) pp. 9–18.
—— *The End of this War*. London: Allen & Unwin, 1941.
—— *Europe to Let*. NY: Macmillan, 1940.
—— 'Fighting the Foes of Civilization'. *Times Literary Supplement* (7 Oct. 1939) p. 571.
—— *The Fort*. London: Cassell, 1942.
—— *The Green Man*. London: Cassell, 1952.
—— 'In Courage Keep Your Heart' (1939). *Women in Wartime: The Role of Women's Magazines 1939–45*. Jane Waller and Michael Vaughan-Rees (eds). London: Optima, 1987, pp. 14–15.
—— 'In the End'. *Challenge to Death*, pp. 322–32; in *Civil Journey*, pp. 212–25.
—— *In the Second Year*. NY: Macmillan, 1936.
—— *The Journey of Mary Hervey Russell*. London: Macmillan, 1945.
—— *Journey From the North* Vol. 1. London: Collins, 1969.
—— *Journey From the North* Vol. 2. London: Virago, 1984.
—— 'The Last Night'. *Lidice: A Tribute by Members of the International PEN*. London: Allen & Unwin, 1944, pp. 50–84.
—— Letter to Vera Brittain. 6 August 1940. Vera Brittain Papers, McMaster University.
—— Letter to Vera Brittain. 4 Sept. 1941. VB Papers.
—— 'Man the Helpmate'. *Man, Proud Man*. Mabel Ulrich (ed.). London: Hamish Hamilton, 1932, pp. 105–36.
—— *Mirror of Darkness: Company Parade*. London: Cassell, 1934; Virago, 1984; *Love in Winter*. Cassell, 1935; Virago, 1984; *None Turn Back*. Cassell, 1936; Virago, 1984.
—— 'The New Europe'. *Fortnightly* (Jan. 1940) pp. 68–79.
—— *No Time Like the Present*. London: Cassell, 1933.

—— *The Other Side*. London: Macmillan, 1946.
—— 'A Popular Front'. *Time and Tide* (6 June 1936) p. 811.
—— 'The Responsibilities of a Writer'. *The Writer's Situation*, pp. 164–79.
—— 'Silchester'. *Times Literary Supplement* (30 Oct. 1943) p. 525.
—— *Then We Shall Hear Singing: A Fantasy in C Major*. London: Macmillan, 1942.
—— 'The Twilight of Reason'. *Challenge to Death*, pp. 1–20.
—— 'To a Labour Party Official'. *Left Review* (2 Nov. 1934) p. 29.
—— 'Women On the Spot'. *Atlantic Monthly* (Feb. 1941) pp. 169–76.
—— as William Lamb. *The World Ends*. London: John Dent, 1937.
—— as James Hill. *No Victory For the Soldier*. NY: Doubleday, 1939.
Kaye, Barbara. *The Company We Kept*. London: Werner Shaw, 1986.
Kennedy, Margaret. *Where Stands a Winged Sentry*. New Haven: Yale University Press, 1941.
Laski, Marghanita. *Love on the Supertax*. London: Cresset, 1944.
Lehmann, Rosamond. 'When the Waters Came'. *The Penguin New Writing* 3 (Feb. 1941), pp. 108–13; *The Gipsy's Baby*. London: Virago, 1982, pp. 91–8.
Lorna Lewis. Letter to *Time and Tide* (1 March 1941) p. 170.
Lister, Elizabeth. 'Goering and Beethoven'. *The Listener* (18 Sept. 1941) p. 403.
Lyon, Lilian Bowes. Letter and Reprint of 'England. By Anna'. *Time and Tide* (10 Aug. 1940) p. 821.
Macaulay, Rose. 'Consolations of the War'. *The Listener* (16 Jan. 1941) p. 75.
—— 'Losing One's Books'. *Articles of War: The Spectator Book of World War II*. Fiona Glass and Philip Marsden-Smedly (eds). London: Grafton, 1989, pp. 184–6.
—— 'Miss Anstruther's Letters'. *Wave Me Goodbye*, pp. 40–7.
—— 'Moral Indignation'. *The English Genius*. Hugh Kingsmell (ed.). London: The Right Book Club, 1939.
—— 'Notes Along the Way'. *Time and Tide* (5 Oct. 1940) p. 982.
Mannin, Ethel. *Bavarian Story*. London: Jarrolds, 1948.
—— *Brief Voices*. London: Hutchinson 1959.
—— *Christianity – or Chaos*. London: Jarrolds, 1940.
—— *The Dark Forest*. London: Hutchinson, 1946.
—— *Privileged Spectator*. London: Jarrolds, 1939.
Manning, Olivia. *The Balkan Trilogy*. Harmondsworth: Penguin, 1984.
—— 'In a Winter Landscape'. *A Romantic Hero*. London: Mandarin Paperbacks, 1992, pp. 85–104.
—— 'The Journey'. *Wave Me Goodbye*, pp. 61–73.
—— 'Last Civilian Ship'. *The Windmill* (1945) pp. 117–19.
—— *The Levant Trilogy*. Harmondsworth: Penguin, 1984.
—— 'Olivia Manning on the Perils of the Female Writer'. *The Spectator* (7 Dec. 1974) pp. 734–5.
—— *School For Love*. Harmondsworth: Penguin, 1951.
Miller, Betty. *On the Side of the Angels*. London: Virago, 1986.
Mitchison, Naomi. *All Change Here: Girlhood and Marriage*. London: Bodley Head, 1975.
—— *Among You Taking Notes: The Wartime Diary of Naomi Mitchison*. Dorothy Sheridan (ed.). London: Gollancz, 1985.

—— *The Blood of the Martyrs* (London: Constable, 1939) London: Canongate Classics, 1988.

—— *The Corn King and the Spring Queen*. London: Cape, 1931; Virago, 1983.

—— 'Eye Opener'. *New Statesman* (27 Jan. 1984) p. 25.

—— 'The Fourth Pig: A Fable of Europe 1935'. *Time and Tide* (5 Oct. 1935) pp. 1395–6.

—— 'I Have Five Children'. *Lilliput Goes to War*. Kay Webb (ed.). London: Hutchinson, 1985, pp. 17–20.

—— *The Home and a Changing Civilization*. London: Lane, 1934.

—— 'The Home'. *Times Literary Supplement* (20 Sept. 1934) p. 631.

—— Letter to *Times Literary Supplement* (25 April 1935) p. 270.

—— Letter to *Times Literary Supplement* (4 May 1935) p. 656.

—— Letters to *Time and Tide* (11 Nov. 1939) p. 1436; (18 Nov. 1939) p. 1446; (25 Nov. 1939) pp. 1488–9; (9 Dec. 1939) p. 1584; (30 Dec. 1939) p. 1651.

—— *The Moral Basis of Politics*. London: Constable, 1938.

—— 'The Reluctant Feminists'. *The Left Review* (3 Dec. 1934) pp. 93–4.

—— 'Talking With Alison Hennegan'. *Writing Lives: Conversations Between Women Writers*. Mary Chamberlain (ed.). London: Virago, 1988, pp. 169–80.

—— '1940'. *Living Through the Blitz*. Tom Harrisson (ed.). London: Penguin, 1990, p. 44.

—— *Vienna Diary*. NY: Smith and Haas, 1934.

—— *We Have Been Warned*. London: Constable, 1935.

—— *You May Well Ask: A Memoir 1920–1940*. London: Fontana, 1975.

Muir, Willa. 'What Should We Tell the Children?' *The Listener* (14 March 1940) pp. 535–6.

O'Brien, Kate. 'The Village and the War'. *Fortnightly* (June 1944) pp. 577–84.

Panter-Downes, Mollie. *London War Notes 1939–45*. NY: Farrar Strauss, 1971.

Partridge, Frances. *A Pacifist's War*. London: Robin Clark, 1983.

Ratcliffe, Dorothy Una. *Mrs Buffey in Wartime*. London: Thomas Nelson, 1942.

Rathbone, Eleanor. *Falsehoods and Facts About the Jews*. London: Gollancz, 1944.

—— *Rescue the Perishing*. London: The National Committee for Rescue from Nazi Terror, 1943.

Ridler, Anne. 'Poem for a Birthday'. *New Writing and Daylight*. John Lehmann (ed.) (Summer 1942) p. 83.

Sackville-West, Vita. 'July 1940'. *Country Notes in Wartime*. London: Hogarth Press, 1940, p. 70.

—— *Grand Canyon*. London: Michael Joseph, 1942.

Sayers, Dorothy L. 'Aerial Reconnaissance'. *Fortnightly* 160 (1943) p. 270.

—— *Begin Here: A War-time Essay*. London: Gollancz, 1940.

—— *Creed Or Chaos?* Address delivered at the Biennial Festival of the Church Tutorial Classes Association in Derby, 4 May 1940. London: Hodder and Stoughton, 1940.

—— 'The English War' (1940). *The Terrible Rain: The War Poets 1939–45*. Ed. Brian Gardner. London: Methuen, 1966, pp. 45–7.
—— *The Mysterious English*. London: Macmillan, 1941.
—— 'Notes on the Way'. *Time and Tide* (15 June 1940) pp. 633–4.
Scannell, Dorothy. *Dolly's War*. London: Macmillan, 1975.
Smith, Stevie. 'Beside the Seaside: a Holiday with Children'. (*Holidays and Happy Days*, 1949). *Me Again: Uncollected Writings of Stevie Smith*. Jack Barbera and William McBrien (eds). NY: Vintage, 1983, pp. 13–25.
—— 'Brittain and the British' (1941). *Me Again*, pp. 176–7.
—— *The Holiday*. NY: Pinnacle, 1982.
—— 'In the Beginning of the War'. (*Life and Letters Today*, August 1942). *Me Again*, pp. 28–30.
—— 'Mosaic'. *Eve's Journal* (March 1939). *Me Again*, pp. 105–7.
—— *Novel on Yellow Paper* NY: Pinnacle, 1982.
—— *Over the Frontier* NY: Pinnacle, 1982.
—— 'To School in Germany'. *Evening Standard* (12 May 1955). *Me Again*, pp. 35–8.
Spender, Stephen. *The Thirties and After: Poetry, Politics, People (1933–75)*. London: Macmillan, 1978.
Steen, Marguerite. *Shelter*. NY: Sun Dial Press, 1942.
—— *Pier Glass: More Autobiography*. London: Longmans, Green, 1968.
Stern, G.B. *Trumpet Voluntary*. NY: Macmillan, 1944.
Streatfeild, Noel. 'From My Diary: The Beginning of London's Blitz'. *London Calling: A Salute to America*. Storm Jameson (ed.). NY and London: Harper, 1942, pp. 35–52.
Taylor, Elizabeth. *At Mrs Lippincote's*. London: Davies, 1945.
Thirkell, Angela. *Cheerfulness Breaks In*. NY: Carroll & Graf, 1990.
—— *Marling Hall*. NY: Carroll & Graf, 1990.
—— *Northbridge Rectory*. NY: Carroll & Graf, 1991.
Townsend-Warner, Sylvia. 'Rainbow Villa'. *Garland of Straw*. NY: Viking, 1943, pp. 35–43.
—— 'Sweethearts and Wives'. *Wave Me Goodbye*, pp. 159–67.
West, Rebecca. 'A Challenge to the Left'. *Time and Tide* (16 December 1939) pp. 1606–7.
—— 'Differences that Divide and Bind'. *The Listener* (19 April 1939) pp. 562–3.
—— 'Hitler Promised Them Husbands'. *The Listener* (2 April 1943) p. 143.
—— 'I believe'. *I Believe: The Personal Philosophies of Twenty-Three Eminent Men and Women of Our Time*. London: Allen & Unwin, 1940, pp. 371–90.
—— Letters to *Time and Tide* (18 November 1939) pp. 1466–7; (2 December 1939) pp. 1519–20; (30 December 1939) p. 1652.
—— 'The Necessity and Grandeur of the International Idea'. *Challenge to Death*, pp. 240–60.
Woolf, Virginia. *Between the Acts* NY: Harcourt Brace, 1953.
—— *The Diary of Virginia Woolf* Vol. 5: 1936–1941 Anne Olivier Bell (ed.). NY: Harcourt Brace, 1984.
—— 'The Duchess and the Jeweller'. *Collected Stories of Virginia Woolf*. Susan Dick (ed.). London: Hogarth, 1989.

—— *The Letters of Virginia Woolf* Vols. 1, 2, 6. Nigel Nicolson and Joanne Trautmann (eds). NY: Harcourt, Brace, 1975.
—— 'Thoughts on Peace in an Air Raid'. *The Death of the Moth and Other Essays*. London: Hogarth Press, 1942.
—— *Three Guineas* (1938). NY: Harcourt Brace, 1986.
—— *A Writer's Diary*. Leonard Woolf (ed.). NY: Harcourt Brace, 1954.

Select Bibliography

Alberti, Johanna. 'Keep the Candle Burning: Some British Feminists Between Two Wars'. *Suffrage and Beyond: International Perspectives.* Caroline Daley and Melanie Nolan (eds). NY: New York University Press, 1994.

Albinski, Nan. *Women's Utopias in British and American Fiction.* London: Routledge, 1988.

Albinski, Nan. 'Thomas and Peter: Society and Politics in Four British Utopian Novels'. *Utopian Studies* 1 Gorman Beauchamp, Kenneth Roemer, Nicholas Smith (eds). Boston: University Press of America, 1987. pp. 11–22.

Anon. 'A Second General Strike': Review of Storm Jameson's *In the Second Year. The Times Literary Supplement* (1 February 1936) p. 92.

Anon. Review of Phyllis Bottome's *The Mortal Storm. The Times Literary Supplement* (9 October 1937) p. 734.

Anon. Review of Storm Jameson's *In the Second Year. Forum* 95 (April 1936) p. vii.

Anon. Review of Storm Jameson's *In the Second Year. Manchester Guardian* (7 February 1936) p. 7.

Anon. Review of Storm Jameson's *In the Second Year. Times Literary Supplement* (1 February 1936) p. 92.

Anon. Review of Vita Sackville-West's *Grand Canyon. Nation* (2 January 1943) p. 31.

Balakian, Nona. 'Portrait of Our Time'. *The New York Times Book Review* (16 May 1948) p. 16.

Barbera, Jack and William McBrien, *Stevie: A Biography of Stevie Smith.* London: Heinemann, 1988.

Bazin, Nancy Topping & Jane H. Lauter. 'Virginia Woolf's Keen Sensitivity to War'. *Virginia Woolf and War: Fiction, Reality, and Myth.* Mark Hussey (ed.). Syracuse: Syracuse University Press, 1991. pp. 14–39.

Bell, Quentin. *Virginia Woolf: A Biography*. NY: Harcourt Brace, 1972.

Bennett, Yvonne A. 'Vera Brittain: Feminism, Pacifism and Problems of Class, 1900–1953'. *Atlantis* 12 (Spring 1987) pp. 18–23.

Benton, Jill. *Naomi Mitchison: A Biography*. London: Pandora, 1990.

Berry, Paul and Mark Bostridge. *Vera Brittain: A Life*. London: Chatto & Windus, 1995.

Birkett, Jennifer. 'Doubly Determined: The Ambition of Storm Jameson'. *Determined Women: Studies in the Construction of the Female Subject, 1990–90*. Eds Jennifer Birkett and Elizabeth Harvey. Savage, Md.: Barnes and Noble, 1991. pp. 68–94.

Bowlby, Rachel. *Virginia Woolf: Feminists Destinations*. Oxford: Blackwell, 1988.

Brabazon, James. *Dorothy L. Sayers*. NY: Scribners, 1981.

Brothers, Barbara. 'British Women Write the Story of the Nazis: A Conspiracy of Silence'. *Rediscovering Forgotten Radicals: British Women Writers, 1889–1939*. Angela Ingram and Daphne Patai (eds). Chapel Hill: University of North Carolina Press, 1993. pp. 244–64.

Cadogan, Mary & Patricia Craig. *Women and Children First*. London: Gollancz, 1978.

Ceadel, Martin. 'Popular Fiction and the Next War, 1918–39'. *Class, Culture and Social Change*. Frank Gloversmith (ed.). Sussex: Harvester, 1980. pp. 161–84.

Cooper, Helen M. Adrienne A. Munich, & Susan M. Squier. *Arms and the Woman: War, Gender, and Literary Representation*. Chapel Hill: University of North Carolina Press, 1989.

Cowley, Malcolm. Review Storm Jameson's *In the Second Year*. *The New Republic* (29 January 1936) p. 85.

Croft, Andy. 'Ethel Mannin: The Red Rose of Love and the Red Flower of Liberty'. *Rediscovering Forgotten Radicals*.

Croft, Andy. *Red Letter Days: British Fiction in the 1930s*. London: Lawrence & Wishart, 1990.

Crosland, Margaret. *Beyond the Lighthouse: English Women Novelists in the Twentieth Century*. NY: Taplinger, 1981.

Dick, Kay. *Friends and Friendship: Conversations and Reflections*. London: Sidgwick & Jackson, 1974.

Dickson Beth. 'From Personal to Global: The Fiction of Naomi Mitchison'. *Chapman* 10 (1987) pp. 34–40.

Duthie, Eric. Review *The Mortal Storm*. *The Left Review* (4 December 1937) pp. 694–6.

Gattens, Marie-Louise. *Women Writers and Fascism*. Gainsville: University Press of Florida, 1995.

Gillette, Jane Brown. 'What a Something Web We Weave: The Novels of Elizabeth Taylor'. *Twentieth Century Literature* 35 (Spring 1989) pp. 94–112.

Glendinning, Victoria. *Vita: A Biography*. NY: Knopf, 1983.

Gorham, Deborah. '"Have We Really Rounded Seraglio Point?": Vera Brittain and Inter-War Feminism'. *British Feminism in the Twentieth Century*. Harold L. Smith (ed.). Amherst: University of Massachusetts Press, 1990. pp. 84–103.

Gorham, Deborah. *Vera Brittain*. Oxford: Blackwell, 1996.

Hoder-Salmon, Marilyn. 'Phyllis Bottome'. *British Novelists, 1919–1939*. George M. Johnson (ed.). Columbia, South Carolina: Bruccoli Clark Layman, Inc., 1997.

Hone, Ralph. *Dorothy L. Sayers: A Literary Biography*. Kent, Ohio: Kent State University Press, 1979.

Hussey, Mark. *Virginia Woolf and War: Fiction, Reality and Myth*. NY: Syracuse University Press, 1991.

Jackson, J.H. Review of Vita Sackville-West's *Grand Canyon*. *Books* (1 November 1942) p. 14.

Johnston, Judith L. 'The Remediable Flaw: Revisioning Cultural History in *Between the Acts*'. *Virginia Woolf and Bloomsbury: A Centenary Celebration*. Jane Marcus (ed.). Houndmills: Macmillan, 1987. pp. 253–77.

Leclercq, Florence. *Elizabeth Taylor*. Boston: Twayne, 1985.

Laing, Stuart. 'Popular Fiction and the Next War, 1918–39'. *Class, Culture, and Social Change*. pp. 142–60.

Lassner, Phyllis. '"Between the Gaps": Sex, Class, and Anarchy in the British Comic Novel of World War II'. *Look Who's Laughing: Gender and Comedy*. Gail Finney (ed.). NY: Gordon & Breach, 1994. pp. 205–20.

Lassner, Phyllis. *Elizabeth Bowen: A Study of the Short Fiction*. Boston: Twayne, 1991.

Lassner, Phyllis. 'The "Milk of Mother's Kindness Has Ceased to Flow": Virginia Woolf, Stevie Smith, and the Representation of the Jew'. *Between "Race" and Culture: Representations of "the Jew" in English and American Literature*. Bryan Cheyette (ed.). Stanford: Stanford University Press, 1996.

Leavis, Q.D. 'Lady Novelists and the Lower Orders'. *Scrutiny* 4 (September 1935) pp. 112–32.

LeClerck, Florence. *Elizabeth Taylor*. Boston: Twayne, 1985.

Macneil, Helen. 'Lost Words'. *The New Statesman* (26 September 1980).

Martin Gyde C. 'Olivia Manning: A Bibliography'. *Bulletin of Bibliography* 46 (September 1989) pp. 160–70.

Montefiore, Janet. *Men and Women Writers of the 1930s*. London: Routledge, 1996.

Mooney, Harry J. 'Olivia Manning: Witness to History'. *Twentieth Century Women Novelists*. Thomas F. Staley (ed.). London: Macmillan, 1982. pp. 39–60.

Morris, Robert K. *Continuous and Change: The Contemporary British Novel Sequence*. Carbondale: Southern Illinois University Press, 1972.

O'Brien, Kate. Review. *The Mortal Storm*. *The Spectator* (22 October 1937) p. 700.

Owens, Olga. Review, *The Mortal Storm*. *Boston Transcript* (4 September 1938) p. 1.

Pagetti, Carlo. 'In the Year of Our Lord Hitler 720: Katherine Burdekin's *Swastika Night*'. *Sciences Fiction Studies* 17 (1990) pp. 360–9.

Patai, Daphne. 'British and American Utopias by Women: 1836–1979'. *Alternative Futures* 4 (Spring-Summer 1981) pp. 184–206.

Patai, Daphne. 'Orwell's Despair, Burdekin's Hope: Gender and Power in Dystopia'. *Women's Studies International Forum* 7 (1984) pp. 85–95.

Patai, Daphne. 'Imagining Reality: The Utopian Fiction of Katharine Burdekin'. *Rediscovering Forgotten Radicals*. pp. 226–43.

Patterson, Nancy. 'Images of Judaism and Anti-Semitism in the Novels of Dorothy L. Sayers'. *Sayers Review* 2.2 (June 1978) pp. 17–23.

Plain, Gill. *Women's Fiction of the Second World War*. Edinburgh: Edinburgh University Press, 1996.

Poole, Roger. 'We All Put Up With You Virginia'. *Virginia Woolf and War*. pp. 79–100.

Robillard, Douglas. 'Storm Jameson as Novelist and Critic'. *Essays in Arts and Science* (17 May 1988) pp. 63–73.

Sargent, Lyman Tower. *British and American Utopian Literature 1516–1975: an annotated bibliography*. Boston: G.K. Hall, 1979.

Sargent, Lyman Tower. 'The War Years: British Utopianism 1915–1950'.

Just the Other Day: Essays on the Suture of the Future. Ed. Luk de Vos. Antwerp: EXA, 1985. pp. 161–85.

Schneider, Karen. 'Of Two Minds: Woolf, the War and *Between the Acts*. *Journal of Modern Literature* XVI:1 (Summer 1989) pp. 93–112.

Silver, Brenda. '*Three Guineas* Before and After: Further Answers to Correspondents'. *Virginia Woolf: A Feminist Slant*. Jane Marcus (ed.). Lincoln: University of Nebraska Press, 1983.

Smith, Alison. 'The Woman From the Big House: The Autobiographical Writings of Naomi Mitchison'. *Chapman* 10 (1987) pp. 10–17.

Smith, Constance Babington. *Rose Macaulay*. London: Collins, 1972.

Smith, David. *Socialist Propaganda in the Twentieth-Century British Novel*. Houndmills: Macmillan, 1978.

Smith, Harrison. 'Berlin Tragedy'. *The Saturday Review* (1 May 1948) p. 16.

Spalding, Frances. *Stevie Smith*. NY: Norton, 1989.

Watson, George. *Politics and Literature in Modern Britain*. Totowa, NJ: Rowman and Littlefield, 1977.

Index

95 still uneasy state of Jews in England; insistence on difference troubling; 'antisemitism of tolerance' (19?);
See 1919 Aliens Act
97 Smith antiFascist, for Jews; 200 her visits to Germany 1929 + 31 saw antisemitism consolidating;
02 Bowen's House in Paris (1935) - role of Jews.
06 Britain slow to abandon antisemitic stance
208 Europe to Let - English made to feel complicit in pogroms
x 11 (209) male narrator involves women - as does Smith (she says); insists on seeing Cousin Honoré ~~as~~ fable re Britain (212); - crazy dating, in 1941 as 'hopeful'...
213 Cloudless May; The Fort (214) - gets plot quite wrong
216 Bottome: The Mortal Storm blockbuster here + in US (219);
226 Within the Cup (1943); Adler (229)
230 The Lifeline (1946) - sees Christian Jews as mere extension
232 Manning's postwar trilogy of war. - Sasha + woman both marginalised (234) - Otherness;
239 M's School for Love (1951) - based in Jerusalem
241 Ann Bridge + Helen MacInnes - ~~good~~ 90 novels by sound of it
246 SJ The Black Laurel 1947 + Before the Crossing
249 Crucial to see the Other in ourselves. Smith + Bettie Miller fellows - 1949
250 SJ The Green Man
251 Return to shifting heart after war - DEPENDS ON GENERATION

See Acknowledgements for Archives.

[Manning's novels not simply rehash of her non fiction (46) as Lassner suggests – strange complication creeps in.
47 Storm Jameson for outsider/victim – turns from pacifism.
48 Macaulay too shifted – still loathes war, but sees this one as defensive. (Partridge + Russell other pacifists (52);
53 West + Mitchison as pacifists – they argue – M thinks war may be replay, W sees Fascism as genuine enemy – both very concerned for others; West's stance paradoxical (54); many
55 women come to think of victims beyond borders eg
56 Bryher's continental perspective (+ Naomi Jacob).
57 For many women, war destroys boundaries
59 Many of most popular writers not into politics (see n.3)
61 30s gt decade for dystopias
62 SO MANY OUT OF PRINT [put in introduction)
66 Jameson + Mitchison
67 Jameson not so feminist in fiction.[76] See fn 34 on Lassner's reaction to M + J
(85) See Fourth Pig · 87 SJ as critic of Labour Party
95 See SJ's 2nd yr: Sacker's wife Lotte delivers stillborn son on day General Strike begins (check).
97 Reviews of 2nd yr decry its Englishness cp The World Ends (1937) + No Victory for the Soldier (1938) re spousal war
105 SJ's Then We Shall Hear Singing – gen distorted, written pub after destruction of Lidice (109 Vita Sackville West's dystopia Grand Canyon (1942)) – seen as 'profoundly defeatist' (113))
114 Swastika Night [see book in 1984]; see links w The End of this Day's Business (124); she links gender + racial politics (125);
130 Treatment of village home front; Goudge writes of disenchantment – Castle on the Hill (1942) SEE QUOTE, ... – nurturing – Btwn the Acts (136) – Jew (check); Susan Ertz (132); private life ceases to be 'subconscious Hitlerism' (141). Marghanita Laski's novel, Love retreat (148); see Heart of the Dog (150); on the Superlax – satire (149); Shelter (1940).
see Marguerite Steen's Dallo Black Bethlehem v fine novel – no real examination
161 of its structure. Frame not acknowledged – gets story utterly wrong – heavily simplified
167 Betty Miller. Andrew's damaged heart's very symbol of effects of war (169); Eliz Taylor (172) see significance of Julia choosing Woolf recipe (173) – no mention of other woman in home (176); short look at pop romances (179);
192 Despite pop romances w bad foreigners, 30s saw West, SJ, Bottome, Smith, Manning etc really knew central Europe (193); 3 guineas sees is linking fascism – not just sexes but races (194);

(2) Pamphlet of 1941 'Why not War Writers?'
(3) Too essentialist in lumping together British writers - most of key g...
(4) Too often all women lumped under pacifism - + canon exclud...
// xx Good point on changing aesthetics: [see p254 on Laura Marc... 255] //xx (5) VIP new definitions of modernism.
(6) VIP WOMEN + WAR.
(8) War, gender + the historical moment. See fn 20 p 256 + fn 21
(10) Important not to oversimplify war in gender terms
(11) All meanings of war etc dissected by women
(12) Importance of separating WW1 + WW2 (see Brittain, ... Mannin v others who changed their minds - Jameson e...
Siting of women's issues w/in war context - VIP
(13) Uses of non realism - more earthbound than men
(14) See Jamesons Then We Shall Hear Singing - spillo...
(15) from home to street
(16) Domestic disorder under strain of war. IDENTIFIC... more IMPORTANT THAN IDENTITY
(17) Jameson + Rathbone - identification w OTHERS - in proc... redefine patriotism
(19) stress on importance of OTHER to women. See Levin... See re JEWS
(20) Women's complex way of using plight of OTHERS - + WA... OF WRITING (RICOEUR)
Interesting but muddled introduction
(24) Rebecca West - from WW1 → WW2 + Jameson - ra... + necessary war. 25 Bottome + Mannin
Perception of different war - but many difft points ...
26 → Woolf + her war correspondents
(27) Three Guineas, Woolf + feminism
(29) Woolf not sole voice of home grown anti semitism
(30) Frank awareness of some pacifists to reluctan... on patriotism. Most of some pacifists to reluctan...
(31) backing of war effort eg SJ, Bryher, RW. No conse... Brittain + Stevie Smith. Brittain's pacifism
(32) Vera Brittain + Stevie Smith. Xianity - not romantic
Xianity - not happy w Brittain's England's Hou...
(36) Delafield, like Smith, not happy w Brittain's ... - v Shaw.
(37) Analysis of Smith - v Shaw.
(38) Sayers + Mannin; Sayers 'valorized military agg... (40); good crit by James Brabazon (41); she + Mann... call on Xian ethos (42/3); praise of Mannin (43) + pow... of spirit; remained pacifist like Brittain + but pro Repu... in Spain (44); less than pleasing try to minimise Jews...
x // suffering + Fascist atrocities (45); MANNINS Dark Forest not insignificant of her ideas (45)